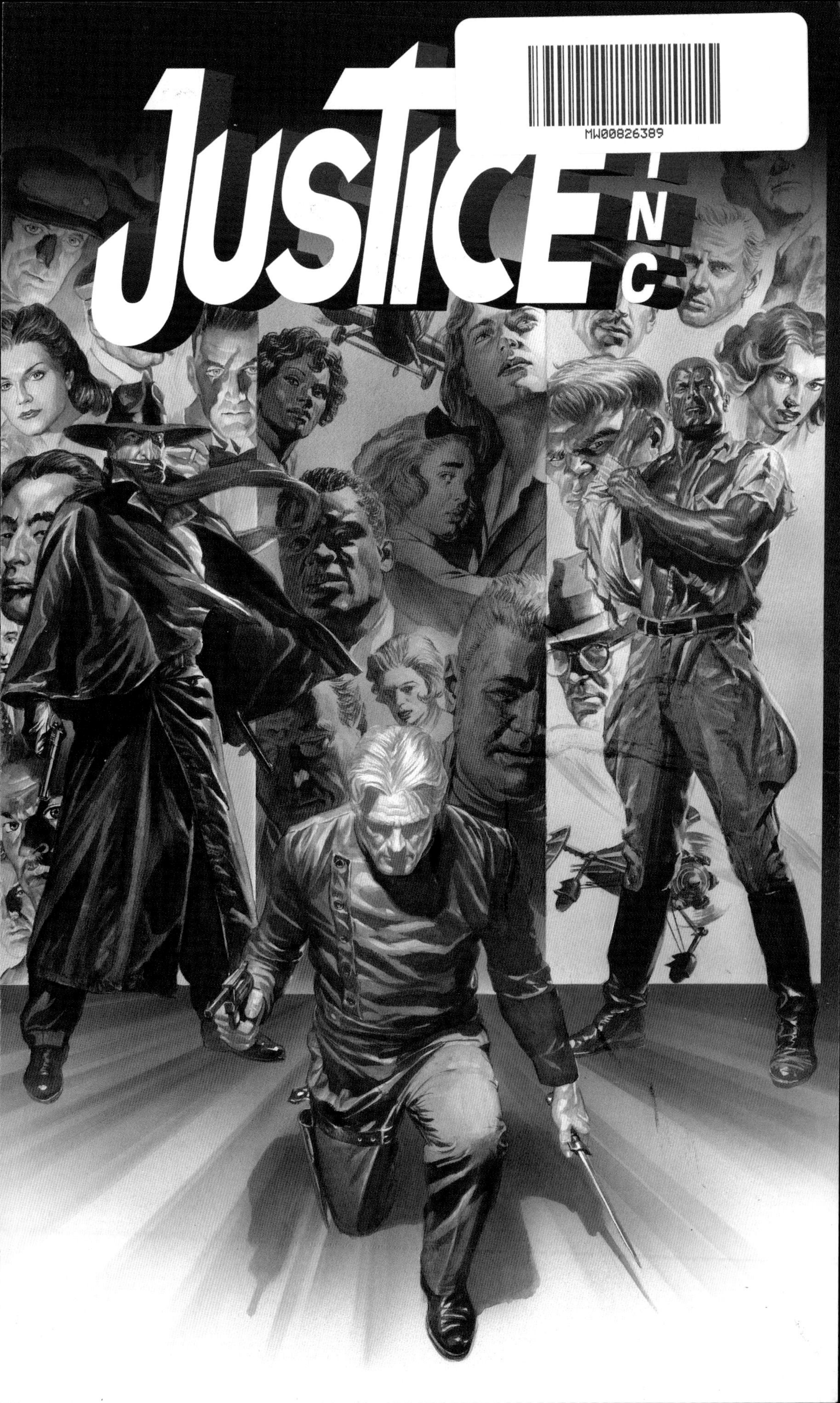
JUSTICE
INC

DYNAMITE®

Nick Barrucci, CEO / Publisher
Juan Collado, President / COO
Rich Young, Director Business Development
Keith Davidsen, Marketing Manager

Joe Rybandt, Senior Editor
Hannah Elder, Associate Editor
Molly Mahan, Associate Editor

Jason Ullmeyer, Design Director
Katie Hidalgo, Graphic Designer
Chris Caniano, Digital Associate
Rachel Kilbury, Digital Assistant

Online at **www.DYNAMITE.com**
On Twitter **@dynamitecomics**
On Facebook **/Dynamitecomics**
On YouTube **/Dynamitecomics**
On Tumblr **dynamitecomics.tumblr.com**

ISBN-10: 1-60690-662-3
ISBN-13:978-1-60690-662-0
First Printing 10 9 8 7 6 5 4 3 2 1

For information regarding press, media rights, foreign rights, licensing, promotions, and advertising e-mail: marketing@dynamite.com

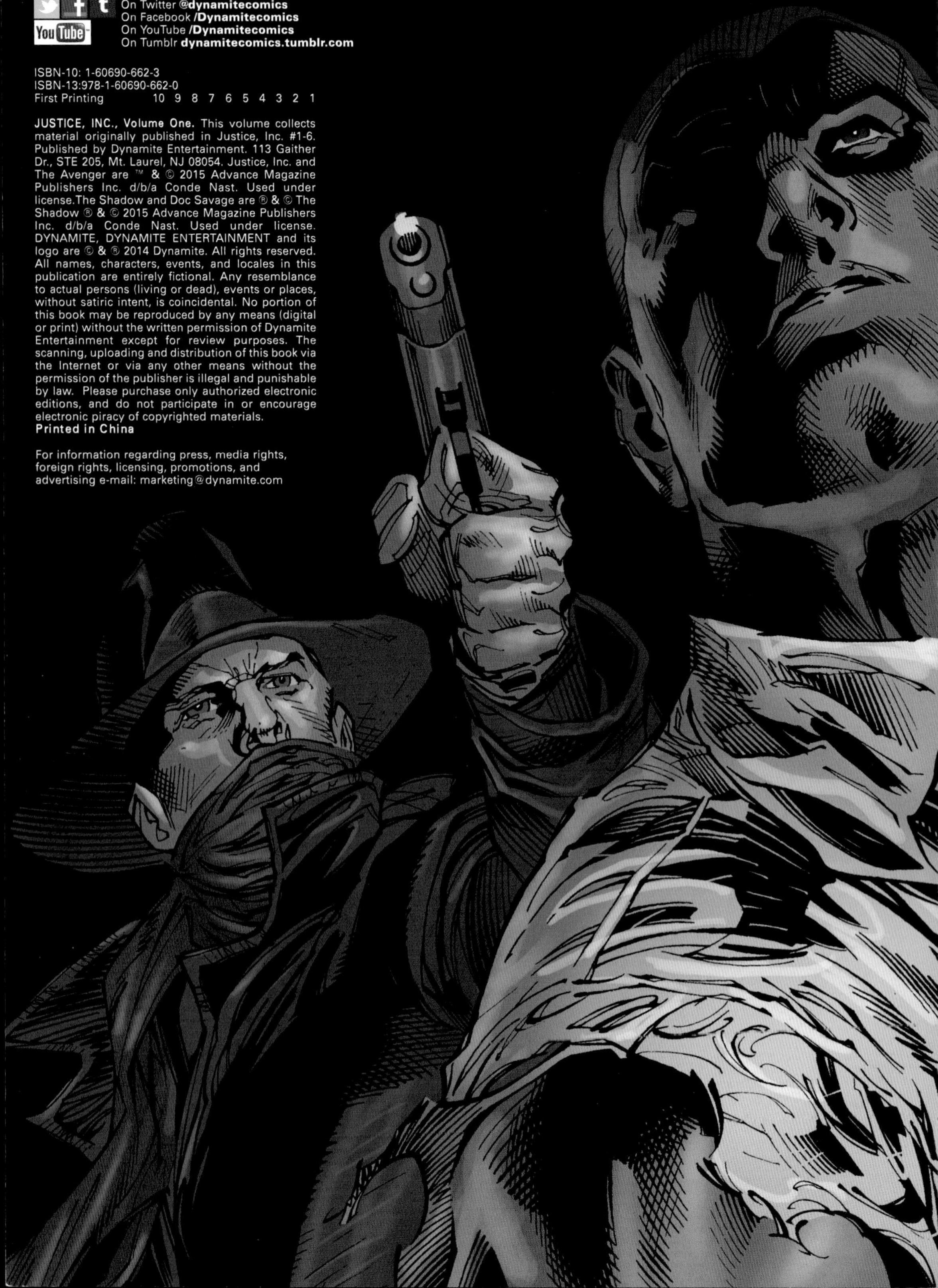

written by **MICHAEL USLAN**
illustrated by **GIOVANNI TIMPANO**
colored by **MARCO LESKO**
lettered by **SIMON BOWLAND**
collection cover by **ALEX ROSS**

special thanks to **JERRY BIRENZ** and **ANTHONY TOLLIN**

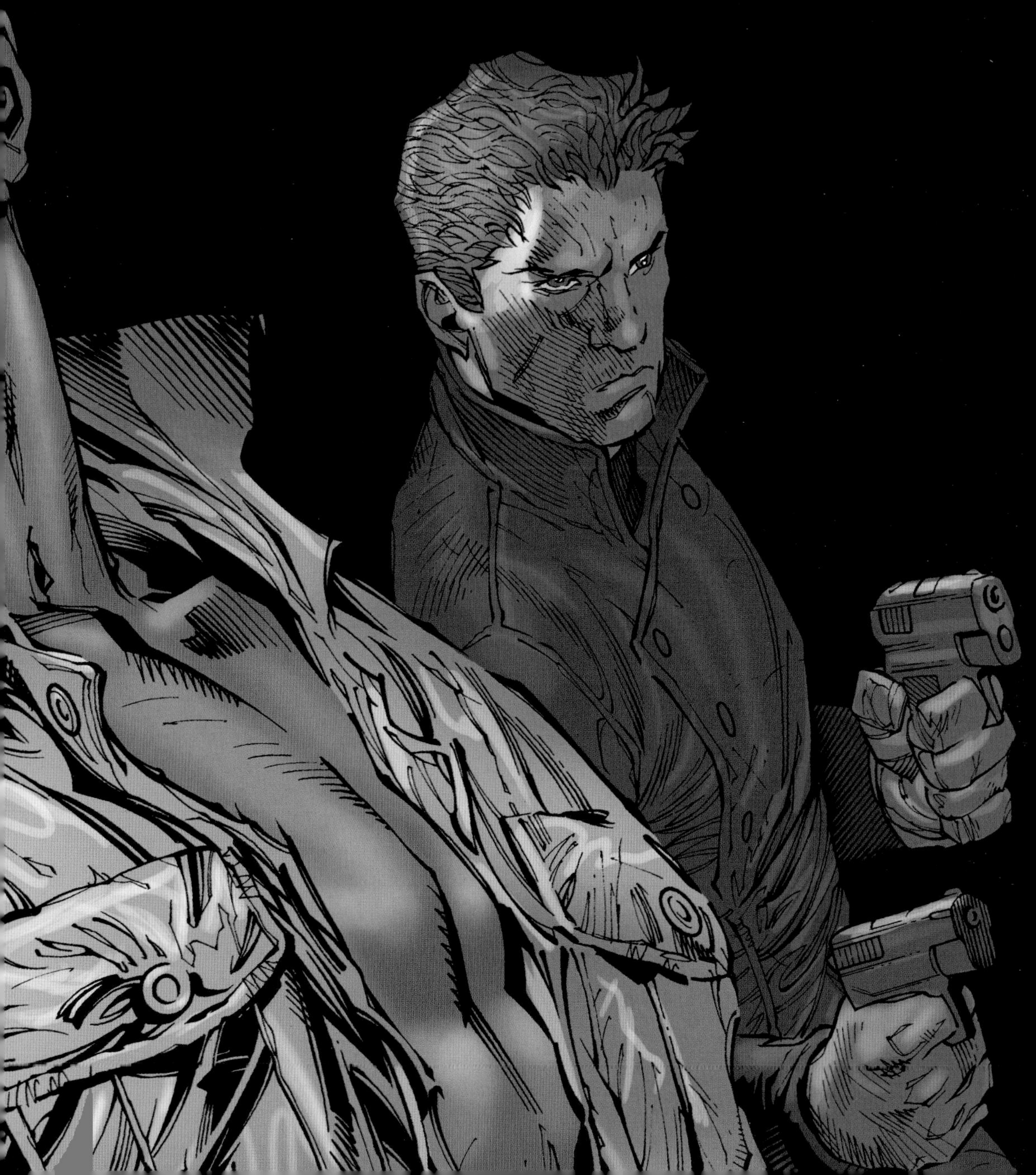

ONE

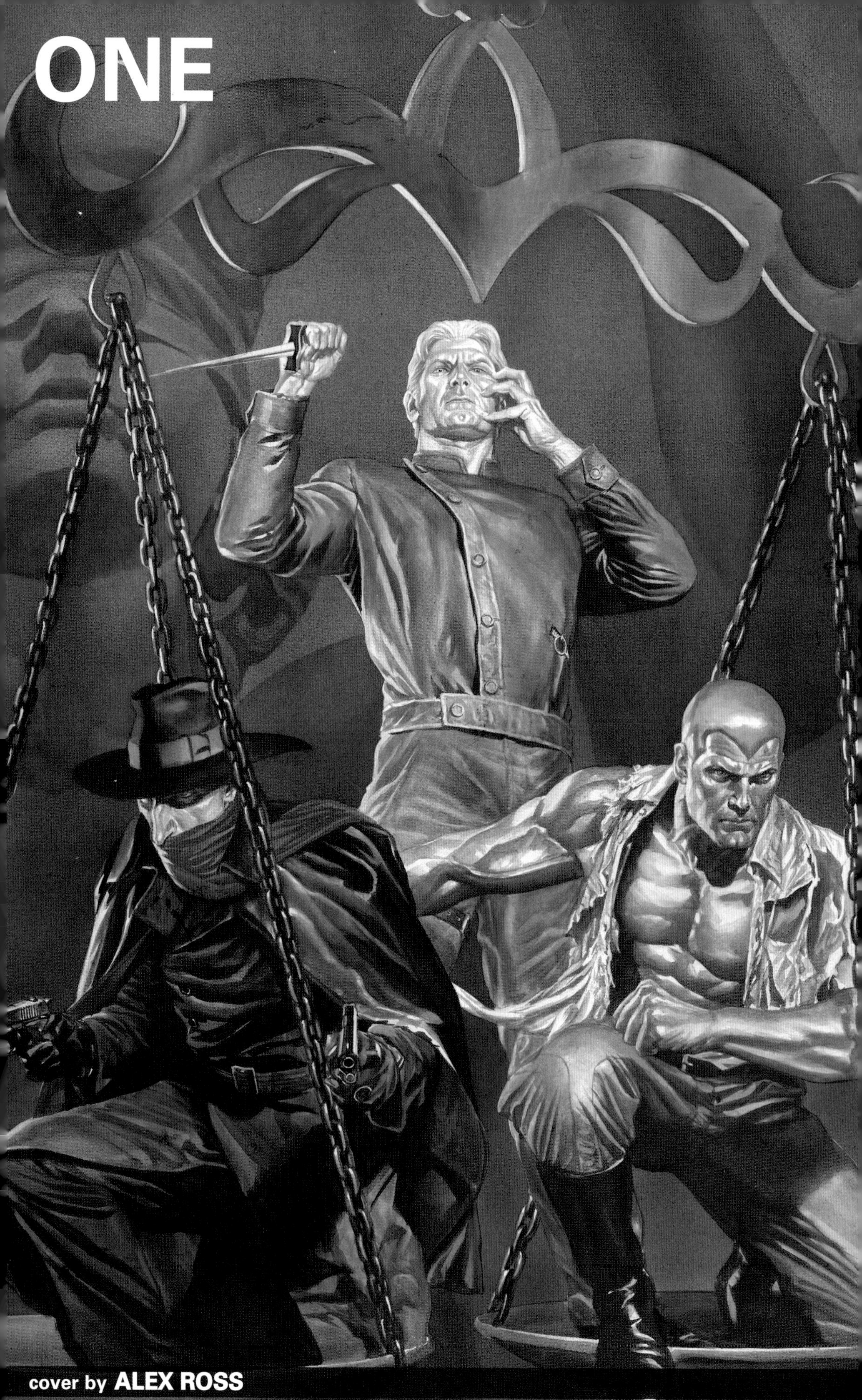

cover by **ALEX ROSS**

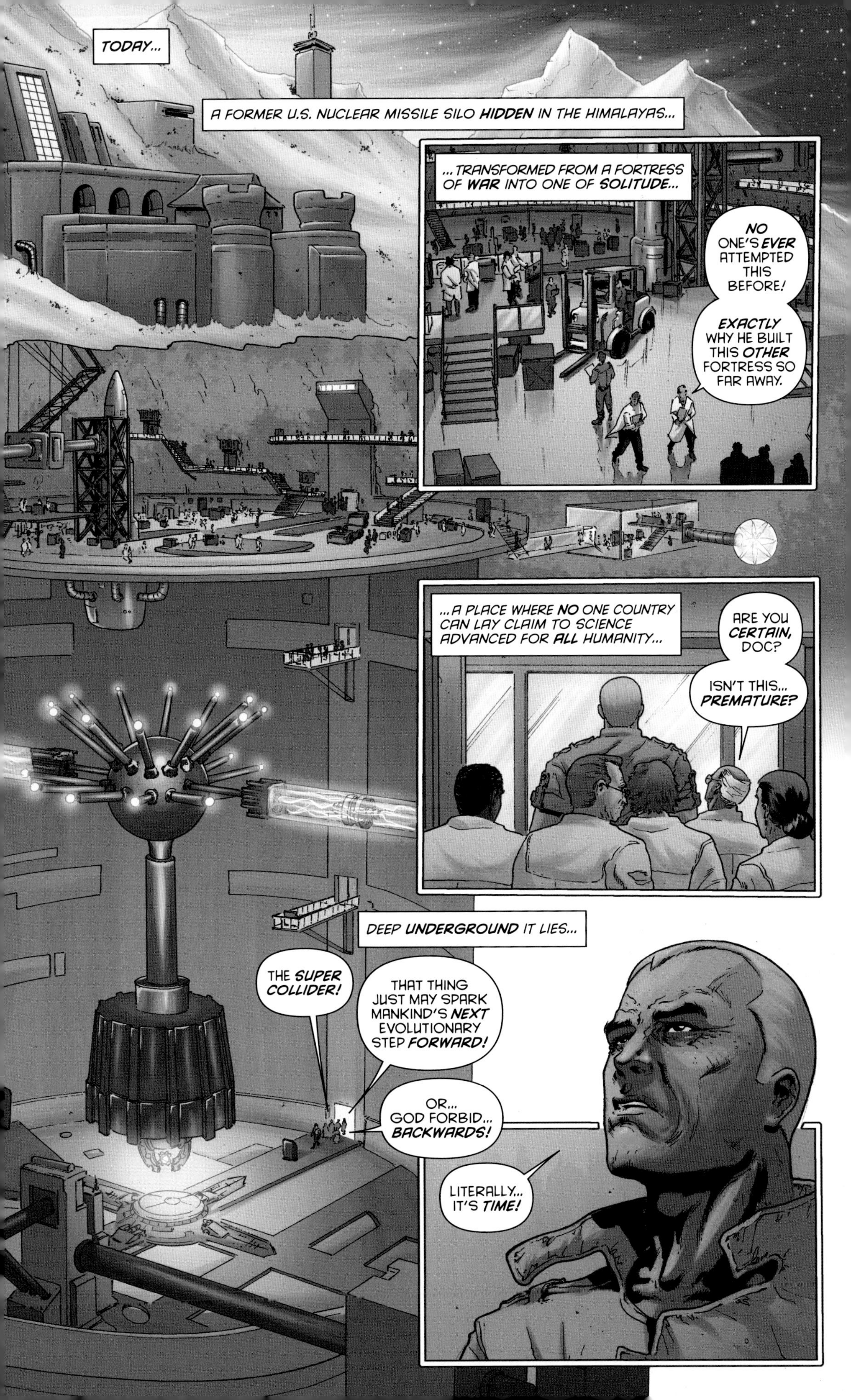
TODAY...
A FORMER U.S. NUCLEAR MISSILE SILO HIDDEN IN THE HIMALAYAS...
...TRANSFORMED FROM A FORTRESS OF WAR INTO ONE OF SOLITUDE...
NO ONE'S EVER ATTEMPTED THIS BEFORE!
EXACTLY WHY HE BUILT THIS OTHER FORTRESS SO FAR AWAY.
...A PLACE WHERE NO ONE COUNTRY CAN LAY CLAIM TO SCIENCE ADVANCED FOR ALL HUMANITY...
ARE YOU CERTAIN, DOC?
ISN'T THIS... PREMATURE?
DEEP UNDERGROUND IT LIES...
THE SUPER COLLIDER!
THAT THING JUST MAY SPARK MANKIND'S NEXT EVOLUTIONARY STEP FORWARD!
OR... GOD FORBID... BACKWARDS!
LITERALLY... IT'S TIME!

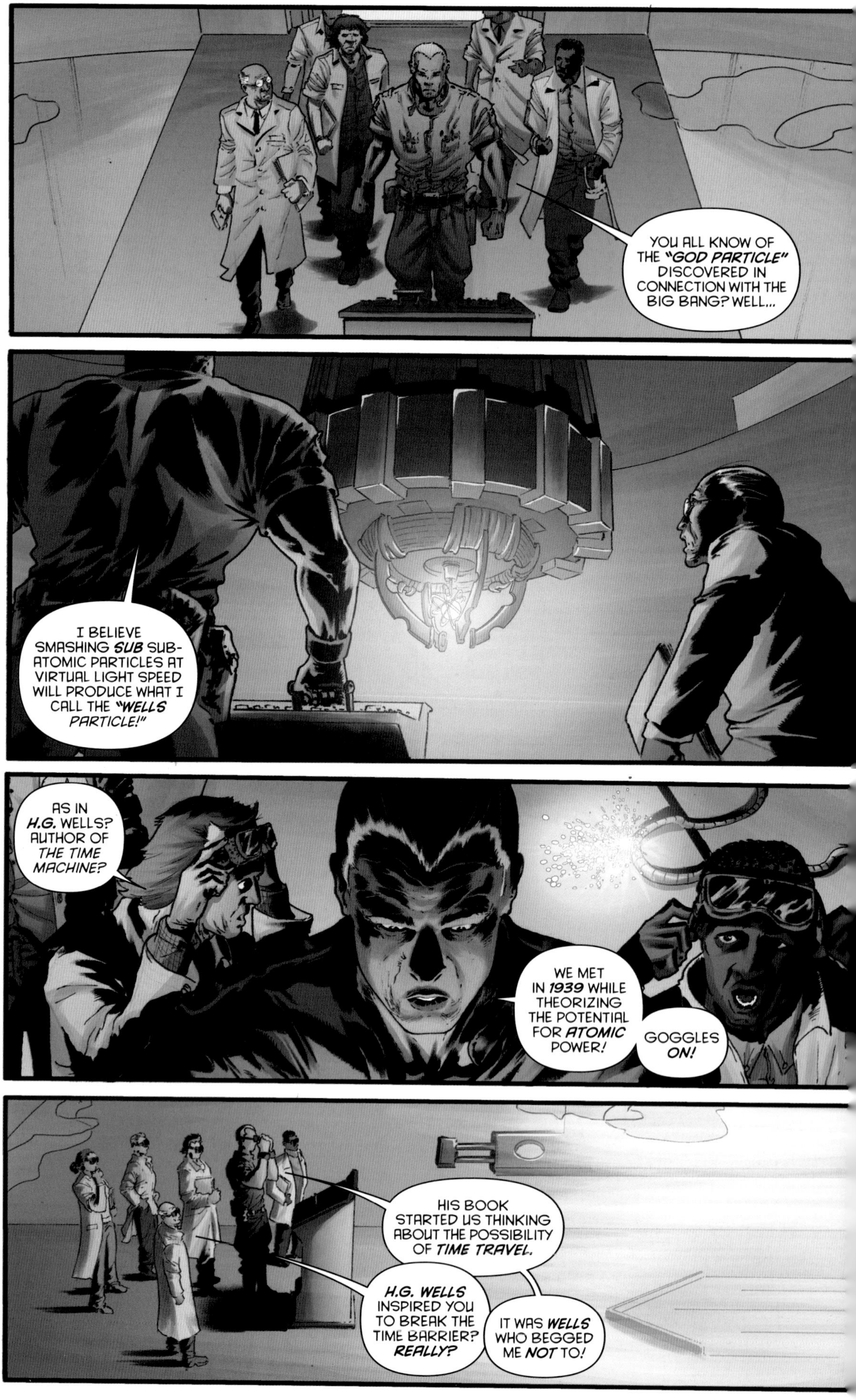

YOU ALL KNOW OF THE "GOD PARTICLE" DISCOVERED IN CONNECTION WITH THE BIG BANG? WELL...
I BELIEVE SMASHING SUB SUB-ATOMIC PARTICLES AT VIRTUAL LIGHT SPEED WILL PRODUCE WHAT I CALL THE "WELLS PARTICLE!"
AS IN H.G. WELLS? AUTHOR OF THE TIME MACHINE?
WE MET IN 1939 WHILE THEORIZING THE POTENTIAL FOR ATOMIC POWER!
GOGGLES ON!
HIS BOOK STARTED US THINKING ABOUT THE POSSIBILITY OF TIME TRAVEL.
H.G. WELLS INSPIRED YOU TO BREAK THE TIME BARRIER? REALLY?
IT WAS WELLS WHO BEGGED ME NOT TO!

IN 2014, A *UNIVERSAL QUANTUM MACHINE* PRODUCED A ROTATION MATRIX. ROTATIONS BEING *REVERSIBLE*, IT PROVED *TIME* IS NOT A STRAIGHT LINE BUT *CURVED*.

SO WHAT WILL YOUR *ADVANCED* UQM PROVE?

THAT EVERYTHING EXISTS *SIMULTANEOUSLY* IN *TIME*. IT SIMPLY DEPENDS ON *WHERE* WE CHOOSE TO LOOK.

YOU'VE *NEVER* SAID HOW YOU AFFORDED THIS. THE COST IS *BEYOND*--

A *MASSIVE* ENDOWMENT MADE *SEVENTY-FIVE* YEARS AGO WITH COMPOUNDED INTEREST.

THE GOVERNMENT?

NO. THE *SAME* MAN WHO FUNDED ME IN *'39* ON OUR SECRET *ATOMIC* WORK...

...*RICHARD HENRY BENSON!*

RICHARD HENRY BENSON? THE *BILLIONAIRE* INDUSTRIALIST?

NO. RICHARD HENRY BENSON...

...*THE AVENGER!*

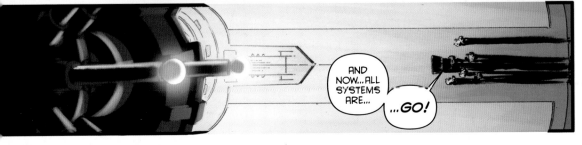

AND NOW...ALL SYSTEMS ARE...

...*GO!*

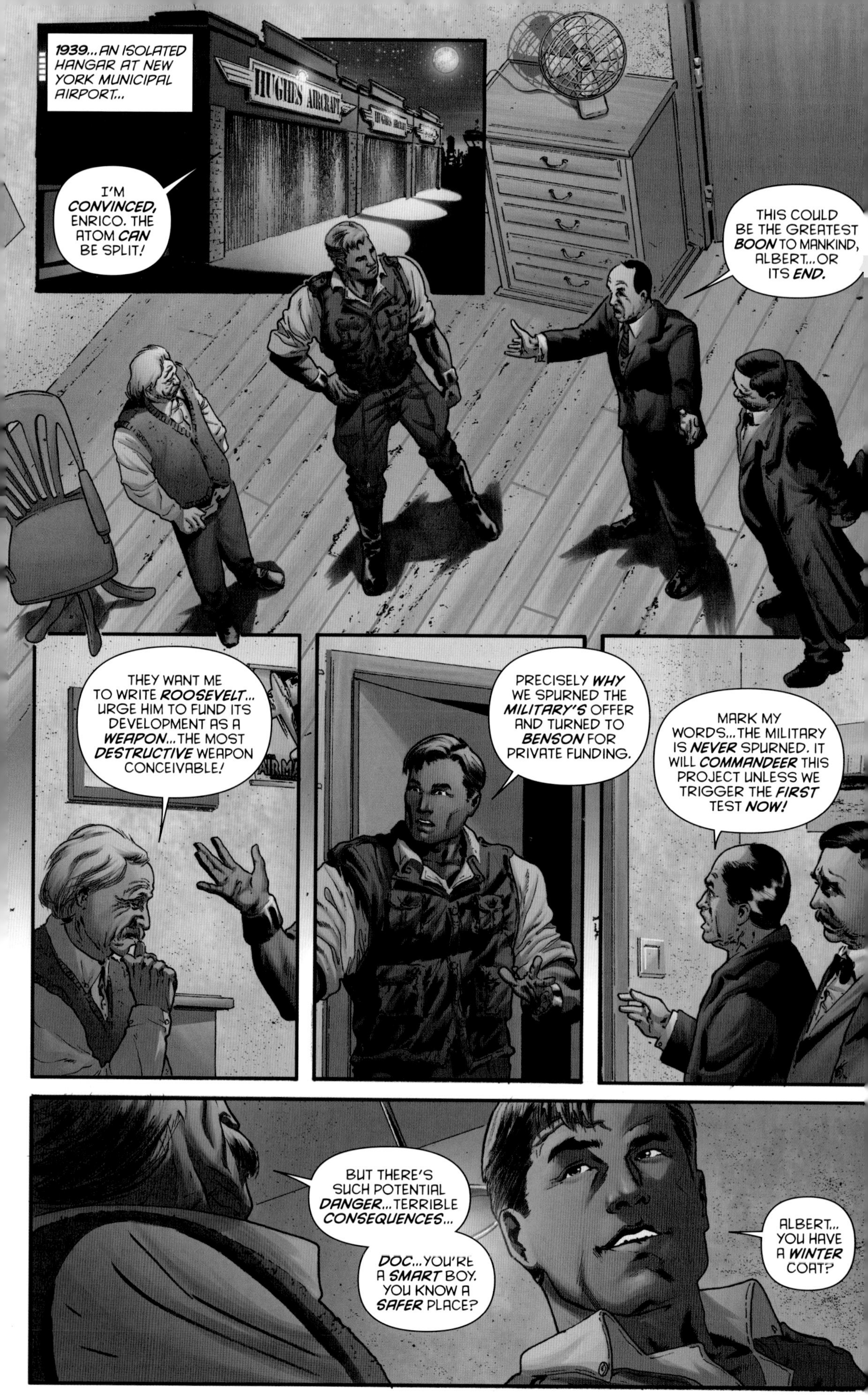
1939... AN ISOLATED HANGAR AT NEW YORK MUNICIPAL AIRPORT...
HUGHES AIRCRAFT
I'M CONVINCED, ENRICO. THE ATOM CAN BE SPLIT!
THIS COULD BE THE GREATEST BOON TO MANKIND, ALBERT...OR ITS END.
THEY WANT ME TO WRITE ROOSEVELT... URGE HIM TO FUND ITS DEVELOPMENT AS A WEAPON... THE MOST DESTRUCTIVE WEAPON CONCEIVABLE!
PRECISELY WHY WE SPURNED THE MILITARY'S OFFER AND TURNED TO BENSON FOR PRIVATE FUNDING.
MARK MY WORDS... THE MILITARY IS NEVER SPURNED. IT WILL COMMANDEER THIS PROJECT UNLESS WE TRIGGER THE FIRST TEST NOW!
BUT THERE'S SUCH POTENTIAL DANGER... TERRIBLE CONSEQUENCES...
DOC... YOU'RE A SMART BOY. YOU KNOW A SAFER PLACE?
ALBERT... YOU HAVE A WINTER COAT?

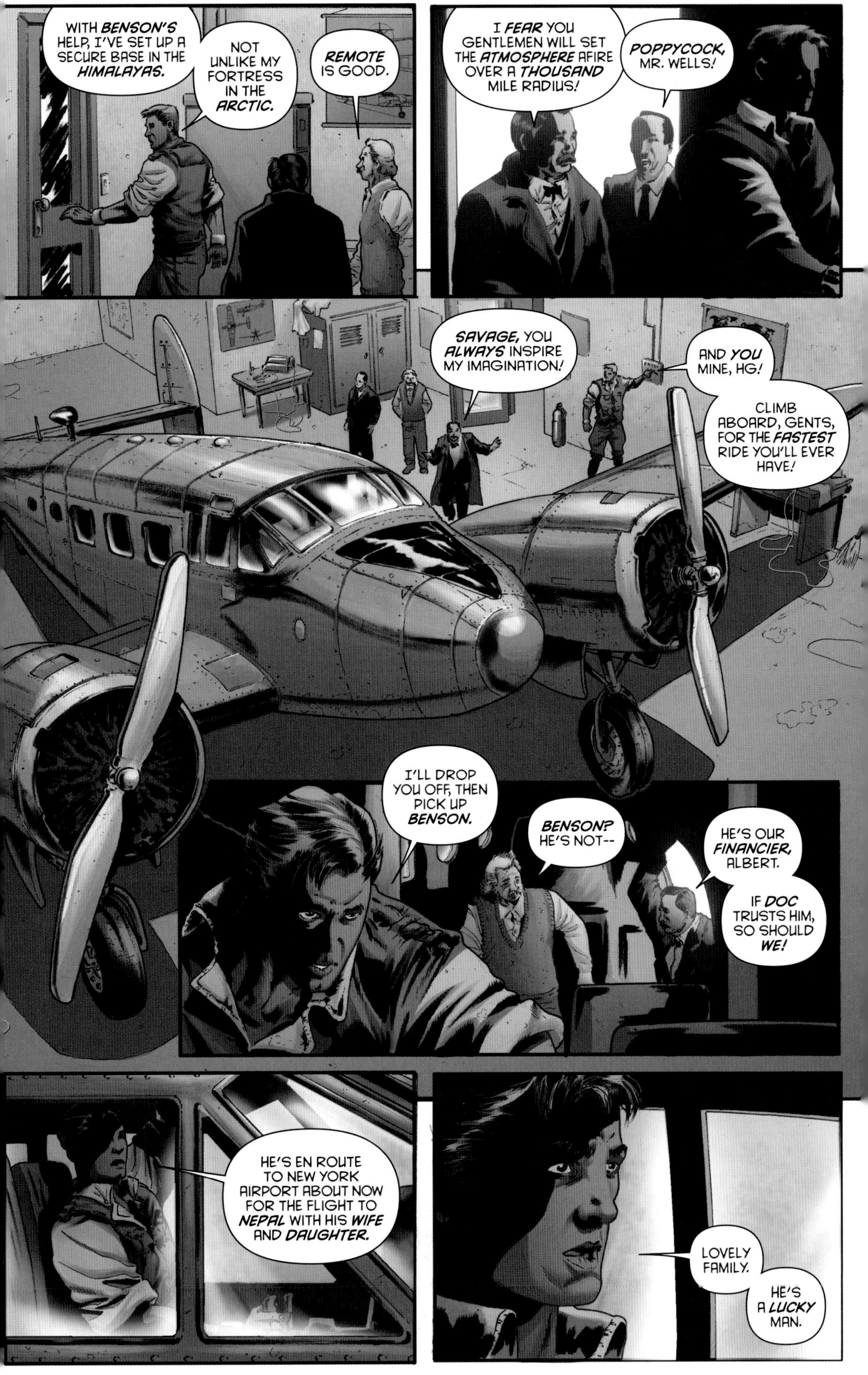
WITH BENSON'S HELP, I'VE SET UP A SECURE BASE IN THE HIMALAYAS.
NOT UNLIKE MY FORTRESS IN THE ARCTIC.
REMOTE IS GOOD.
I FEAR YOU GENTLEMEN WILL SET THE ATMOSPHERE AFIRE OVER A THOUSAND MILE RADIUS!
POPPYCOCK, MR. WELLS!
SAVAGE, YOU ALWAYS INSPIRE MY IMAGINATION!
AND YOU MINE, HG!
CLIMB ABOARD, GENTS, FOR THE FASTEST RIDE YOU'LL EVER HAVE!
I'LL DROP YOU OFF, THEN PICK UP BENSON.
BENSON? HE'S NOT--
HE'S OUR FINANCIER, ALBERT.
IF DOC TRUSTS HIM, SO SHOULD WE!
HE'S EN ROUTE TO NEW YORK AIRPORT ABOUT NOW FOR THE FLIGHT TO NEPAL WITH HIS WIFE AND DAUGHTER.
LOVELY FAMILY.
HE'S A LUCKY MAN.

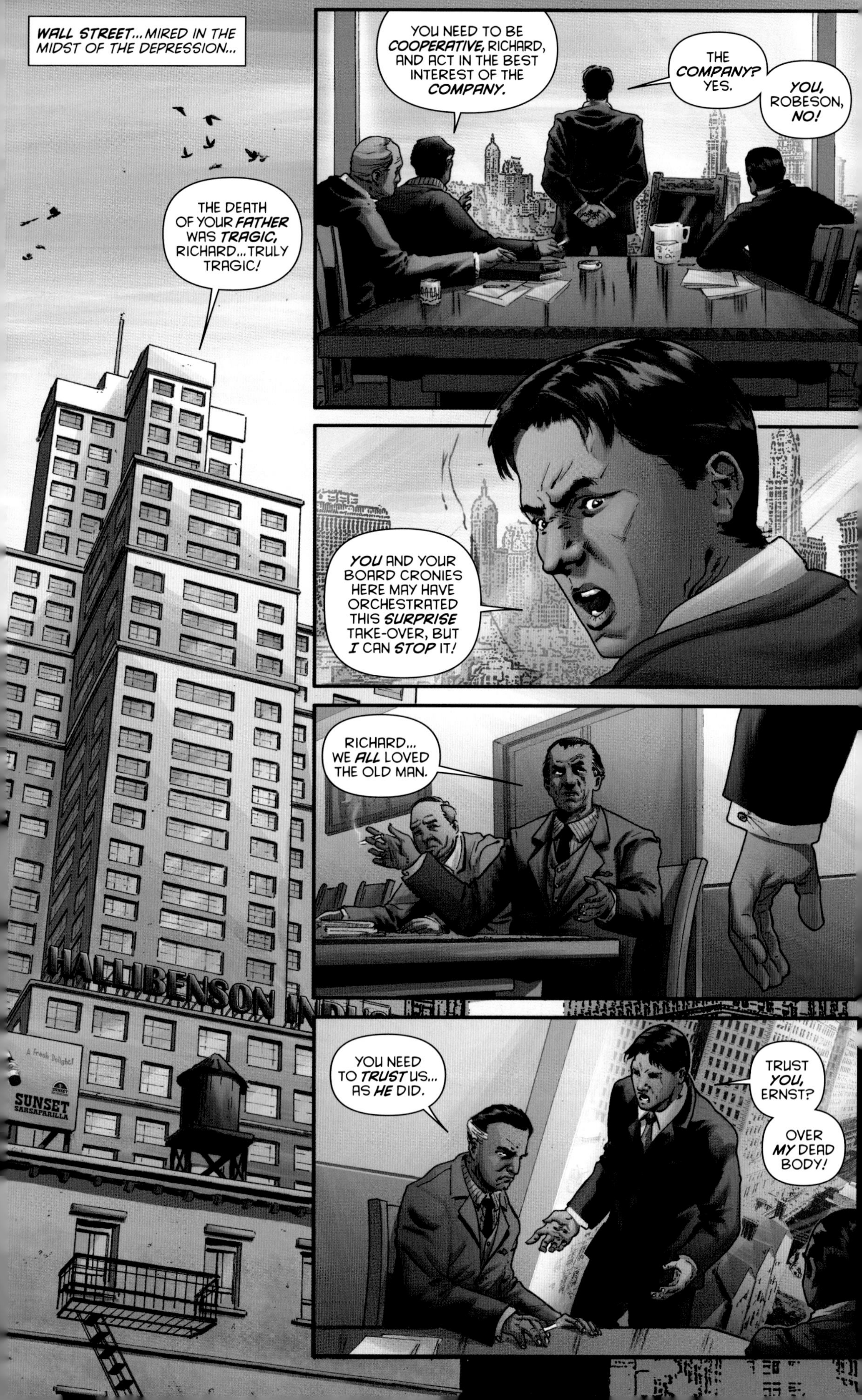
WALL STREET... MIRED IN THE MIDST OF THE DEPRESSION...
THE DEATH OF YOUR FATHER WAS TRAGIC, RICHARD... TRULY TRAGIC!
HALLIBENSON IND
A Fresh Delight!
SUNSET SARSAPARILLA
YOU NEED TO BE COOPERATIVE, RICHARD, AND ACT IN THE BEST INTEREST OF THE COMPANY.
THE COMPANY? YES.
YOU, ROBESON, NO!
YOU AND YOUR BOARD CRONIES HERE MAY HAVE ORCHESTRATED THIS SURPRISE TAKE-OVER, BUT I CAN STOP IT!
RICHARD... WE ALL LOVED THE OLD MAN.
YOU NEED TO TRUST US... AS HE DID.
TRUST YOU, ERNST?
OVER MY DEAD BODY!

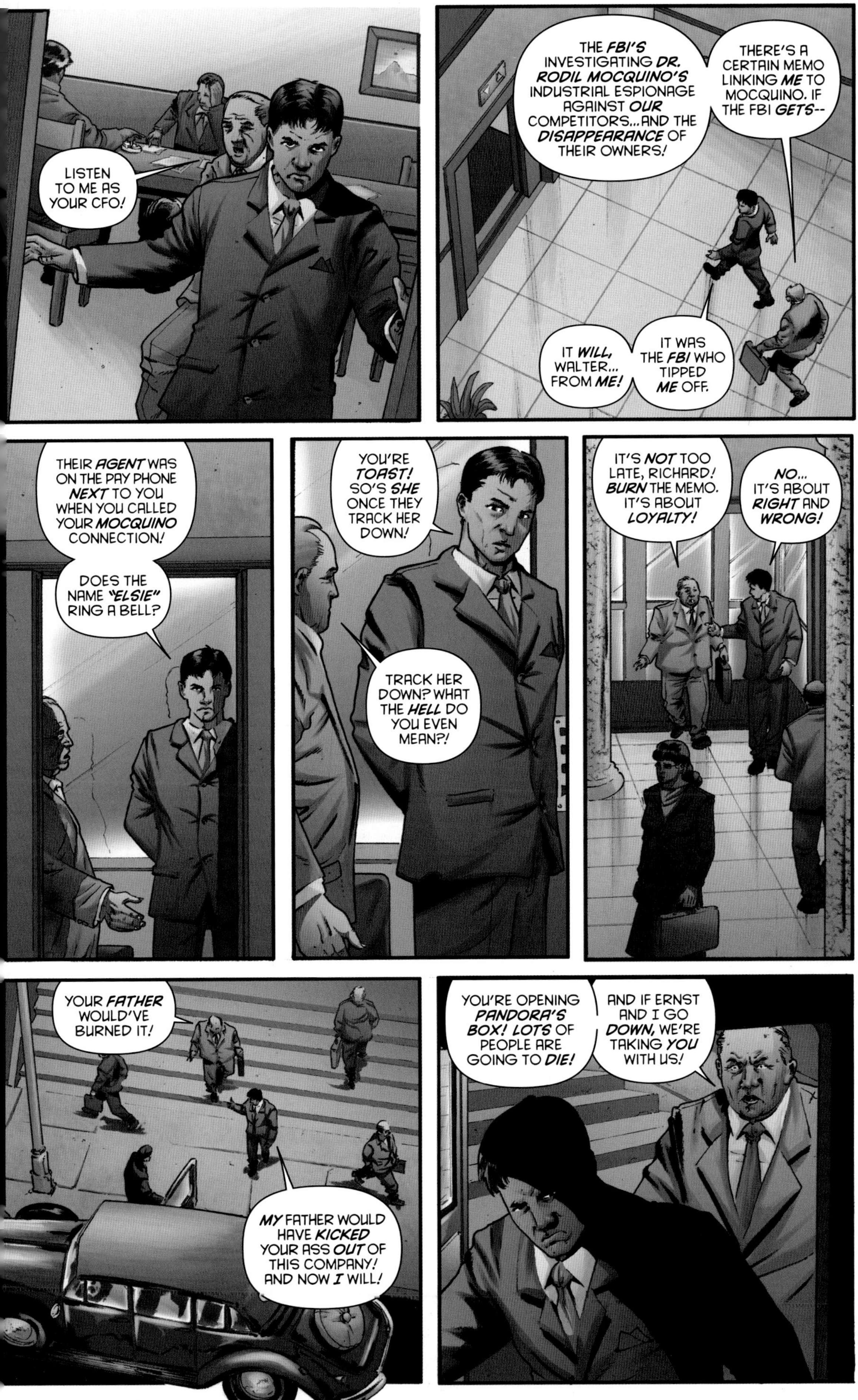

LISTEN TO ME AS YOUR CFO!
THE FBI'S INVESTIGATING DR. RODIL MOCQUINO'S INDUSTRIAL ESPIONAGE AGAINST OUR COMPETITORS...AND THE DISAPPEARANCE OF THEIR OWNERS!
THERE'S A CERTAIN MEMO LINKING ME TO MOCQUINO. IF THE FBI GETS--
IT WILL, WALTER... FROM ME!
IT WAS THE FBI WHO TIPPED ME OFF.
THEIR AGENT WAS ON THE PAY PHONE NEXT TO YOU WHEN YOU CALLED YOUR MOCQUINO CONNECTION!
DOES THE NAME "ELSIE" RING A BELL?
YOU'RE TOAST! SO'S SHE ONCE THEY TRACK HER DOWN!
TRACK HER DOWN? WHAT THE HELL DO YOU EVEN MEAN?!
IT'S NOT TOO LATE, RICHARD! BURN THE MEMO. IT'S ABOUT LOYALTY!
NO... IT'S ABOUT RIGHT AND WRONG!
YOUR FATHER WOULD'VE BURNED IT!
MY FATHER WOULD HAVE KICKED YOUR ASS OUT OF THIS COMPANY! AND NOW I WILL!
YOU'RE OPENING PANDORA'S BOX! LOTS OF PEOPLE ARE GOING TO DIE!
AND IF ERNST AND I GO DOWN, WE'RE TAKING YOU WITH US!

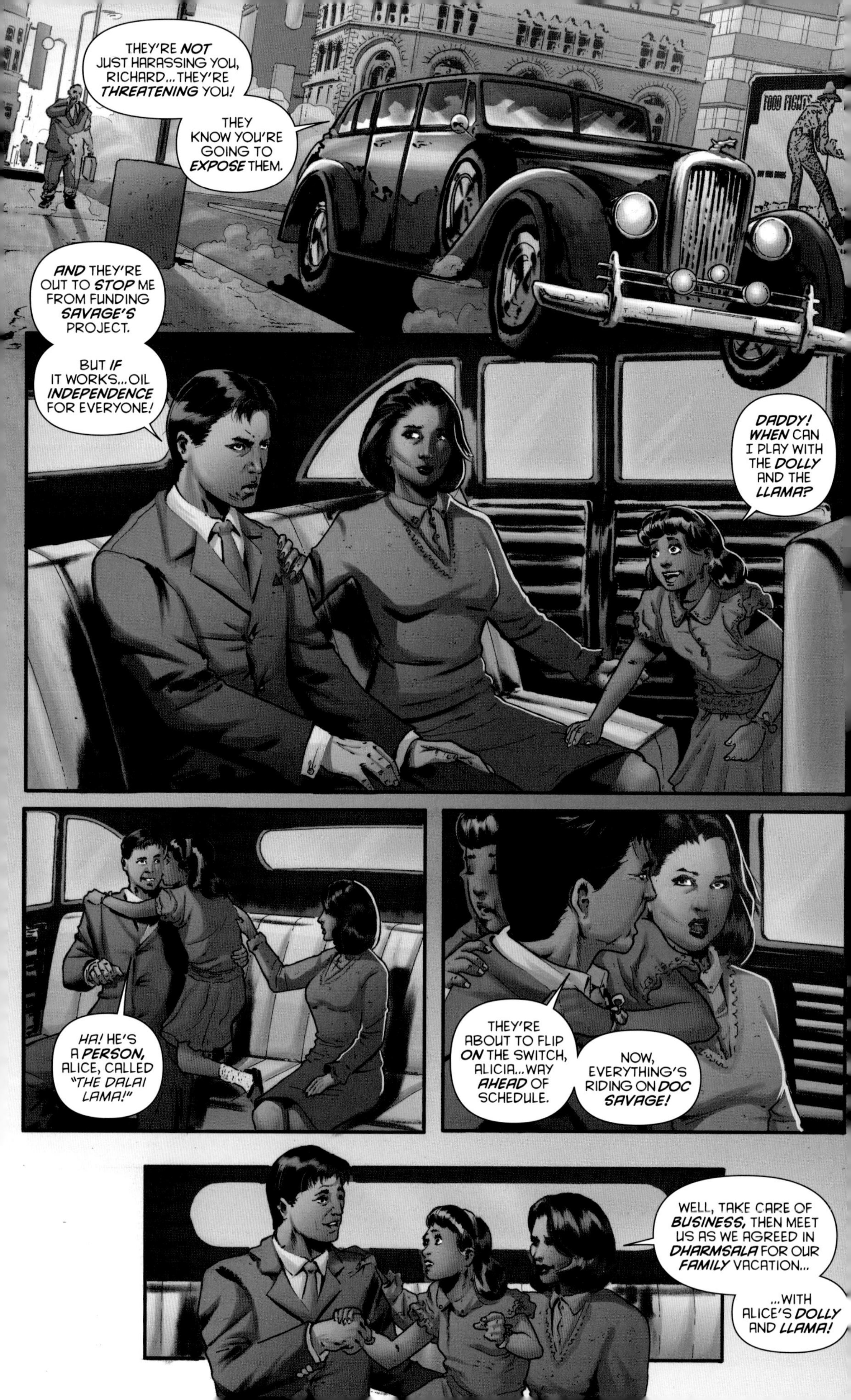
THEY'RE NOT JUST HARASSING YOU, RICHARD... THEY'RE THREATENING YOU!
THEY KNOW YOU'RE GOING TO EXPOSE THEM.
FOOD FIGHTS
AND THEY'RE OUT TO STOP ME FROM FUNDING SAVAGE'S PROJECT.
BUT IF IT WORKS...OIL INDEPENDENCE FOR EVERYONE!
DADDY! WHEN CAN I PLAY WITH THE DOLLY AND THE LLAMA?
HA! HE'S A PERSON, ALICE, CALLED "THE DALAI LAMA!"
THEY'RE ABOUT TO FLIP ON THE SWITCH, ALICIA...WAY AHEAD OF SCHEDULE.
NOW, EVERYTHING'S RIDING ON DOC SAVAGE!
WELL, TAKE CARE OF BUSINESS, THEN MEET US AS WE AGREED IN DHARMSALA FOR OUR FAMILY VACATION...
...WITH ALICE'S DOLLY AND LLAMA!

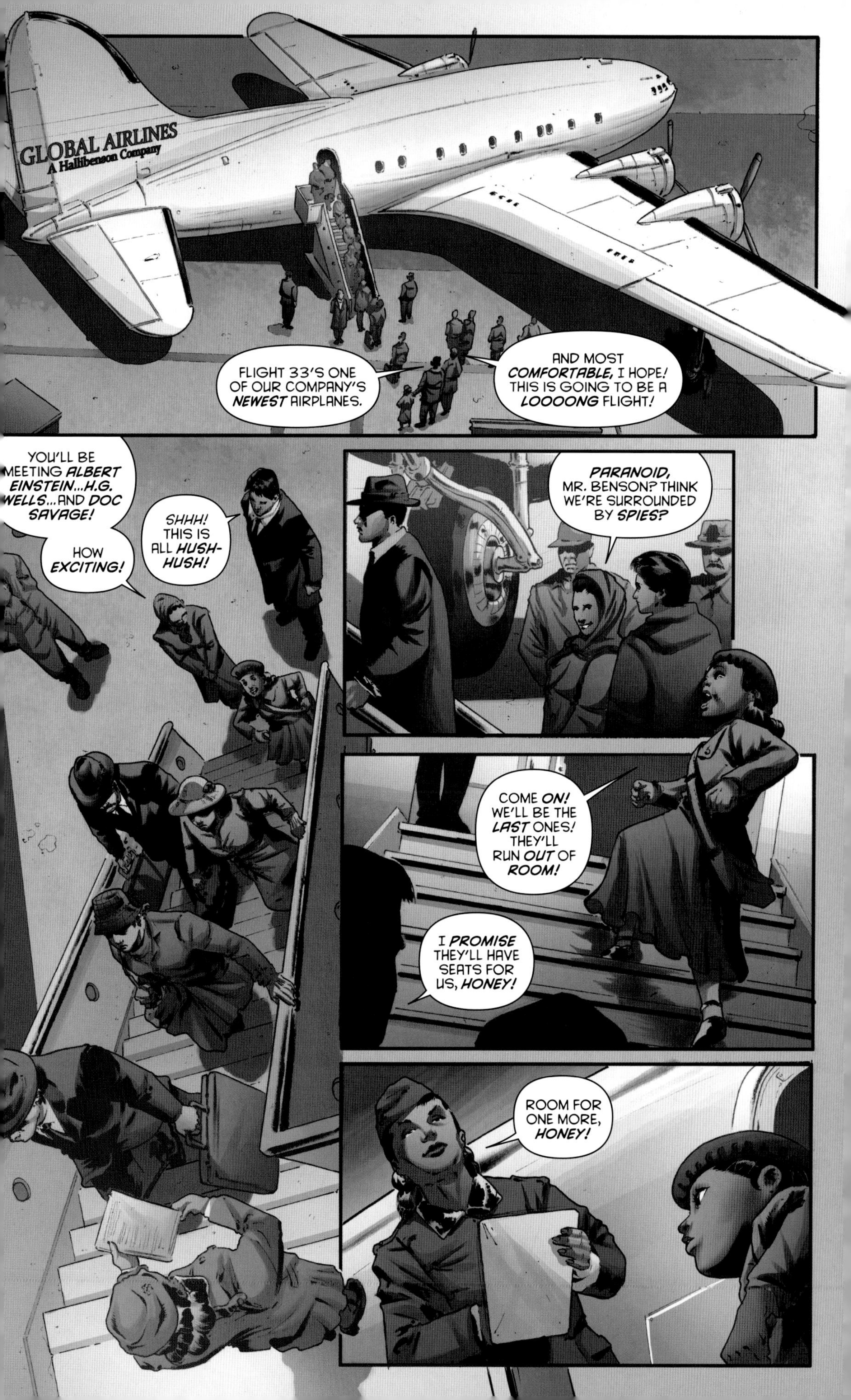
GLOBAL AIRLINES
A Hallibenson Company
FLIGHT 33'S ONE OF OUR COMPANY'S NEWEST AIRPLANES.
AND MOST COMFORTABLE, I HOPE! THIS IS GOING TO BE A LOOOONG FLIGHT!
YOU'LL BE MEETING ALBERT EINSTEIN...H.G. WELLS...AND DOC SAVAGE!
HOW EXCITING!
SHHH! THIS IS ALL HUSH-HUSH!
PARANOID, MR. BENSON? THINK WE'RE SURROUNDED BY SPIES?
COME ON! WE'LL BE THE LAST ONES! THEY'LL RUN OUT OF ROOM!
I PROMISE THEY'LL HAVE SEATS FOR US, HONEY!
ROOM FOR ONE MORE, HONEY!

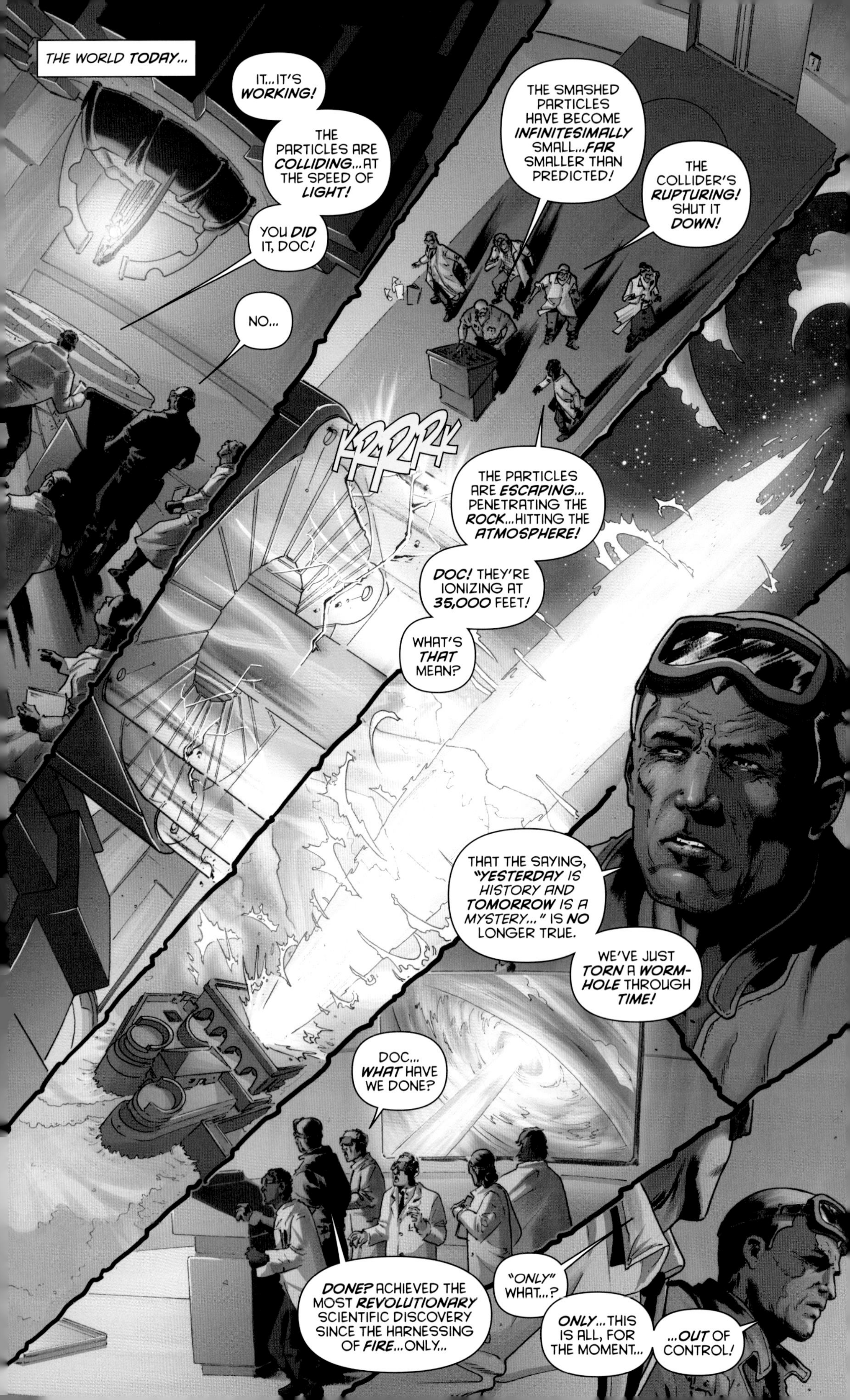
THE WORLD TODAY...
IT...IT'S WORKING!
THE PARTICLES ARE COLLIDING...AT THE SPEED OF LIGHT!
YOU DID IT, DOC!
NO...
THE SMASHED PARTICLES HAVE BECOME INFINITESIMALLY SMALL...FAR SMALLER THAN PREDICTED!
THE COLLIDER'S RUPTURING! SHUT IT DOWN!
KRRRK
THE PARTICLES ARE ESCAPING... PENETRATING THE ROCK...HITTING THE ATMOSPHERE!
DOC! THEY'RE IONIZING AT 35,000 FEET!
WHAT'S THAT MEAN?
THAT THE SAYING, "YESTERDAY IS HISTORY AND TOMORROW IS A MYSTERY..." IS NO LONGER TRUE.
WE'VE JUST TORN A WORM-HOLE THROUGH TIME!
DOC... WHAT HAVE WE DONE?
DONE? ACHIEVED THE MOST REVOLUTIONARY SCIENTIFIC DISCOVERY SINCE THE HARNESSING OF FIRE...ONLY...
"ONLY" WHAT...?
ONLY...THIS IS ALL, FOR THE MOMENT...
...OUT OF CONTROL!

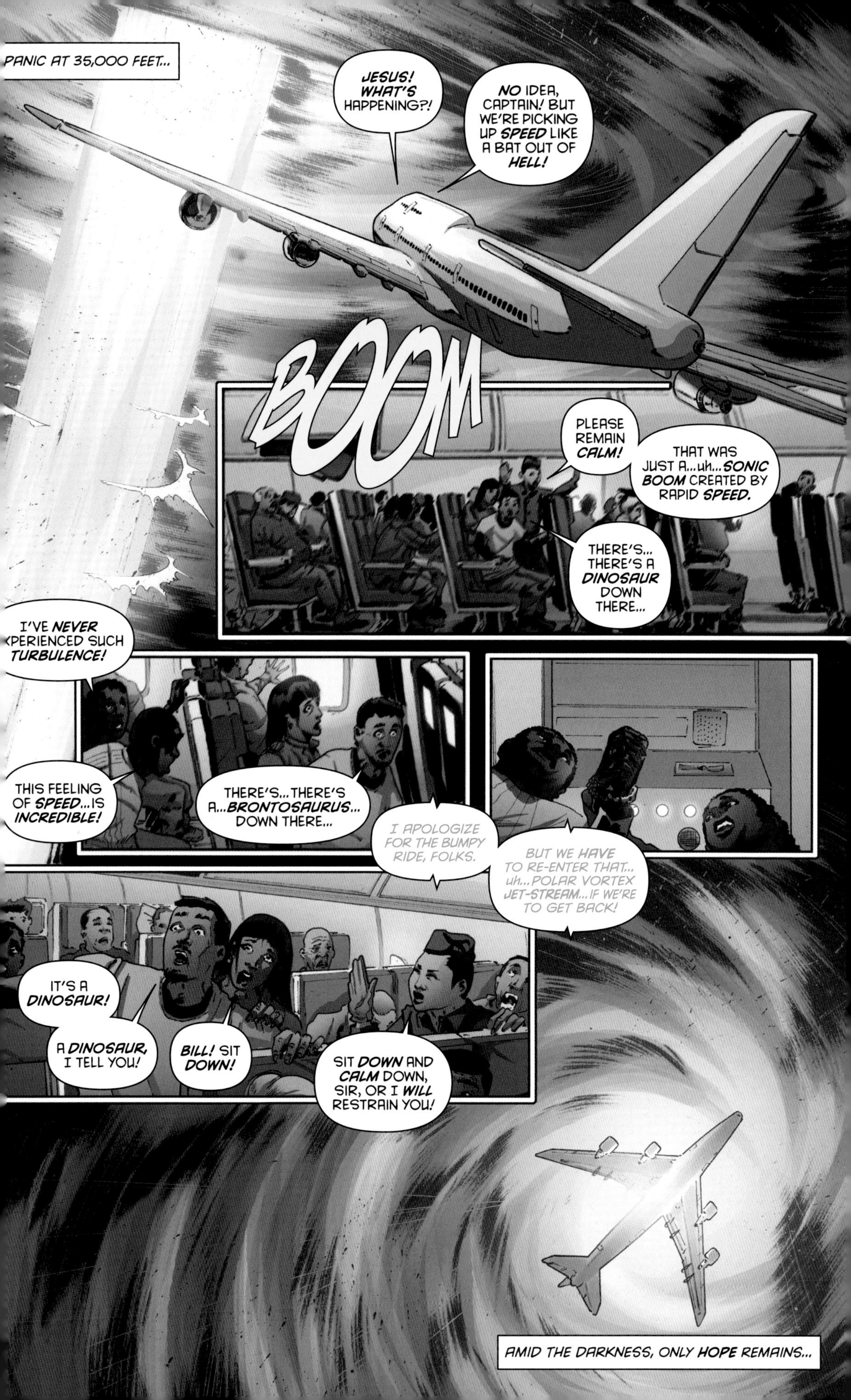
PANIC AT 35,000 FEET...
JESUS! WHAT'S HAPPENING?!
NO IDEA, CAPTAIN! BUT WE'RE PICKING UP SPEED LIKE A BAT OUT OF HELL!
BOOM
PLEASE REMAIN CALM!
THAT WAS JUST A...uh...SONIC BOOM CREATED BY RAPID SPEED.
THERE'S... THERE'S A DINOSAUR DOWN THERE...
I'VE NEVER EXPERIENCED SUCH TURBULENCE!
THIS FEELING OF SPEED...IS INCREDIBLE!
THERE'S... THERE'S A...BRONTOSAURUS... DOWN THERE...
I APOLOGIZE FOR THE BUMPY RIDE, FOLKS.
BUT WE HAVE TO RE-ENTER THAT... uh...POLAR VORTEX JET-STREAM...IF WE'RE TO GET BACK!
IT'S A DINOSAUR!
A DINOSAUR, I TELL YOU!
BILL! SIT DOWN!
SIT DOWN AND CALM DOWN, SIR, OR I WILL RESTRAIN YOU!
AMID THE DARKNESS, ONLY HOPE REMAINS...

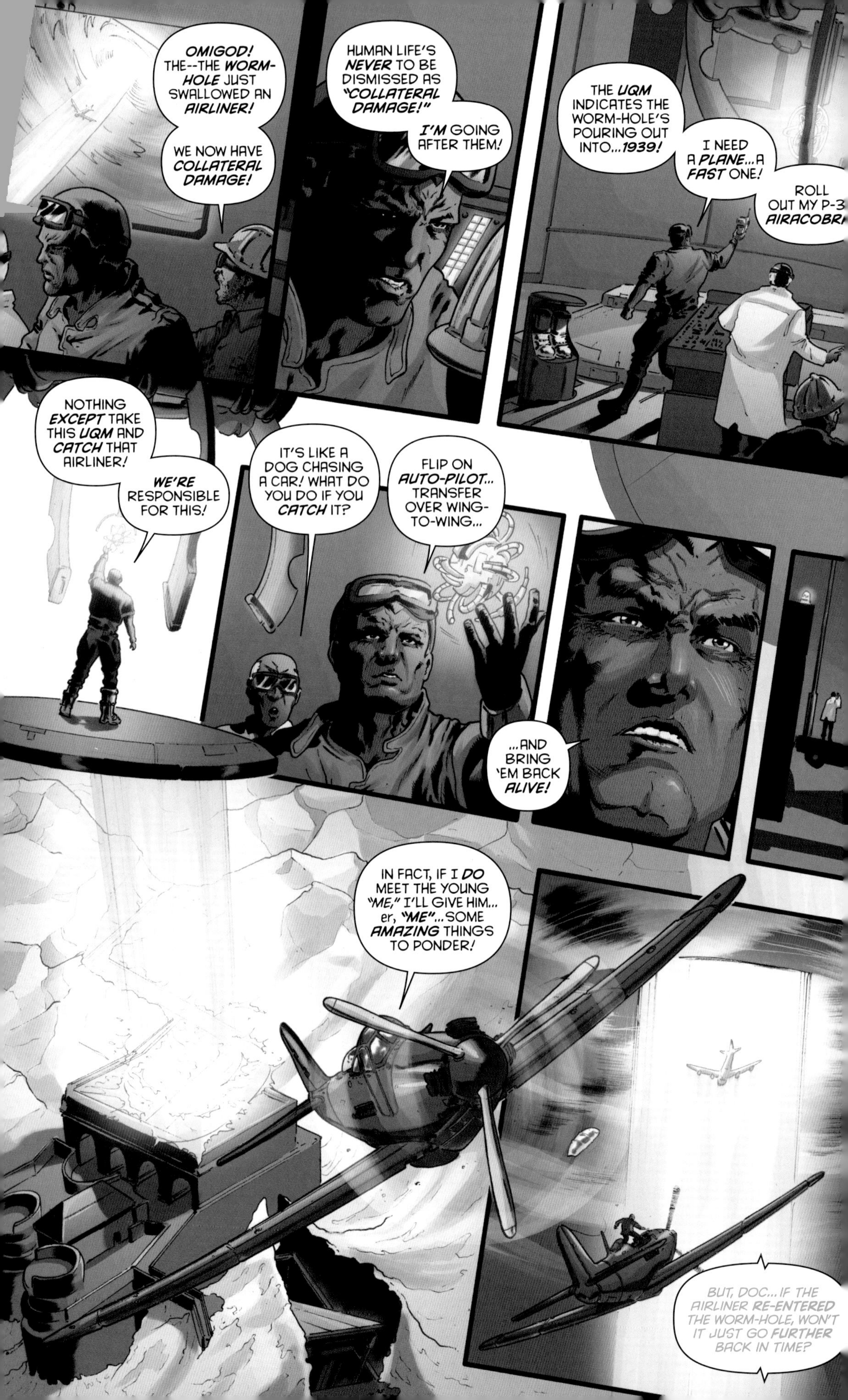
OMIGOD! THE--THE WORM-HOLE JUST SWALLOWED AN AIRLINER!
WE NOW HAVE COLLATERAL DAMAGE!
HUMAN LIFE'S NEVER TO BE DISMISSED AS "COLLATERAL DAMAGE!"
I'M GOING AFTER THEM!
THE UQM INDICATES THE WORM-HOLE'S POURING OUT INTO...1939!
I NEED A PLANE...A FAST ONE!
ROLL OUT MY P-3
AIRACOBR
NOTHING EXCEPT TAKE THIS UQM AND CATCH THAT AIRLINER!
WE'RE RESPONSIBLE FOR THIS!
IT'S LIKE A DOG CHASING A CAR! WHAT DO YOU DO IF YOU CATCH IT?
FLIP ON AUTO-PILOT... TRANSFER OVER WING-TO-WING...
...AND BRING 'EM BACK ALIVE!
IN FACT, IF I DO MEET THE YOUNG "ME," I'LL GIVE HIM... er, "ME"...SOME AMAZING THINGS TO PONDER!
BUT, DOC... IF THE AIRLINER RE-ENTERED THE WORM-HOLE, WON'T IT JUST GO FURTHER BACK IN TIME?

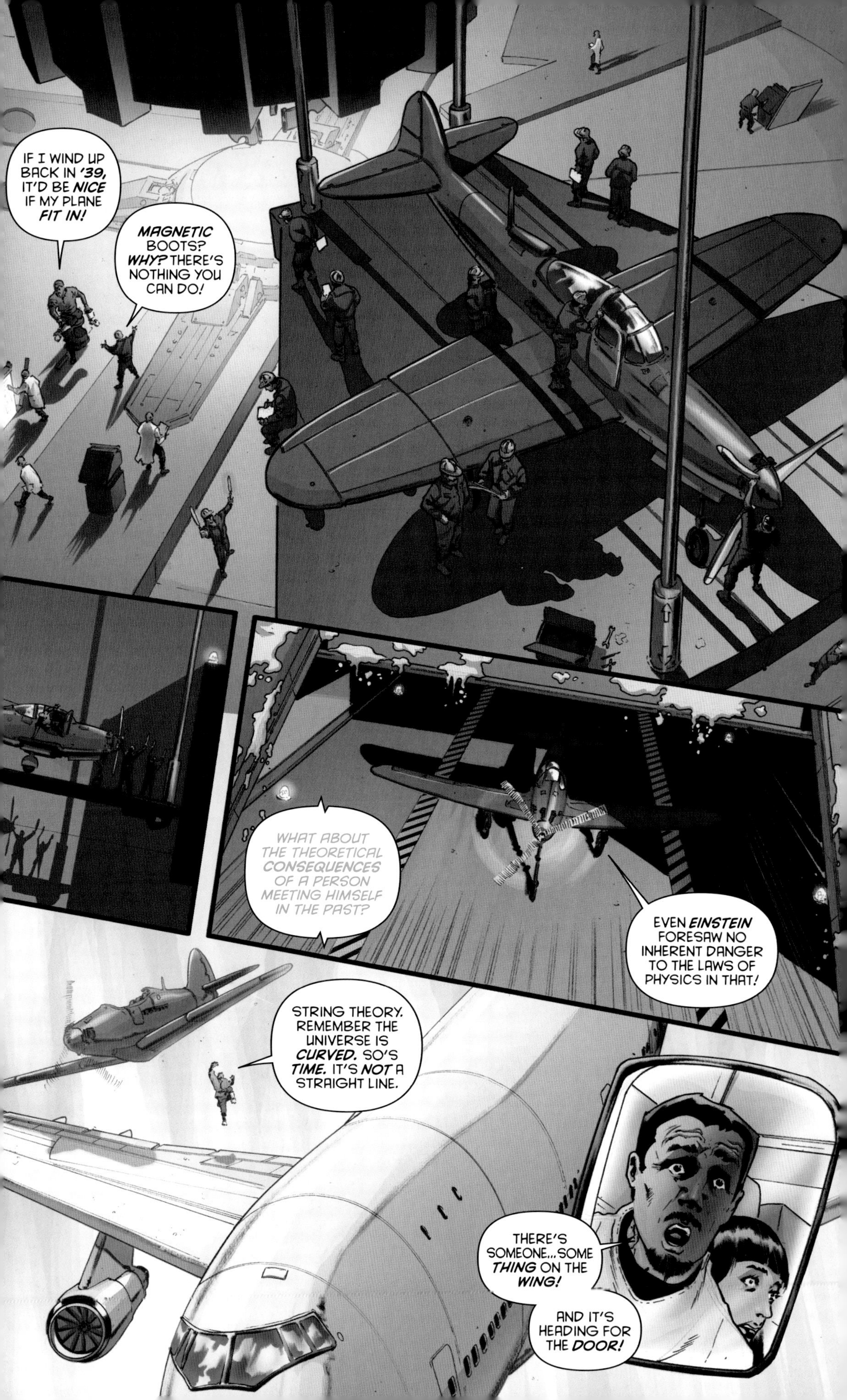
IF I WIND UP BACK IN '39, IT'D BE NICE IF MY PLANE FIT IN!
MAGNETIC BOOTS? WHY? THERE'S NOTHING YOU CAN DO!
WHAT ABOUT THE THEORETICAL CONSEQUENCES OF A PERSON MEETING HIMSELF IN THE PAST?
EVEN EINSTEIN FORESAW NO INHERENT DANGER TO THE LAWS OF PHYSICS IN THAT!
STRING THEORY. REMEMBER THE UNIVERSE IS CURVED. SO'S TIME. IT'S NOT A STRAIGHT LINE.
THERE'S SOMEONE... SOME THING ON THE WING!
AND IT'S HEADING FOR THE DOOR!

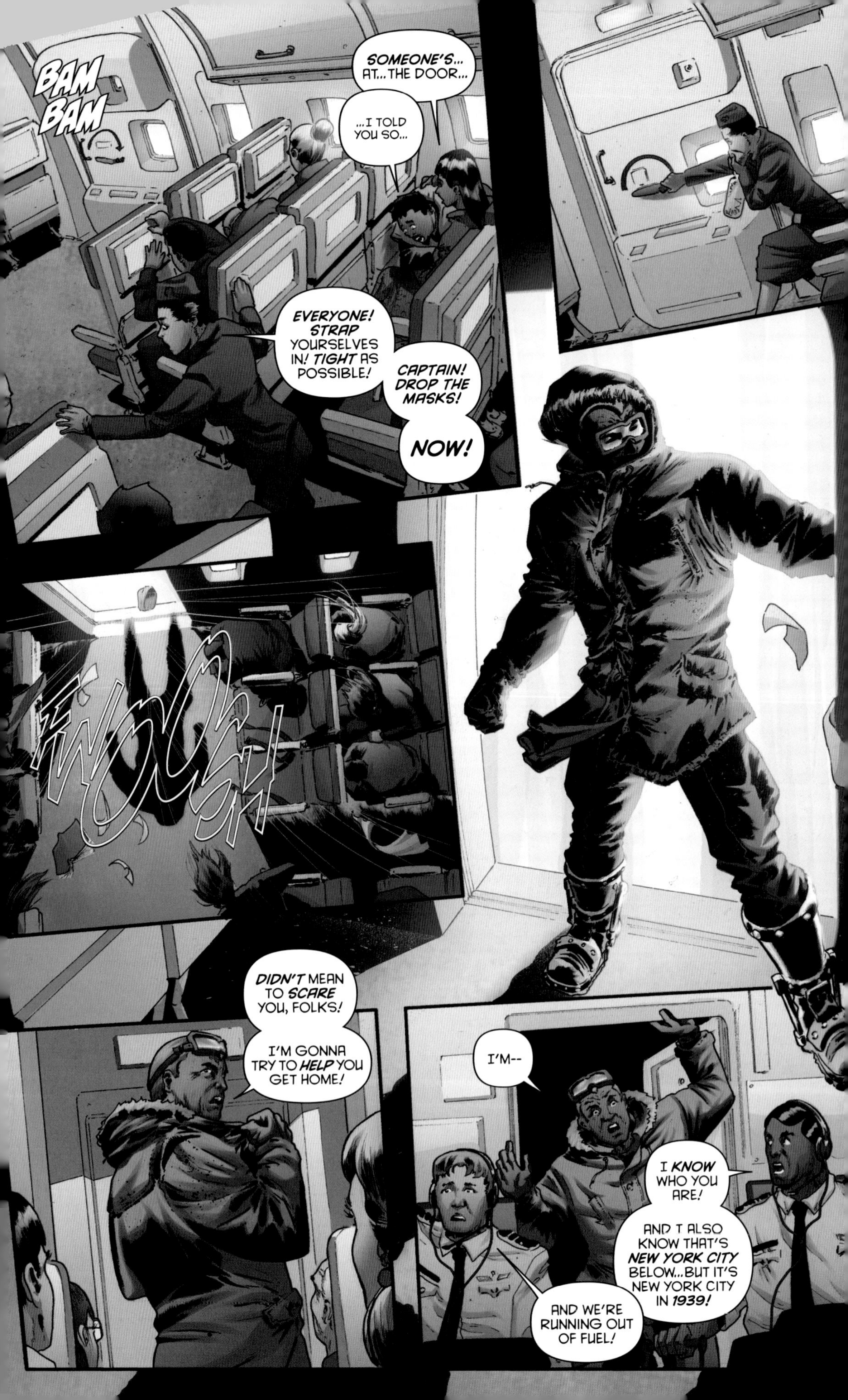
BAM BAM
SOMEONE'S... AT... THE DOOR...
...I TOLD YOU SO...
EVERYONE! STRAP YOURSELVES IN! TIGHT AS POSSIBLE!
CAPTAIN! DROP THE MASKS!
NOW!
FWOOSH
DIDN'T MEAN TO SCARE YOU, FOLKS!
I'M GONNA TRY TO HELP YOU GET HOME!
I'M--
I KNOW WHO YOU ARE!
AND I ALSO KNOW THAT'S NEW YORK CITY BELOW...BUT IT'S NEW YORK CITY IN 1939!
AND WE'RE RUNNING OUT OF FUEL!

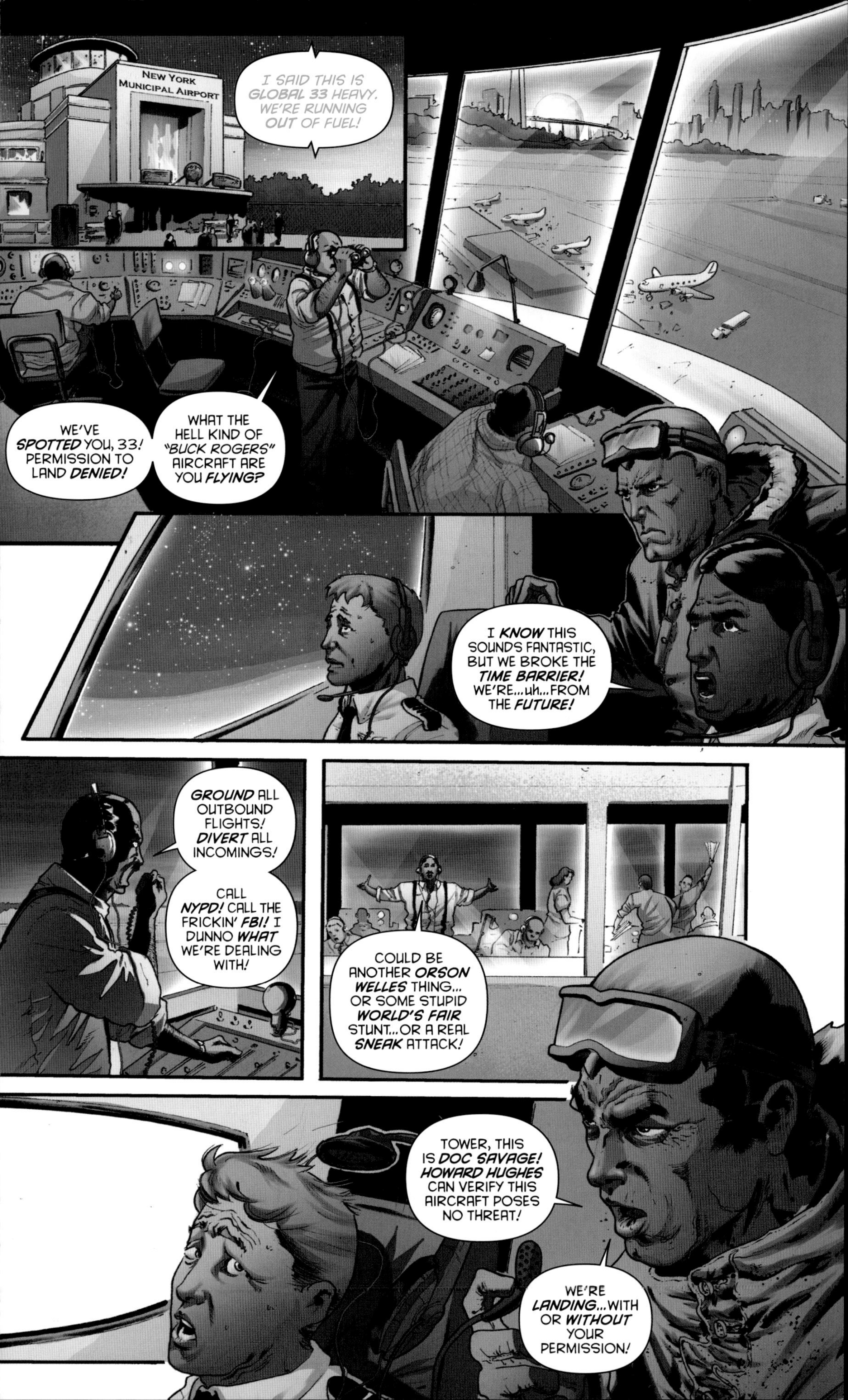
NEW YORK MUNICIPAL AIRPORT
I SAID THIS IS GLOBAL 33 HEAVY. WE'RE RUNNING OUT OF FUEL!
WE'VE SPOTTED YOU, 33! PERMISSION TO LAND DENIED!
WHAT THE HELL KIND OF "BUCK ROGERS" AIRCRAFT ARE YOU FLYING?
I KNOW THIS SOUNDS FANTASTIC, BUT WE BROKE THE TIME BARRIER! WE'RE...uh...FROM THE FUTURE!
GROUND ALL OUTBOUND FLIGHTS! DIVERT ALL INCOMINGS!
CALL NYPD! CALL THE FRICKIN' FBI! I DUNNO WHAT WE'RE DEALING WITH!
COULD BE ANOTHER ORSON WELLES THING... OR SOME STUPID WORLD'S FAIR STUNT...OR A REAL SNEAK ATTACK!
TOWER, THIS IS DOC SAVAGE! HOWARD HUGHES CAN VERIFY THIS AIRCRAFT POSES NO THREAT!
WE'RE LANDING...WITH OR WITHOUT YOUR PERMISSION!

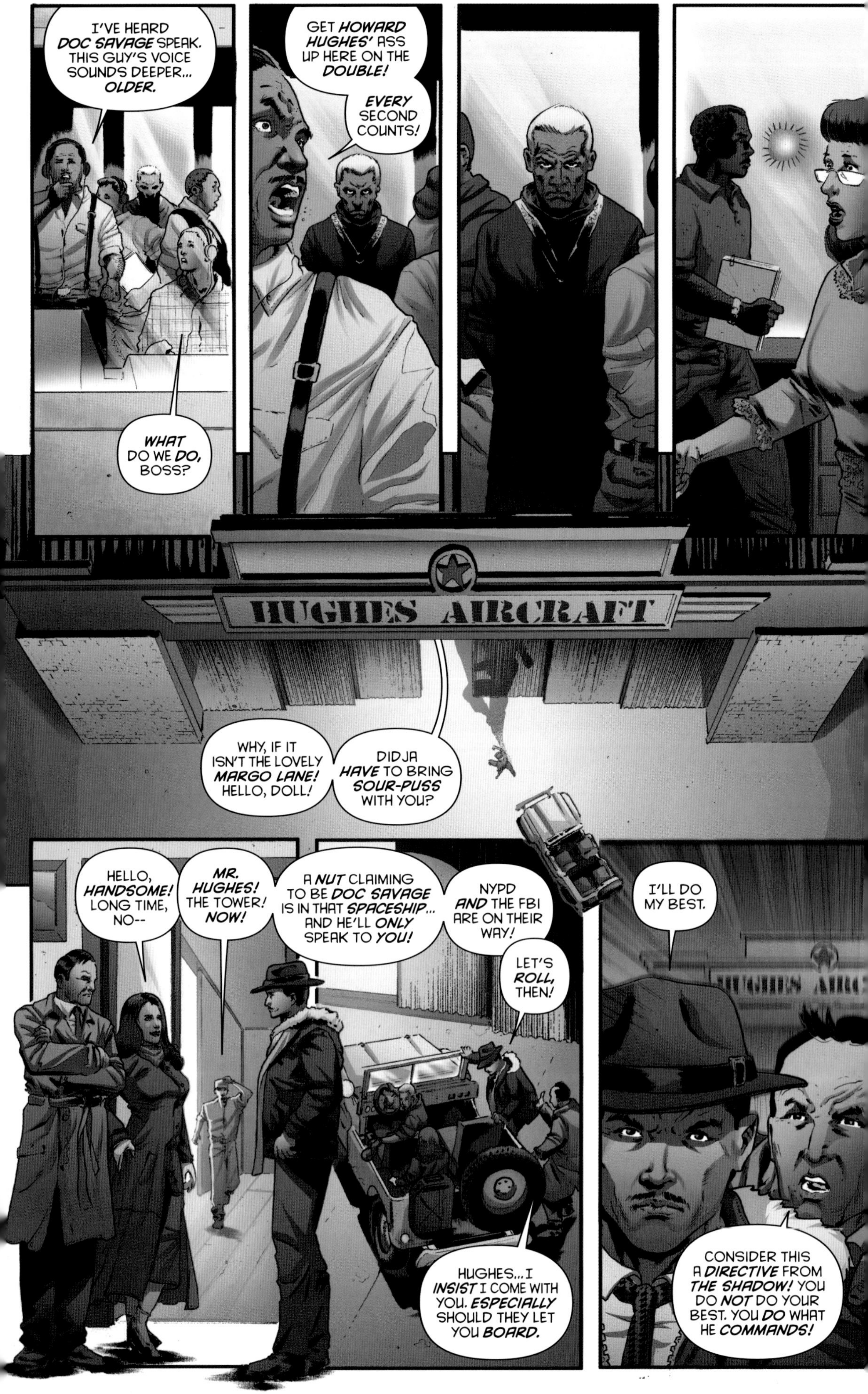
I'VE HEARD DOC SAVAGE SPEAK. THIS GUY'S VOICE SOUNDS DEEPER... OLDER.
WHAT DO WE DO, BOSS?
GET HOWARD HUGHES' ASS UP HERE ON THE DOUBLE!
EVERY SECOND COUNTS!
HUGHES AIRCRAFT
WHY, IF IT ISN'T THE LOVELY MARGO LANE! HELLO, DOLL!
DIDJA HAVE TO BRING SOUR-PUSS WITH YOU?
HELLO, HANDSOME! LONG TIME, NO--
MR. HUGHES! THE TOWER! NOW!
A NUT CLAIMING TO BE DOC SAVAGE IS IN THAT SPACESHIP... AND HE'LL ONLY SPEAK TO YOU!
NYPD AND THE FBI ARE ON THEIR WAY!
LET'S ROLL, THEN!
HUGHES...I INSIST I COME WITH YOU. ESPECIALLY SHOULD THEY LET YOU BOARD.
I'LL DO MY BEST.
CONSIDER THIS A DIRECTIVE FROM THE SHADOW! YOU DO NOT DO YOUR BEST. YOU DO WHAT HE COMMANDS!

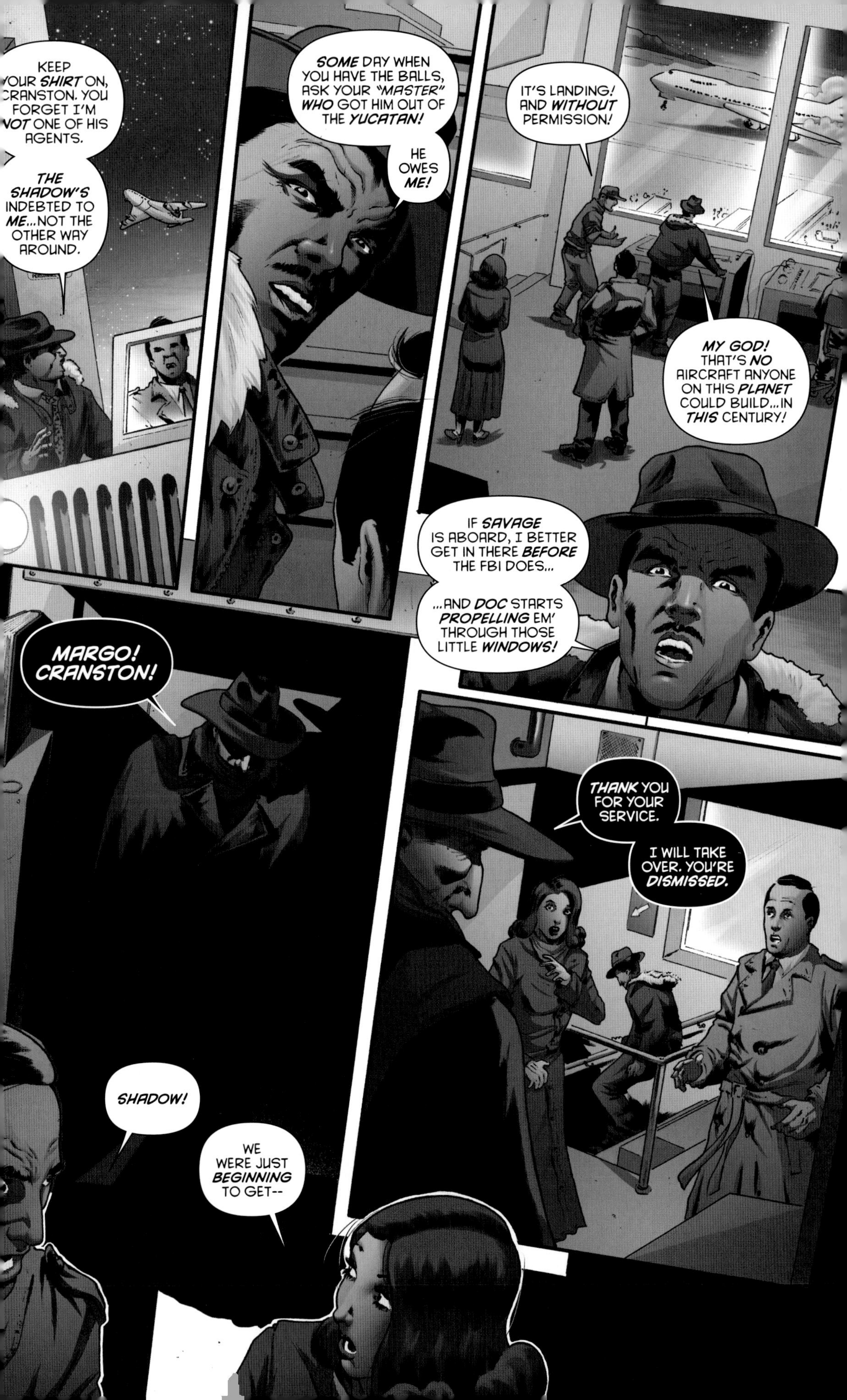
KEEP YOUR SHIRT ON, CRANSTON. YOU FORGET I'M NOT ONE OF HIS AGENTS.
THE SHADOW'S INDEBTED TO ME...NOT THE OTHER WAY AROUND.
SOME DAY WHEN YOU HAVE THE BALLS, ASK YOUR "MASTER" WHO GOT HIM OUT OF THE YUCATAN!
HE OWES ME!
IT'S LANDING! AND WITHOUT PERMISSION!
MY GOD! THAT'S NO AIRCRAFT ANYONE ON THIS PLANET COULD BUILD...IN THIS CENTURY!
IF SAVAGE IS ABOARD, I BETTER GET IN THERE BEFORE THE FBI DOES...
...AND DOC STARTS PROPELLING EM' THROUGH THOSE LITTLE WINDOWS!
MARGO! CRANSTON!
THANK YOU FOR YOUR SERVICE.
I WILL TAKE OVER. YOU'RE DISMISSED.
SHADOW!
WE WERE JUST BEGINNING TO GET--

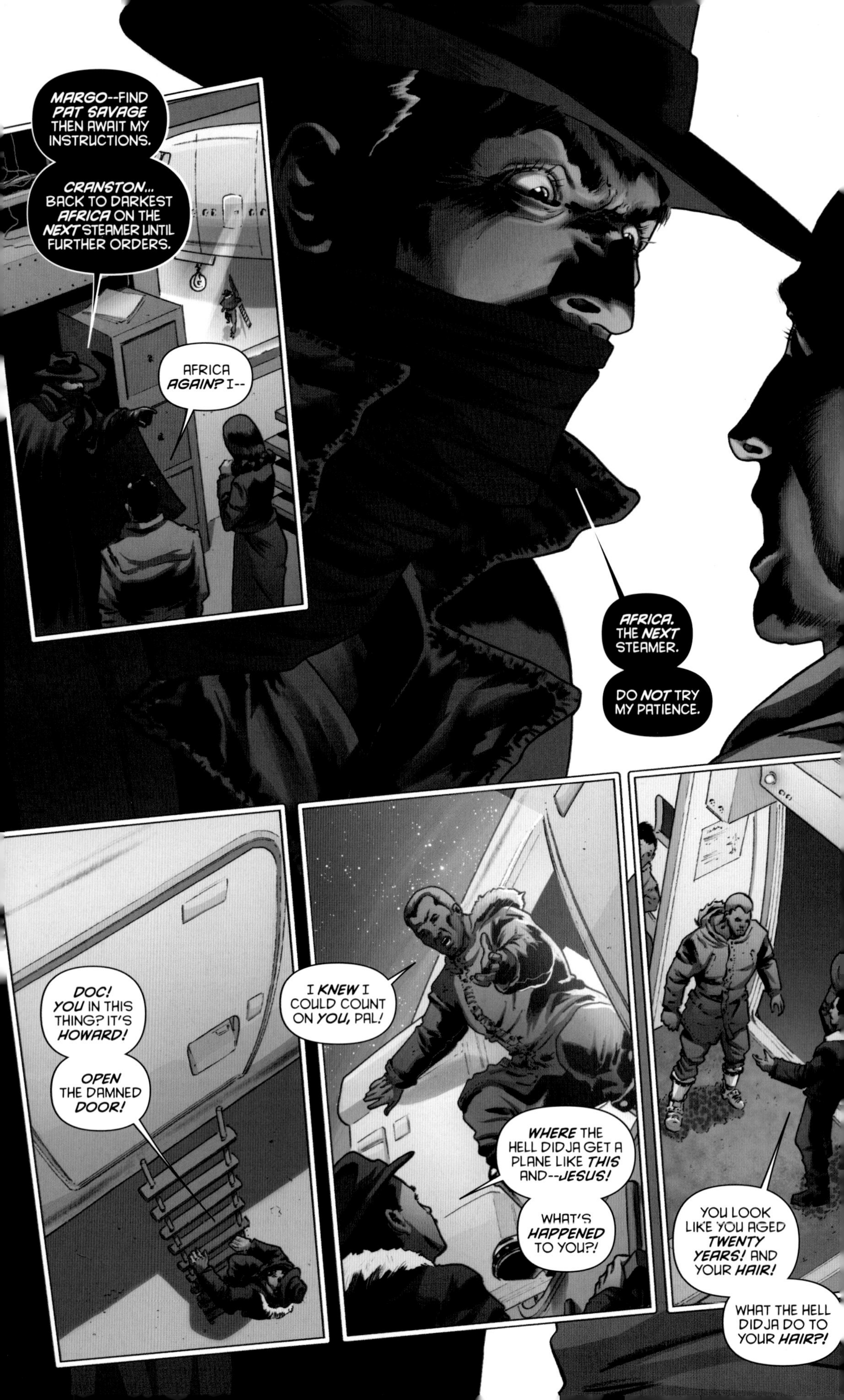

MARGO--FIND PAT SAVAGE THEN AWAIT MY INSTRUCTIONS.
CRANSTON... BACK TO DARKEST AFRICA ON THE NEXT STEAMER UNTIL FURTHER ORDERS.
AFRICA AGAIN? I--
AFRICA. THE NEXT STEAMER.
DO NOT TRY MY PATIENCE.
DOC! YOU IN THIS THING? IT'S HOWARD!
OPEN THE DAMNED DOOR!
I KNEW I COULD COUNT ON YOU, PAL!
WHERE THE HELL DIDJA GET A PLANE LIKE THIS AND--JESUS!
WHAT'S HAPPENED TO YOU?!
YOU LOOK LIKE YOU AGED TWENTY YEARS! AND YOUR HAIR!
WHAT THE HELL DIDJA DO TO YOUR HAIR?!

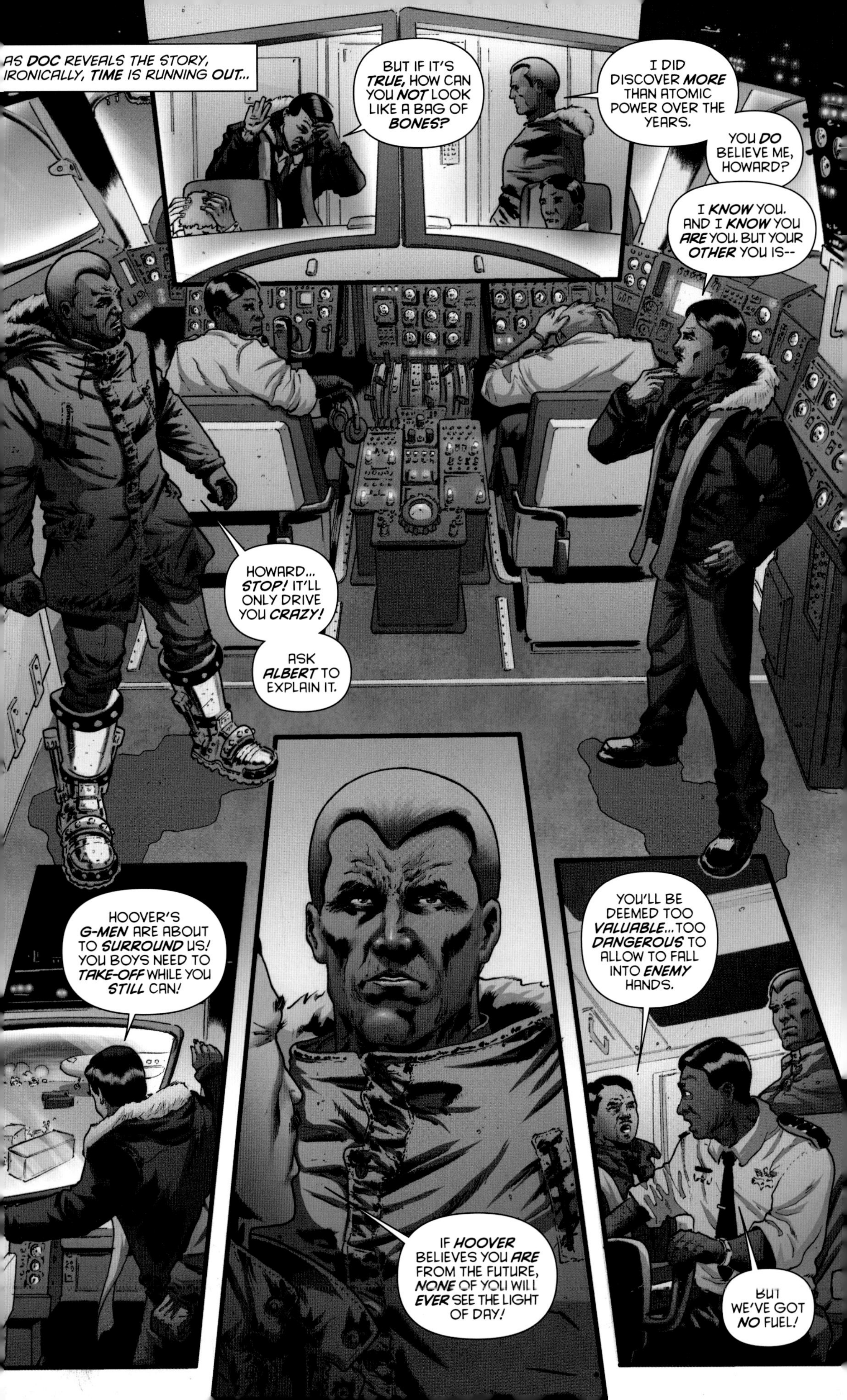
AS DOC REVEALS THE STORY, IRONICALLY, TIME IS RUNNING OUT...
BUT IF IT'S TRUE, HOW CAN YOU NOT LOOK LIKE A BAG OF BONES?
I DID DISCOVER MORE THAN ATOMIC POWER OVER THE YEARS.
YOU DO BELIEVE ME, HOWARD?
I KNOW YOU. AND I KNOW YOU ARE YOU. BUT YOUR OTHER YOU IS--
HOWARD... STOP! IT'LL ONLY DRIVE YOU CRAZY!
ASK ALBERT TO EXPLAIN IT.
HOOVER'S G-MEN ARE ABOUT TO SURROUND US! YOU BOYS NEED TO TAKE-OFF WHILE YOU STILL CAN!
IF HOOVER BELIEVES YOU ARE FROM THE FUTURE, NONE OF YOU WILL EVER SEE THE LIGHT OF DAY!
YOU'LL BE DEEMED TOO VALUABLE...TOO DANGEROUS TO ALLOW TO FALL INTO ENEMY HANDS.
BUT WE'VE GOT NO FUEL!

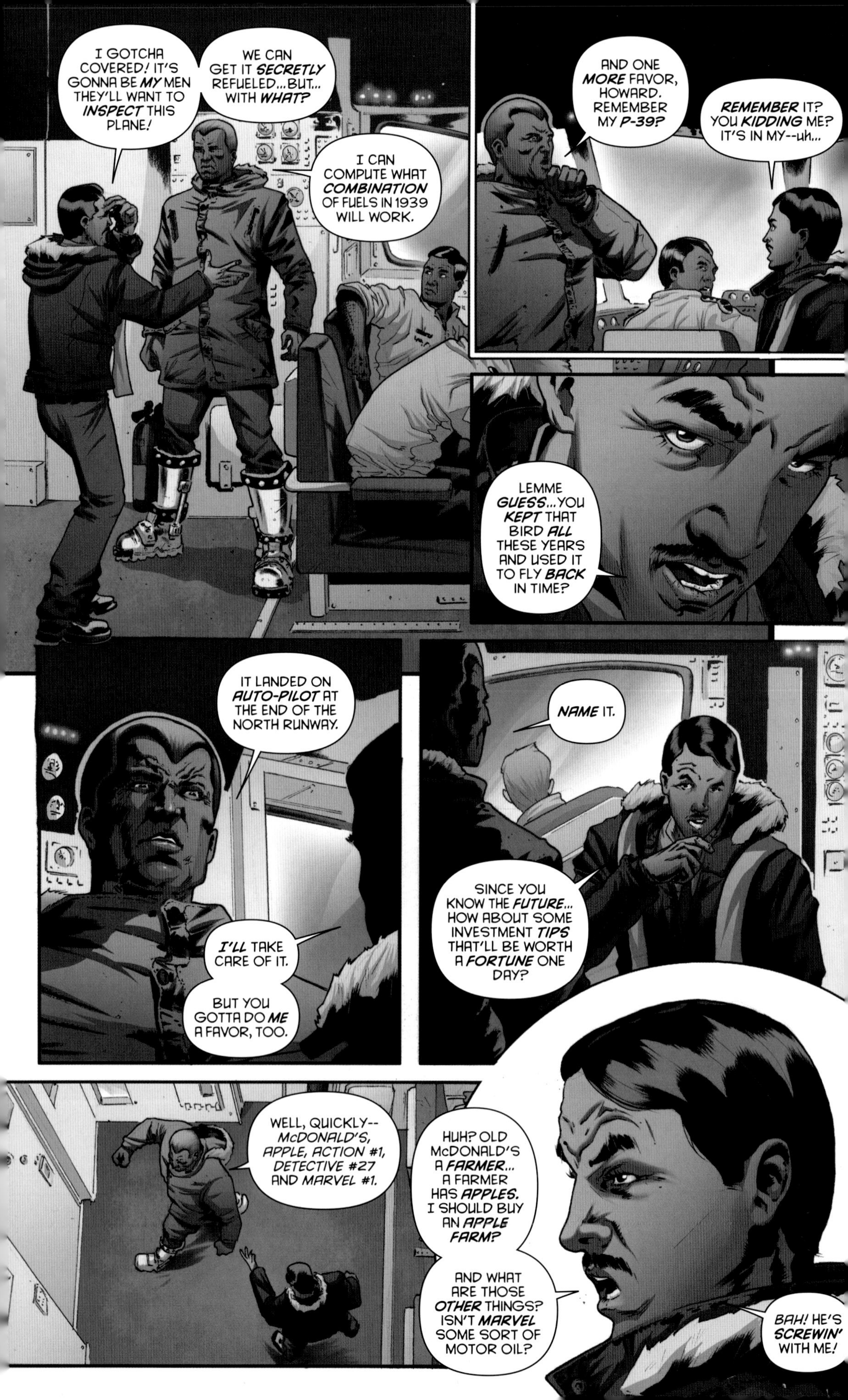
I GOTCHA COVERED! IT'S GONNA BE MY MEN THEY'LL WANT TO INSPECT THIS PLANE!
WE CAN GET IT SECRETLY REFUELED...BUT... WITH WHAT?
I CAN COMPUTE WHAT COMBINATION OF FUELS IN 1939 WILL WORK.
AND ONE MORE FAVOR, HOWARD. REMEMBER MY P-39?
REMEMBER IT? YOU KIDDING ME? IT'S IN MY--uh...
LEMME GUESS...YOU KEPT THAT BIRD ALL THESE YEARS AND USED IT TO FLY BACK IN TIME?
IT LANDED ON AUTO-PILOT AT THE END OF THE NORTH RUNWAY.
I'LL TAKE CARE OF IT.
BUT YOU GOTTA DO ME A FAVOR, TOO.
NAME IT.
SINCE YOU KNOW THE FUTURE... HOW ABOUT SOME INVESTMENT TIPS THAT'LL BE WORTH A FORTUNE ONE DAY?
WELL, QUICKLY-- McDONALD'S, APPLE, ACTION #1, DETECTIVE #27 AND MARVEL #1.
HUH? OLD McDONALD'S A FARMER... A FARMER HAS APPLES. I SHOULD BUY AN APPLE FARM?
AND WHAT ARE THOSE OTHER THINGS? ISN'T MARVEL SOME SORT OF MOTOR OIL?
BAH! HE'S SCREWIN' WITH ME!

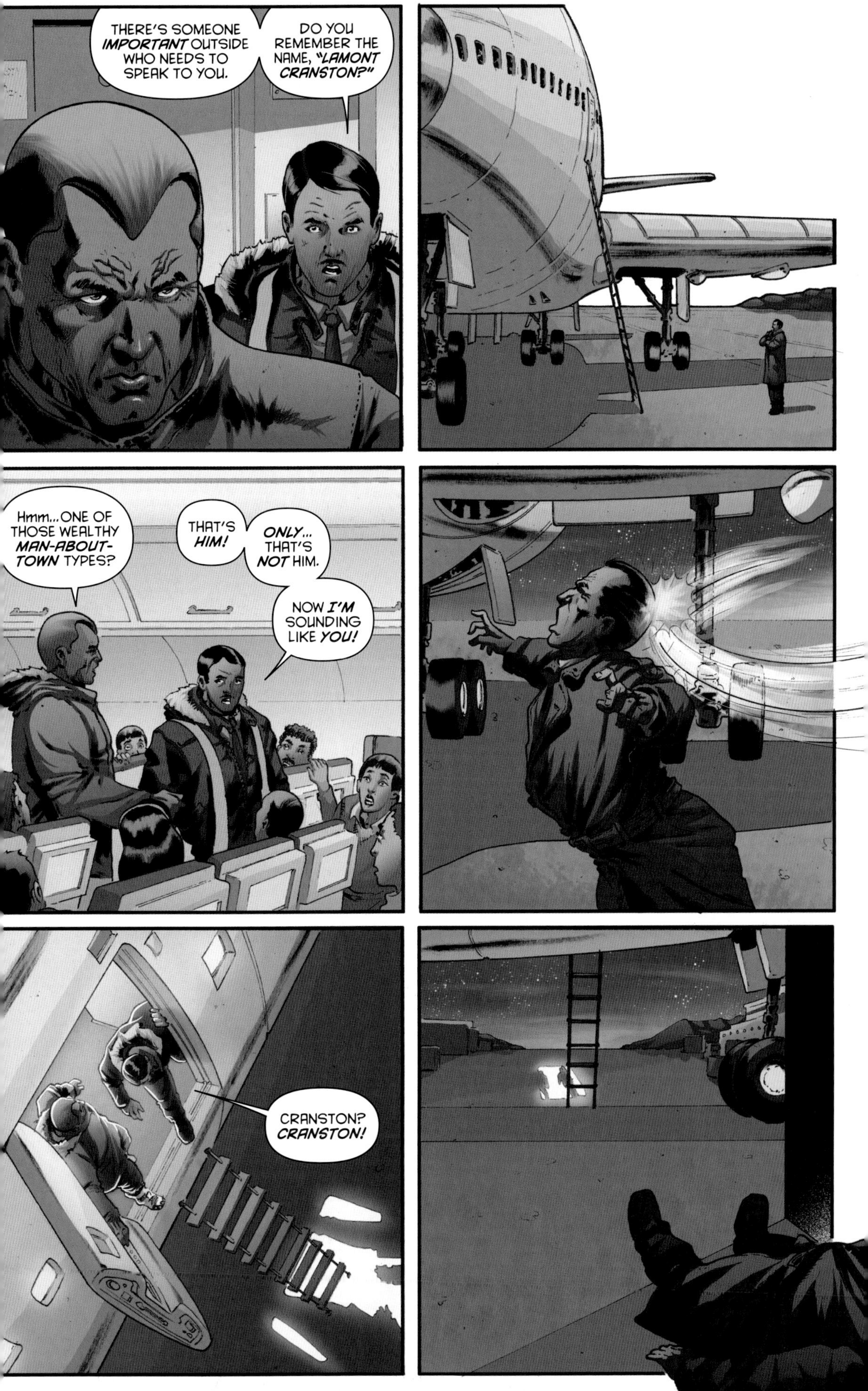

THERE'S SOMEONE *IMPORTANT* OUTSIDE WHO NEEDS TO SPEAK TO YOU.
DO YOU REMEMBER THE NAME, *"LAMONT CRANSTON?"*
Hmm... ONE OF THOSE WEALTHY *MAN-ABOUT-TOWN* TYPES?
THAT'S *HIM!*
ONLY... THAT'S *NOT* HIM.
NOW *I'M* SOUNDING LIKE *YOU!*
CRANSTON? *CRANSTON!*

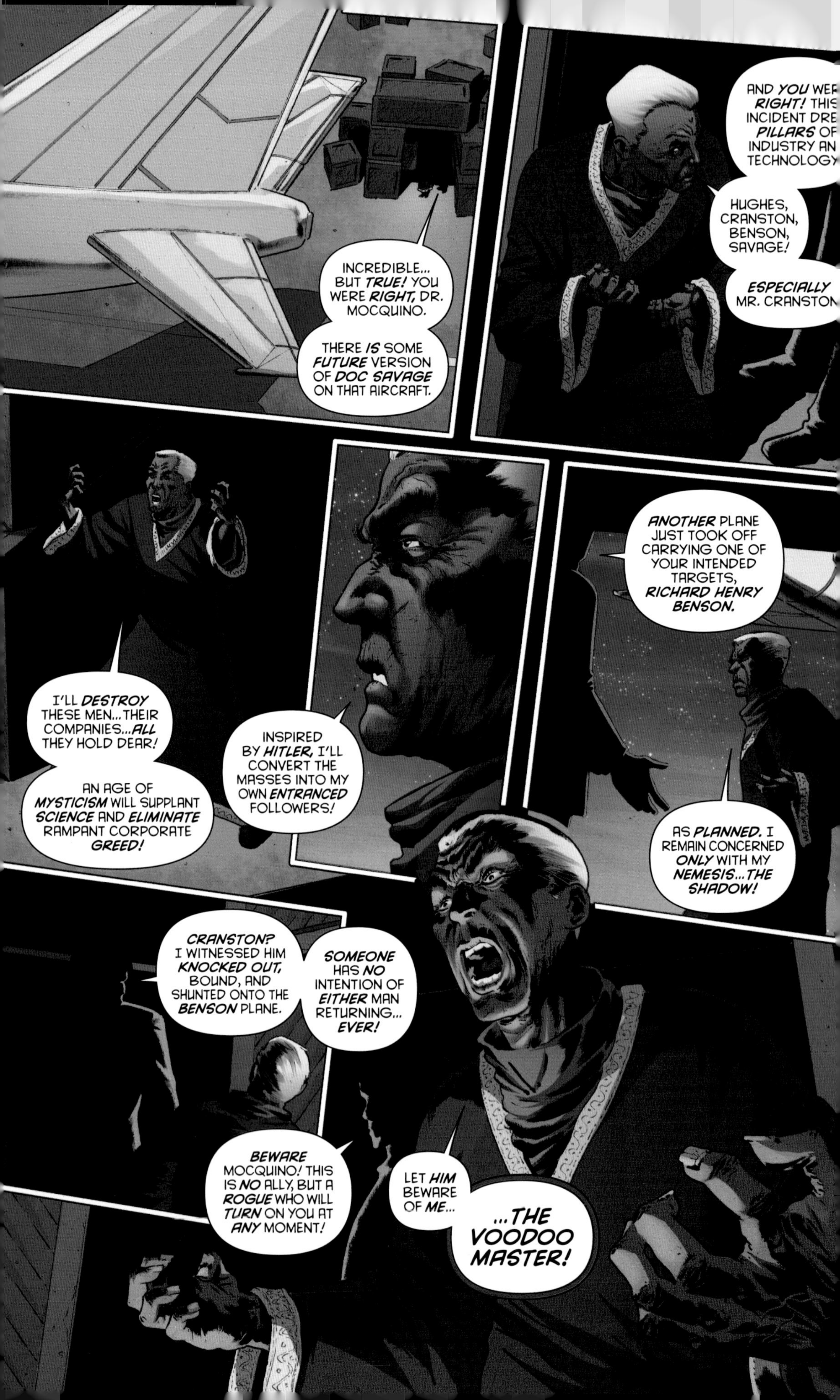

INCREDIBLE... BUT TRUE! YOU WERE RIGHT, DR. MOCQUINO.
THERE IS SOME FUTURE VERSION OF DOC SAVAGE ON THAT AIRCRAFT.
AND YOU WER RIGHT! THIS INCIDENT DRE PILLARS OF INDUSTRY AN TECHNOLOGY
HUGHES, CRANSTON, BENSON, SAVAGE!
ESPECIALLY MR. CRANSTON
I'LL DESTROY THESE MEN... THEIR COMPANIES... ALL THEY HOLD DEAR!
AN AGE OF MYSTICISM WILL SUPPLANT SCIENCE AND ELIMINATE RAMPANT CORPORATE GREED!
INSPIRED BY HITLER, I'LL CONVERT THE MASSES INTO MY OWN ENTRANCED FOLLOWERS!
ANOTHER PLANE JUST TOOK OFF CARRYING ONE OF YOUR INTENDED TARGETS, RICHARD HENRY BENSON.
AS PLANNED. I REMAIN CONCERNED ONLY WITH MY NEMESIS... THE SHADOW!
CRANSTON? I WITNESSED HIM KNOCKED OUT, BOUND, AND SHUNTED ONTO THE BENSON PLANE.
SOMEONE HAS NO INTENTION OF EITHER MAN RETURNING... EVER!
BEWARE MOCQUINO! THIS IS NO ALLY, BUT A ROGUE WHO WILL TURN ON YOU AT ANY MOMENT!
LET HIM BEWARE OF ME...
...THE VOODOO MASTER!

TWO

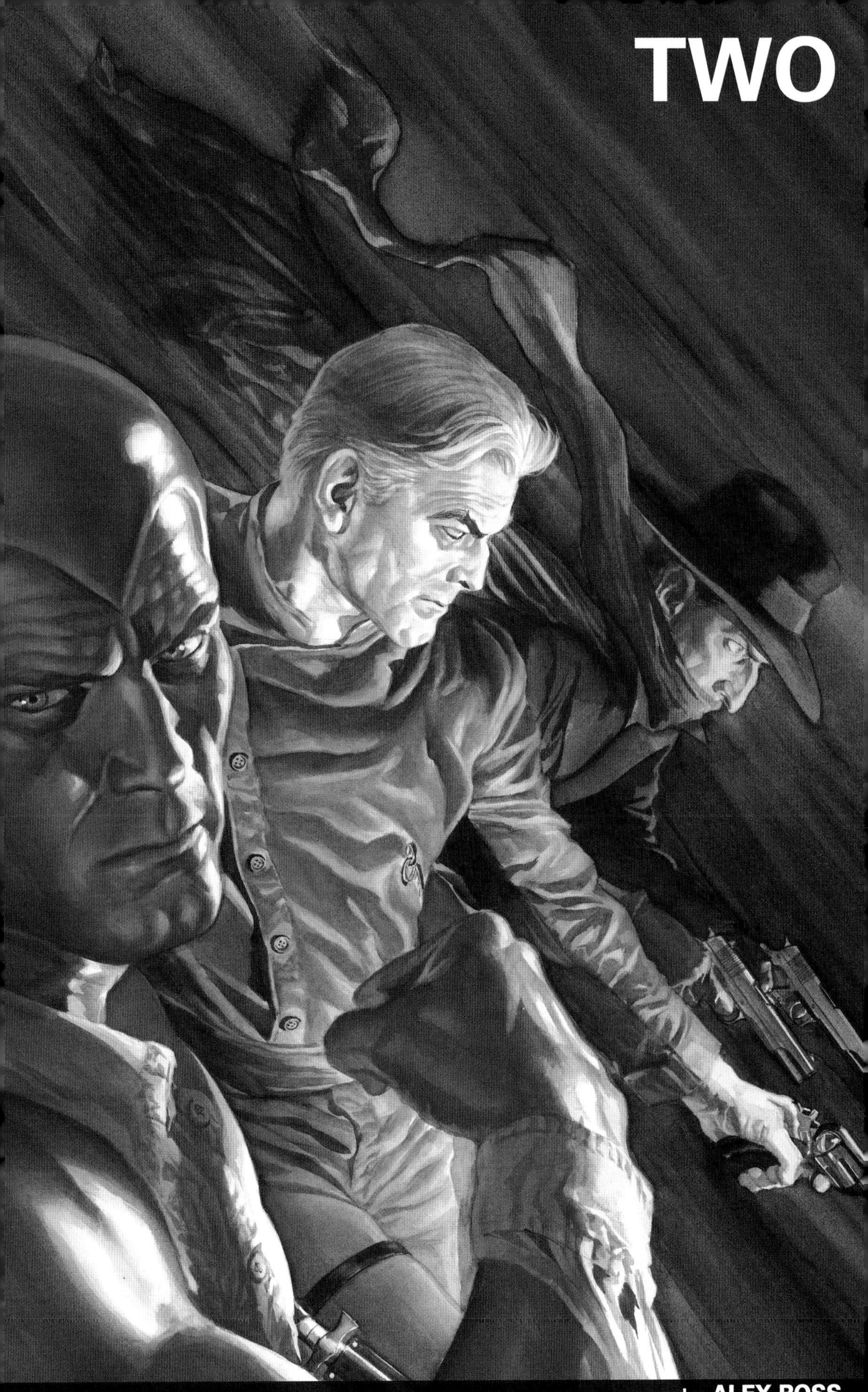

cover by **ALEX ROSS**

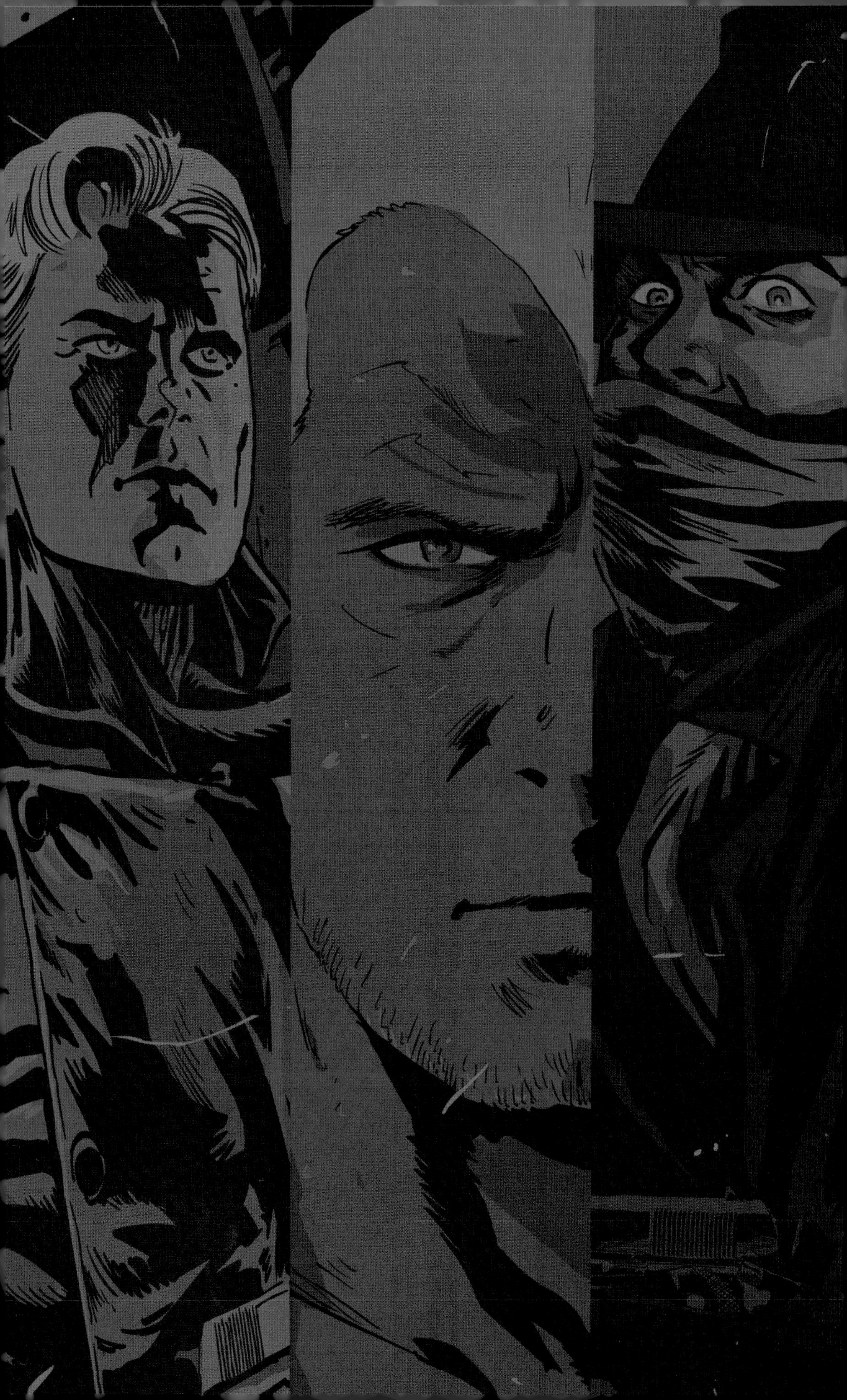

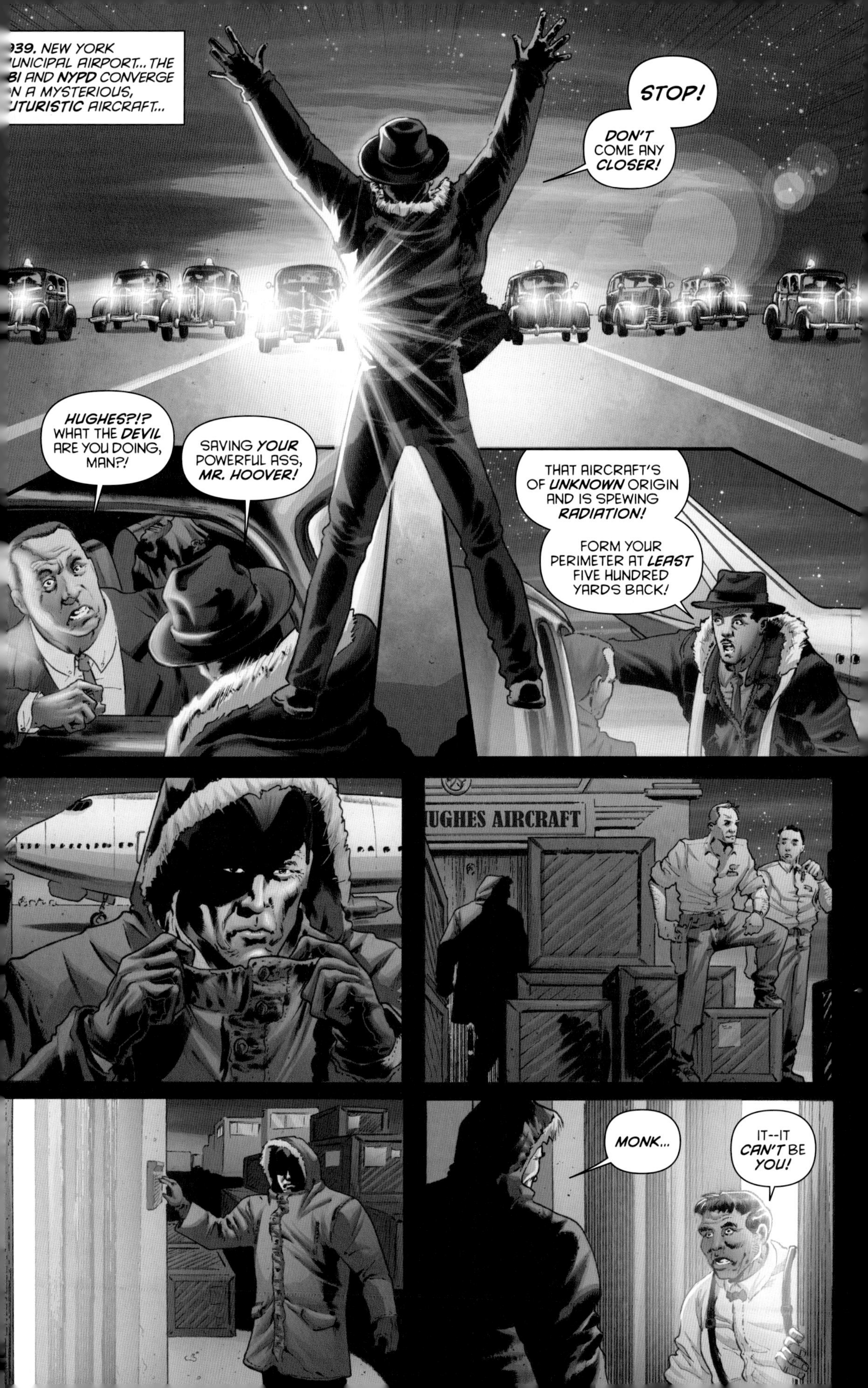

939. NEW YORK
UNICIPAL AIRPORT... THE
BI AND NYPD CONVERGE
N A MYSTERIOUS,
UTURISTIC AIRCRAFT...
STOP!
DON'T COME ANY CLOSER!
HUGHES?!? WHAT THE DEVIL ARE YOU DOING, MAN?!
SAVING YOUR POWERFUL ASS, MR. HOOVER!
THAT AIRCRAFT'S OF UNKNOWN ORIGIN AND IS SPEWING RADIATION!
FORM YOUR PERIMETER AT LEAST FIVE HUNDRED YARDS BACK!
HUGHES AIRCRAFT
MONK...
IT--IT CAN'T BE YOU!

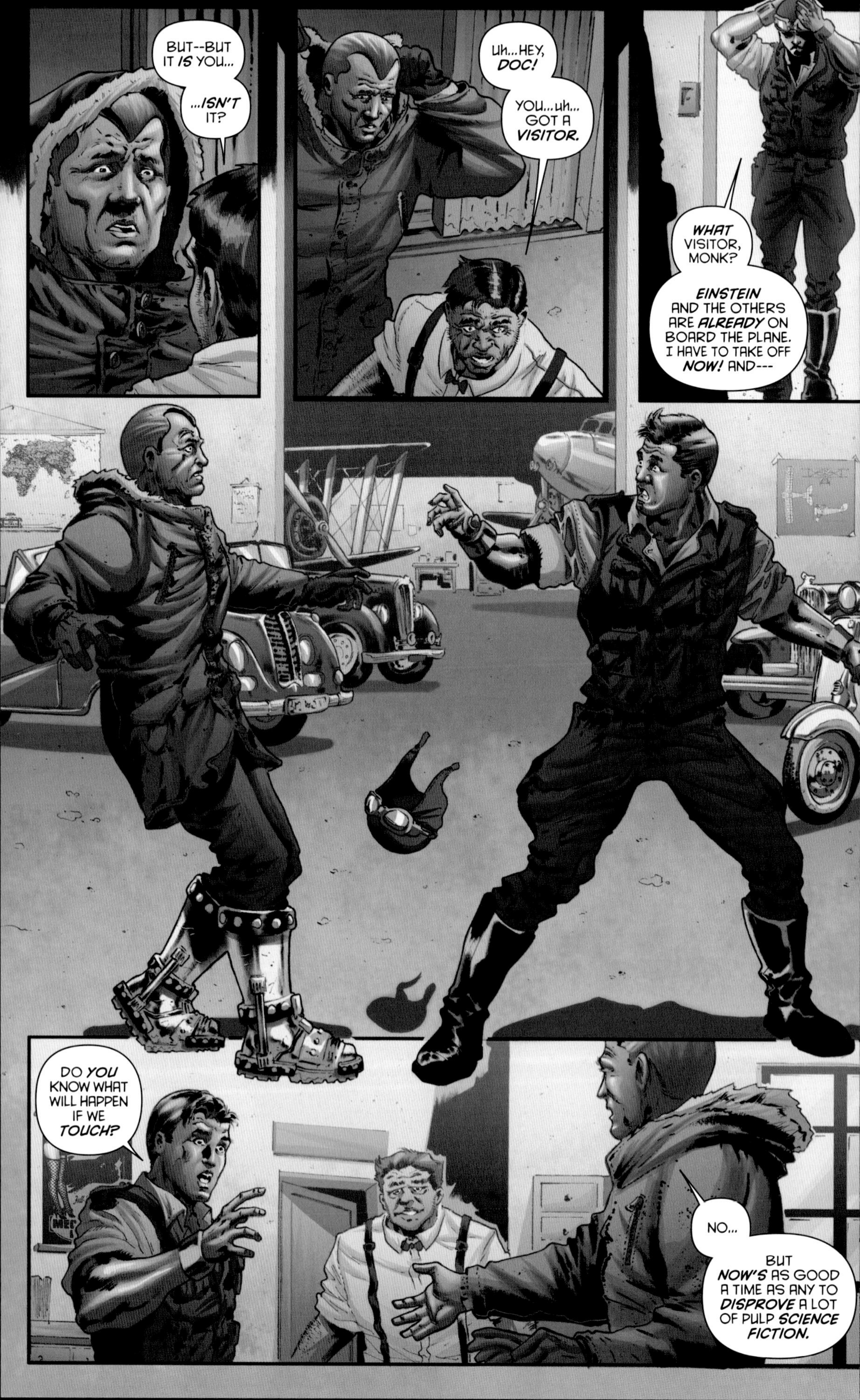
BUT--BUT IT IS YOU...
...ISN'T IT?
Uh...HEY, DOC!
YOU...uh... GOT A VISITOR.
WHAT VISITOR, MONK?
EINSTEIN AND THE OTHERS ARE ALREADY ON BOARD THE PLANE. I HAVE TO TAKE OFF NOW! AND---
DO YOU KNOW WHAT WILL HAPPEN IF WE TOUCH?
NO...
BUT NOW'S AS GOOD A TIME AS ANY TO DISPROVE A LOT OF PULP SCIENCE FICTION.

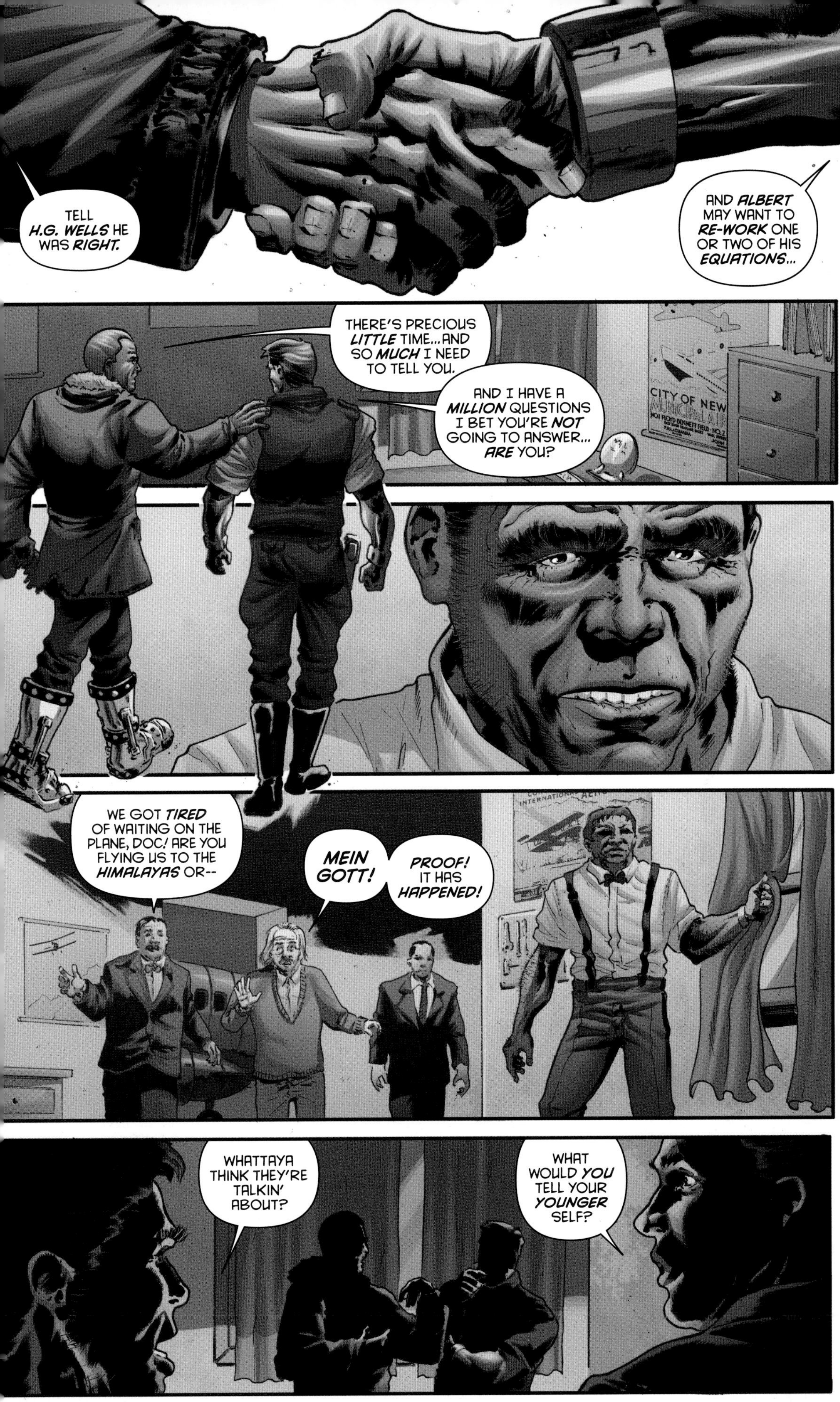
TELL H.G. WELLS HE WAS RIGHT.
AND ALBERT MAY WANT TO RE-WORK ONE OR TWO OF HIS EQUATIONS...
THERE'S PRECIOUS LITTLE TIME...AND SO MUCH I NEED TO TELL YOU.
AND I HAVE A MILLION QUESTIONS I BET YOU'RE NOT GOING TO ANSWER... ARE YOU?
CITY OF NEW
MUNICIPAL AI
WE GOT TIRED OF WAITING ON THE PLANE, DOC! ARE YOU FLYING US TO THE HIMALAYAS OR--
MEIN GOTT!
PROOF! IT HAS HAPPENED!
WHATTAYA THINK THEY'RE TALKIN' ABOUT?
WHAT WOULD YOU TELL YOUR YOUNGER SELF?

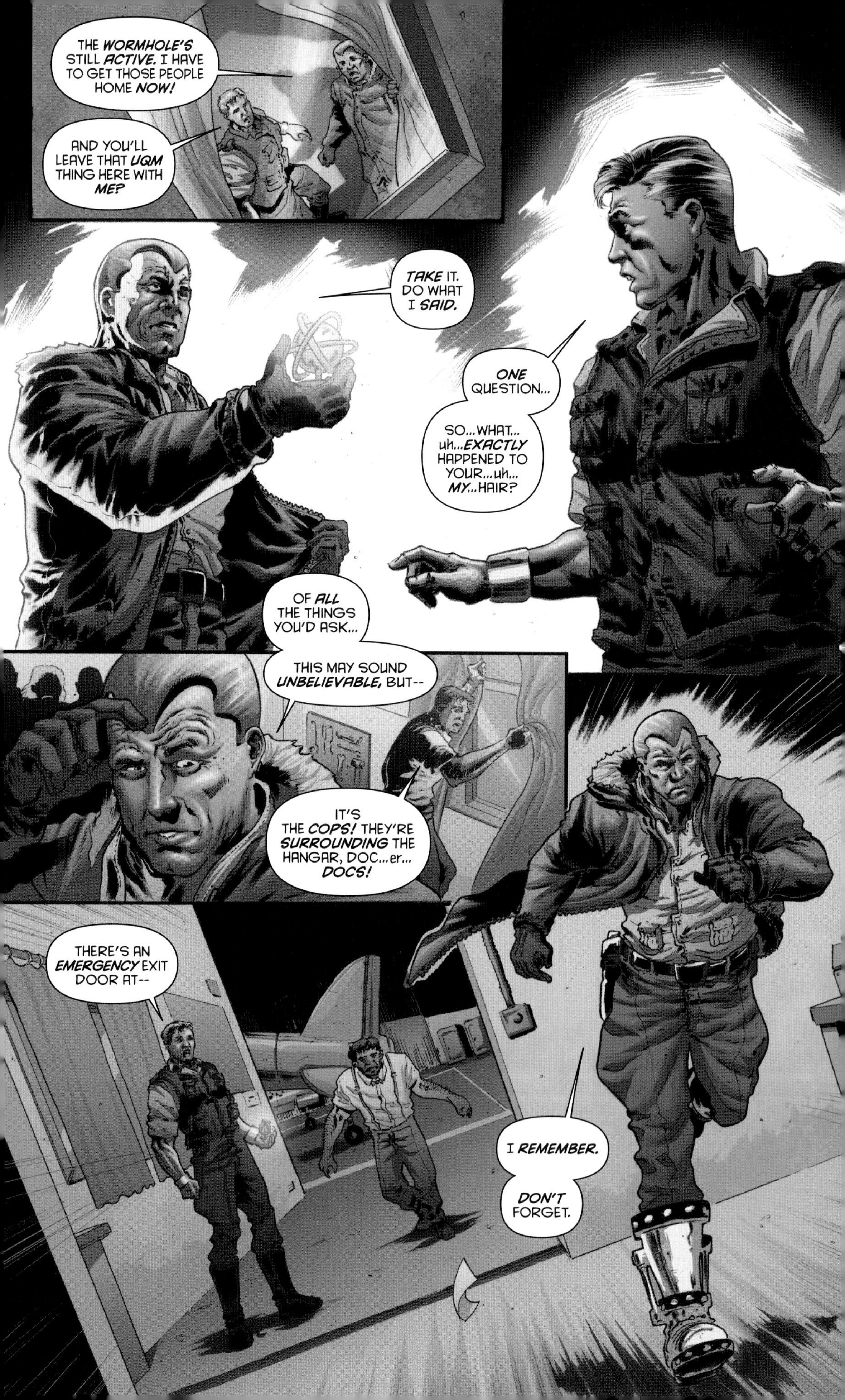
THE WORMHOLE'S STILL ACTIVE. I HAVE TO GET THOSE PEOPLE HOME NOW!
AND YOU'LL LEAVE THAT UQM THING HERE WITH ME?
TAKE IT. DO WHAT I SAID.
ONE QUESTION...
SO...WHAT... uh...EXACTLY HAPPENED TO YOUR...uh... MY...HAIR?
OF ALL THE THINGS YOU'D ASK...
THIS MAY SOUND UNBELIEVABLE, BUT--
IT'S THE COPS! THEY'RE SURROUNDING THE HANGAR, DOC...er... DOCS!
THERE'S AN EMERGENCY EXIT DOOR AT--
I REMEMBER.
DON'T FORGET.

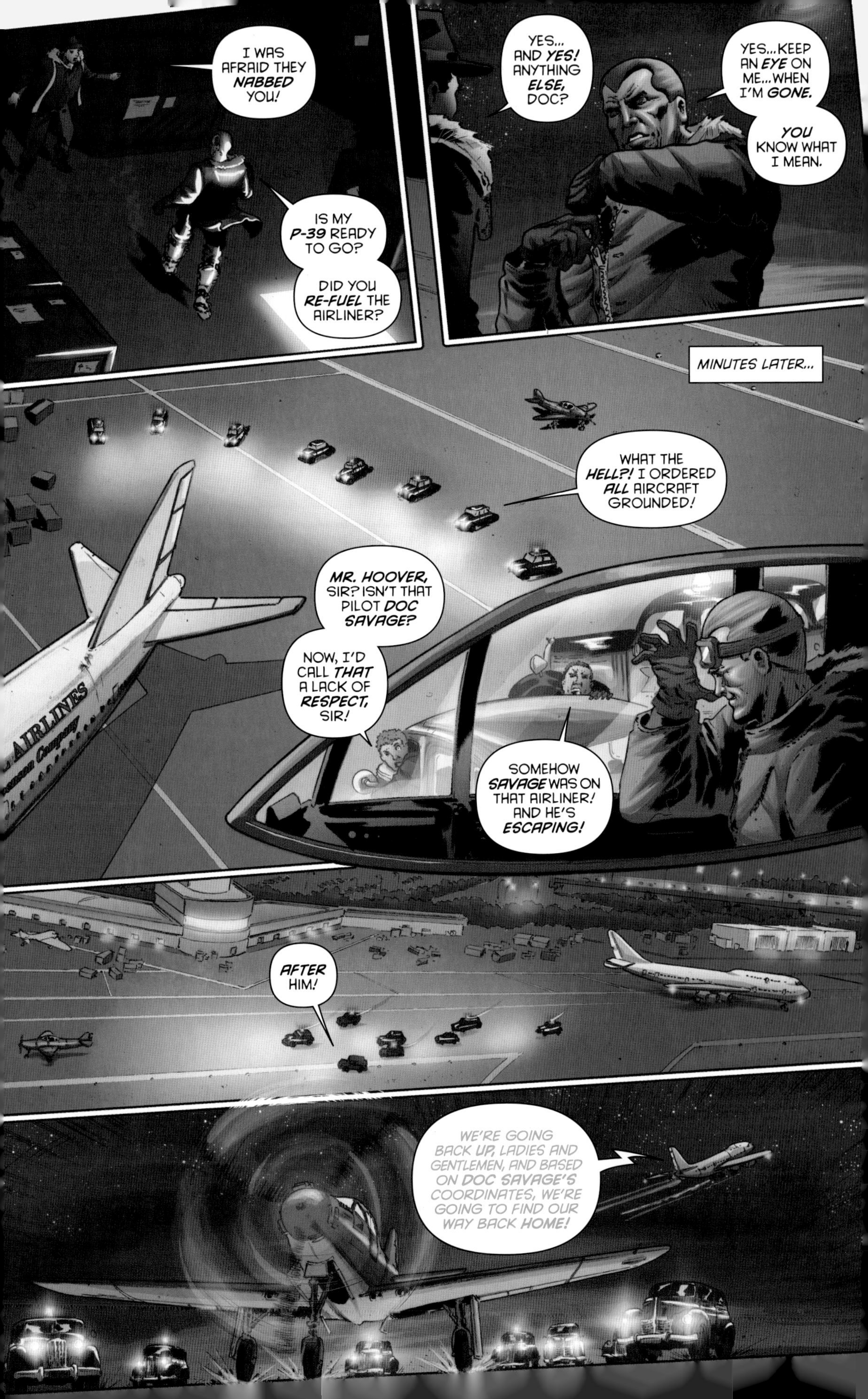
I WAS AFRAID THEY NABBED YOU!
IS MY P-39 READY TO GO?
DID YOU RE-FUEL THE AIRLINER?
YES... AND YES! ANYTHING ELSE, DOC?
YES...KEEP AN EYE ON ME...WHEN I'M GONE.
YOU KNOW WHAT I MEAN.
MINUTES LATER...
WHAT THE HELL?! I ORDERED ALL AIRCRAFT GROUNDED!
MR. HOOVER, SIR? ISN'T THAT PILOT DOC SAVAGE?
NOW, I'D CALL THAT A LACK OF RESPECT, SIR!
SOMEHOW SAVAGE WAS ON THAT AIRLINER! AND HE'S ESCAPING!
AIRLINES
AFTER HIM!
WE'RE GOING BACK UP, LADIES AND GENTLEMEN, AND BASED ON DOC SAVAGE'S COORDINATES, WE'RE GOING TO FIND OUR WAY BACK HOME!

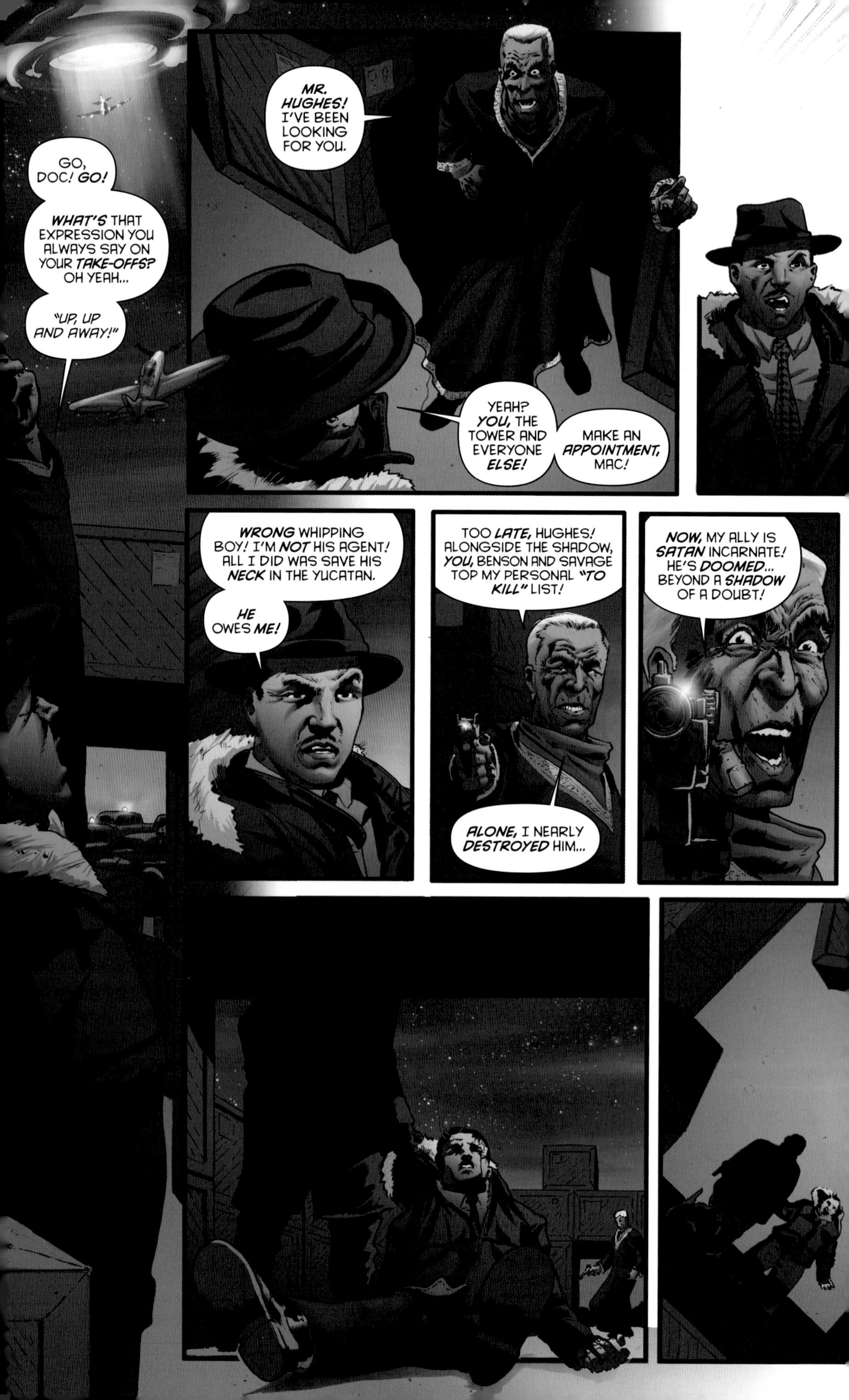

GO, DOC! GO!
WHAT'S THAT EXPRESSION YOU ALWAYS SAY ON YOUR TAKE-OFFS? OH YEAH...
"UP, UP AND AWAY!"
MR. HUGHES! I'VE BEEN LOOKING FOR YOU.
YEAH? YOU, THE TOWER AND EVERYONE ELSE!
MAKE AN APPOINTMENT, MAC!
WRONG WHIPPING BOY! I'M NOT HIS AGENT! ALL I DID WAS SAVE HIS NECK IN THE YUCATAN.
HE OWES ME!
TOO LATE, HUGHES! ALONGSIDE THE SHADOW, YOU, BENSON AND SAVAGE TOP MY PERSONAL "TO KILL" LIST!
ALONE, I NEARLY DESTROYED HIM...
NOW, MY ALLY IS SATAN INCARNATE! HE'S DOOMED... BEYOND A SHADOW OF A DOUBT!

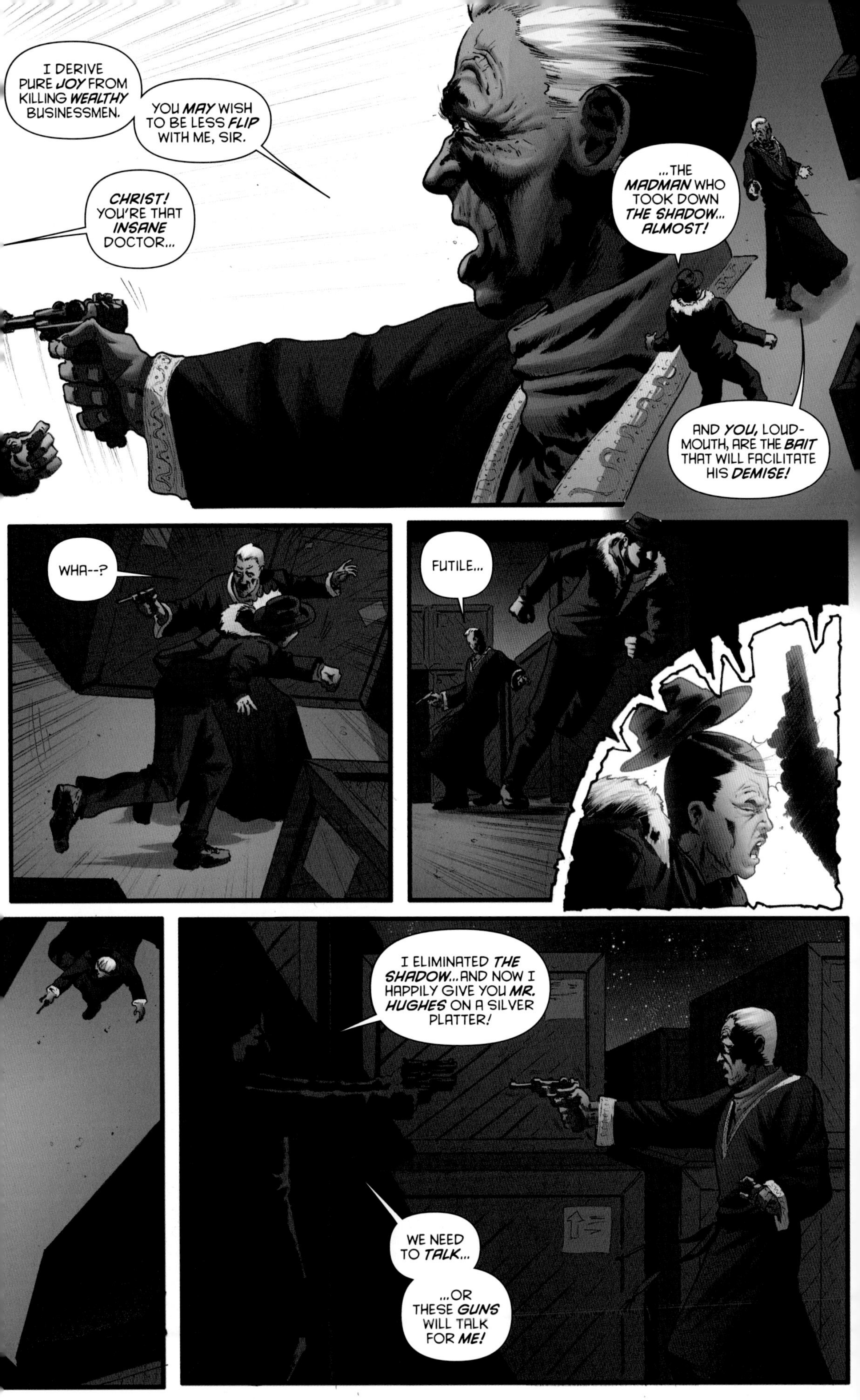
I DERIVE PURE JOY FROM KILLING WEALTHY BUSINESSMEN.
YOU MAY WISH TO BE LESS FLIP WITH ME, SIR.
CHRIST! YOU'RE THAT INSANE DOCTOR...
...THE MADMAN WHO TOOK DOWN THE SHADOW... ALMOST!
AND YOU, LOUD-MOUTH, ARE THE BAIT THAT WILL FACILITATE HIS DEMISE!
WHA--?
FUTILE...
I ELIMINATED THE SHADOW...AND NOW I HAPPILY GIVE YOU MR. HUGHES ON A SILVER PLATTER!
WE NEED TO TALK...
...OR THESE GUNS WILL TALK FOR ME!

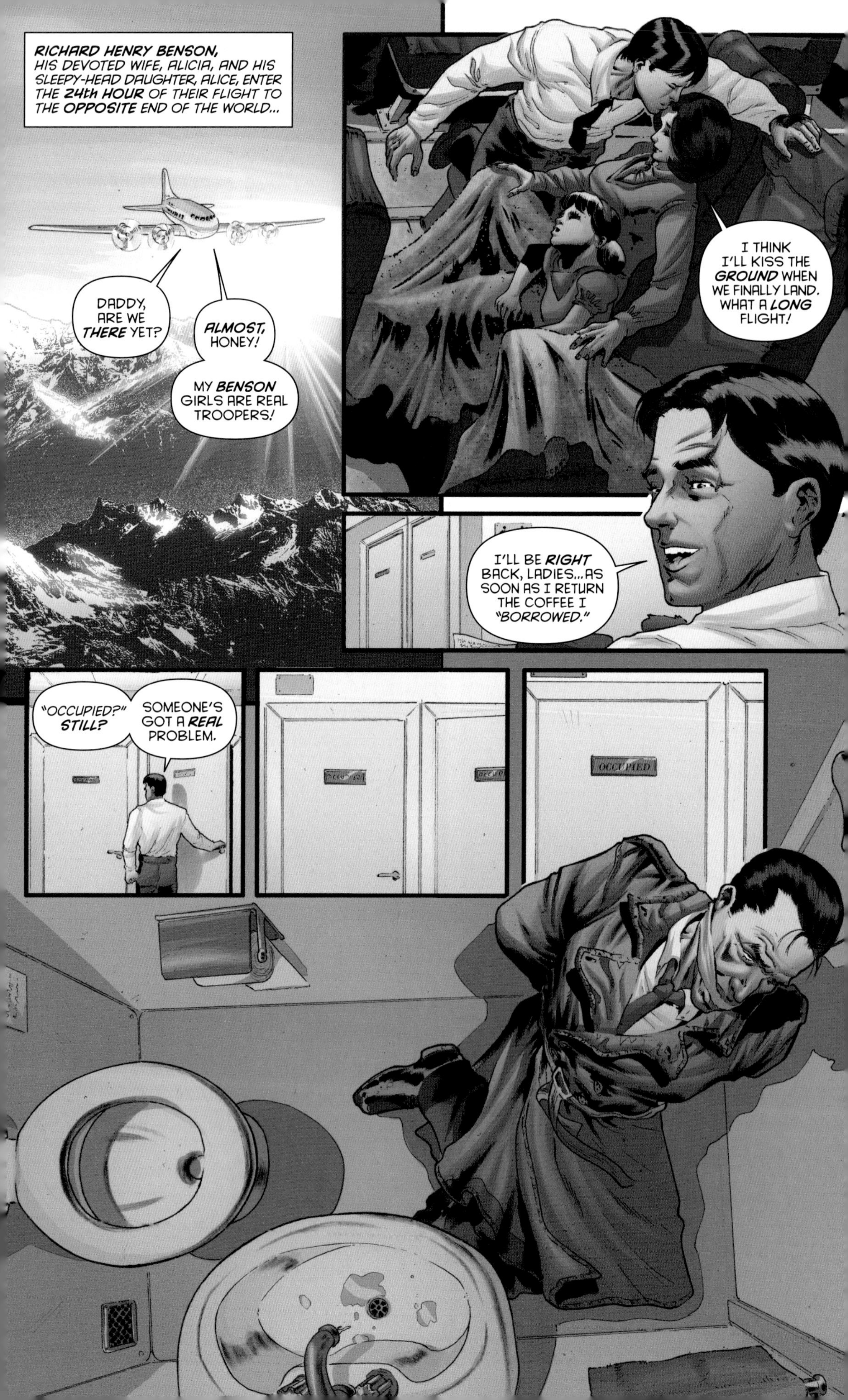

RICHARD HENRY BENSON, HIS DEVOTED WIFE, ALICIA, AND HIS SLEEPY-HEAD DAUGHTER, ALICE, ENTER THE 24th HOUR OF THEIR FLIGHT TO THE OPPOSITE END OF THE WORLD...
DADDY, ARE WE THERE YET?
ALMOST, HONEY!
MY BENSON GIRLS ARE REAL TROOPERS!
I THINK I'LL KISS THE GROUND WHEN WE FINALLY LAND. WHAT A LONG FLIGHT!
I'LL BE RIGHT BACK, LADIES...AS SOON AS I RETURN THE COFFEE I "BORROWED."
"OCCUPIED?" STILL?
SOMEONE'S GOT A REAL PROBLEM.
OCCUPIED

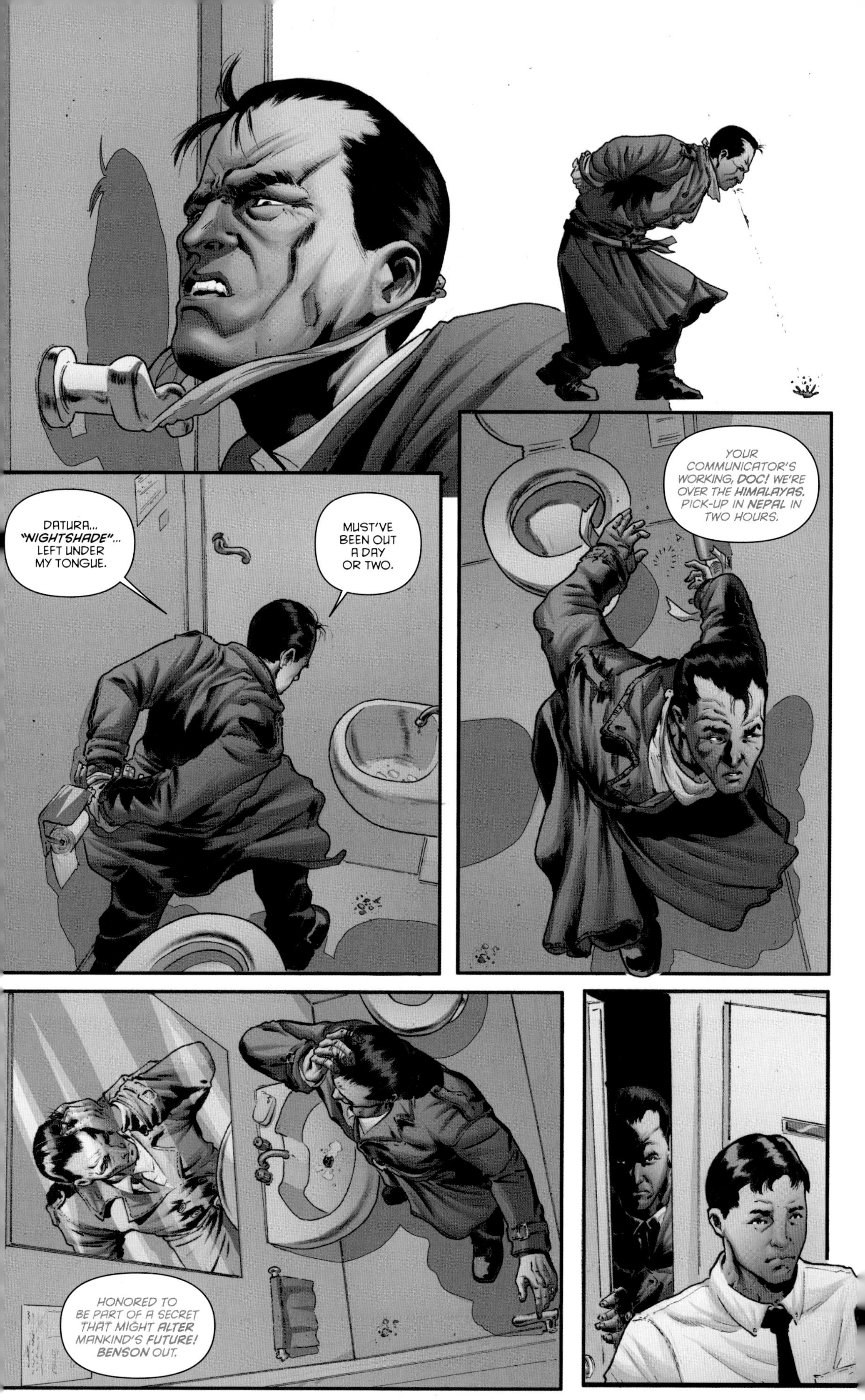
DATURA... "NIGHTSHADE"... LEFT UNDER MY TONGUE.
MUST'VE BEEN OUT A DAY OR TWO.
YOUR COMMUNICATOR'S WORKING, DOC! WE'RE OVER THE HIMALAYAS. PICK-UP IN NEPAL IN TWO HOURS.
HONORED TO BE PART OF A SECRET THAT MIGHT ALTER MANKIND'S FUTURE! BENSON OUT.

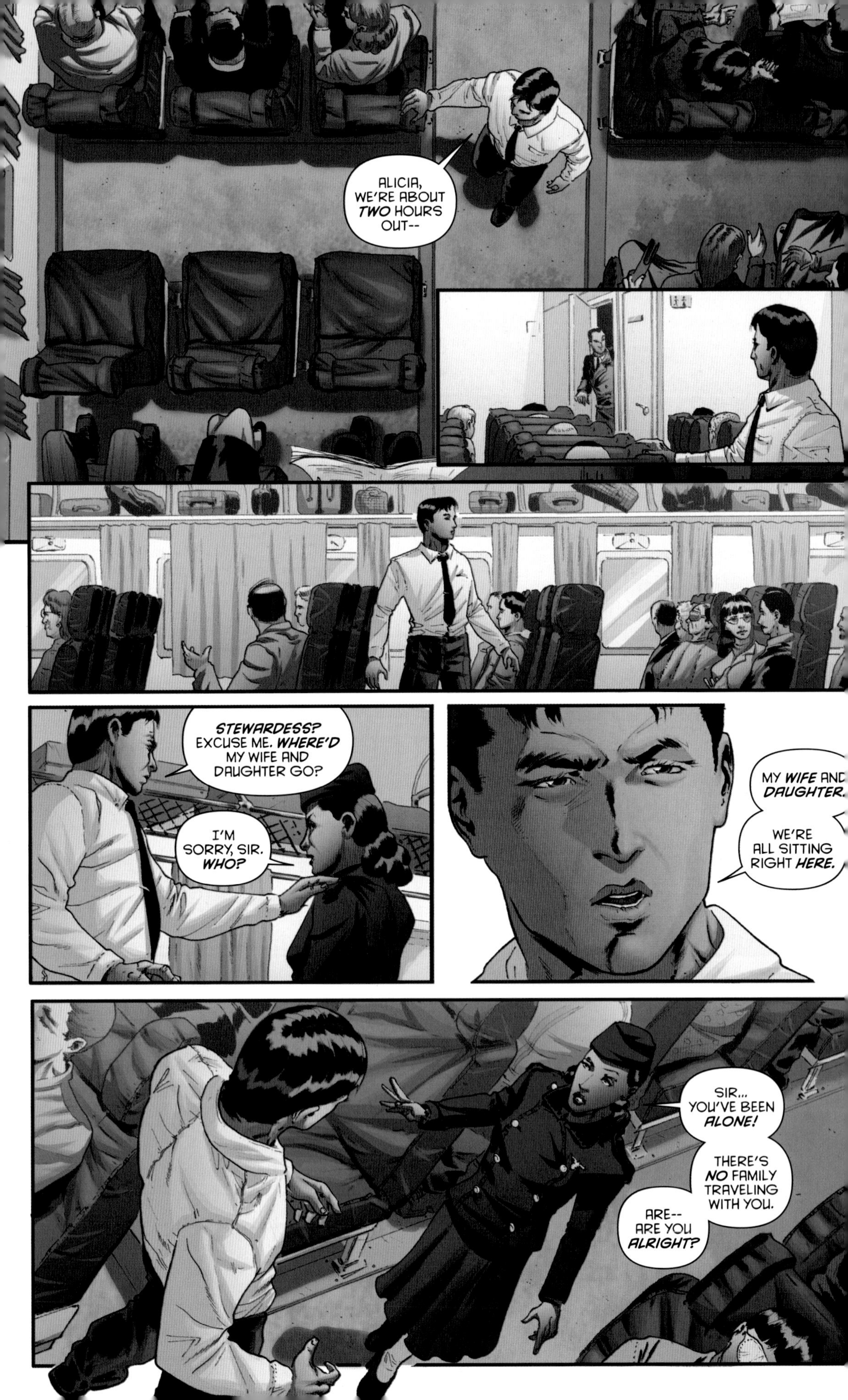
ALICIA, WE'RE ABOUT *TWO* HOURS OUT--
STEWARDESS? EXCUSE ME. *WHERE'D* MY WIFE AND DAUGHTER GO?
I'M SORRY, SIR. *WHO?*
MY *WIFE* AND *DAUGHTER.*
WE'RE ALL SITTING RIGHT *HERE.*
SIR... YOU'VE BEEN *ALONE!*
THERE'S *NO* FAMILY TRAVELING WITH YOU.
ARE-- ARE YOU *ALRIGHT?*

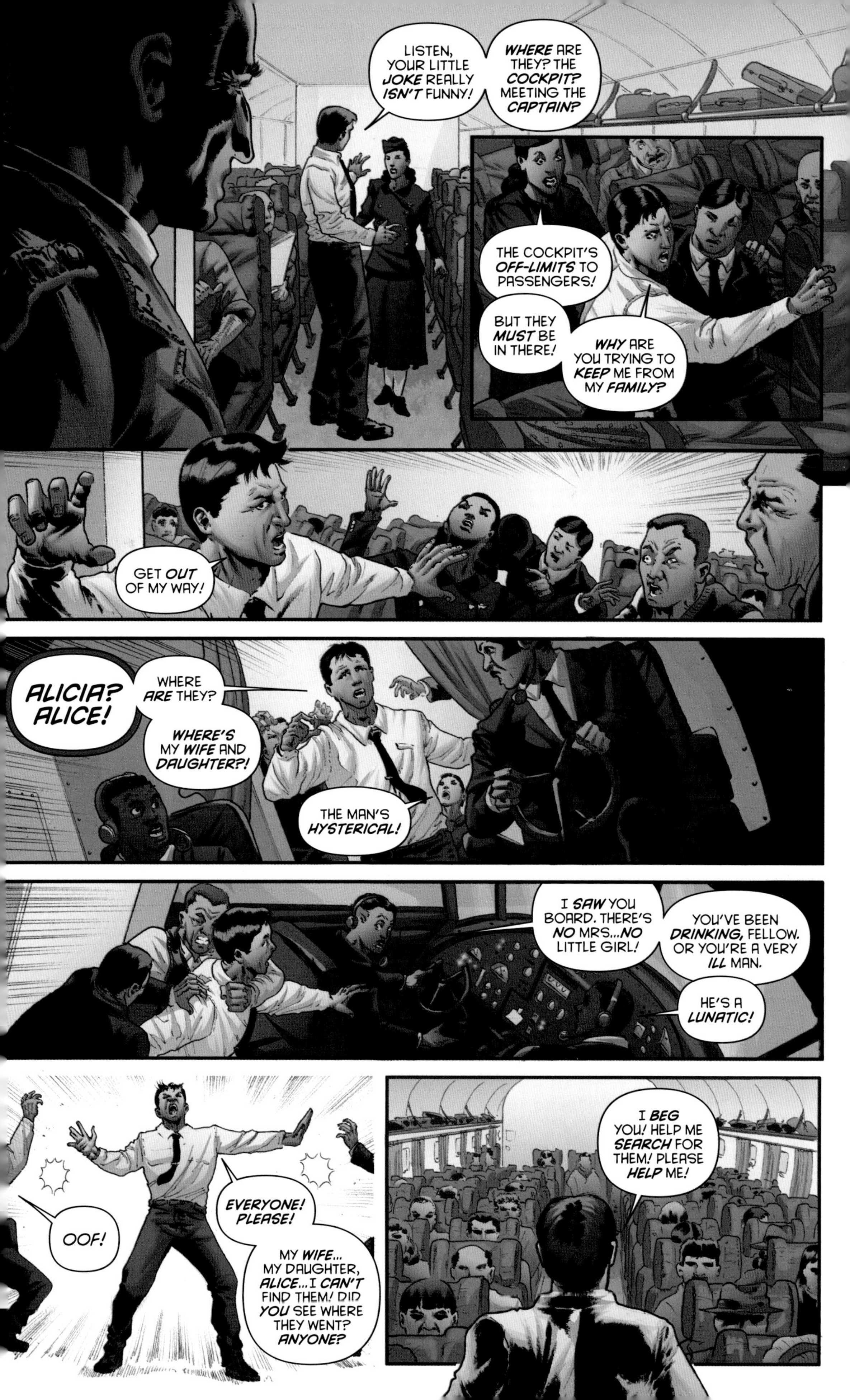

LISTEN, YOUR LITTLE JOKE REALLY ISN'T FUNNY!
WHERE ARE THEY? THE COCKPIT? MEETING THE CAPTAIN?
THE COCKPIT'S OFF-LIMITS TO PASSENGERS!
BUT THEY MUST BE IN THERE!
WHY ARE YOU TRYING TO KEEP ME FROM MY FAMILY?
GET OUT OF MY WAY!
ALICIA? ALICE!
WHERE ARE THEY?
WHERE'S MY WIFE AND DAUGHTER?!
THE MAN'S HYSTERICAL!
I SAW YOU BOARD. THERE'S NO MRS...NO LITTLE GIRL!
YOU'VE BEEN DRINKING, FELLOW. OR YOU'RE A VERY ILL MAN.
HE'S A LUNATIC!
OOF!
EVERYONE! PLEASE!
MY WIFE... MY DAUGHTER, ALICE...I CAN'T FIND THEM! DID YOU SEE WHERE THEY WENT? ANYONE?
I BEG YOU! HELP ME SEARCH FOR THEM! PLEASE HELP ME!

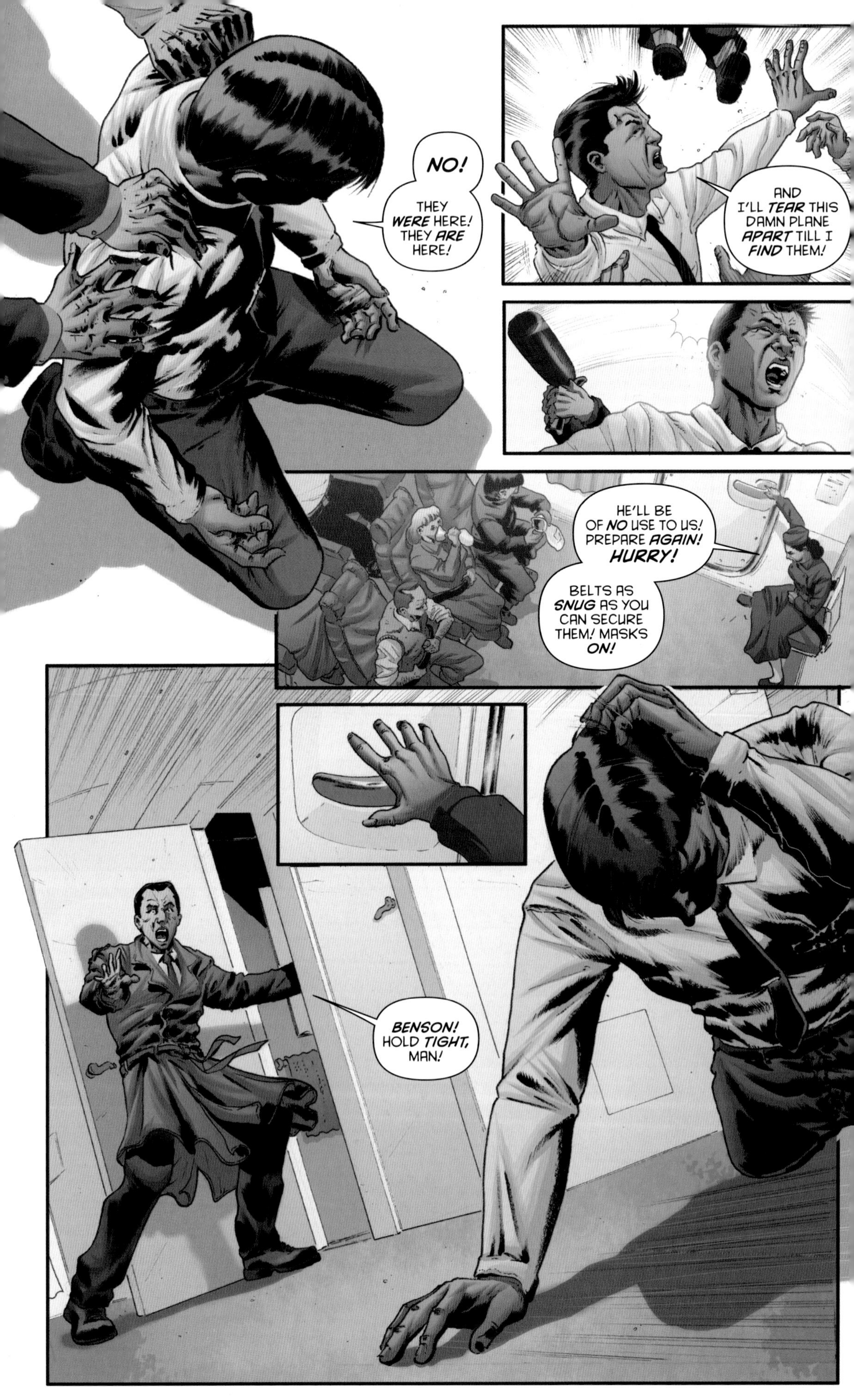

NO!
THEY WERE HERE! THEY ARE HERE!
AND I'LL TEAR THIS DAMN PLANE APART TILL I FIND THEM!
HE'LL BE OF NO USE TO US! PREPARE AGAIN! HURRY!
BELTS AS SNUG AS YOU CAN SECURE THEM! MASKS ON!
BENSON! HOLD TIGHT, MAN!

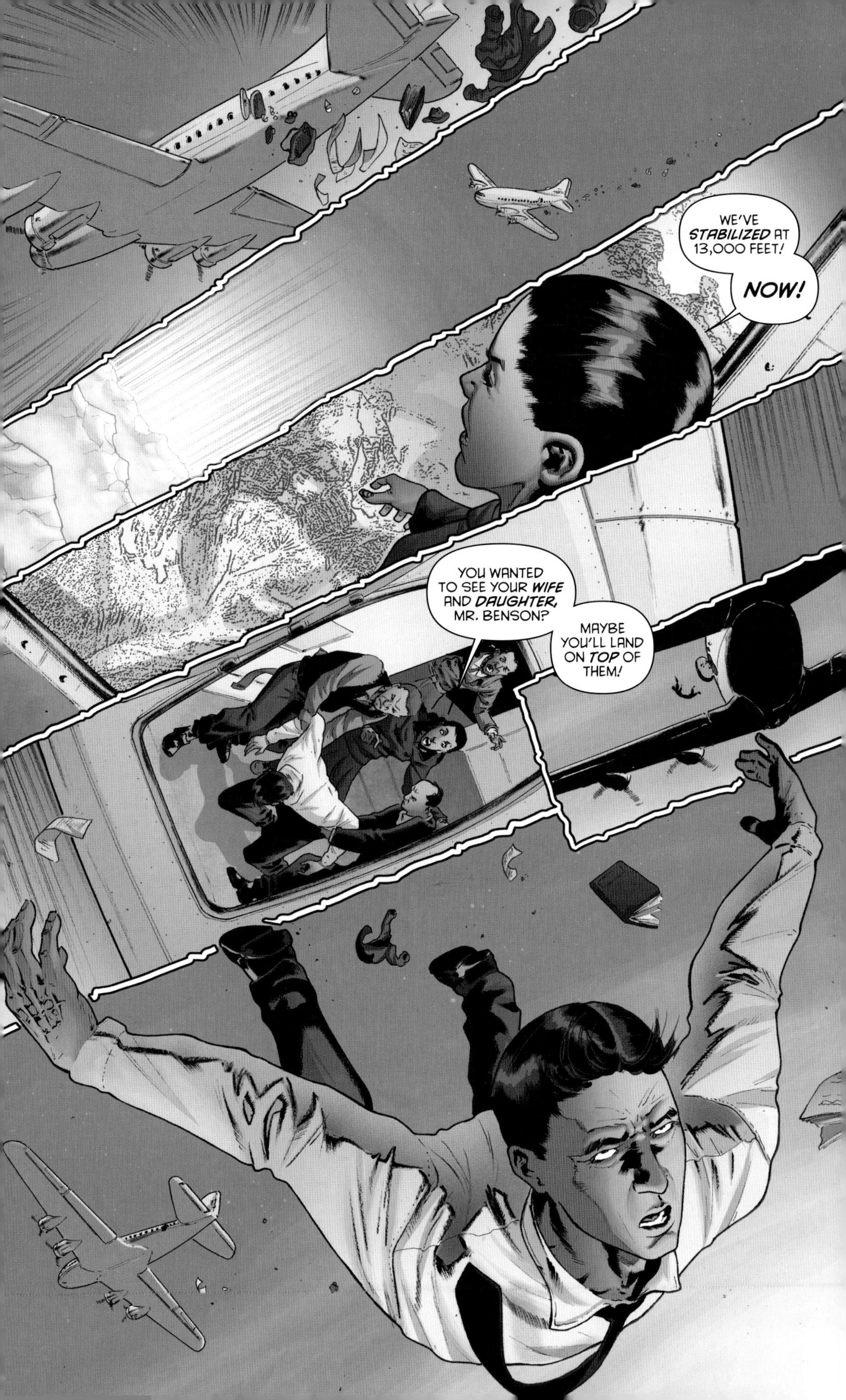

WE'VE STABILIZED AT 13,000 FEET!
NOW!
YOU WANTED TO SEE YOUR WIFE AND DAUGHTER, MR. BENSON?
MAYBE YOU'LL LAND ON TOP OF THEM!

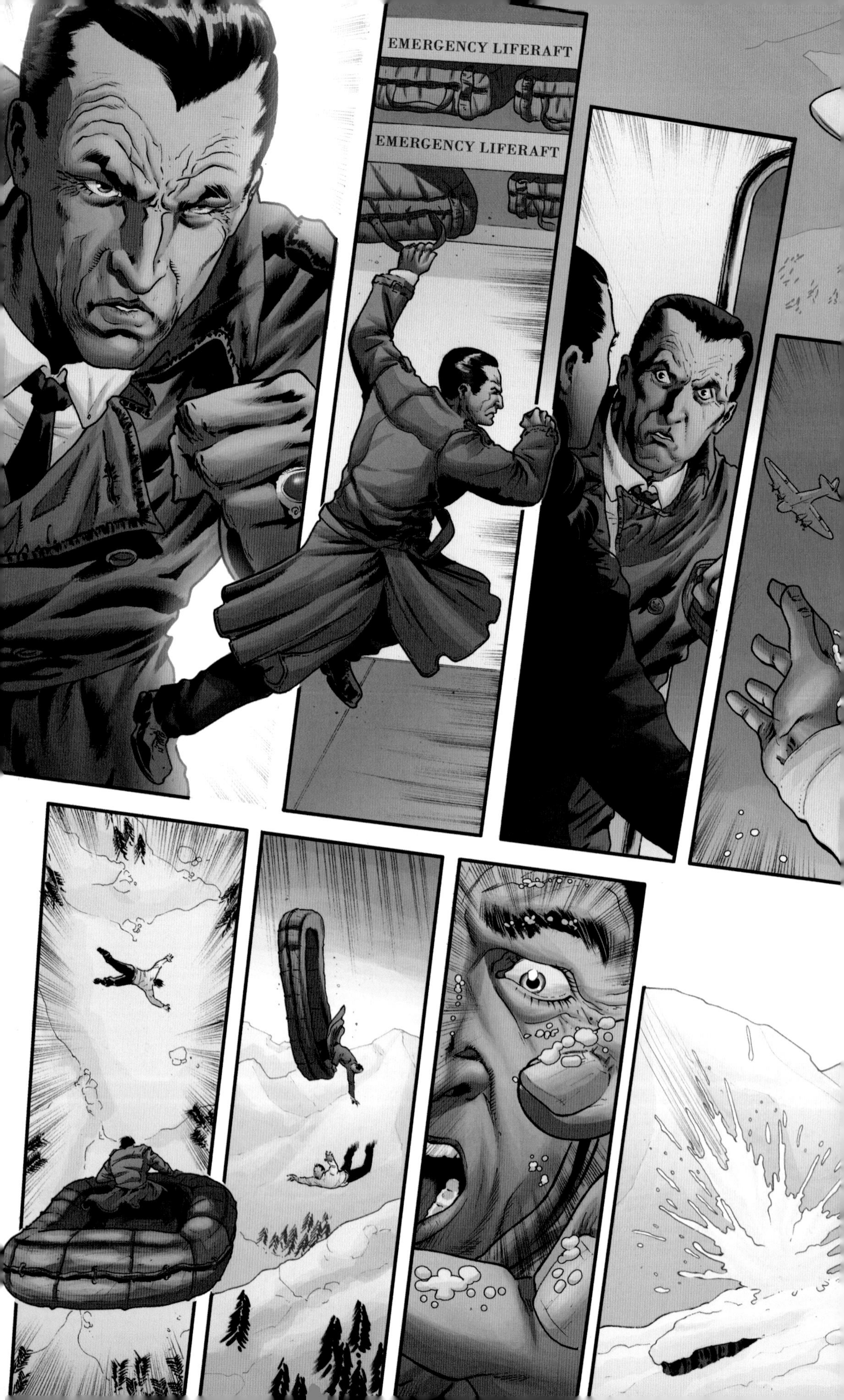
EMERGENCY LIFERAFT
EMERGENCY LIFERAFT

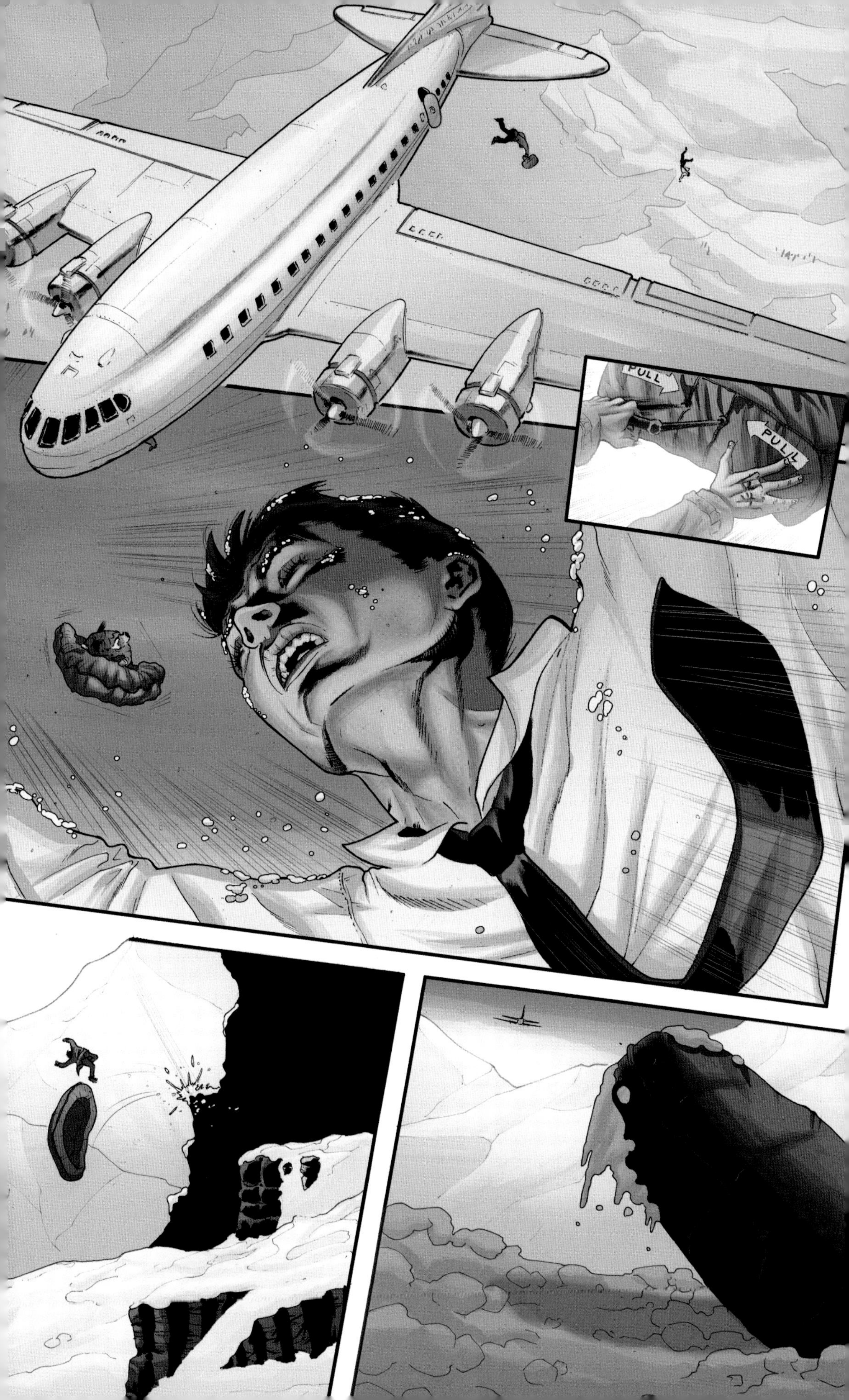
PULL
PULL

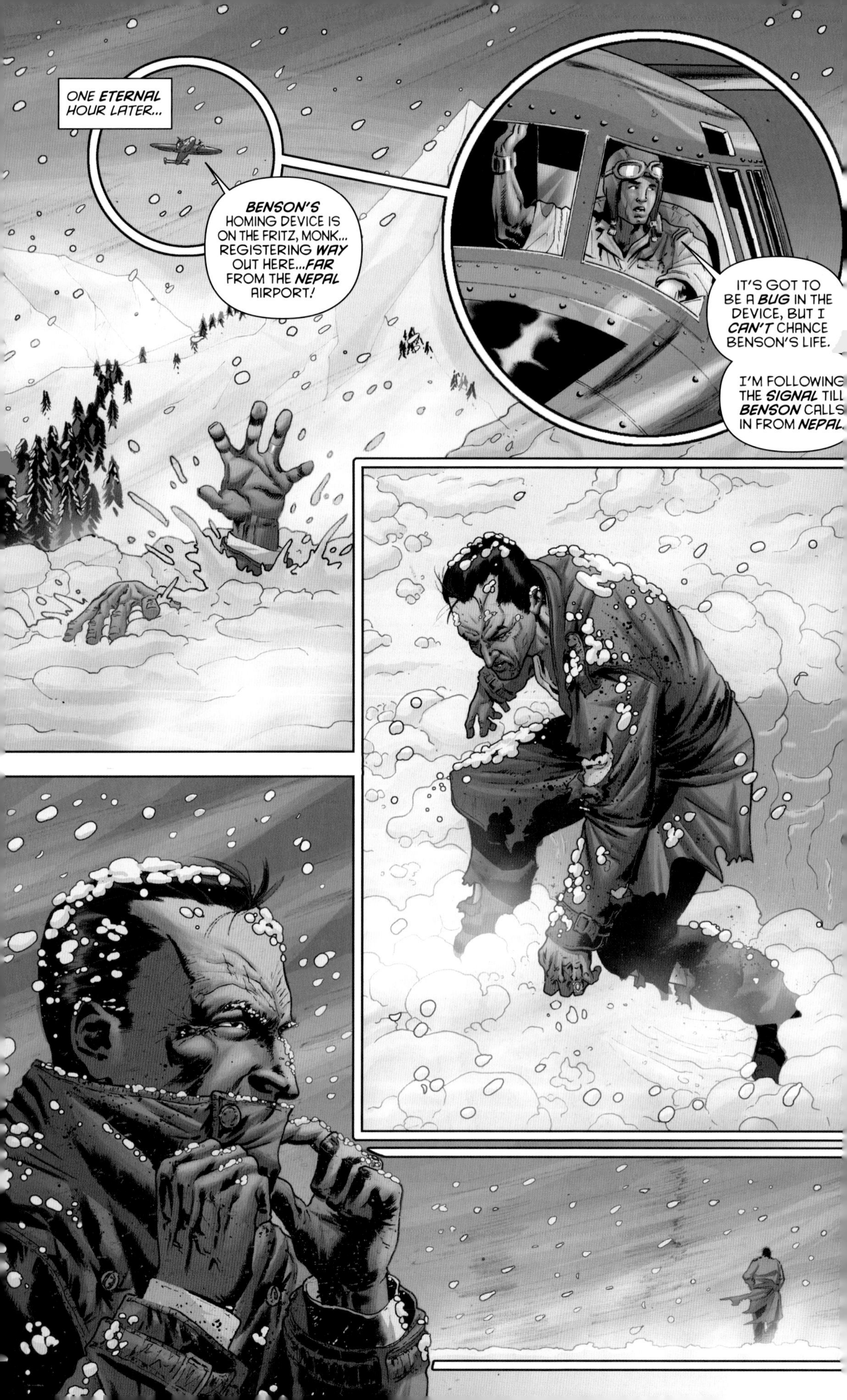

ONE ETERNAL HOUR LATER...
BENSON'S HOMING DEVICE IS ON THE FRITZ, MONK... REGISTERING WAY OUT HERE...FAR FROM THE NEPAL AIRPORT!
IT'S GOT TO BE A BUG IN THE DEVICE, BUT I CAN'T CHANCE BENSON'S LIFE.
I'M FOLLOWING THE SIGNAL TILL BENSON CALLS IN FROM NEPAL.

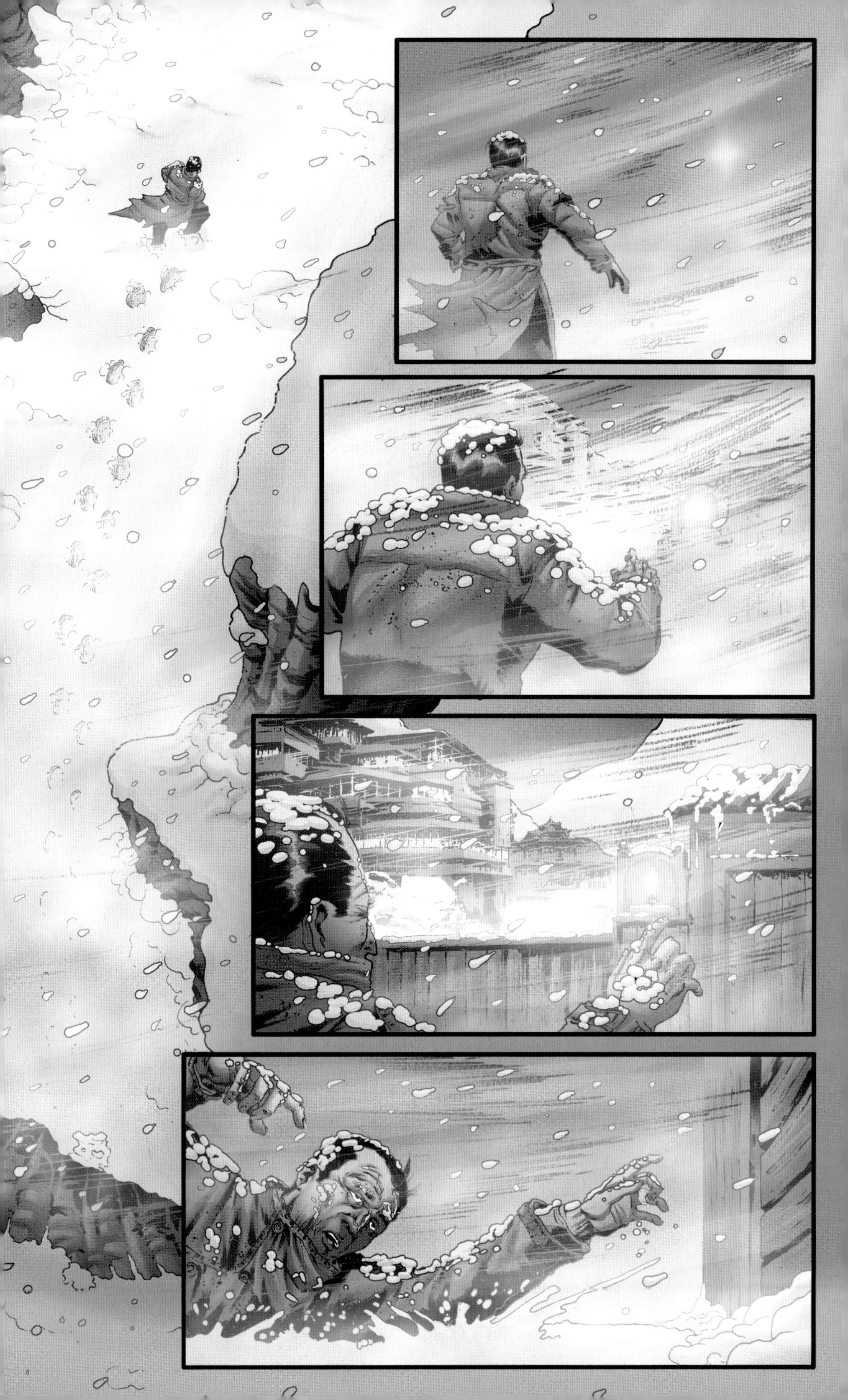

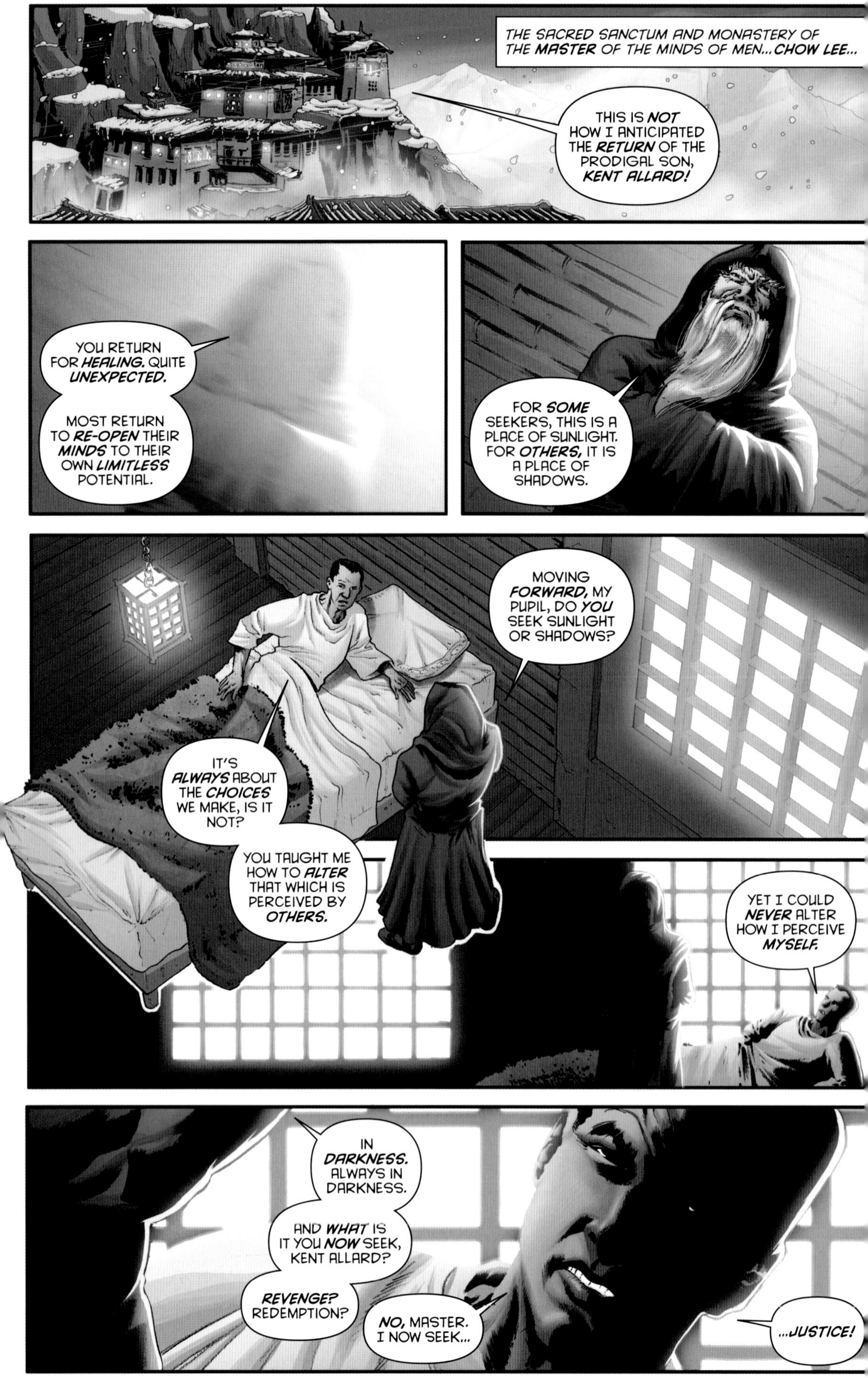
THE SACRED SANCTUM AND MONASTERY OF THE MASTER OF THE MINDS OF MEN...CHOW LEE...
THIS IS NOT HOW I ANTICIPATED THE RETURN OF THE PRODIGAL SON, KENT ALLARD!
YOU RETURN FOR HEALING. QUITE UNEXPECTED.
MOST RETURN TO RE-OPEN THEIR MINDS TO THEIR OWN LIMITLESS POTENTIAL.
FOR SOME SEEKERS, THIS IS A PLACE OF SUNLIGHT. FOR OTHERS, IT IS A PLACE OF SHADOWS.
MOVING FORWARD, MY PUPIL, DO YOU SEEK SUNLIGHT OR SHADOWS?
IT'S ALWAYS ABOUT THE CHOICES WE MAKE, IS IT NOT?
YOU TAUGHT ME HOW TO ALTER THAT WHICH IS PERCEIVED BY OTHERS.
YET I COULD NEVER ALTER HOW I PERCEIVE MYSELF.
IN DARKNESS. ALWAYS IN DARKNESS.
AND WHAT IS IT YOU NOW SEEK, KENT ALLARD?
REVENGE? REDEMPTION?
NO, MASTER. I NOW SEEK...
...JUSTICE!

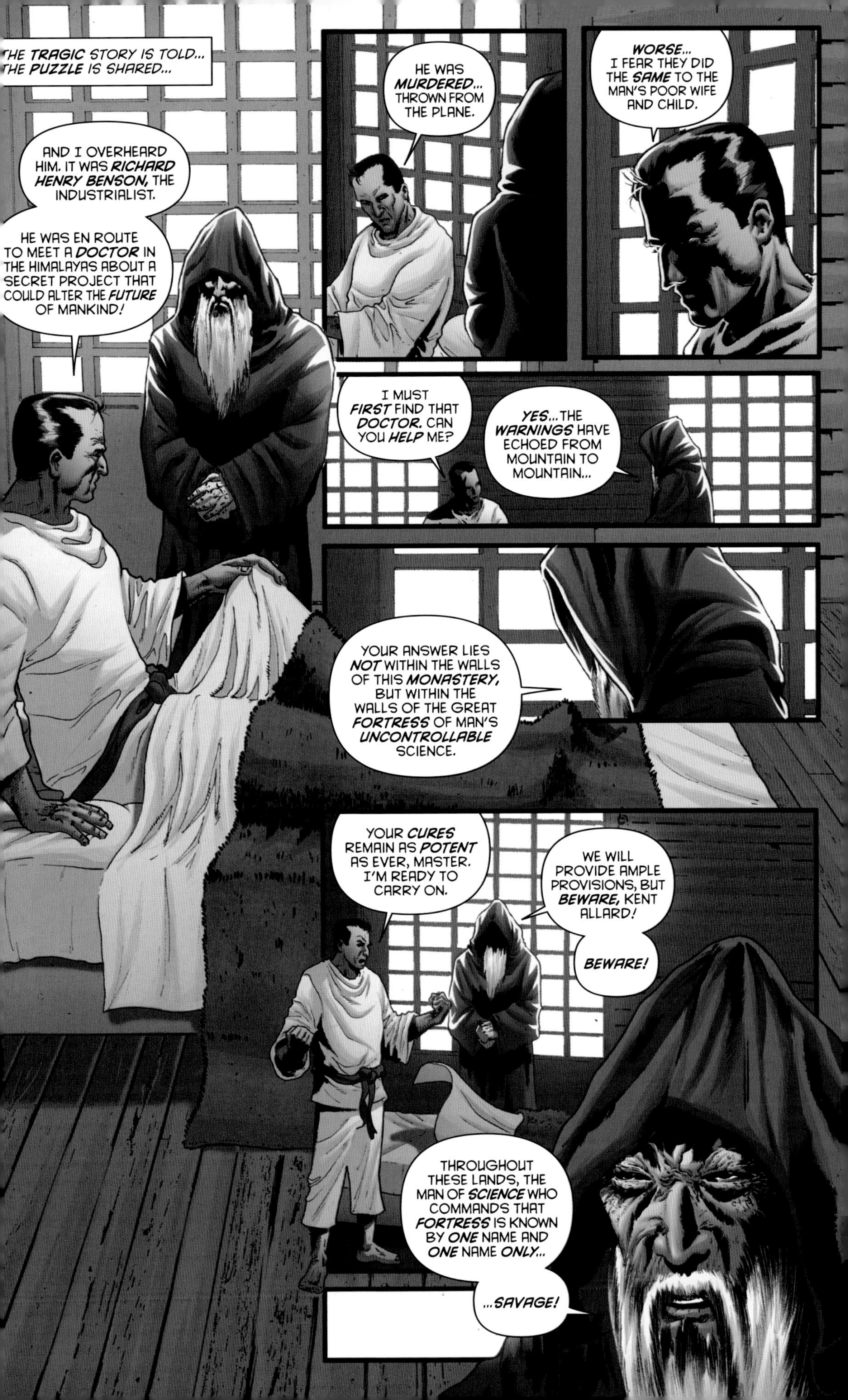
THE TRAGIC STORY IS TOLD... THE PUZZLE IS SHARED...
AND I OVERHEARD HIM. IT WAS RICHARD HENRY BENSON, THE INDUSTRIALIST.
HE WAS EN ROUTE TO MEET A DOCTOR IN THE HIMALAYAS ABOUT A SECRET PROJECT THAT COULD ALTER THE FUTURE OF MANKIND!
HE WAS MURDERED... THROWN FROM THE PLANE.
WORSE... I FEAR THEY DID THE SAME TO THE MAN'S POOR WIFE AND CHILD.
I MUST FIRST FIND THAT DOCTOR. CAN YOU HELP ME?
YES... THE WARNINGS HAVE ECHOED FROM MOUNTAIN TO MOUNTAIN...
YOUR ANSWER LIES NOT WITHIN THE WALLS OF THIS MONASTERY, BUT WITHIN THE WALLS OF THE GREAT FORTRESS OF MAN'S UNCONTROLLABLE SCIENCE.
YOUR CURES REMAIN AS POTENT AS EVER, MASTER. I'M READY TO CARRY ON.
WE WILL PROVIDE AMPLE PROVISIONS, BUT BEWARE, KENT ALLARD!
BEWARE!
THROUGHOUT THESE LANDS, THE MAN OF SCIENCE WHO COMMANDS THAT FORTRESS IS KNOWN BY ONE NAME AND ONE NAME ONLY...
...SAVAGE!

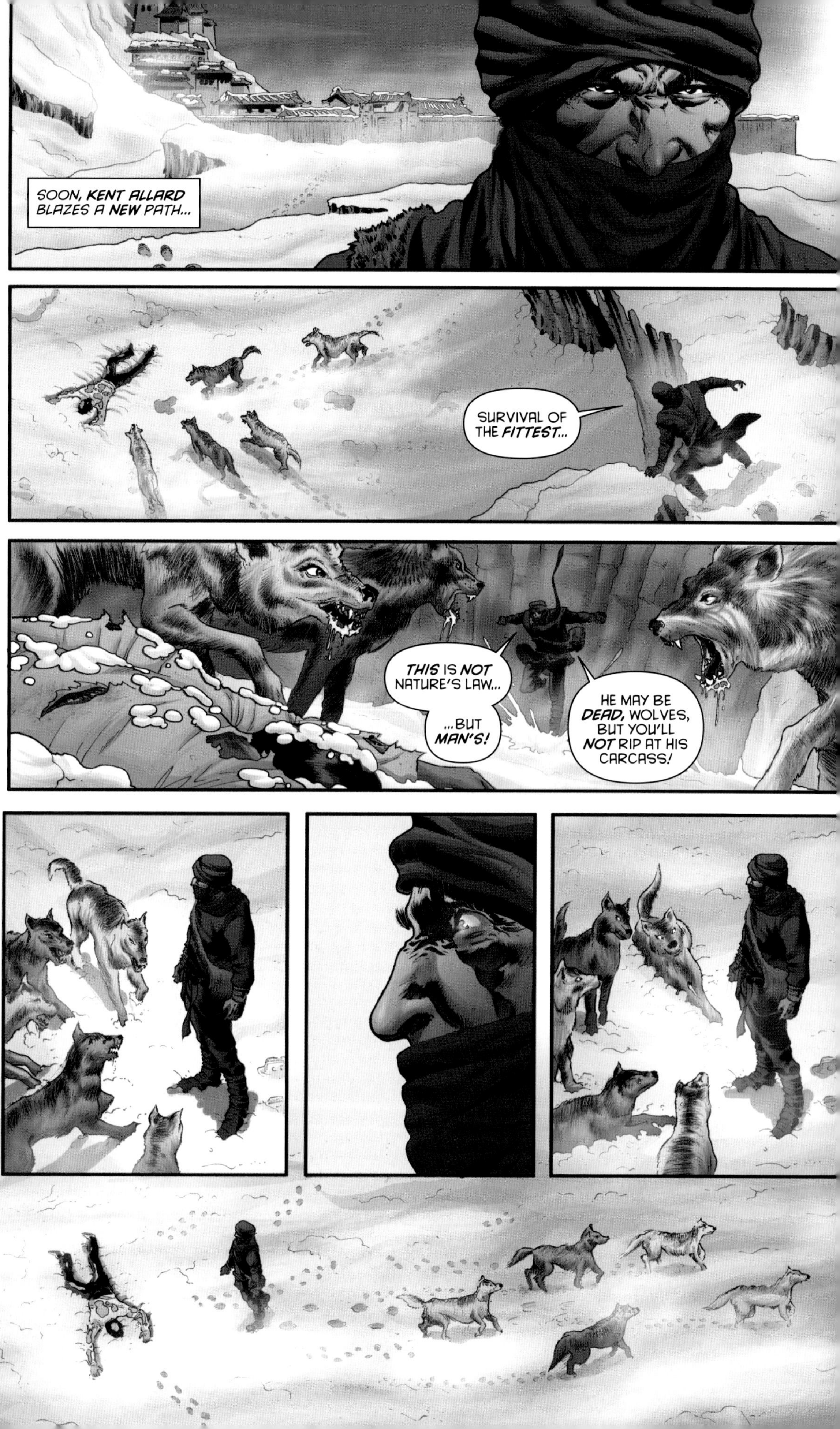
SOON, KENT ALLARD BLAZES A NEW PATH...
SURVIVAL OF THE FITTEST...
THIS IS NOT NATURE'S LAW...
...BUT MAN'S!
HE MAY BE DEAD, WOLVES, BUT YOU'LL NOT RIP AT HIS CARCASS!

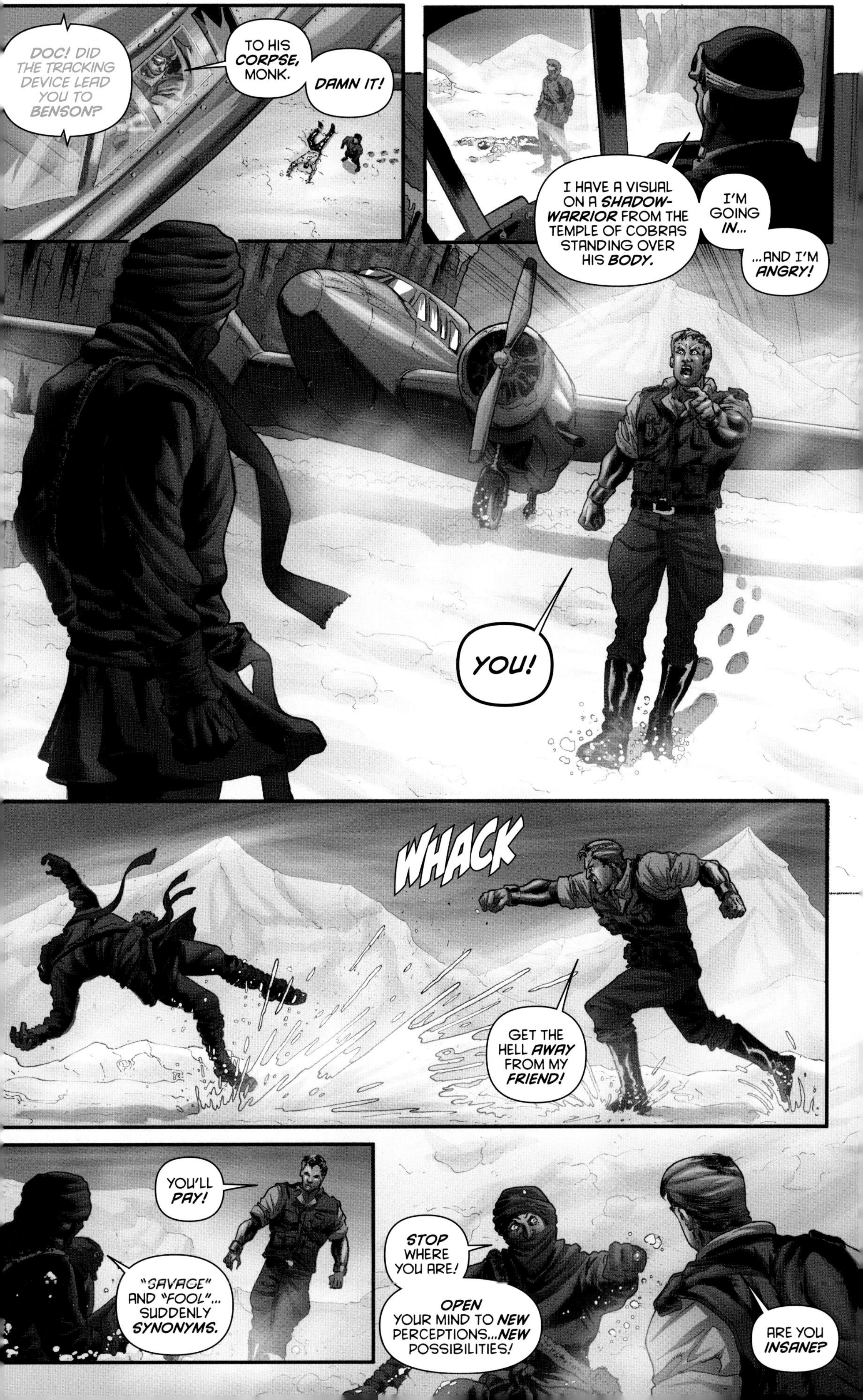
DOC! DID THE TRACKING DEVICE LEAD YOU TO BENSON?
TO HIS CORPSE, MONK.
DAMN IT!
I HAVE A VISUAL ON A SHADOW-WARRIOR FROM THE TEMPLE OF COBRAS STANDING OVER HIS BODY.
I'M GOING IN...
...AND I'M ANGRY!
YOU!
WHACK
GET THE HELL AWAY FROM MY FRIEND!
YOU'LL PAY!
"SAVAGE" AND "FOOL"... SUDDENLY SYNONYMS.
STOP WHERE YOU ARE!
OPEN YOUR MIND TO NEW PERCEPTIONS...NEW POSSIBILITIES!
ARE YOU INSANE?

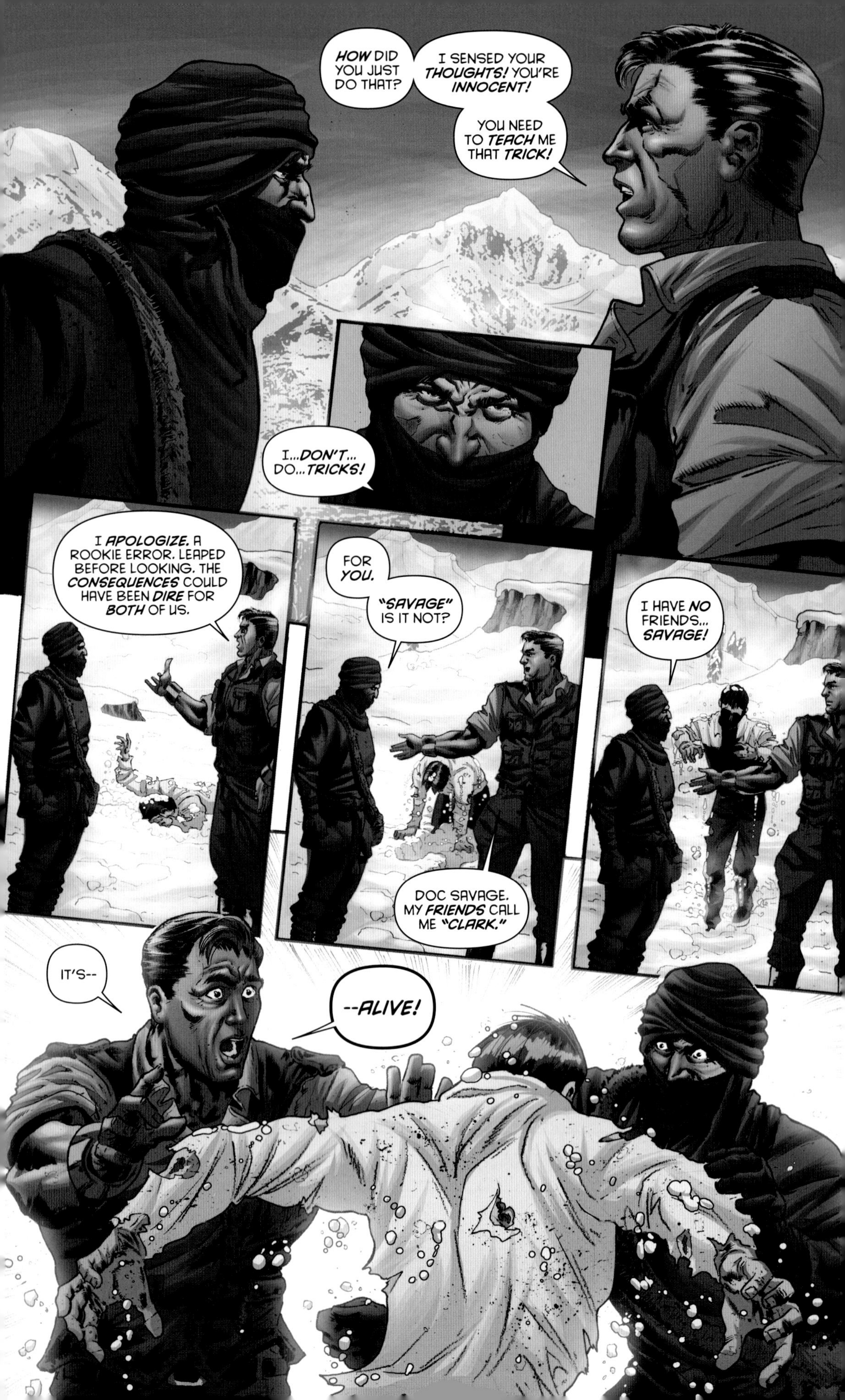

HOW DID YOU JUST DO THAT?
I SENSED YOUR THOUGHTS! YOU'RE INNOCENT!
YOU NEED TO TEACH ME THAT TRICK!
I...DON'T... DO...TRICKS!
I APOLOGIZE. A ROOKIE ERROR. LEAPED BEFORE LOOKING. THE CONSEQUENCES COULD HAVE BEEN DIRE FOR BOTH OF US.
FOR YOU.
"SAVAGE" IS IT NOT?
DOC SAVAGE. MY FRIENDS CALL ME "CLARK."
I HAVE NO FRIENDS... SAVAGE!
IT'S--
--ALIVE!

THREE

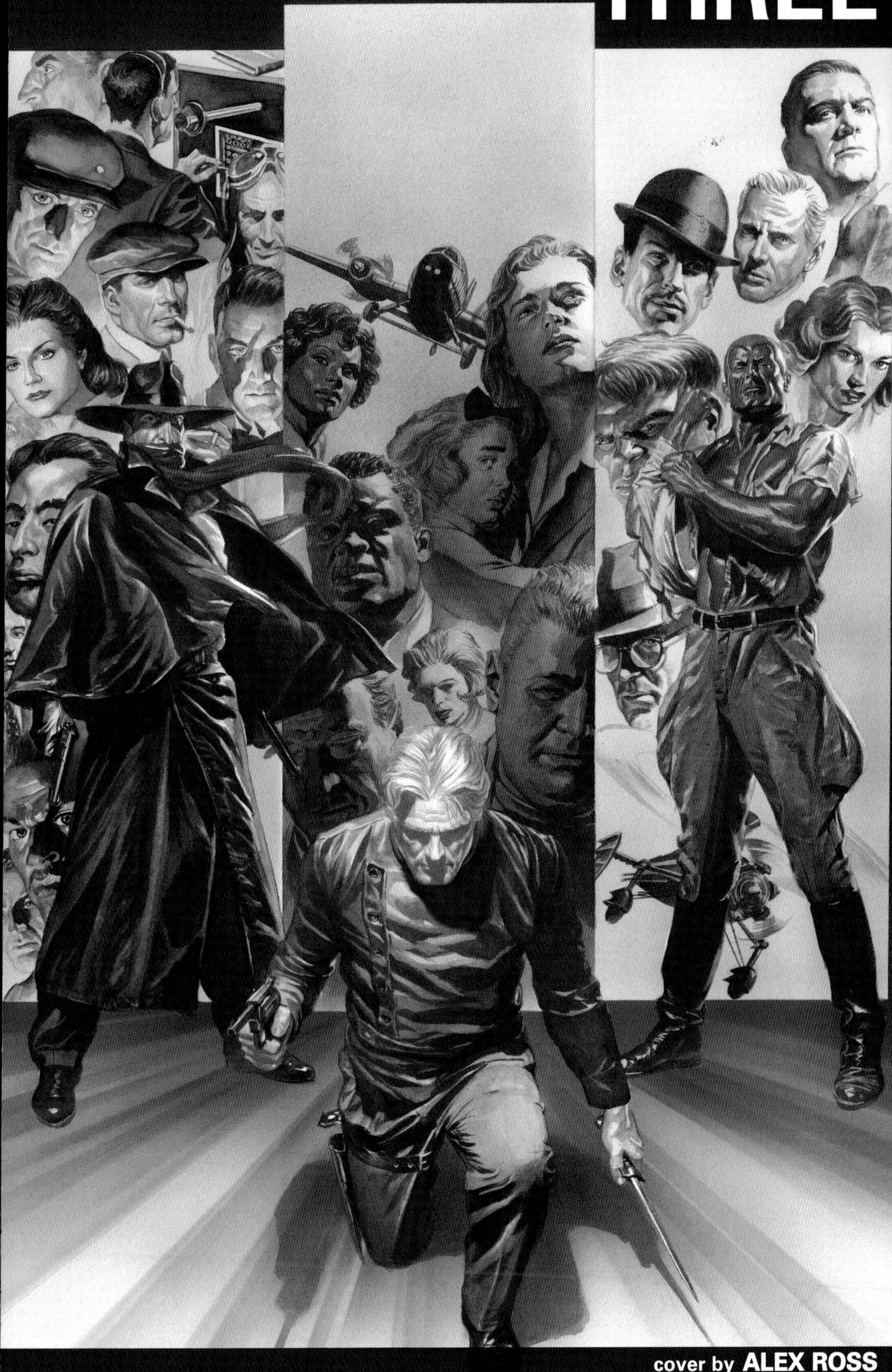

cover by **ALEX ROSS**

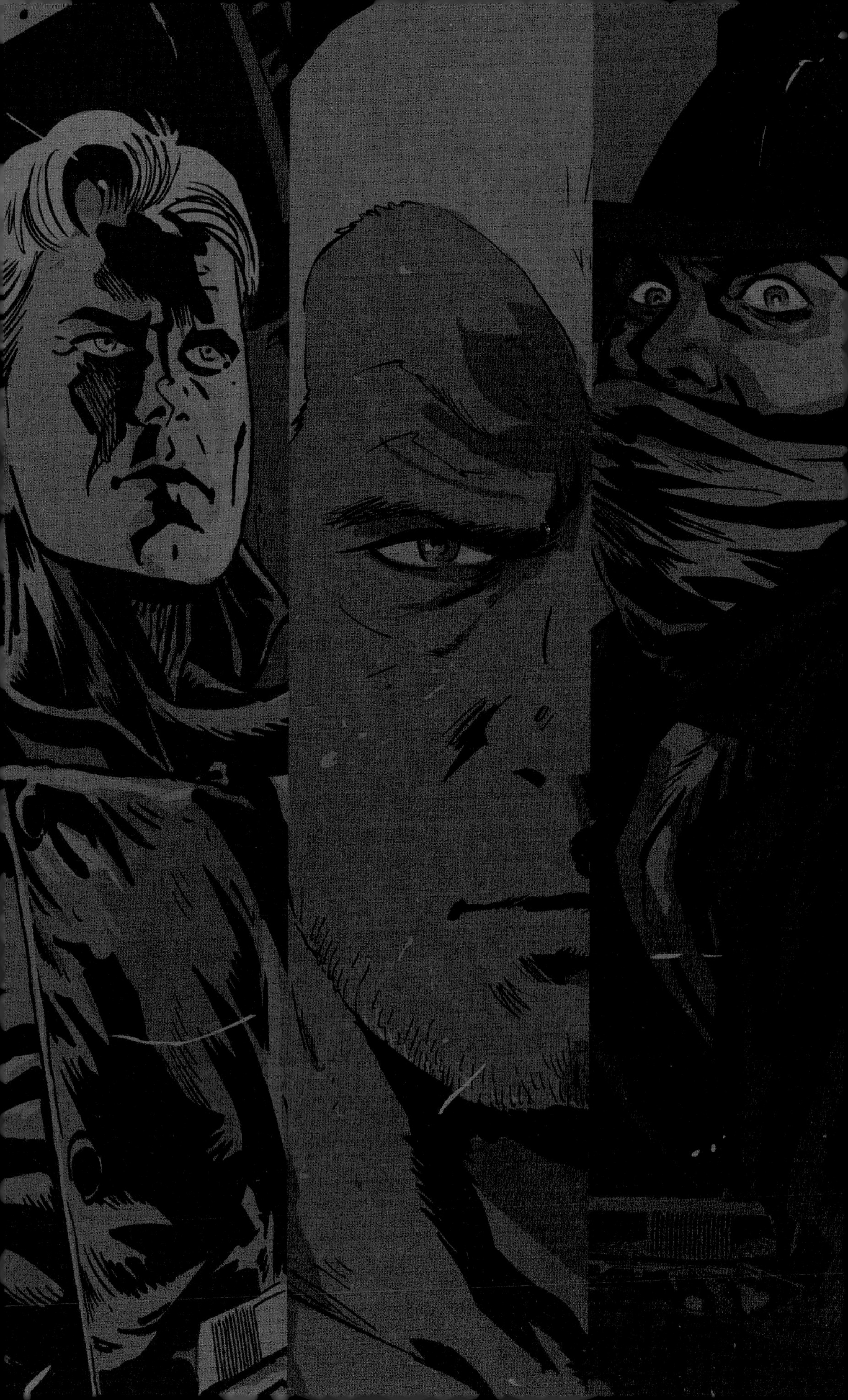

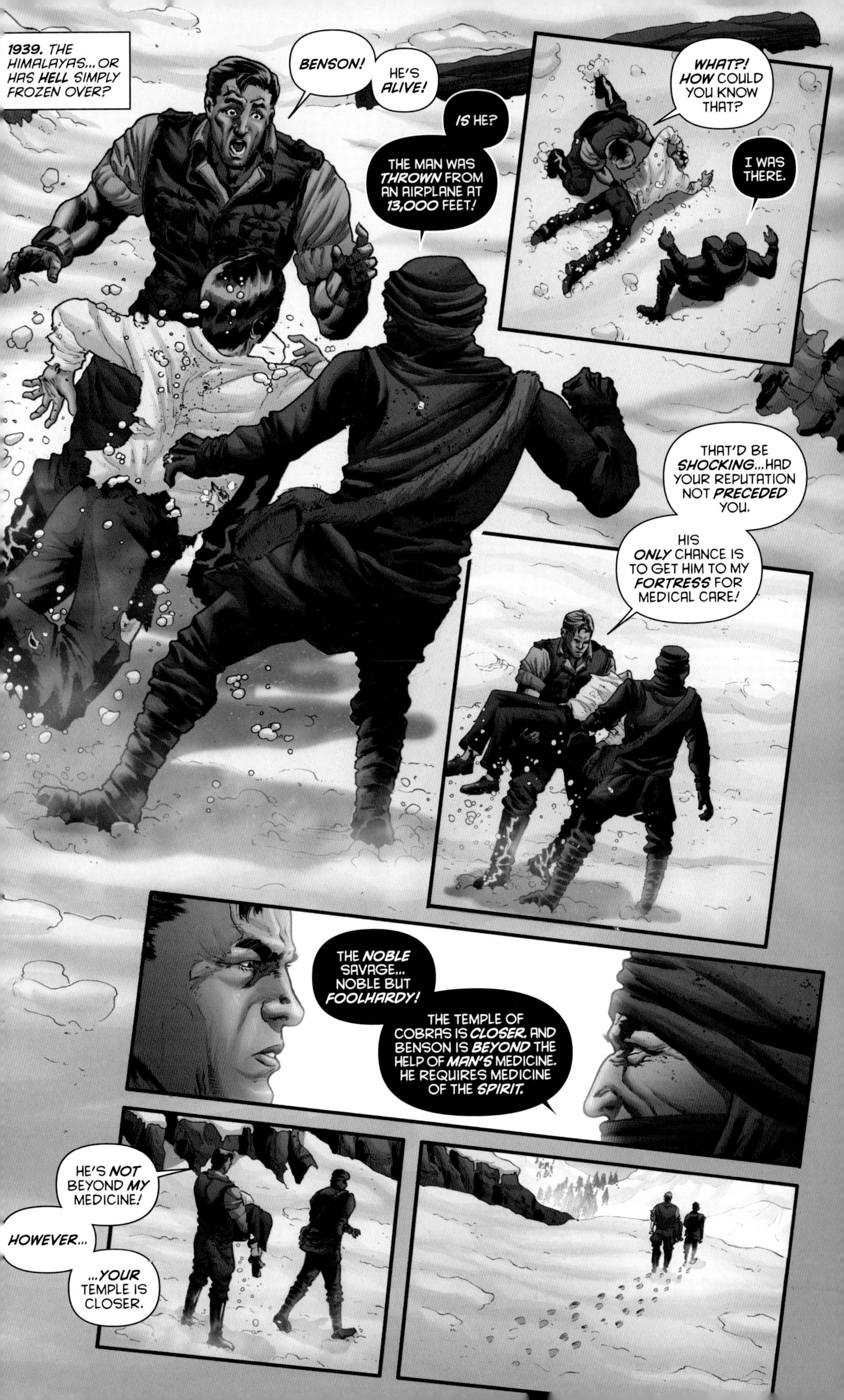
1939. THE HIMALAYAS...OR HAS HELL SIMPLY FROZEN OVER?
BENSON!
HE'S ALIVE!
IS HE?
THE MAN WAS THROWN FROM AN AIRPLANE AT 13,000 FEET!
WHAT?! HOW COULD YOU KNOW THAT?
I WAS THERE.
THAT'D BE SHOCKING...HAD YOUR REPUTATION NOT PRECEDED YOU.
HIS ONLY CHANCE IS TO GET HIM TO MY FORTRESS FOR MEDICAL CARE!
THE NOBLE SAVAGE... NOBLE BUT FOOLHARDY!
THE TEMPLE OF COBRAS IS CLOSER. AND BENSON IS BEYOND THE HELP OF MAN'S MEDICINE. HE REQUIRES MEDICINE OF THE SPIRIT.
HE'S NOT BEYOND MY MEDICINE!
HOWEVER...
...YOUR TEMPLE IS CLOSER.

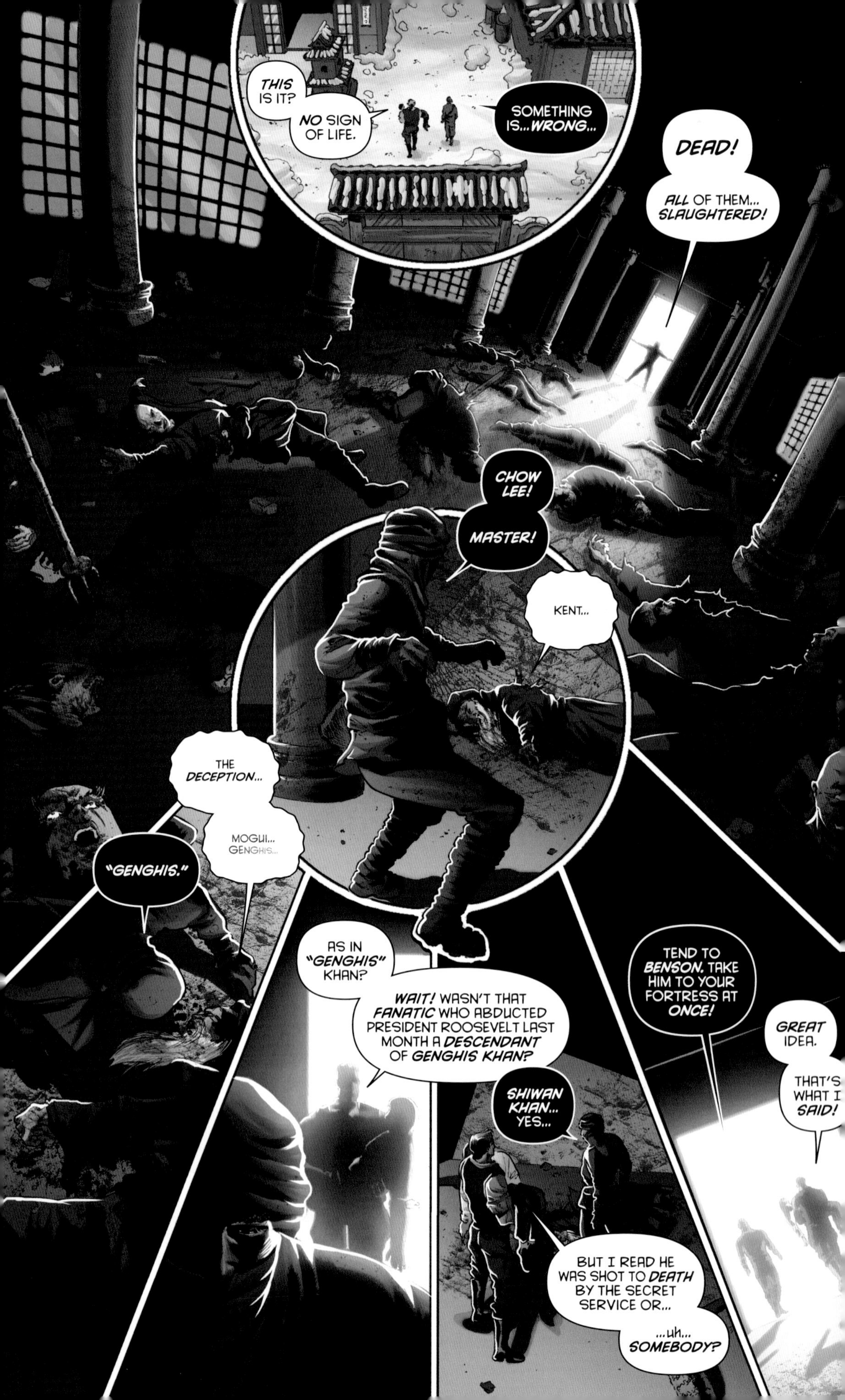
THIS IS IT?
NO SIGN OF LIFE.
SOMETHING IS...WRONG...
DEAD!
ALL OF THEM... SLAUGHTERED!
CHOW LEE!
MASTER!
KENT...
THE DECEPTION...
MOGUI... GENGHIS...
"GENGHIS."
AS IN "GENGHIS" KHAN?
WAIT! WASN'T THAT FANATIC WHO ABDUCTED PRESIDENT ROOSEVELT LAST MONTH A DESCENDANT OF GENGHIS KHAN?
SHIWAN KHAN... YES...
BUT I READ HE WAS SHOT TO DEATH BY THE SECRET SERVICE OR...
...uh... SOMEBODY?
TEND TO BENSON. TAKE HIM TO YOUR FORTRESS AT ONCE!
GREAT IDEA.
THAT'S WHAT I SAID!

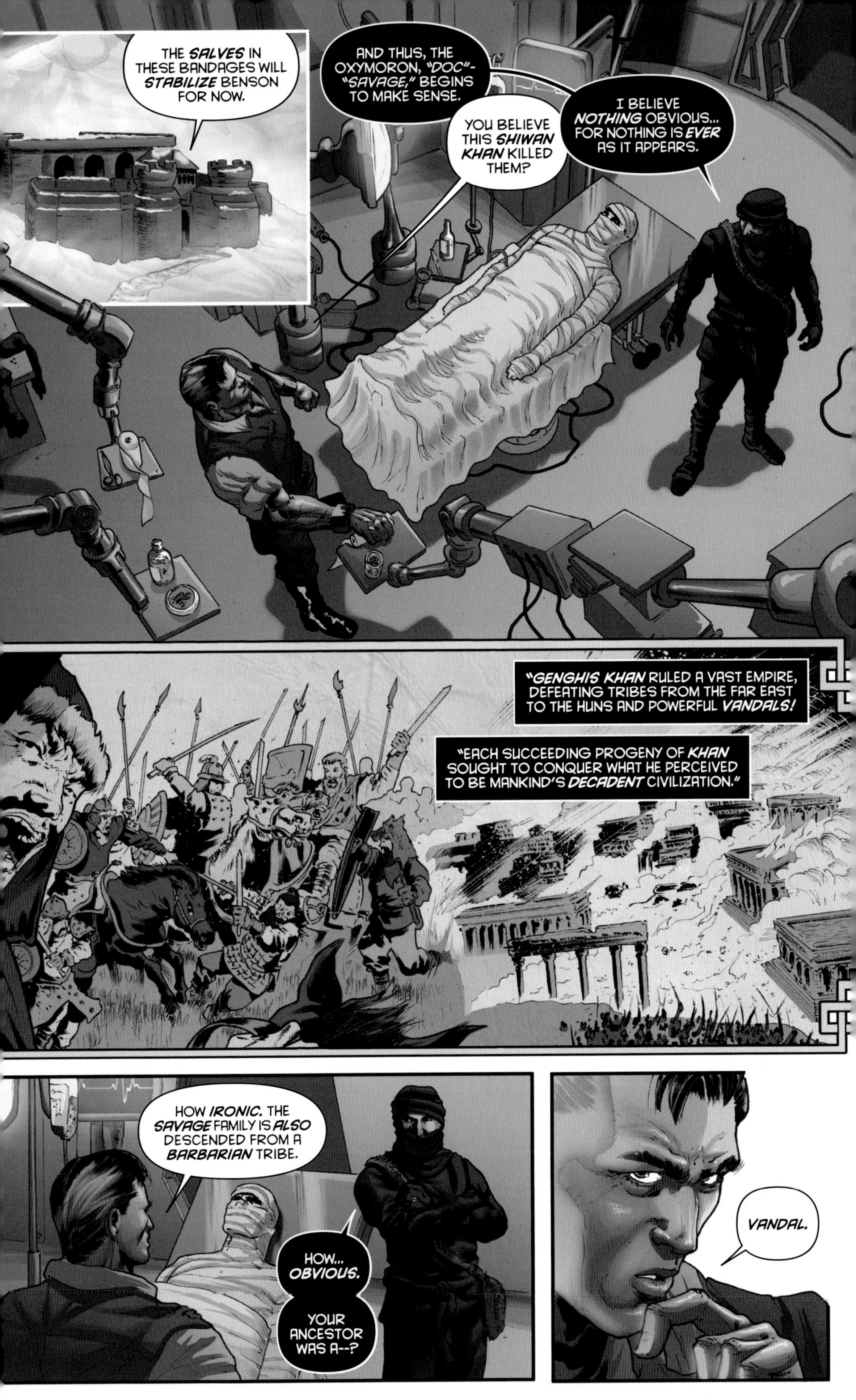
THE SALVES IN THESE BANDAGES WILL STABILIZE BENSON FOR NOW.
AND THUS, THE OXYMORON, "DOC"-"SAVAGE," BEGINS TO MAKE SENSE.
YOU BELIEVE THIS SHIWAN KHAN KILLED THEM?
I BELIEVE NOTHING OBVIOUS... FOR NOTHING IS EVER AS IT APPEARS.
"GENGHIS KHAN RULED A VAST EMPIRE, DEFEATING TRIBES FROM THE FAR EAST TO THE HUNS AND POWERFUL VANDALS!
"EACH SUCCEEDING PROGENY OF KHAN SOUGHT TO CONQUER WHAT HE PERCEIVED TO BE MANKIND'S DECADENT CIVILIZATION."
HOW IRONIC. THE SAVAGE FAMILY IS ALSO DESCENDED FROM A BARBARIAN TRIBE.
HOW... OBVIOUS.
YOUR ANCESTOR WAS A--?
VANDAL.

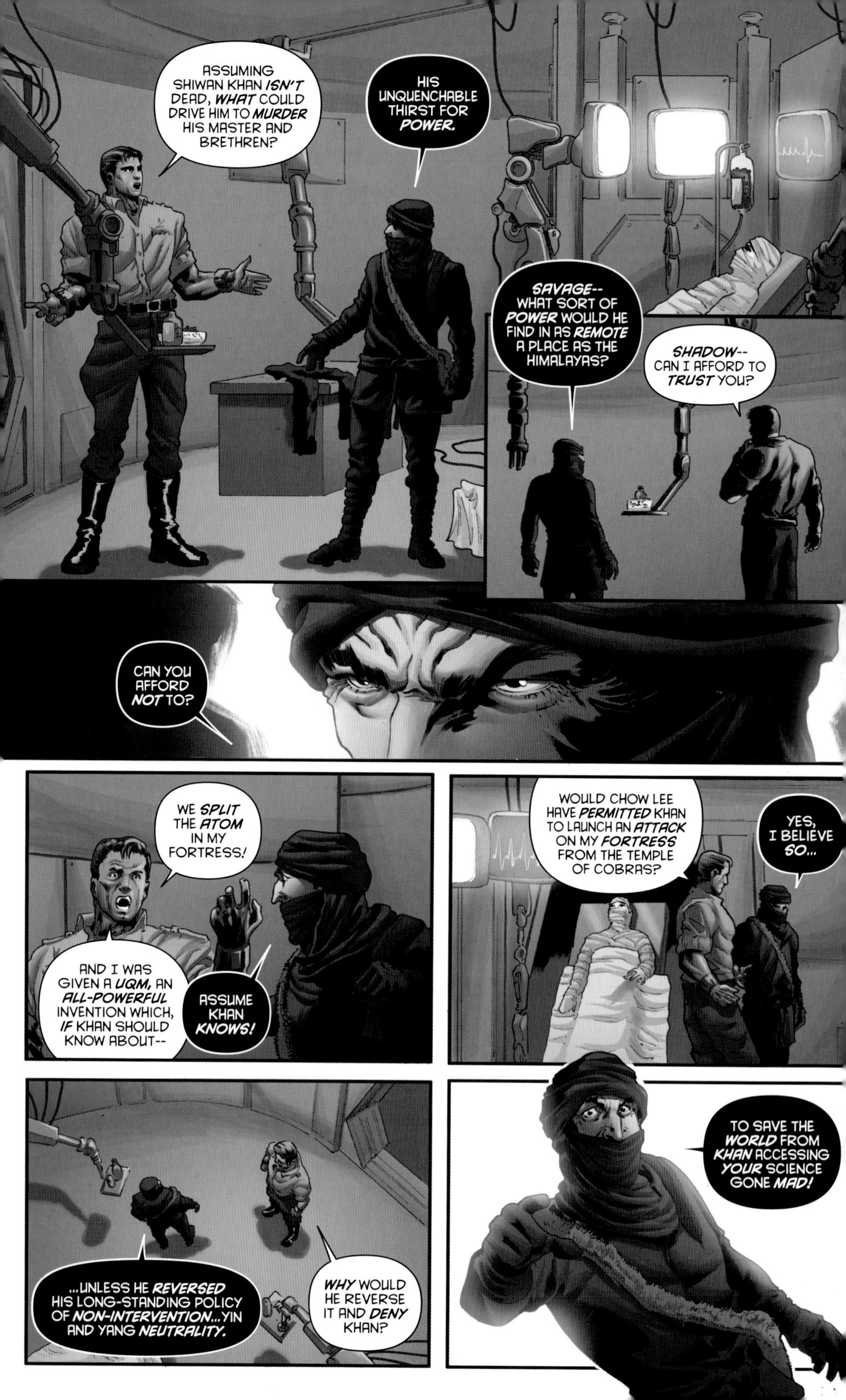
ASSUMING SHIWAN KHAN ISN'T DEAD, WHAT COULD DRIVE HIM TO MURDER HIS MASTER AND BRETHREN?
HIS UNQUENCHABLE THIRST FOR POWER.
SAVAGE-- WHAT SORT OF POWER WOULD HE FIND IN AS REMOTE A PLACE AS THE HIMALAYAS?
SHADOW-- CAN I AFFORD TO TRUST YOU?
CAN YOU AFFORD NOT TO?
WE SPLIT THE ATOM IN MY FORTRESS!
AND I WAS GIVEN A UQM, AN ALL-POWERFUL INVENTION WHICH, IF KHAN SHOULD KNOW ABOUT--
ASSUME KHAN KNOWS!
WOULD CHOW LEE HAVE PERMITTED KHAN TO LAUNCH AN ATTACK ON MY FORTRESS FROM THE TEMPLE OF COBRAS?
YES, I BELIEVE SO...
...UNLESS HE REVERSED HIS LONG-STANDING POLICY OF NON-INTERVENTION...YIN AND YANG NEUTRALITY.
WHY WOULD HE REVERSE IT AND DENY KHAN?
TO SAVE THE WORLD FROM KHAN ACCESSING YOUR SCIENCE GONE MAD!

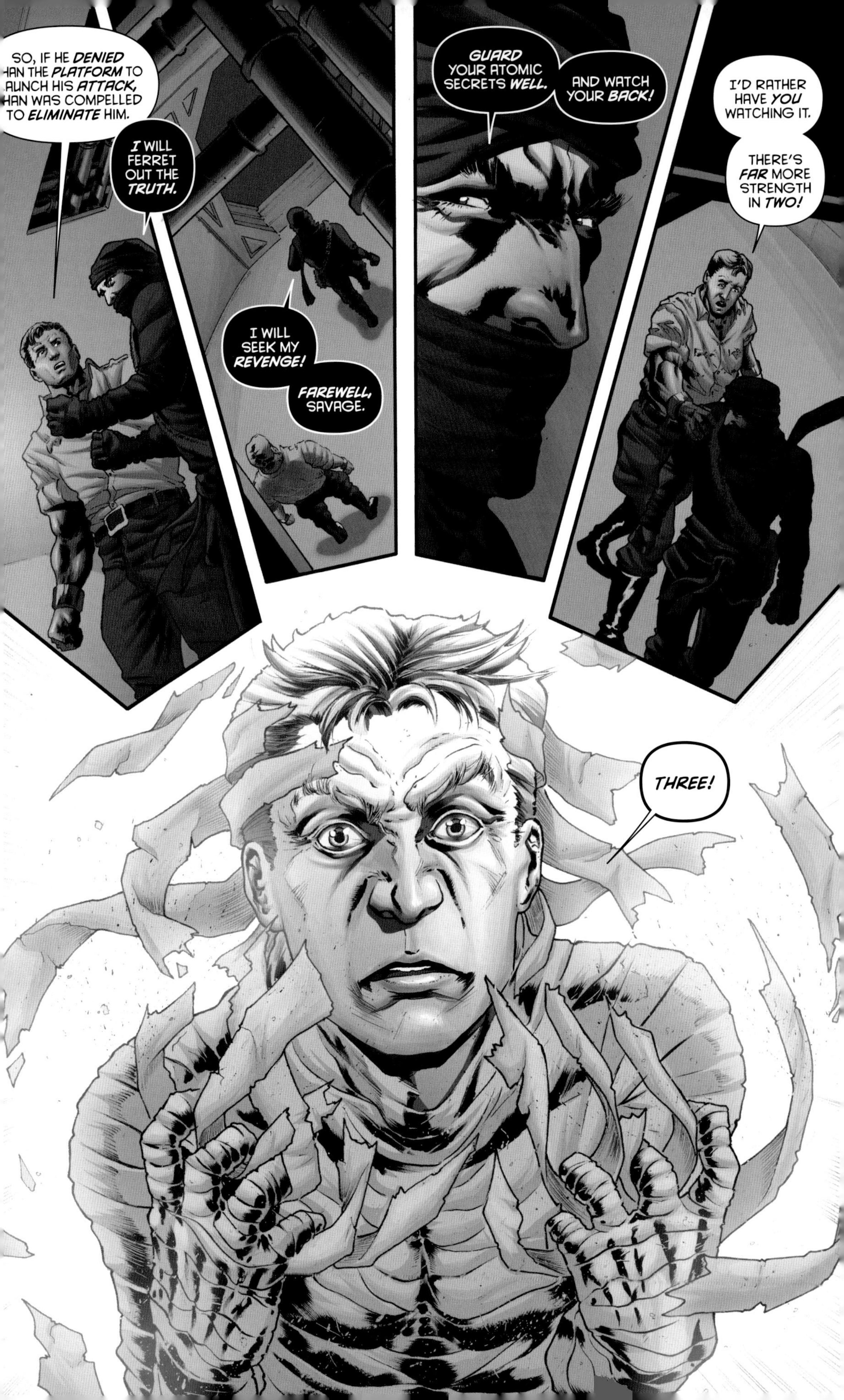
SO, IF HE DENIED
HAN THE PLATFORM TO
AUNCH HIS ATTACK,
HAN WAS COMPELLED
TO ELIMINATE HIM.
I WILL FERRET OUT THE TRUTH.
I WILL SEEK MY REVENGE!
FAREWELL, SAVAGE.
GUARD YOUR ATOMIC SECRETS WELL.
AND WATCH YOUR BACK!
I'D RATHER HAVE YOU WATCHING IT.
THERE'S FAR MORE STRENGTH IN TWO!
THREE!

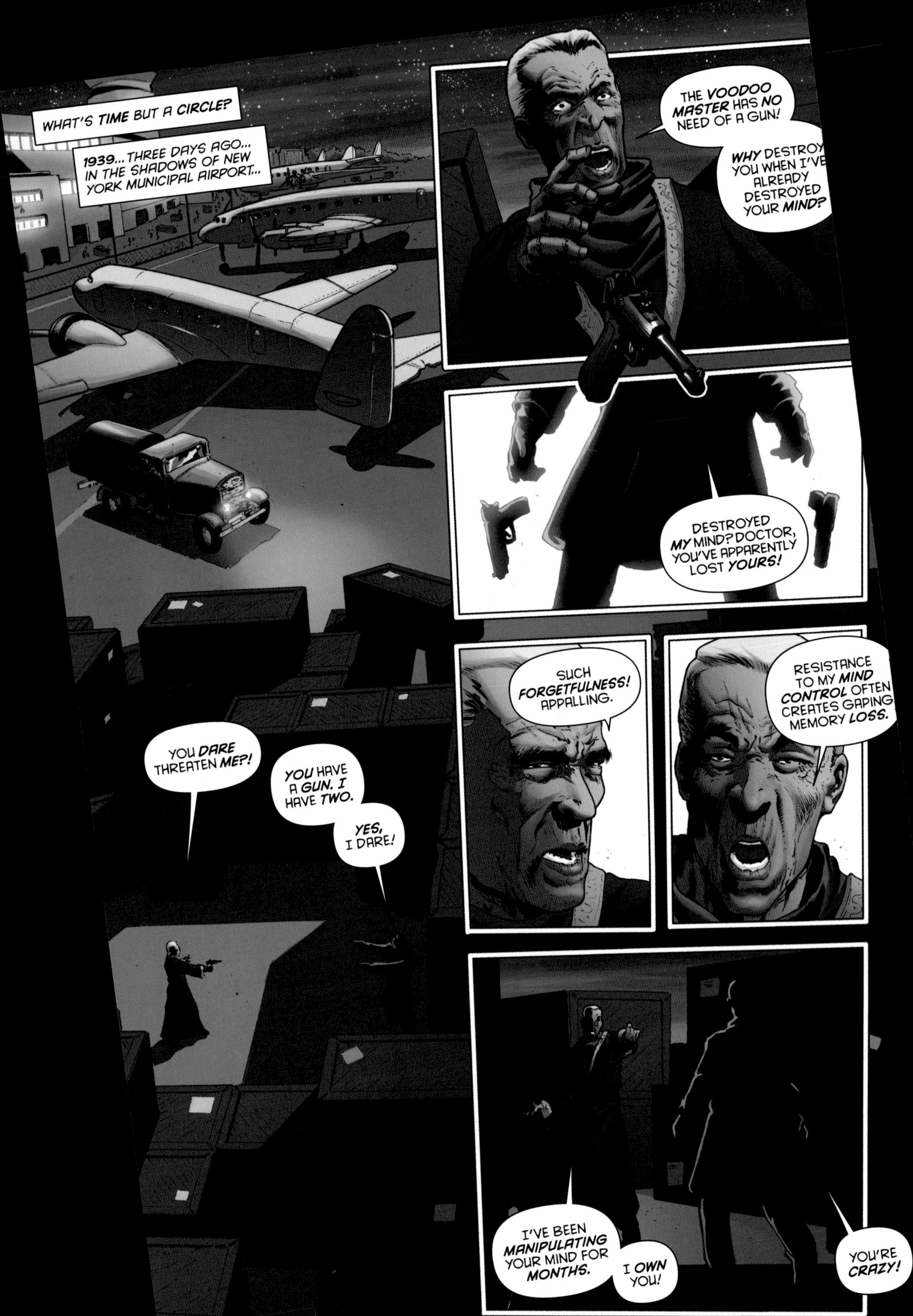
WHAT'S TIME BUT A CIRCLE?
1939... THREE DAYS AGO... IN THE SHADOWS OF NEW YORK MUNICIPAL AIRPORT...
THE VOODOO MASTER HAS NO NEED OF A GUN!
WHY DESTROY YOU WHEN I'VE ALREADY DESTROYED YOUR MIND?
YOU DARE THREATEN ME?!
YOU HAVE A GUN. I HAVE TWO.
YES, I DARE!
DESTROYED MY MIND? DOCTOR, YOU'VE APPARENTLY LOST YOURS!
SUCH FORGETFULNESS! APPALLING.
RESISTANCE TO MY MIND CONTROL OFTEN CREATES GAPING MEMORY LOSS.
I'VE BEEN MANIPULATING YOUR MIND FOR MONTHS.
I OWN YOU!
YOU'RE CRAZY!

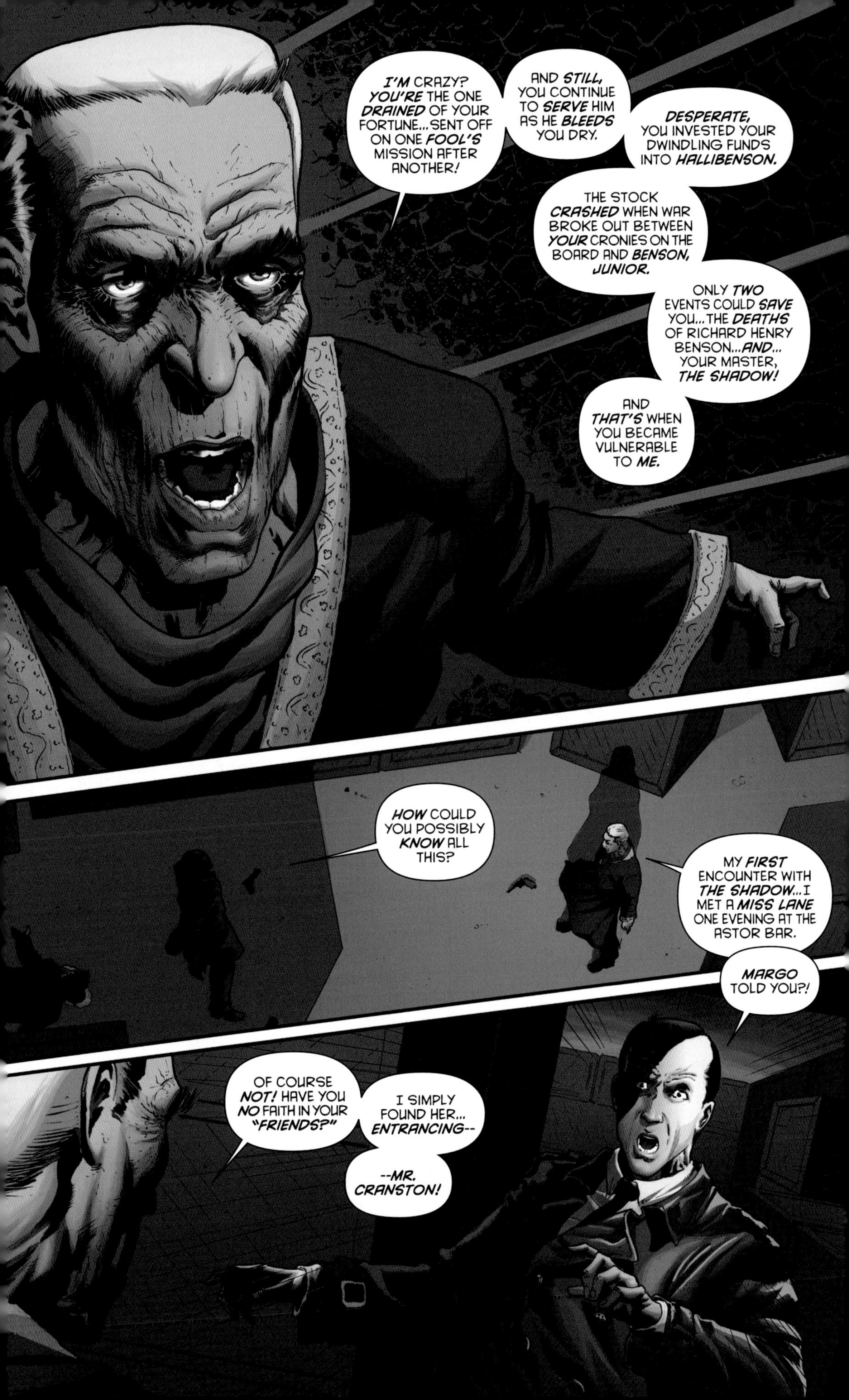
I'M CRAZY? YOU'RE THE ONE DRAINED OF YOUR FORTUNE...SENT OFF ON ONE FOOL'S MISSION AFTER ANOTHER!
AND STILL, YOU CONTINUE TO SERVE HIM AS HE BLEEDS YOU DRY.
DESPERATE, YOU INVESTED YOUR DWINDLING FUNDS INTO HALLIBENSON.
THE STOCK CRASHED WHEN WAR BROKE OUT BETWEEN YOUR CRONIES ON THE BOARD AND BENSON, JUNIOR.
ONLY TWO EVENTS COULD SAVE YOU...THE DEATHS OF RICHARD HENRY BENSON...AND... YOUR MASTER, THE SHADOW!
AND THAT'S WHEN YOU BECAME VULNERABLE TO ME.
HOW COULD YOU POSSIBLY KNOW ALL THIS?
MY FIRST ENCOUNTER WITH THE SHADOW...I MET A MISS LANE ONE EVENING AT THE ASTOR BAR.
MARGO TOLD YOU?!
OF COURSE NOT! HAVE YOU NO FAITH IN YOUR "FRIENDS?"
I SIMPLY FOUND HER... ENTRANCING--
--MR. CRANSTON!

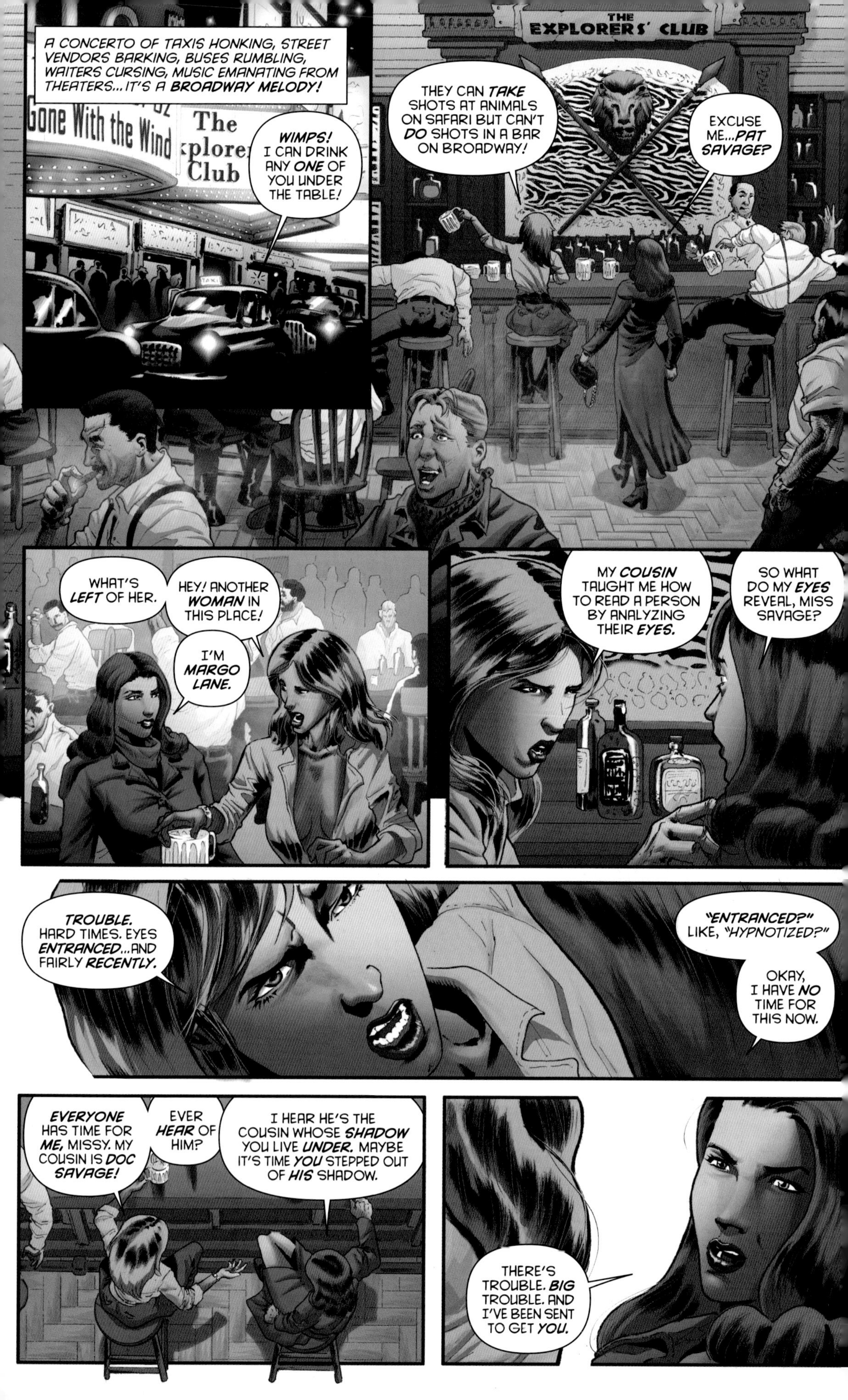
A CONCERTO OF TAXIS HONKING, STREET VENDORS BARKING, BUSES RUMBLING, WAITERS CURSING, MUSIC EMANATING FROM THEATERS...IT'S A BROADWAY MELODY!
Gone With the Wind
The Explorers Club
WIMPS! I CAN DRINK ANY ONE OF YOU UNDER THE TABLE!
THE EXPLORERS' CLUB
THEY CAN TAKE SHOTS AT ANIMALS ON SAFARI BUT CAN'T DO SHOTS IN A BAR ON BROADWAY!
EXCUSE ME...PAT SAVAGE?
WHAT'S LEFT OF HER.
HEY! ANOTHER WOMAN IN THIS PLACE!
I'M MARGO LANE.
MY COUSIN TAUGHT ME HOW TO READ A PERSON BY ANALYZING THEIR EYES.
SO WHAT DO MY EYES REVEAL, MISS SAVAGE?
TROUBLE. HARD TIMES. EYES ENTRANCED...AND FAIRLY RECENTLY.
"ENTRANCED?" LIKE, "HYPNOTIZED?"
OKAY, I HAVE NO TIME FOR THIS NOW.
EVERYONE HAS TIME FOR ME, MISSY. MY COUSIN IS DOC SAVAGE!
EVER HEAR OF HIM?
I HEAR HE'S THE COUSIN WHOSE SHADOW YOU LIVE UNDER. MAYBE IT'S TIME YOU STEPPED OUT OF HIS SHADOW.
THERE'S TROUBLE. BIG TROUBLE. AND I'VE BEEN SENT TO GET YOU.

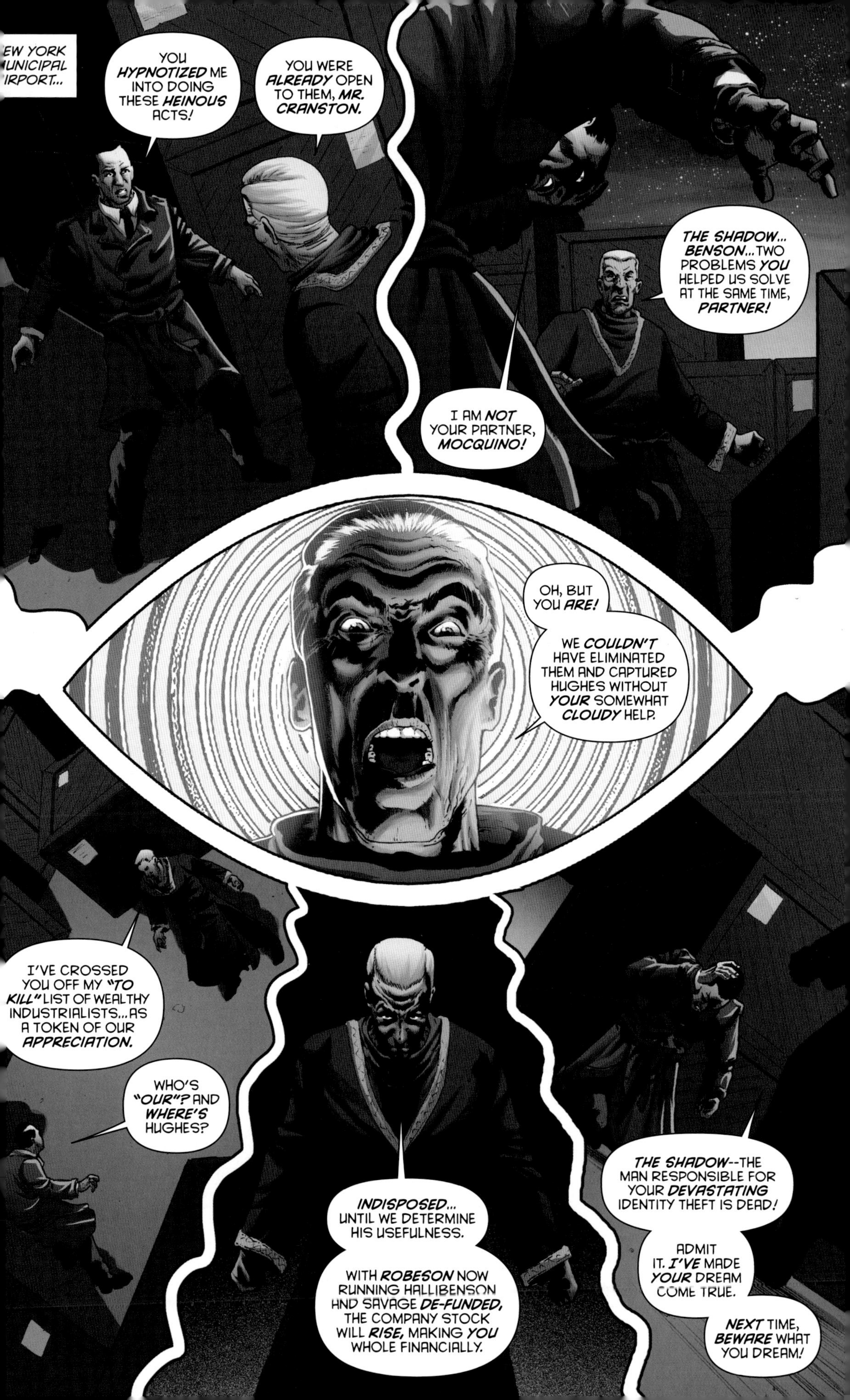

EW YORK UNICIPAL IRPORT...
YOU HYPNOTIZED ME INTO DOING THESE HEINOUS ACTS!
YOU WERE ALREADY OPEN TO THEM, MR. CRANSTON.
THE SHADOW... BENSON...TWO PROBLEMS YOU HELPED US SOLVE AT THE SAME TIME, PARTNER!
I AM NOT YOUR PARTNER, MOCQUINO!
OH, BUT YOU ARE!
WE COULDN'T HAVE ELIMINATED THEM AND CAPTURED HUGHES WITHOUT YOUR SOMEWHAT CLOUDY HELP.
I'VE CROSSED YOU OFF MY "TO KILL" LIST OF WEALTHY INDUSTRIALISTS...AS A TOKEN OF OUR APPRECIATION.
WHO'S "OUR"? AND WHERE'S HUGHES?
INDISPOSED... UNTIL WE DETERMINE HIS USEFULNESS.
WITH ROBESON NOW RUNNING HALLIBENSON AND SAVAGE DE-FUNDED, THE COMPANY STOCK WILL RISE, MAKING YOU WHOLE FINANCIALLY.
THE SHADOW--THE MAN RESPONSIBLE FOR YOUR DEVASTATING IDENTITY THEFT IS DEAD!
ADMIT IT. I'VE MADE YOUR DREAM COME TRUE.
NEXT TIME, BEWARE WHAT YOU DREAM!

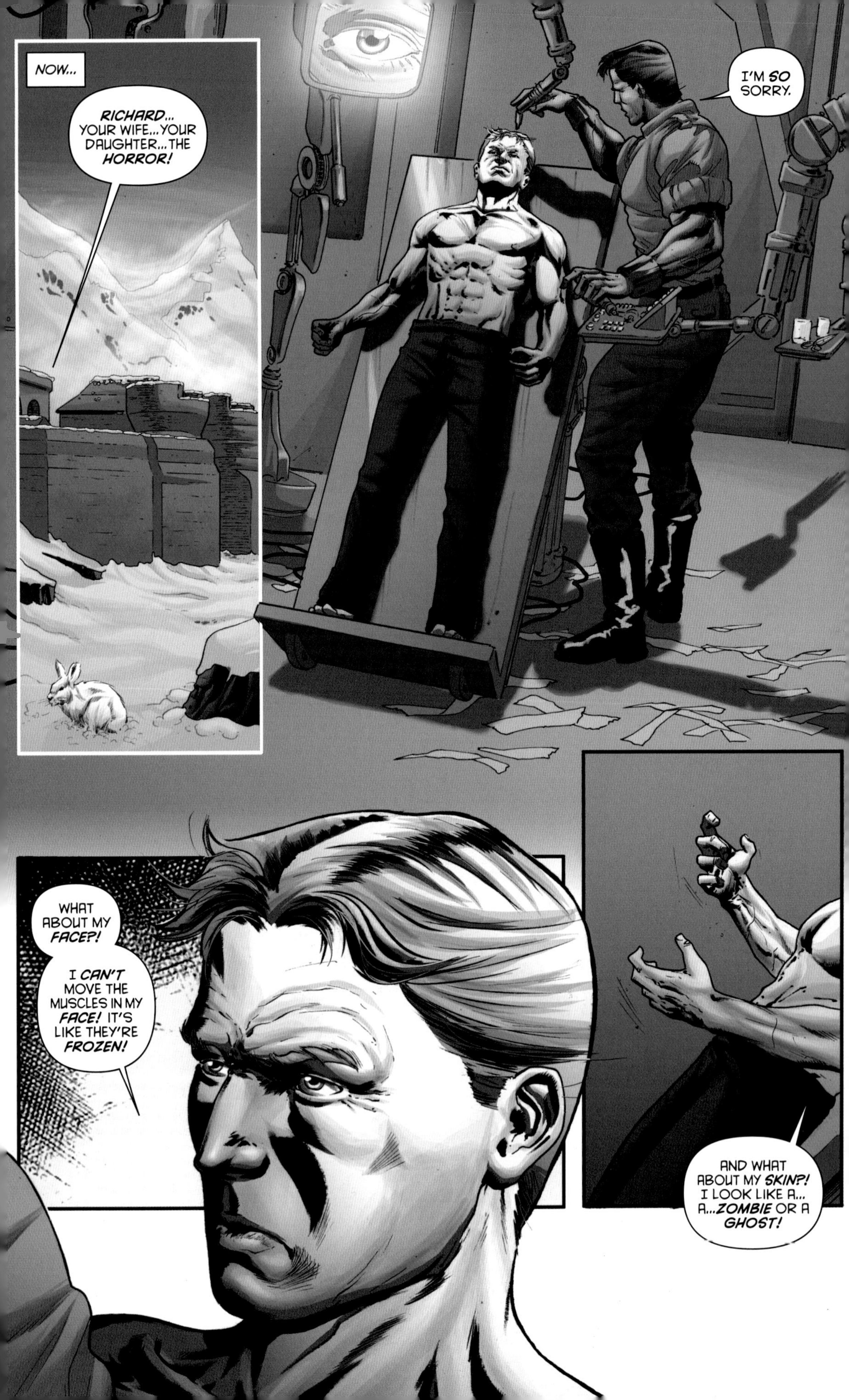
NOW...
RICHARD... YOUR WIFE...YOUR DAUGHTER...THE HORROR!
I'M SO SORRY.
WHAT ABOUT MY FACE?!
I CAN'T MOVE THE MUSCLES IN MY FACE! IT'S LIKE THEY'RE FROZEN!
AND WHAT ABOUT MY SKIN?! I LOOK LIKE A... A...ZOMBIE OR A GHOST!

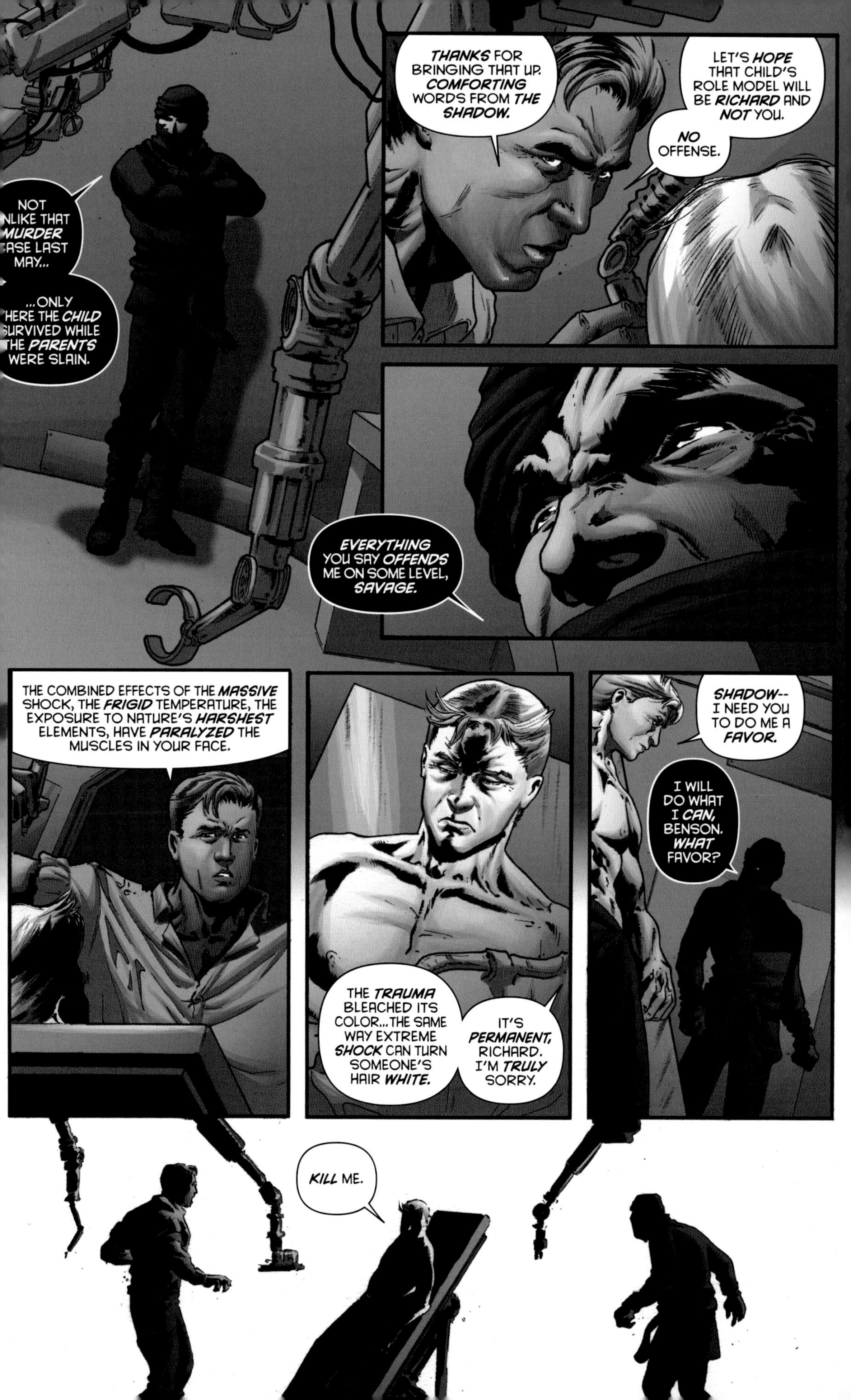
NOT NLIKE THAT MURDER CASE LAST MAY...
...ONLY HERE THE CHILD SURVIVED WHILE THE PARENTS WERE SLAIN.
THANKS FOR BRINGING THAT UP. COMFORTING WORDS FROM THE SHADOW.
LET'S HOPE THAT CHILD'S ROLE MODEL WILL BE RICHARD AND NOT YOU.
NO OFFENSE.
EVERYTHING YOU SAY OFFENDS ME ON SOME LEVEL, SAVAGE.
THE COMBINED EFFECTS OF THE MASSIVE SHOCK, THE FRIGID TEMPERATURE, THE EXPOSURE TO NATURE'S HARSHEST ELEMENTS, HAVE PARALYZED THE MUSCLES IN YOUR FACE.
THE TRAUMA BLEACHED ITS COLOR...THE SAME WAY EXTREME SHOCK CAN TURN SOMEONE'S HAIR WHITE.
IT'S PERMANENT, RICHARD. I'M TRULY SORRY.
SHADOW-- I NEED YOU TO DO ME A FAVOR.
I WILL DO WHAT I CAN, BENSON. WHAT FAVOR?
KILL ME.

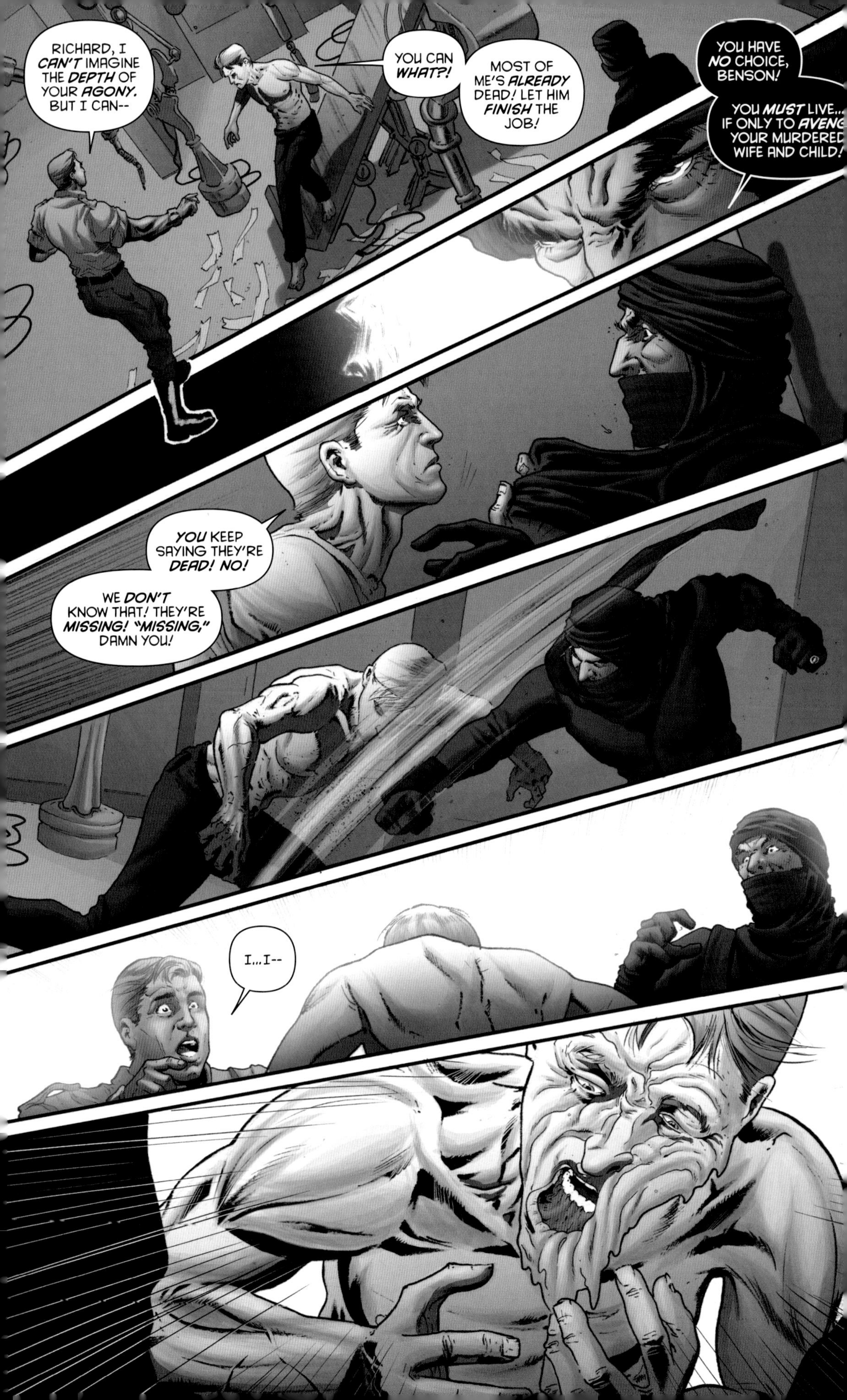
RICHARD, I CAN'T IMAGINE THE DEPTH OF YOUR AGONY. BUT I CAN--
YOU CAN WHAT?!
MOST OF ME'S ALREADY DEAD! LET HIM FINISH THE JOB!
YOU HAVE NO CHOICE, BENSON!
YOU MUST LIVE... IF ONLY TO AVENGE YOUR MURDERED WIFE AND CHILD!
YOU KEEP SAYING THEY'RE DEAD! NO!
WE DON'T KNOW THAT! THEY'RE MISSING! "MISSING," DAMN YOU!
I...I--

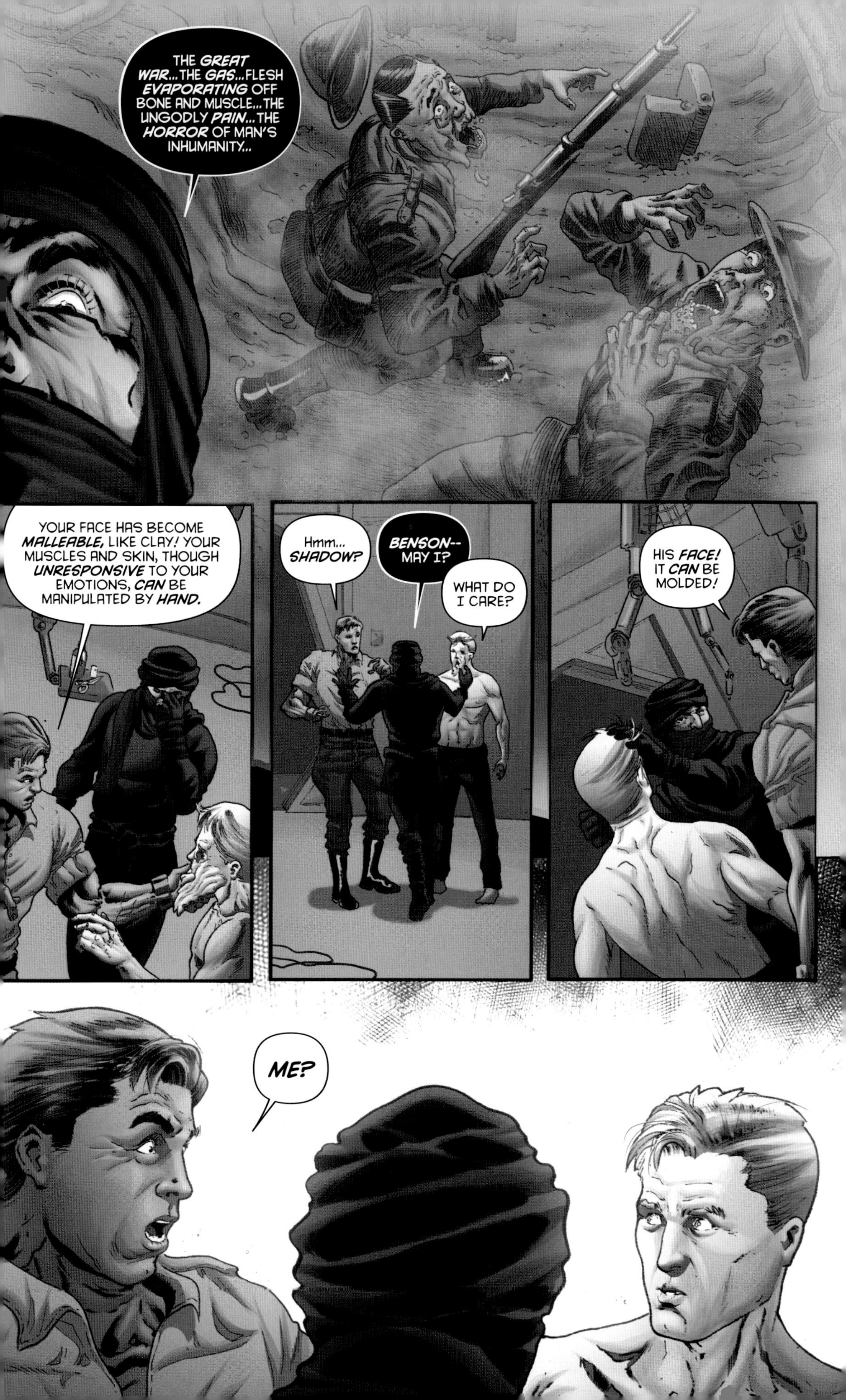
THE *GREAT WAR*... THE *GAS*... FLESH *EVAPORATING* OFF BONE AND MUSCLE... THE UNGODLY *PAIN*... THE *HORROR* OF MAN'S INHUMANITY...
YOUR FACE HAS BECOME *MALLEABLE,* LIKE CLAY! YOUR MUSCLES AND SKIN, THOUGH *UNRESPONSIVE* TO YOUR EMOTIONS, *CAN* BE MANIPULATED BY *HAND.*
Hmm... *SHADOW?*
BENSON-- MAY I?
WHAT DO I CARE?
HIS *FACE!* IT *CAN* BE MOLDED!
ME?

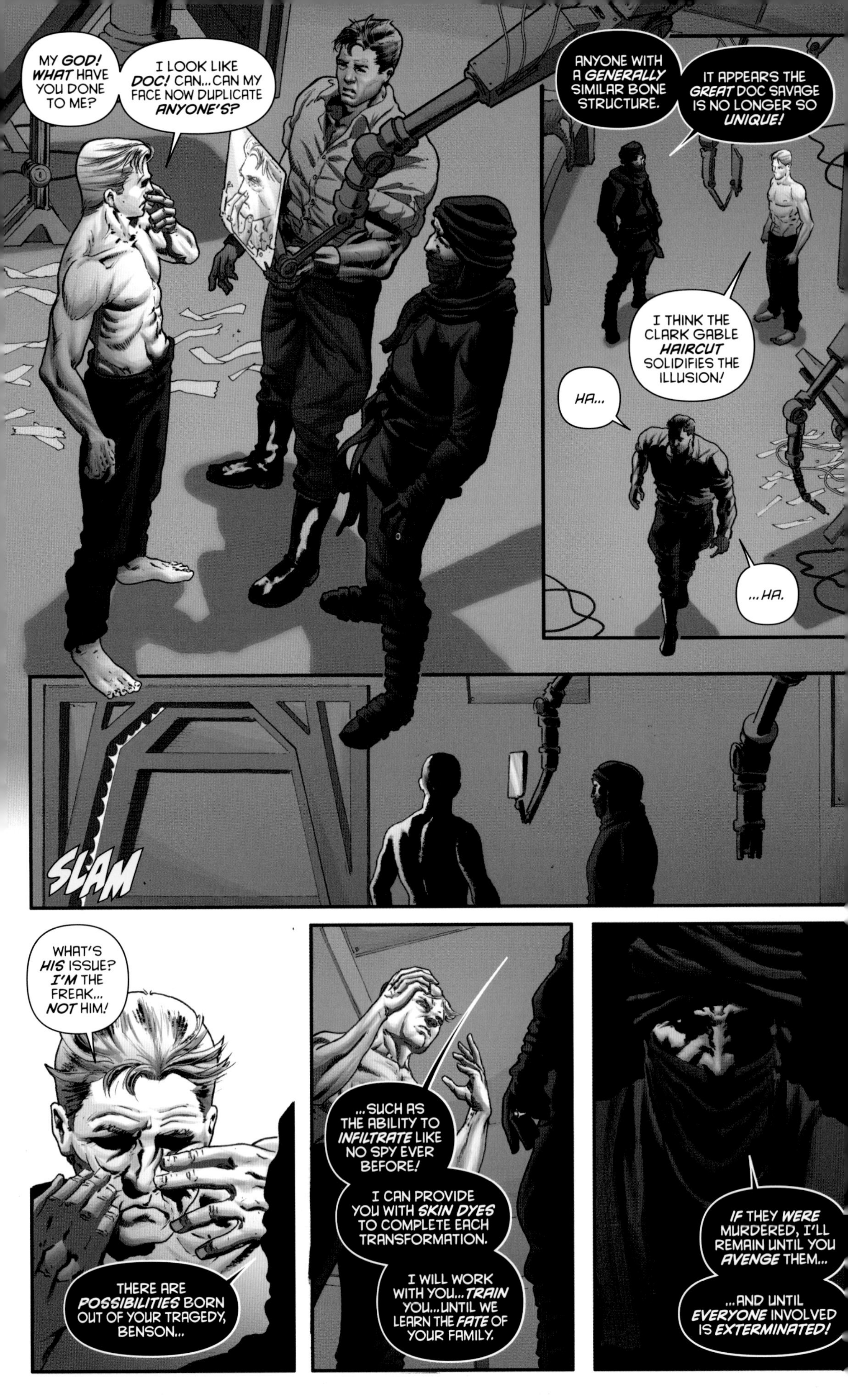
MY GOD! WHAT HAVE YOU DONE TO ME?
I LOOK LIKE DOC! CAN...CAN MY FACE NOW DUPLICATE ANYONE'S?
ANYONE WITH A GENERALLY SIMILAR BONE STRUCTURE.
IT APPEARS THE GREAT DOC SAVAGE IS NO LONGER SO UNIQUE!
I THINK THE CLARK GABLE HAIRCUT SOLIDIFIES THE ILLUSION!
HA...
...HA.
SLAM
WHAT'S HIS ISSUE? I'M THE FREAK... NOT HIM!
THERE ARE POSSIBILITIES BORN OUT OF YOUR TRAGEDY, BENSON...
...SUCH AS THE ABILITY TO INFILTRATE LIKE NO SPY EVER BEFORE!
I CAN PROVIDE YOU WITH SKIN DYES TO COMPLETE EACH TRANSFORMATION.
I WILL WORK WITH YOU...TRAIN YOU...UNTIL WE LEARN THE FATE OF YOUR FAMILY.
IF THEY WERE MURDERED, I'LL REMAIN UNTIL YOU AVENGE THEM...
...AND UNTIL EVERYONE INVOLVED IS EXTERMINATED!

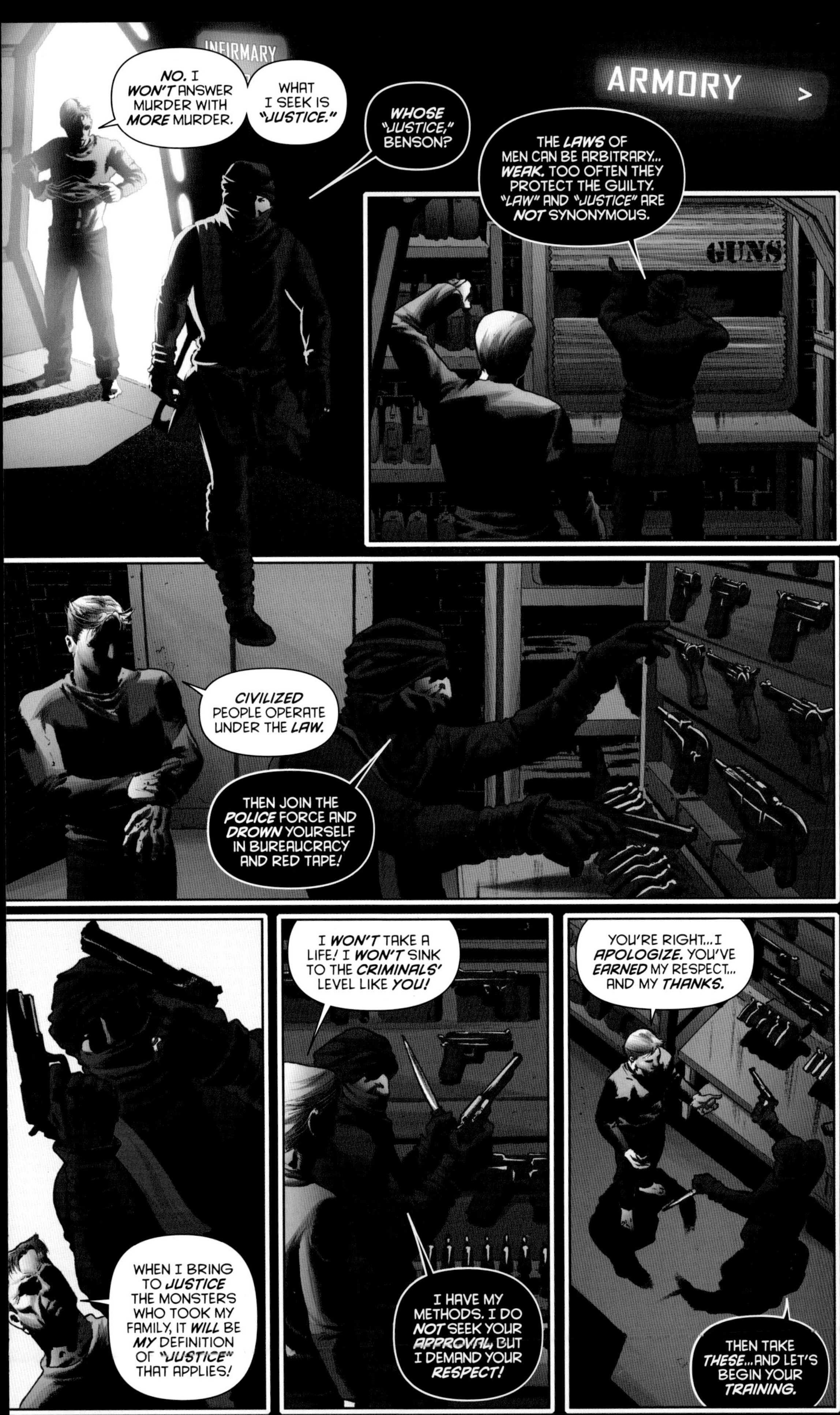
INFIRMARY
ARMORY
NO. I WON'T ANSWER MURDER WITH MORE MURDER.
WHAT I SEEK IS "JUSTICE."
WHOSE "JUSTICE," BENSON?
THE LAWS OF MEN CAN BE ARBITRARY... WEAK. TOO OFTEN THEY PROTECT THE GUILTY. "LAW" AND "JUSTICE" ARE NOT SYNONYMOUS.
GUNS
CIVILIZED PEOPLE OPERATE UNDER THE LAW.
THEN JOIN THE POLICE FORCE AND DROWN YOURSELF IN BUREAUCRACY AND RED TAPE!
WHEN I BRING TO JUSTICE THE MONSTERS WHO TOOK MY FAMILY, IT WILL BE MY DEFINITION OF "JUSTICE" THAT APPLIES!
I WON'T TAKE A LIFE! I WON'T SINK TO THE CRIMINALS' LEVEL LIKE YOU!
I HAVE MY METHODS. I DO NOT SEEK YOUR APPROVAL, BUT I DEMAND YOUR RESPECT!
YOU'RE RIGHT... I APOLOGIZE. YOU'VE EARNED MY RESPECT... AND MY THANKS.
THEN TAKE THESE... AND LET'S BEGIN YOUR TRAINING.

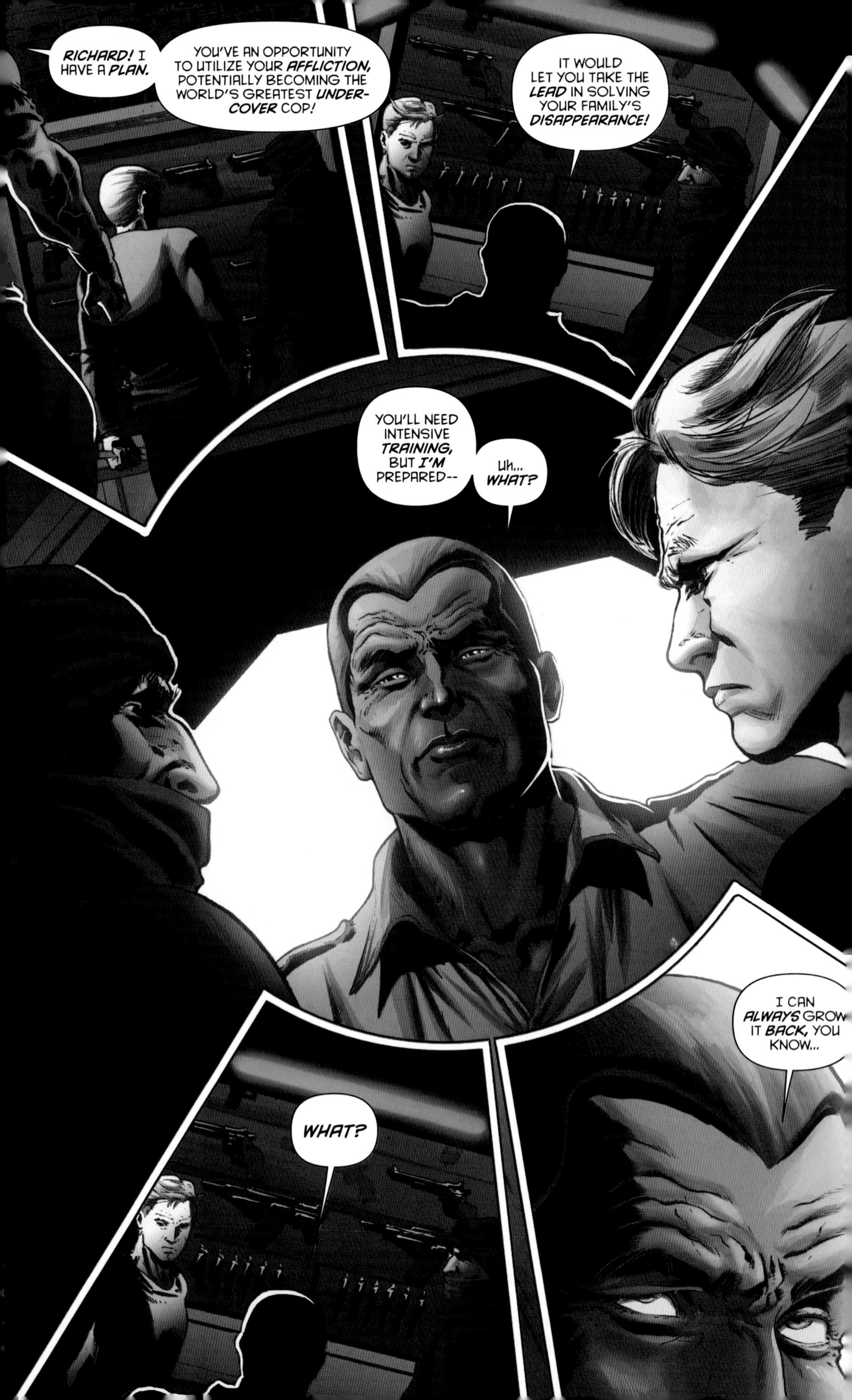
RICHARD! I HAVE A PLAN.
YOU'VE AN OPPORTUNITY TO UTILIZE YOUR AFFLICTION, POTENTIALLY BECOMING THE WORLD'S GREATEST UNDER-COVER COP!
IT WOULD LET YOU TAKE THE LEAD IN SOLVING YOUR FAMILY'S DISAPPEARANCE!
YOU'LL NEED INTENSIVE TRAINING, BUT I'M PREPARED--
UH... WHAT?
WHAT?
I CAN ALWAYS GROW IT BACK, YOU KNOW...

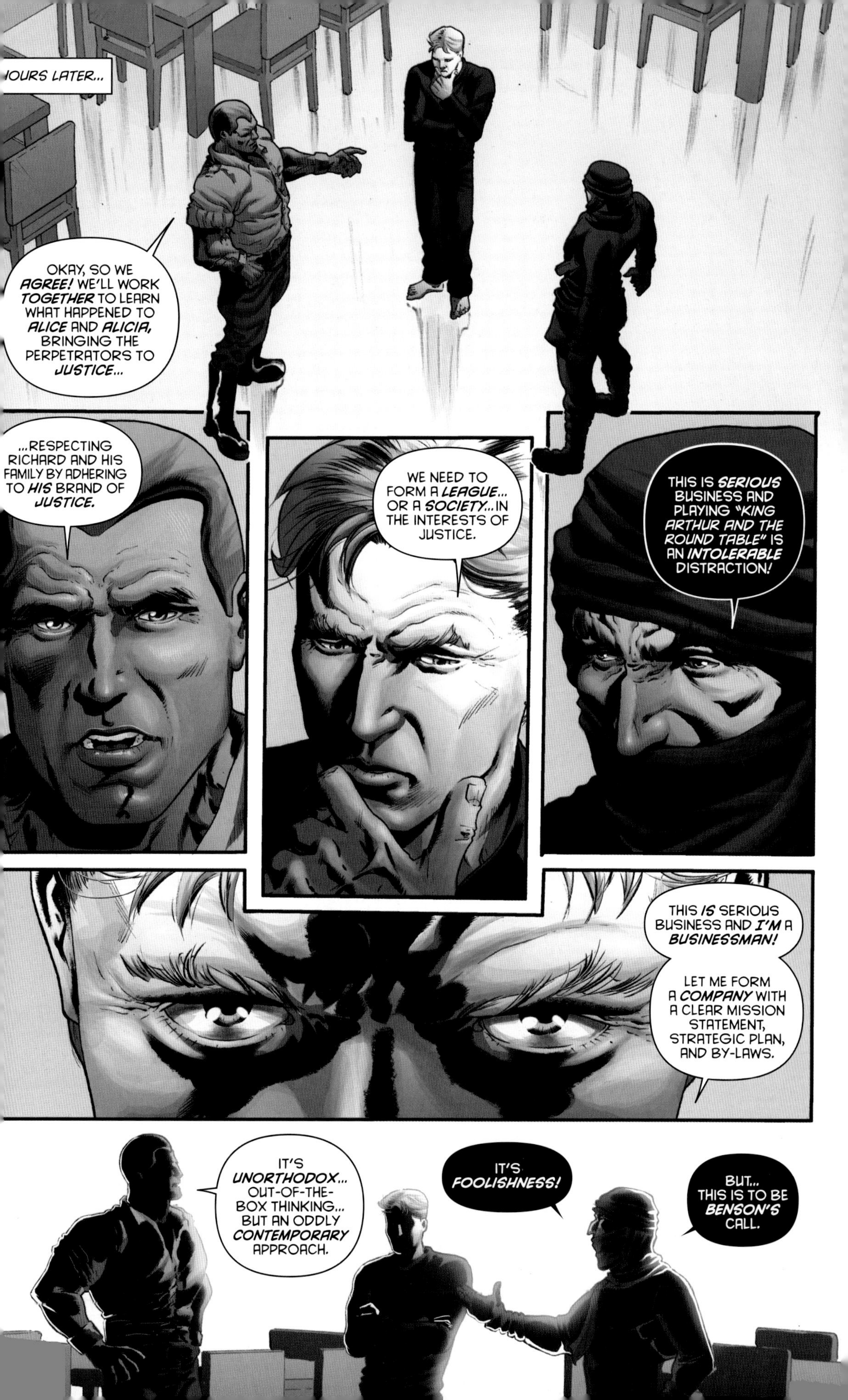

OURS LATER...
OKAY, SO WE AGREE! WE'LL WORK TOGETHER TO LEARN WHAT HAPPENED TO ALICE AND ALICIA, BRINGING THE PERPETRATORS TO JUSTICE...
...RESPECTING RICHARD AND HIS FAMILY BY ADHERING TO HIS BRAND OF JUSTICE.
WE NEED TO FORM A LEAGUE... OR A SOCIETY... IN THE INTERESTS OF JUSTICE.
THIS IS SERIOUS BUSINESS AND PLAYING "KING ARTHUR AND THE ROUND TABLE" IS AN INTOLERABLE DISTRACTION!
THIS IS SERIOUS BUSINESS AND I'M A BUSINESSMAN!
LET ME FORM A COMPANY WITH A CLEAR MISSION STATEMENT, STRATEGIC PLAN, AND BY-LAWS.
IT'S UNORTHODOX... OUT-OF-THE-BOX THINKING... BUT AN ODDLY CONTEMPORARY APPROACH.
IT'S FOOLISHNESS!
BUT... THIS IS TO BE BENSON'S CALL.

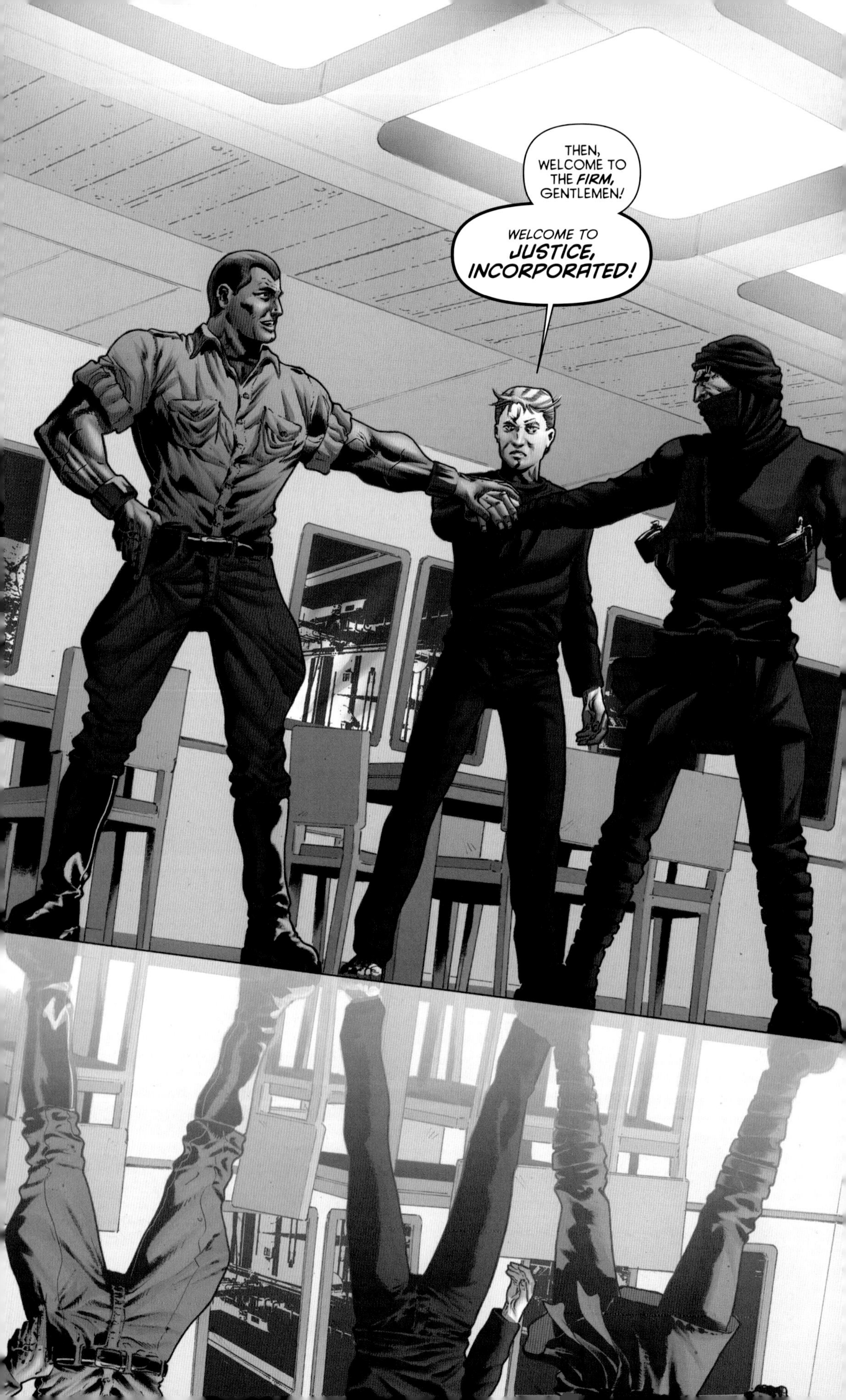
THEN, WELCOME TO THE *FIRM,* GENTLEMEN!
WELCOME TO **JUSTICE, INCORPORATED!**

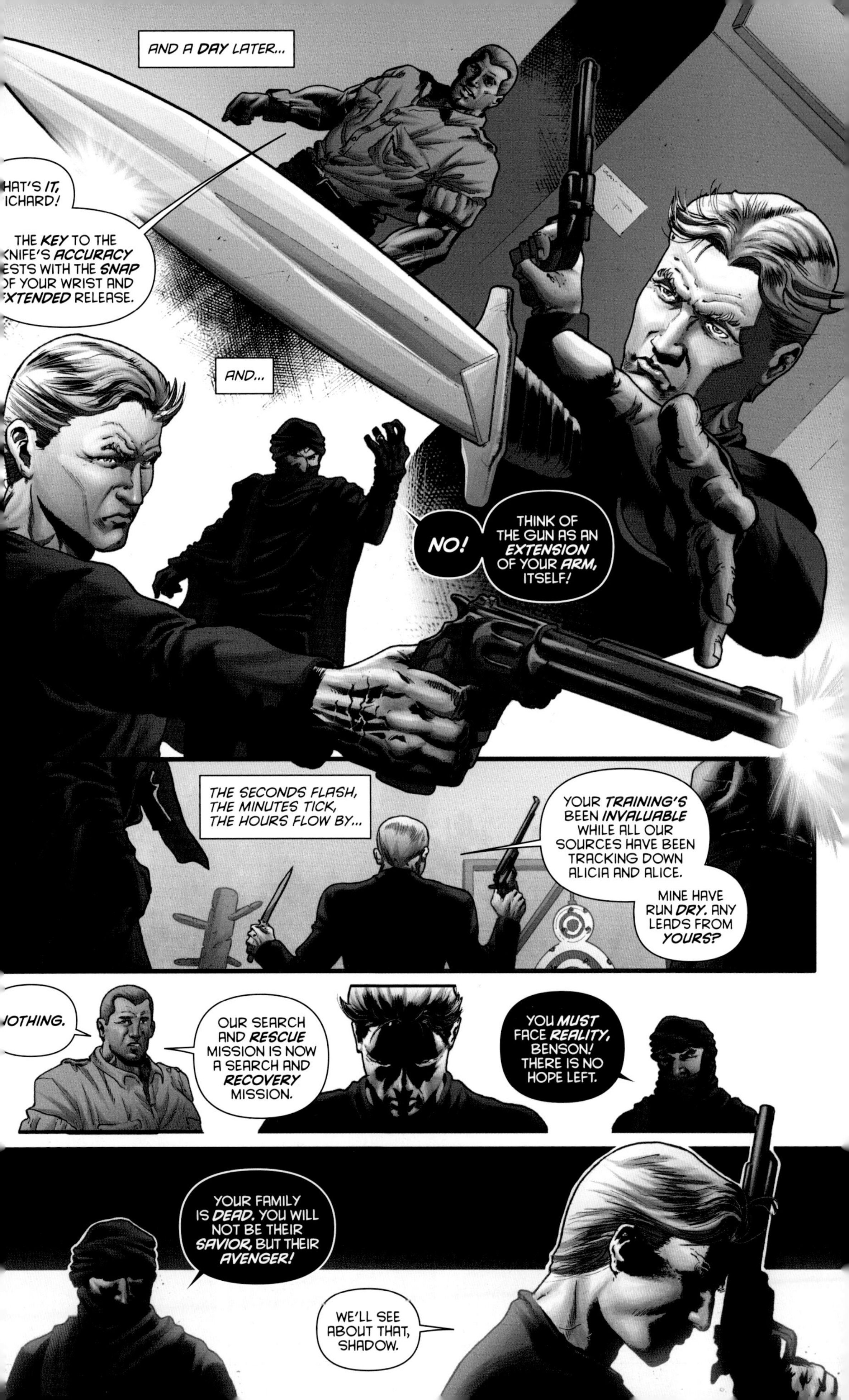
AND A DAY LATER...
HAT'S IT, ICHARD!
THE KEY TO THE KNIFE'S ACCURACY ESTS WITH THE SNAP OF YOUR WRIST AND XTENDED RELEASE.
AND...
NO!
THINK OF THE GUN AS AN EXTENSION OF YOUR ARM, ITSELF!
THE SECONDS FLASH, THE MINUTES TICK, THE HOURS FLOW BY...
YOUR TRAINING'S BEEN INVALUABLE WHILE ALL OUR SOURCES HAVE BEEN TRACKING DOWN ALICIA AND ALICE.
MINE HAVE RUN DRY. ANY LEADS FROM YOURS?
IOTHING.
OUR SEARCH AND RESCUE MISSION IS NOW A SEARCH AND RECOVERY MISSION.
YOU MUST FACE REALITY, BENSON! THERE IS NO HOPE LEFT.
YOUR FAMILY IS DEAD. YOU WILL NOT BE THEIR SAVIOR, BUT THEIR AVENGER!
WE'LL SEE ABOUT THAT, SHADOW.

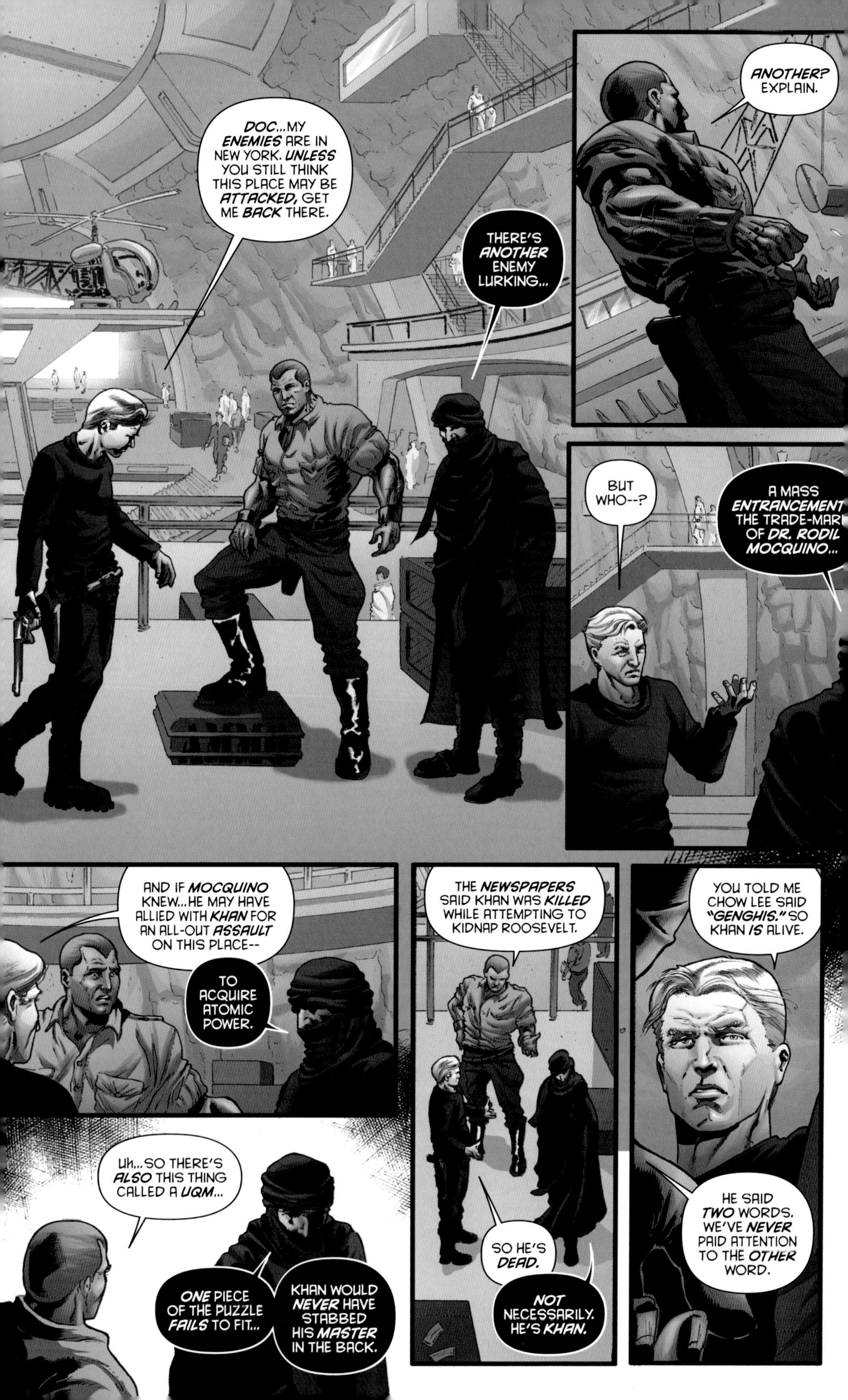
DOC...MY ENEMIES ARE IN NEW YORK. UNLESS YOU STILL THINK THIS PLACE MAY BE ATTACKED, GET ME BACK THERE.
THERE'S ANOTHER ENEMY LURKING...
ANOTHER? EXPLAIN.
BUT WHO--?
A MASS ENTRANCEMENT THE TRADE-MARI OF DR. RODIL MOCQUINO...
AND IF MOCQUINO KNEW...HE MAY HAVE ALLIED WITH KHAN FOR AN ALL-OUT ASSAULT ON THIS PLACE--
TO ACQUIRE ATOMIC POWER.
THE NEWSPAPERS SAID KHAN WAS KILLED WHILE ATTEMPTING TO KIDNAP ROOSEVELT.
SO HE'S DEAD.
NOT NECESSARILY. HE'S KHAN.
YOU TOLD ME CHOW LEE SAID "GENGHIS." SO KHAN IS ALIVE.
HE SAID TWO WORDS. WE'VE NEVER PAID ATTENTION TO THE OTHER WORD.
UH...SO THERE'S ALSO THIS THING CALLED A UQM...
ONE PIECE OF THE PUZZLE FAILS TO FIT...
KHAN WOULD NEVER HAVE STABBED HIS MASTER IN THE BACK.

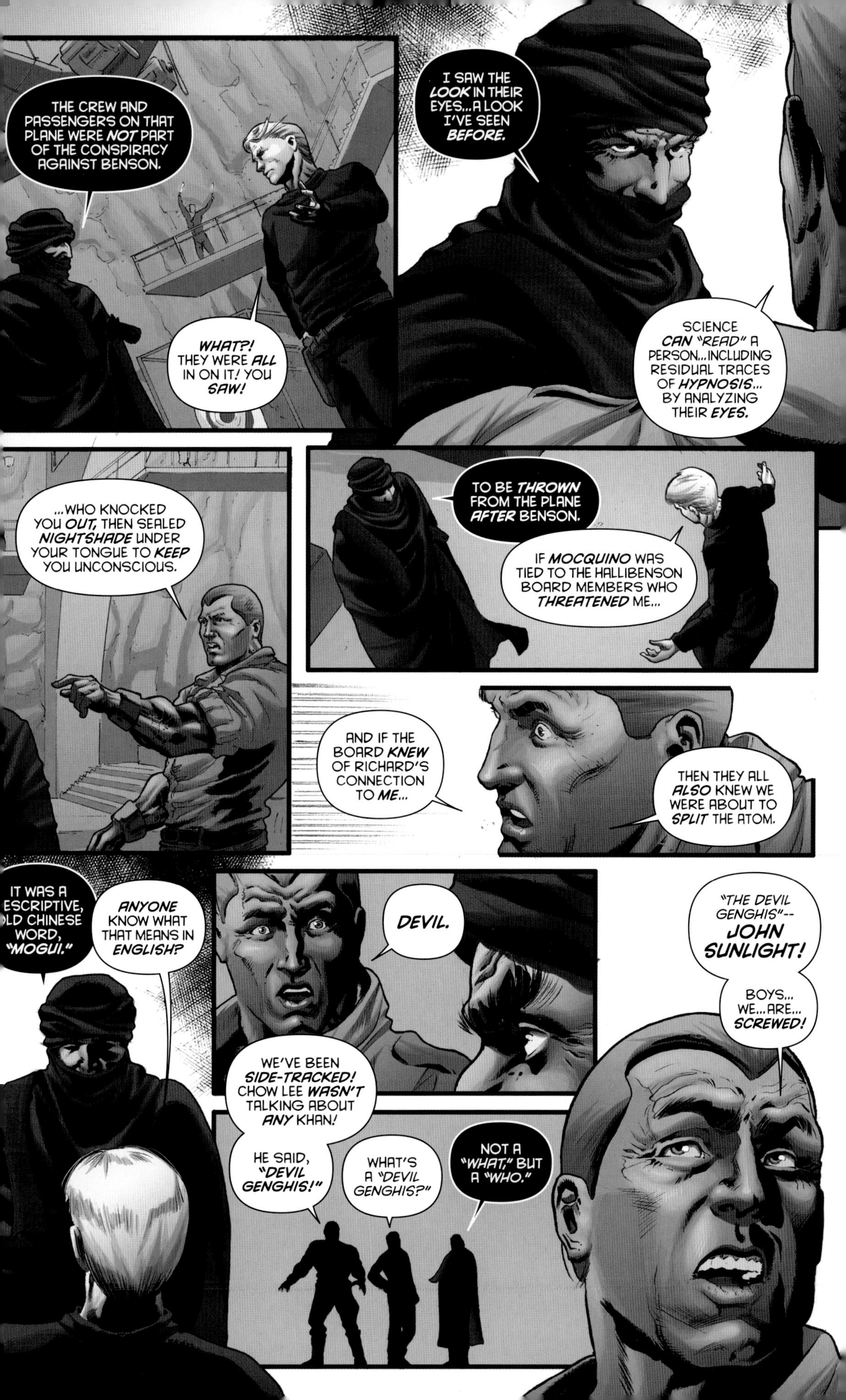

THE CREW AND PASSENGERS ON THAT PLANE WERE NOT PART OF THE CONSPIRACY AGAINST BENSON.
WHAT?! THEY WERE ALL IN ON IT! YOU SAW!
I SAW THE LOOK IN THEIR EYES...A LOOK I'VE SEEN BEFORE.
SCIENCE CAN "READ" A PERSON...INCLUDING RESIDUAL TRACES OF HYPNOSIS... BY ANALYZING THEIR EYES.
...WHO KNOCKED YOU OUT, THEN SEALED NIGHTSHADE UNDER YOUR TONGUE TO KEEP YOU UNCONSCIOUS.
TO BE THROWN FROM THE PLANE AFTER BENSON.
IF MOCQUINO WAS TIED TO THE HALLIBENSON BOARD MEMBERS WHO THREATENED ME...
AND IF THE BOARD KNEW OF RICHARD'S CONNECTION TO ME...
THEN THEY ALL ALSO KNEW WE WERE ABOUT TO SPLIT THE ATOM.
IT WAS A ESCRIPTIVE, LD CHINESE WORD, "MOGUI."
ANYONE KNOW WHAT THAT MEANS IN ENGLISH?
DEVIL.
WE'VE BEEN SIDE-TRACKED! CHOW LEE WASN'T TALKING ABOUT ANY KHAN!
HE SAID, "DEVIL GENGHIS!"
WHAT'S A "DEVIL GENGHIS?"
NOT A "WHAT," BUT A "WHO."
"THE DEVIL GENGHIS"-- JOHN SUNLIGHT!
BOYS... WE...ARE... SCREWED!

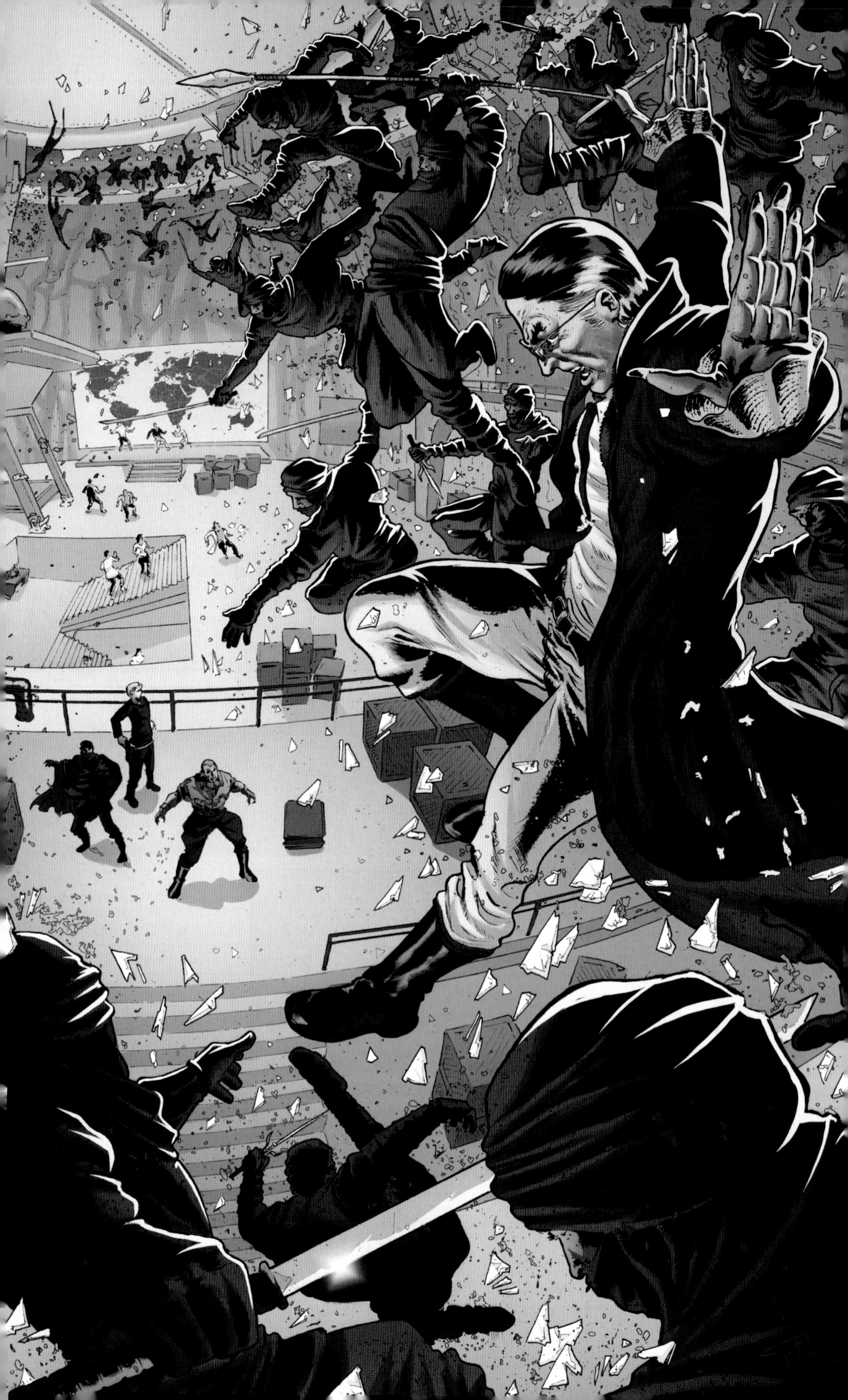

FOUR

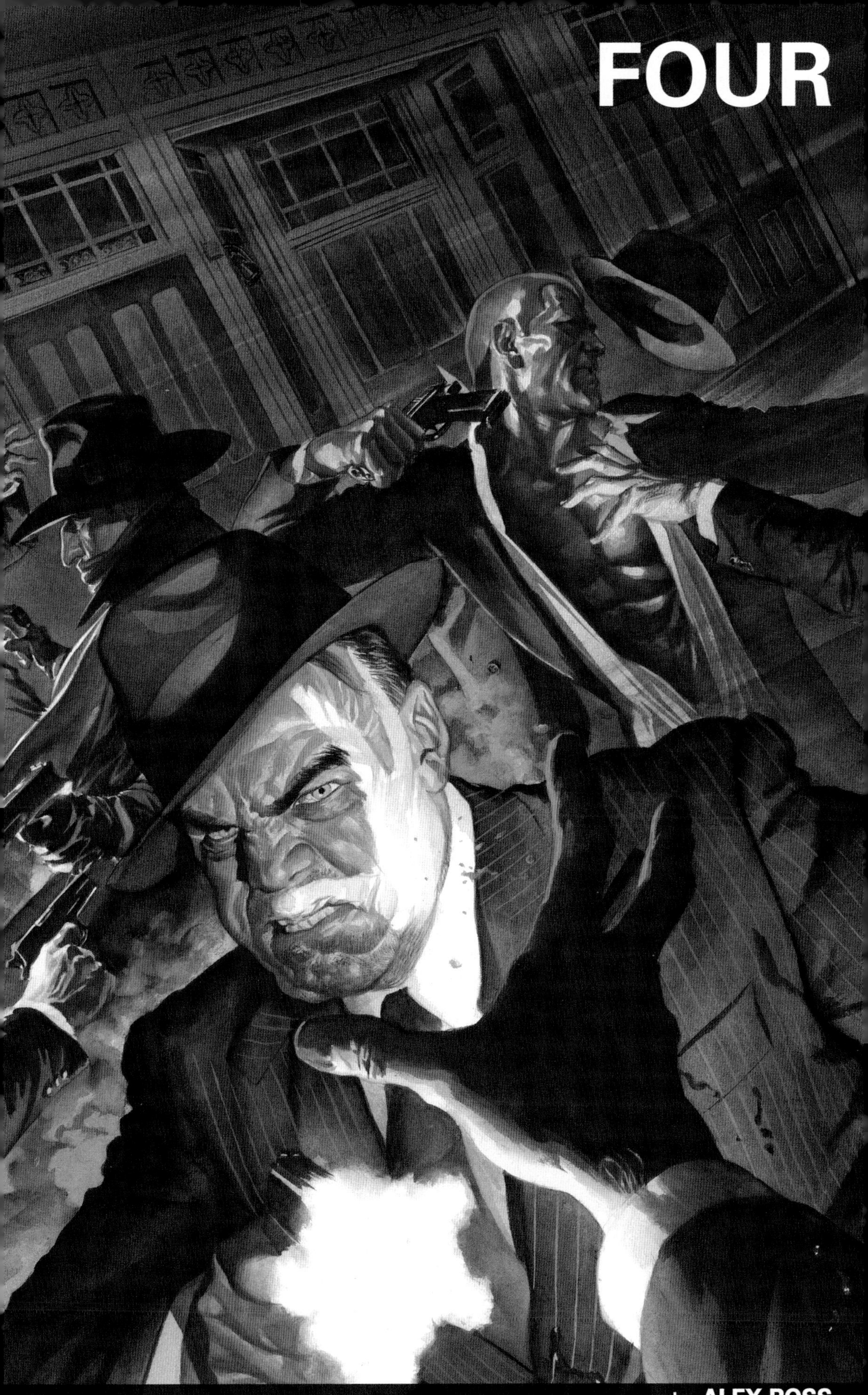

cover by **ALEX ROSS**

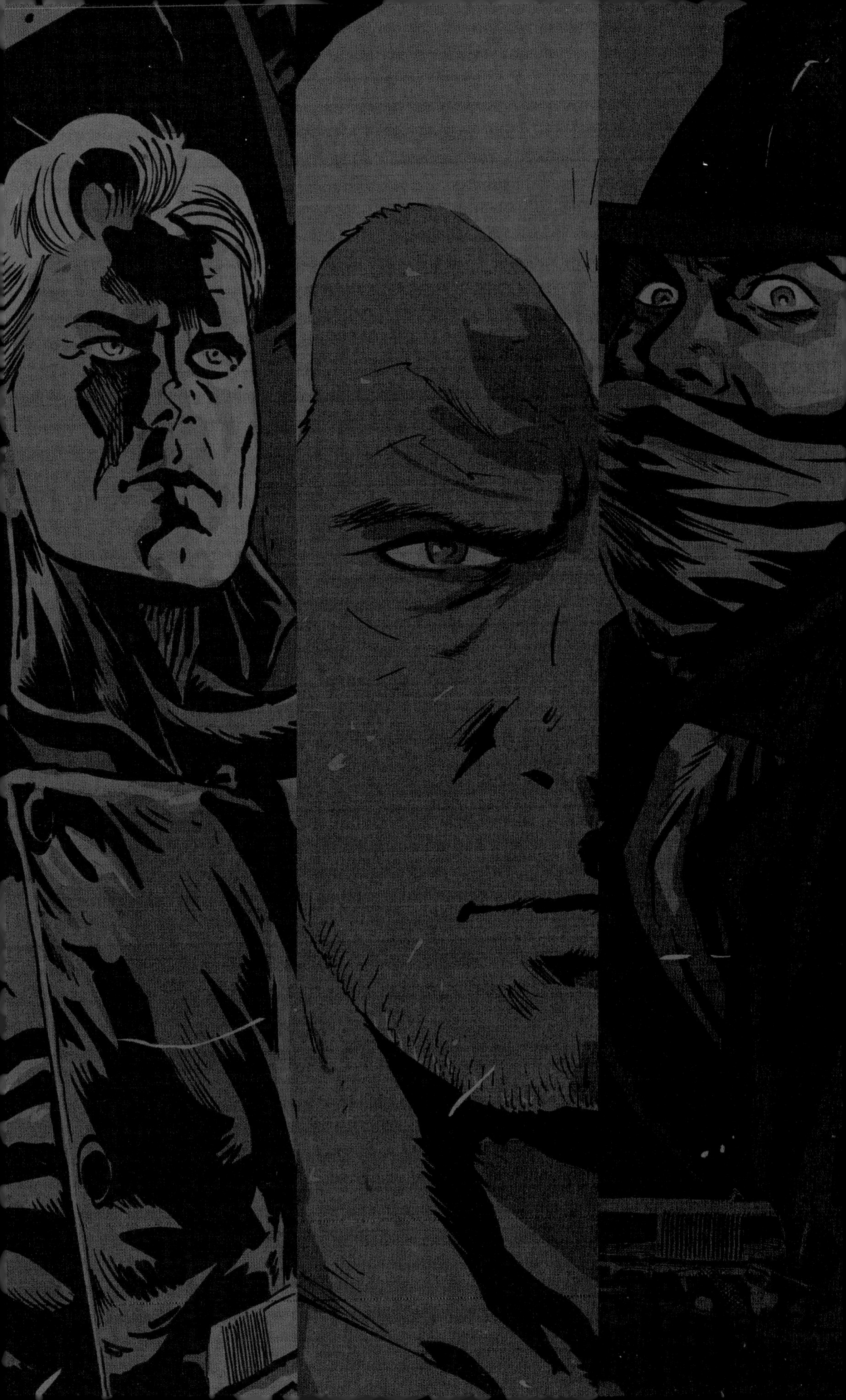

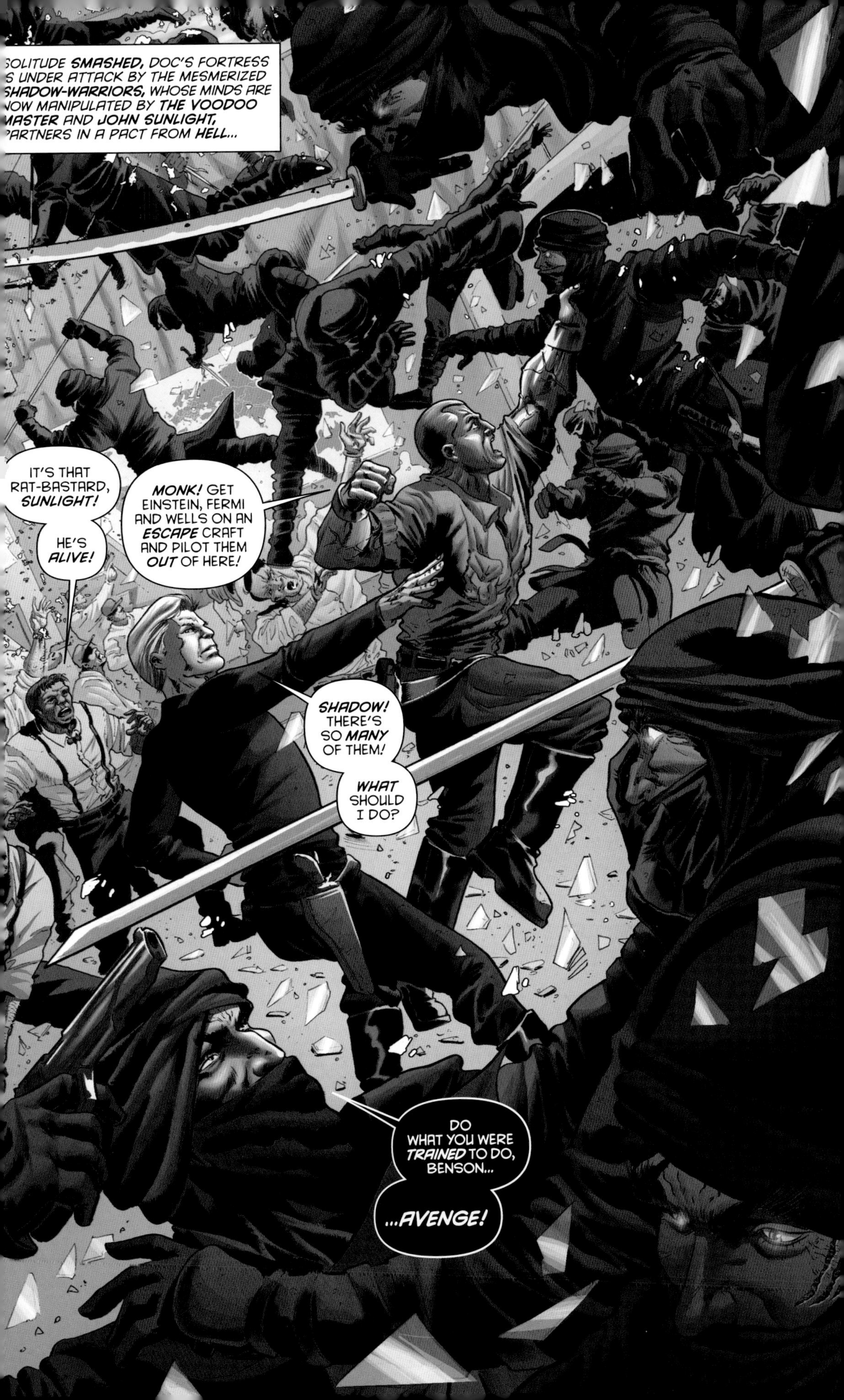
SOLITUDE SMASHED, DOC'S FORTRESS IS UNDER ATTACK BY THE MESMERIZED SHADOW-WARRIORS, WHOSE MINDS ARE NOW MANIPULATED BY THE VOODOO MASTER AND JOHN SUNLIGHT, PARTNERS IN A PACT FROM HELL...
IT'S THAT RAT-BASTARD, SUNLIGHT!
HE'S ALIVE!
MONK! GET EINSTEIN, FERMI AND WELLS ON AN ESCAPE CRAFT AND PILOT THEM OUT OF HERE!
SHADOW! THERE'S SO MANY OF THEM!
WHAT SHOULD I DO?
DO WHAT YOU WERE TRAINED TO DO, BENSON...
...AVENGE!

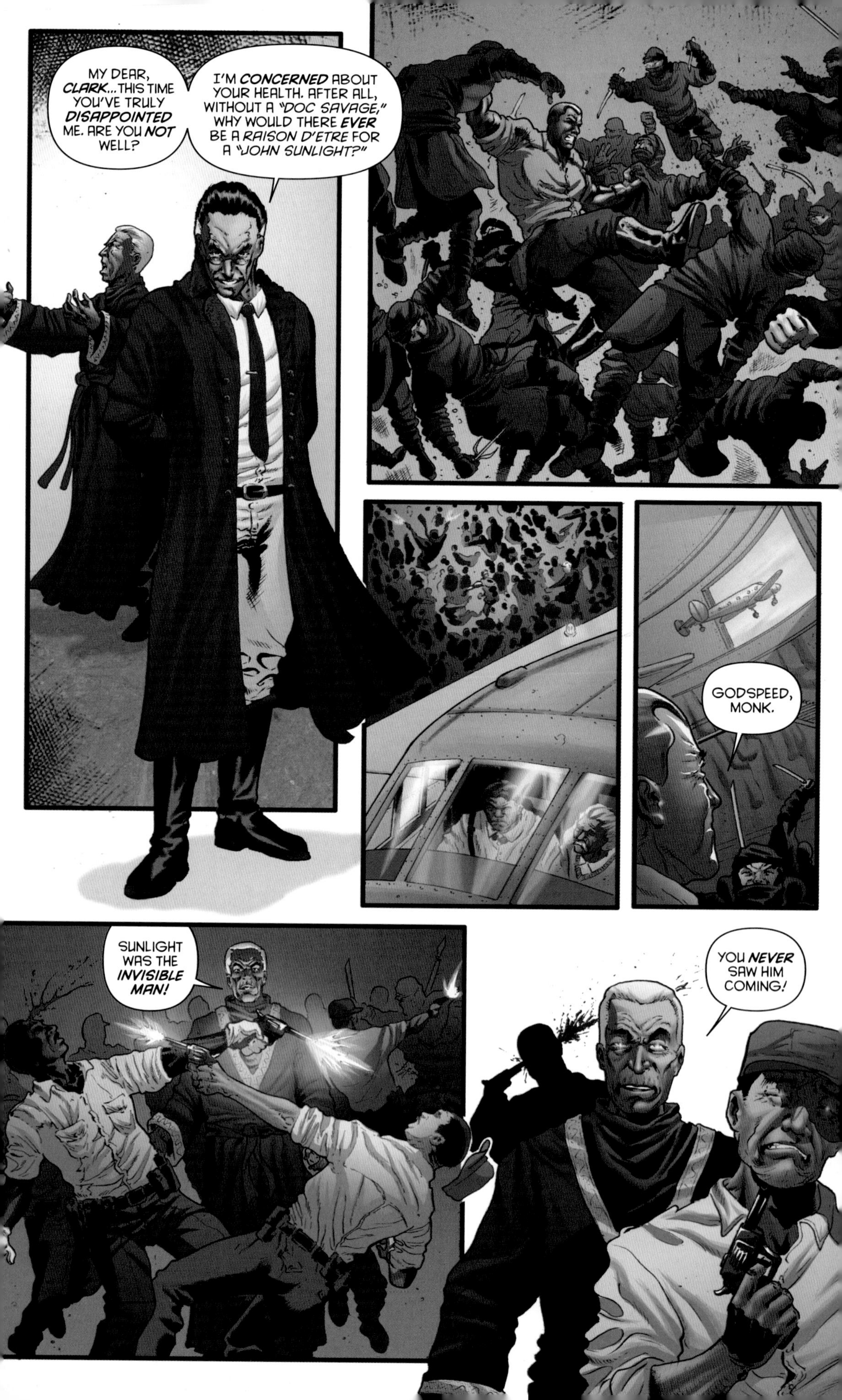
MY DEAR, CLARK...THIS TIME YOU'VE TRULY DISAPPOINTED ME. ARE YOU NOT WELL?
I'M CONCERNED ABOUT YOUR HEALTH. AFTER ALL, WITHOUT A "DOC SAVAGE," WHY WOULD THERE EVER BE A RAISON D'ETRE FOR A "JOHN SUNLIGHT?"
GODSPEED, MONK.
SUNLIGHT WAS THE INVISIBLE MAN!
YOU NEVER SAW HIM COMING!

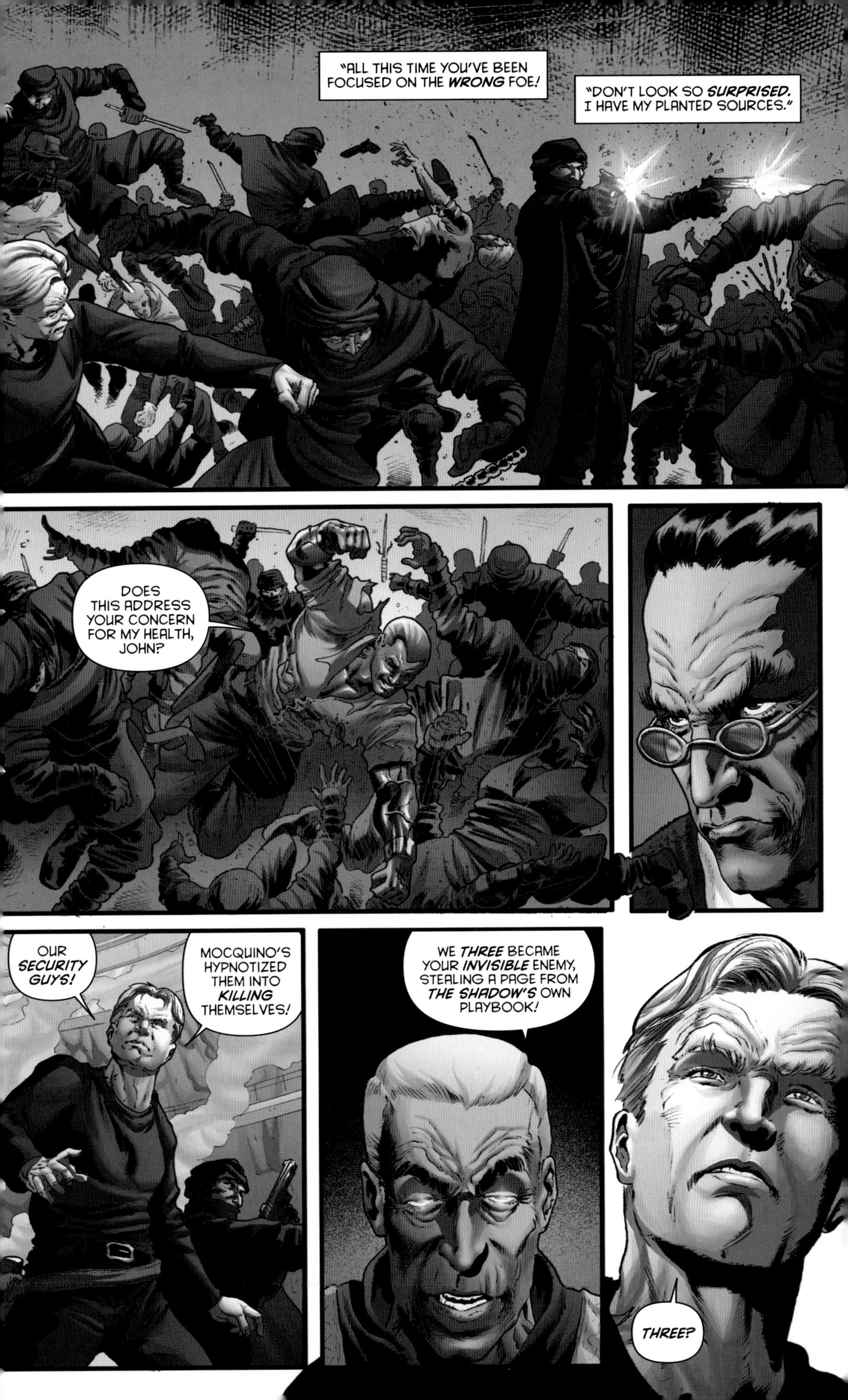
"ALL THIS TIME YOU'VE BEEN FOCUSED ON THE *WRONG* FOE!
"DON'T LOOK SO *SURPRISED.* I HAVE MY PLANTED SOURCES."
DOES THIS ADDRESS YOUR CONCERN FOR MY HEALTH, JOHN?
OUR *SECURITY GUYS!*
MOCQUINO'S HYPNOTIZED THEM INTO *KILLING* THEMSELVES!
WE *THREE* BECAME YOUR *INVISIBLE* ENEMY, STEALING A PAGE FROM *THE SHADOW'S* OWN PLAYBOOK!
THREE?

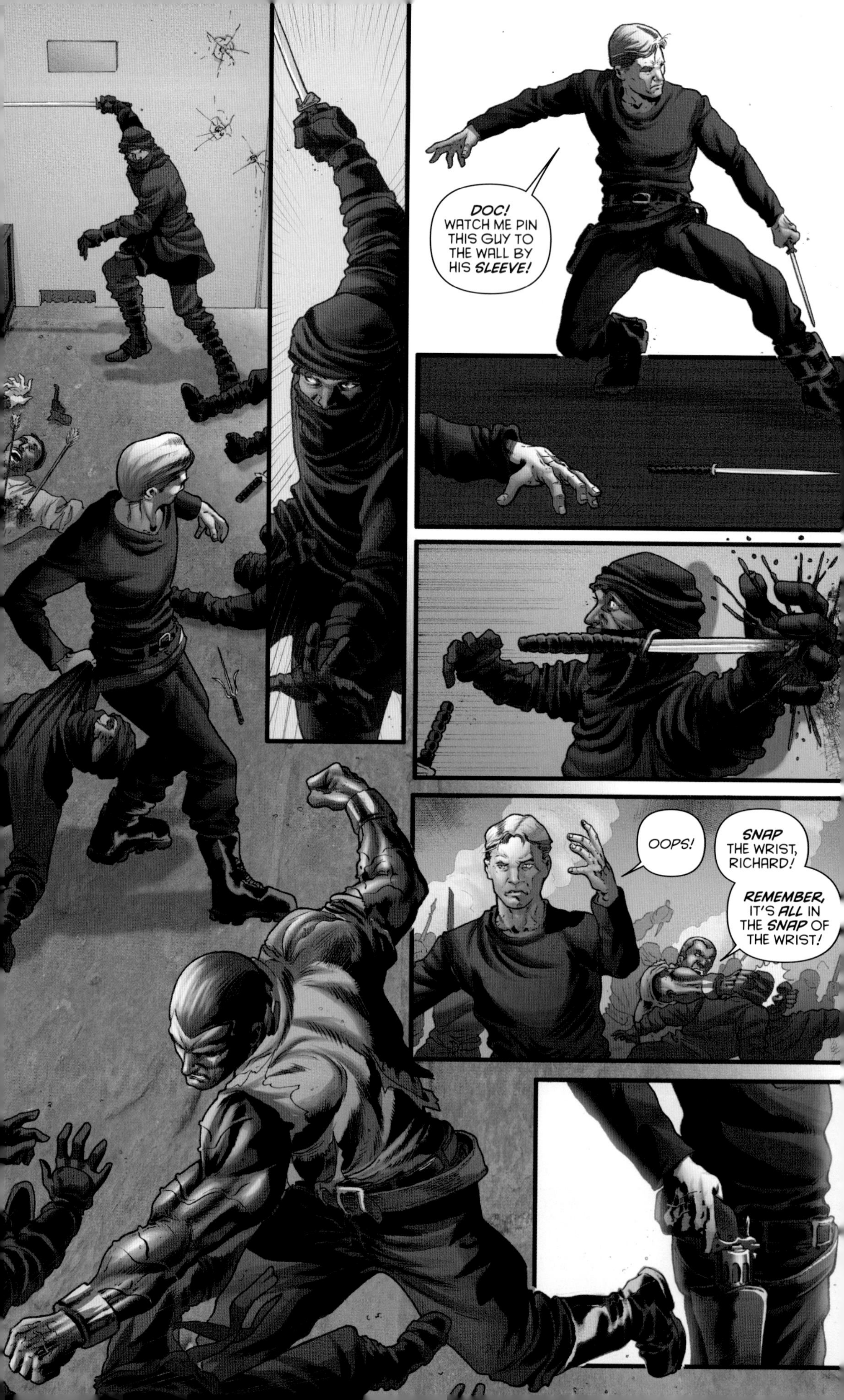
DOC! WATCH ME PIN THIS GUY TO THE WALL BY HIS SLEEVE!
OOPS!
SNAP THE WRIST, RICHARD!
REMEMBER, IT'S ALL IN THE SNAP OF THE WRIST!

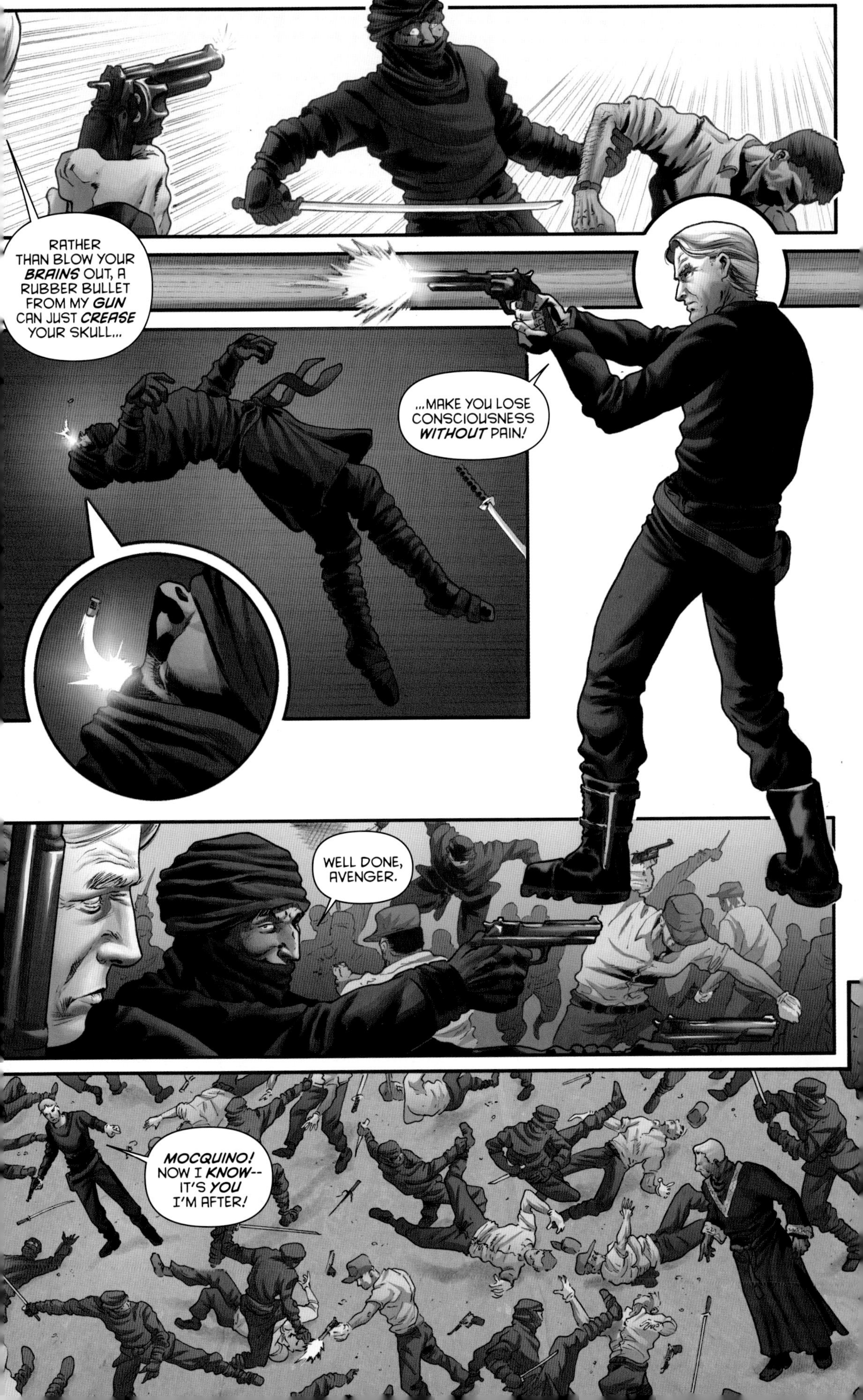
RATHER THAN BLOW YOUR BRAINS OUT, A RUBBER BULLET FROM MY GUN CAN JUST CREASE YOUR SKULL...
...MAKE YOU LOSE CONSCIOUSNESS WITHOUT PAIN!
WELL DONE, AVENGER.
MOCQUINO! NOW I KNOW-- IT'S YOU I'M AFTER!

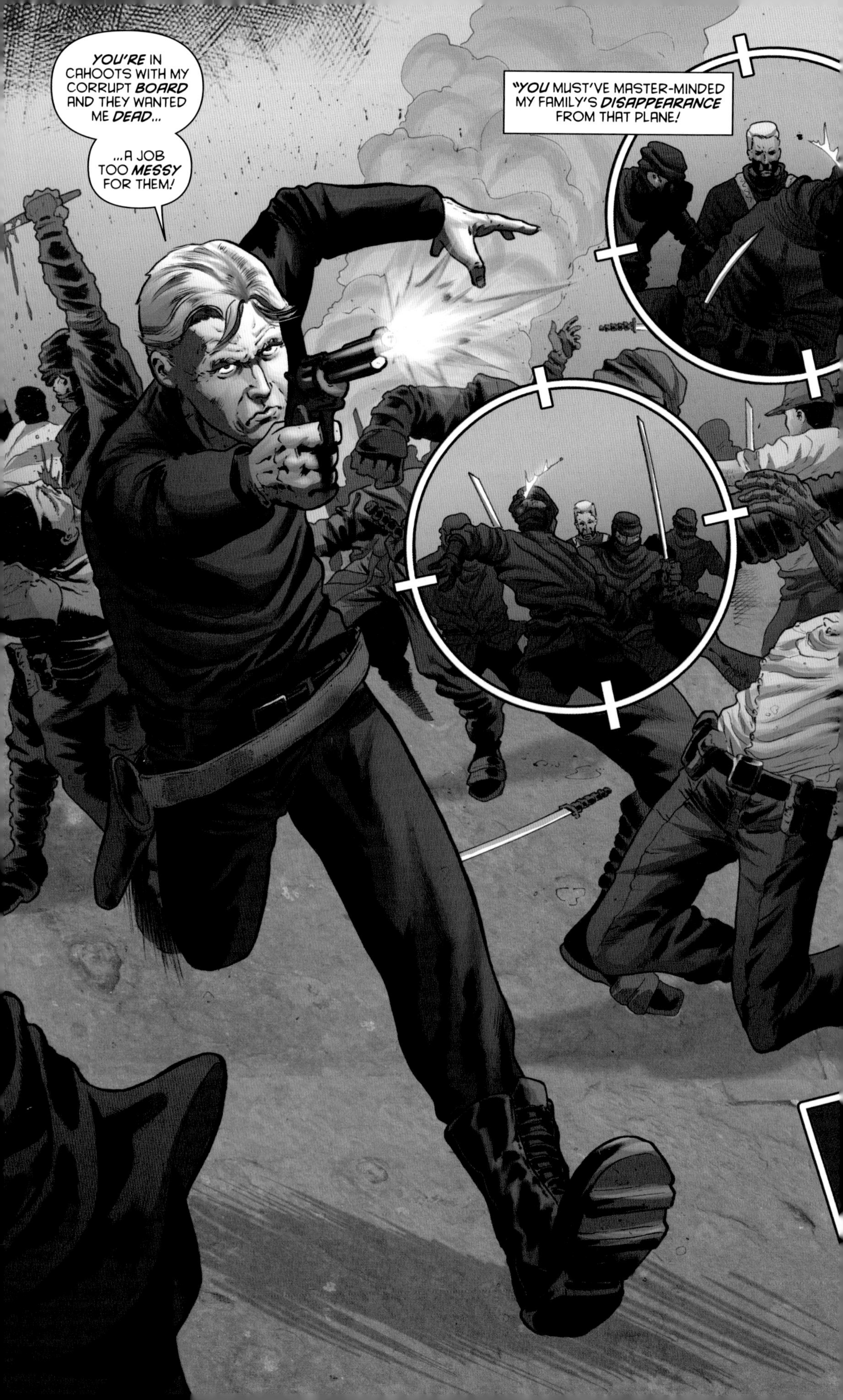
YOU'RE IN CAHOOTS WITH MY CORRUPT BOARD AND THEY WANTED ME DEAD...
...A JOB TOO MESSY FOR THEM!
"YOU MUST'VE MASTER-MINDED MY FAMILY'S DISAPPEARANCE FROM THAT PLANE!

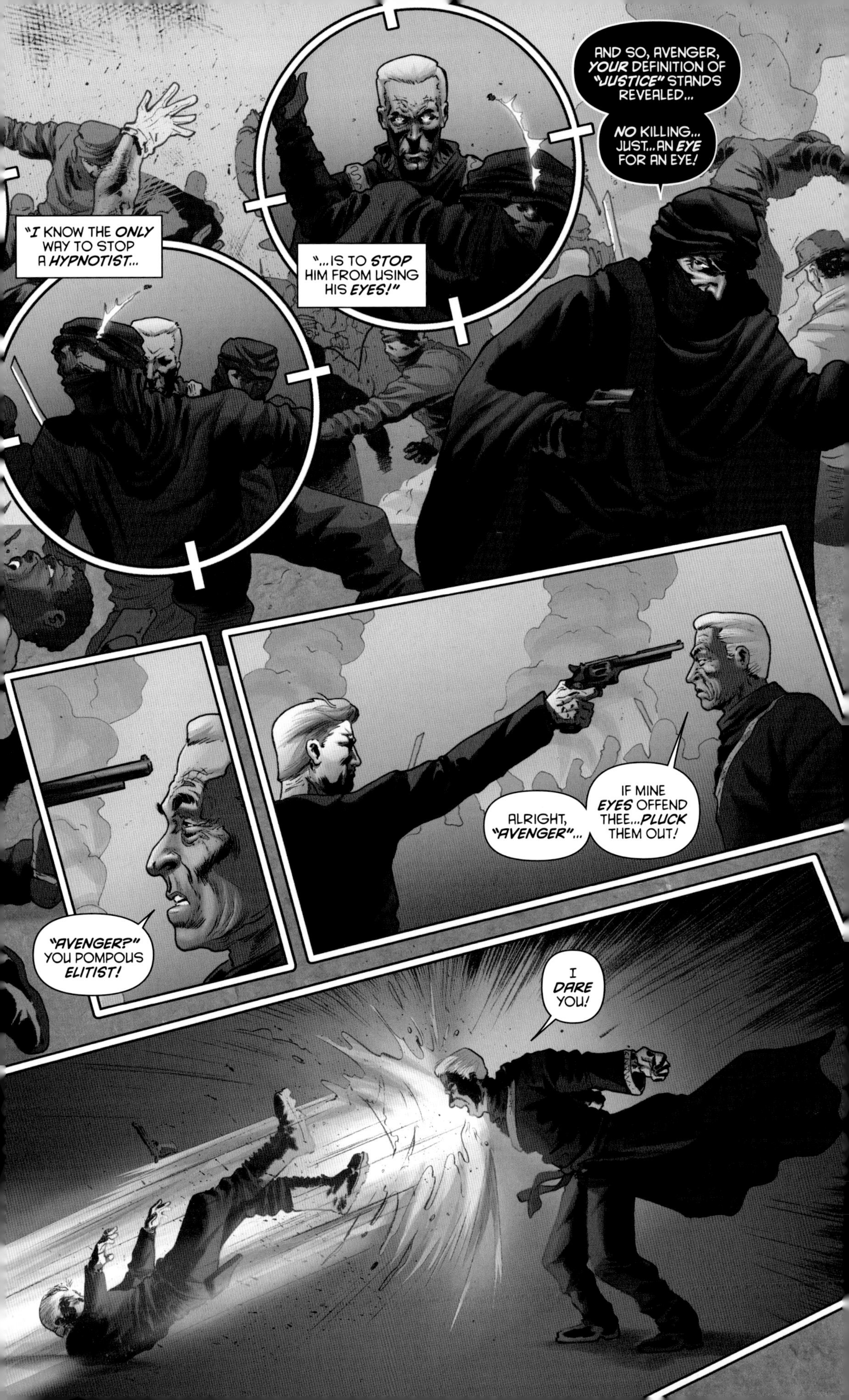
"I KNOW THE ONLY WAY TO STOP A HYPNOTIST...
"...IS TO STOP HIM FROM USING HIS EYES!"
AND SO, AVENGER, YOUR DEFINITION OF "JUSTICE" STANDS REVEALED...
NO KILLING... JUST...AN EYE FOR AN EYE!
"AVENGER?" YOU POMPOUS ELITIST!
ALRIGHT, "AVENGER"...
IF MINE EYES OFFEND THEE...PLUCK THEM OUT!
I DARE YOU!

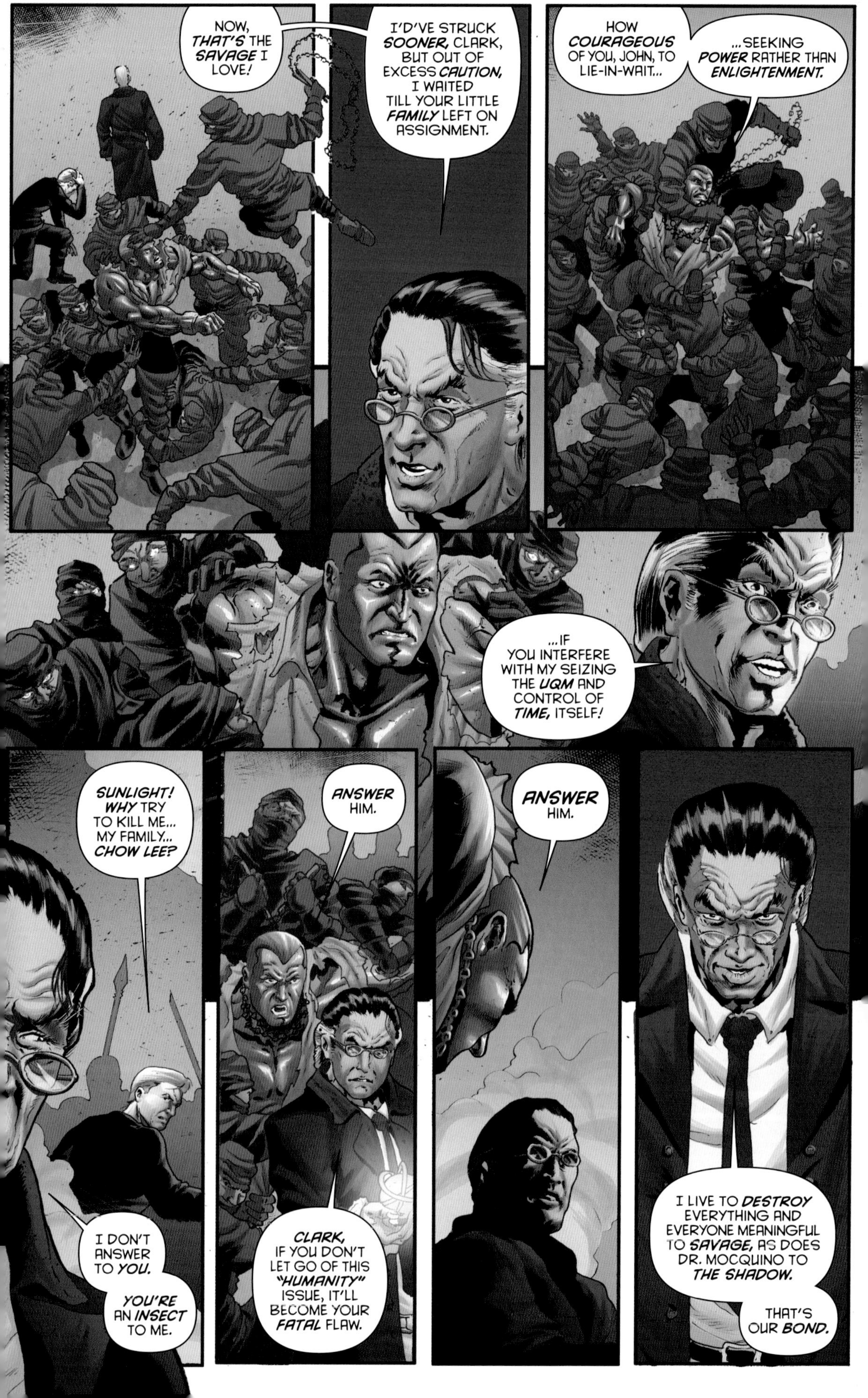
NOW, THAT'S THE SAVAGE I LOVE!
I'D'VE STRUCK SOONER, CLARK, BUT OUT OF EXCESS CAUTION, I WAITED TILL YOUR LITTLE FAMILY LEFT ON ASSIGNMENT.
HOW COURAGEOUS OF YOU, JOHN, TO LIE-IN-WAIT...
...SEEKING POWER RATHER THAN ENLIGHTENMENT.
...IF YOU INTERFERE WITH MY SEIZING THE UQM AND CONTROL OF TIME, ITSELF!
SUNLIGHT! WHY TRY TO KILL ME... MY FAMILY... CHOW LEE?
I DON'T ANSWER TO YOU.
YOU'RE AN INSECT TO ME.
ANSWER HIM.
CLARK, IF YOU DON'T LET GO OF THIS "HUMANITY" ISSUE, IT'LL BECOME YOUR FATAL FLAW.
ANSWER HIM.
I LIVE TO DESTROY EVERYTHING AND EVERYONE MEANINGFUL TO SAVAGE, AS DOES DR. MOCQUINO TO THE SHADOW.
THAT'S OUR BOND.

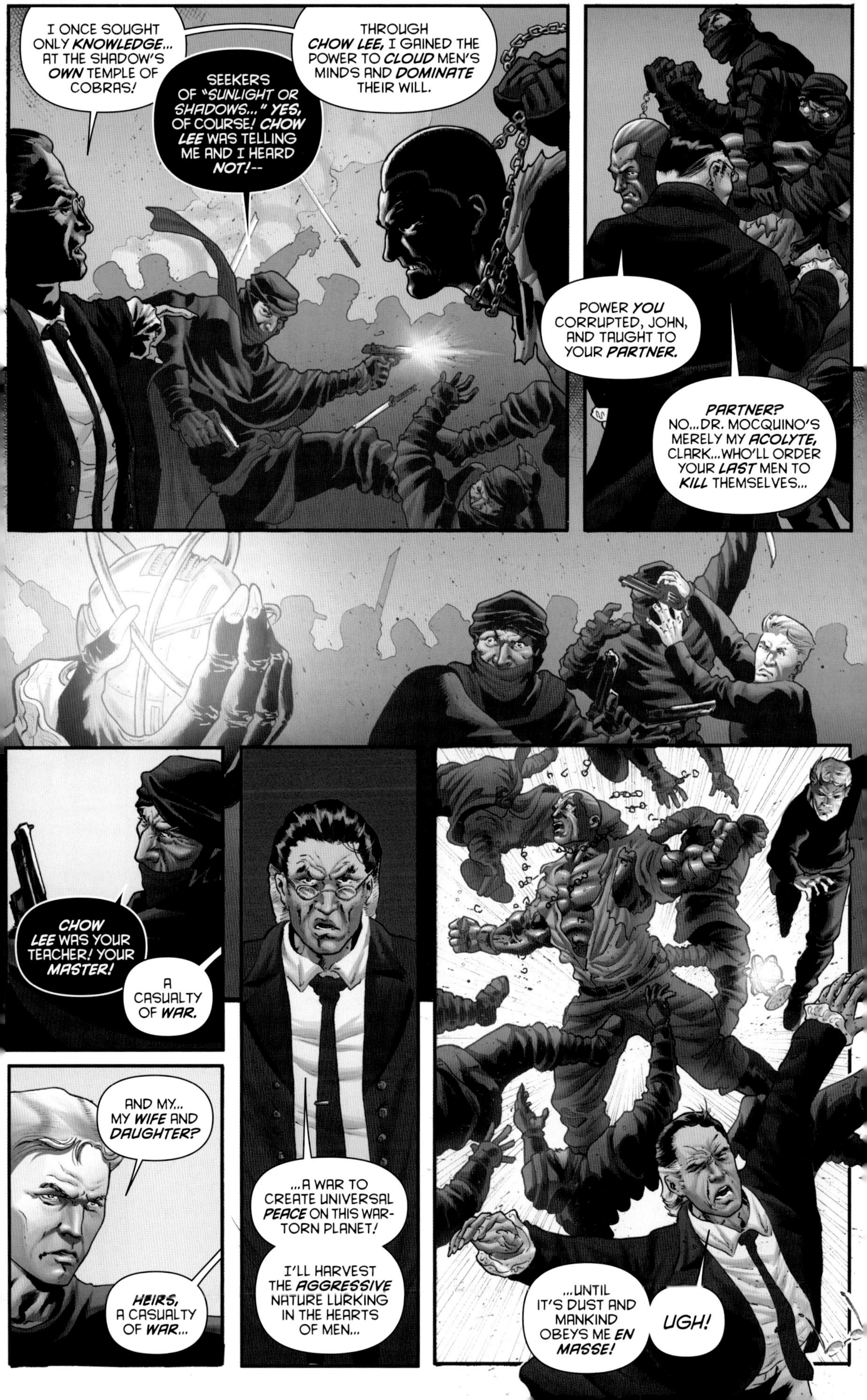
I ONCE SOUGHT ONLY KNOWLEDGE... AT THE SHADOW'S OWN TEMPLE OF COBRAS!
THROUGH CHOW LEE, I GAINED THE POWER TO CLOUD MEN'S MINDS AND DOMINATE THEIR WILL.
SEEKERS OF "SUNLIGHT OR SHADOWS..." YES, OF COURSE! CHOW LEE WAS TELLING ME AND I HEARD NOT!--
POWER YOU CORRUPTED, JOHN, AND TAUGHT TO YOUR PARTNER.
PARTNER? NO...DR. MOCQUINO'S MERELY MY ACOLYTE, CLARK...WHO'LL ORDER YOUR LAST MEN TO KILL THEMSELVES...
CHOW LEE WAS YOUR TEACHER! YOUR MASTER!
A CASUALTY OF WAR.
AND MY... MY WIFE AND DAUGHTER?
HEIRS, A CASUALTY OF WAR...
...A WAR TO CREATE UNIVERSAL PEACE ON THIS WAR-TORN PLANET!
I'LL HARVEST THE AGGRESSIVE NATURE LURKING IN THE HEARTS OF MEN...
...UNTIL IT'S DUST AND MANKIND OBEYS ME EN MASSE!
UGH!

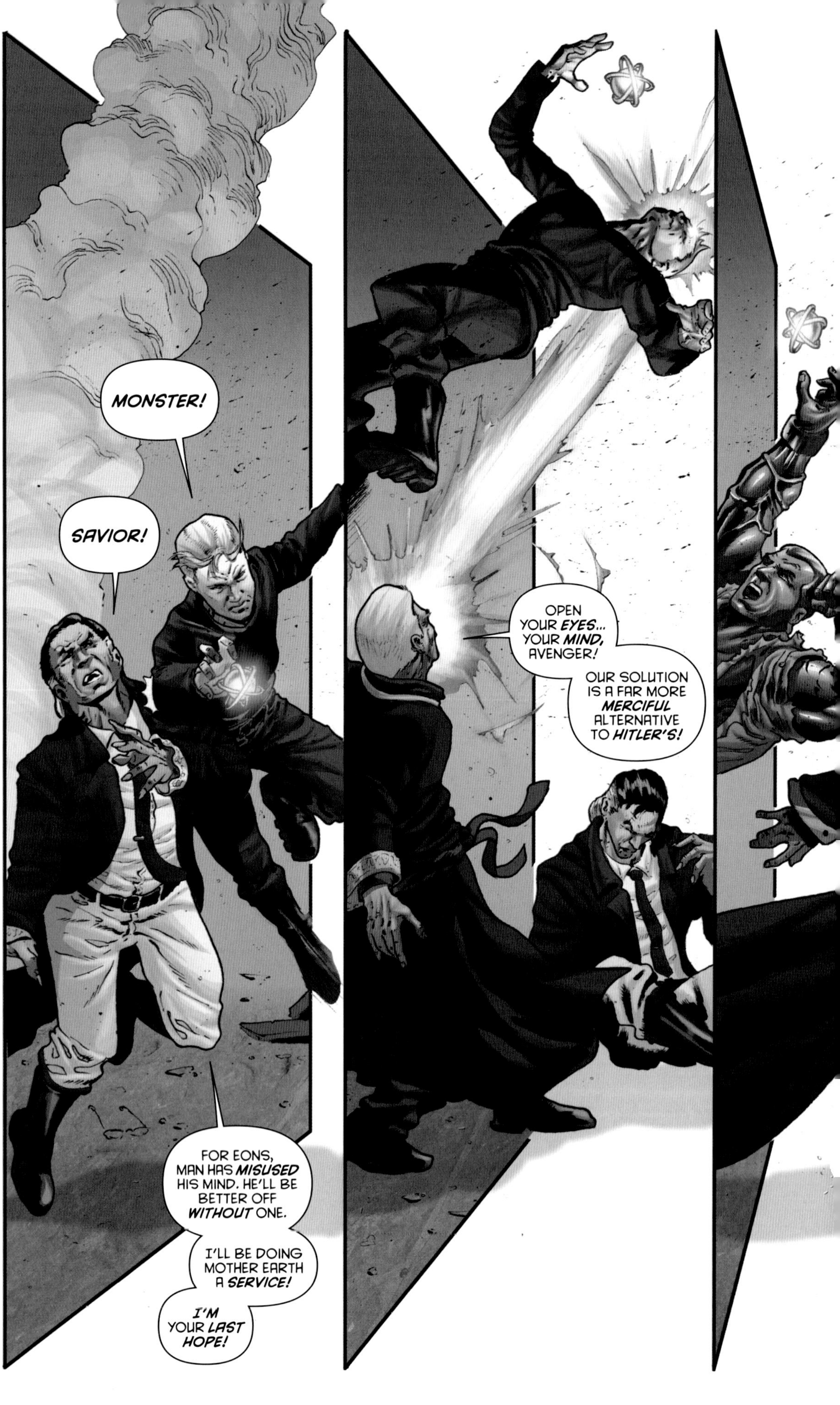
MONSTER!
SAVIOR!
FOR EONS, MAN HAS MISUSED HIS MIND. HE'LL BE BETTER OFF WITHOUT ONE.
I'LL BE DOING MOTHER EARTH A SERVICE!
I'M YOUR LAST HOPE!
OPEN YOUR EYES... YOUR MIND, AVENGER!
OUR SOLUTION IS A FAR MORE MERCIFUL ALTERNATIVE TO HITLER'S!

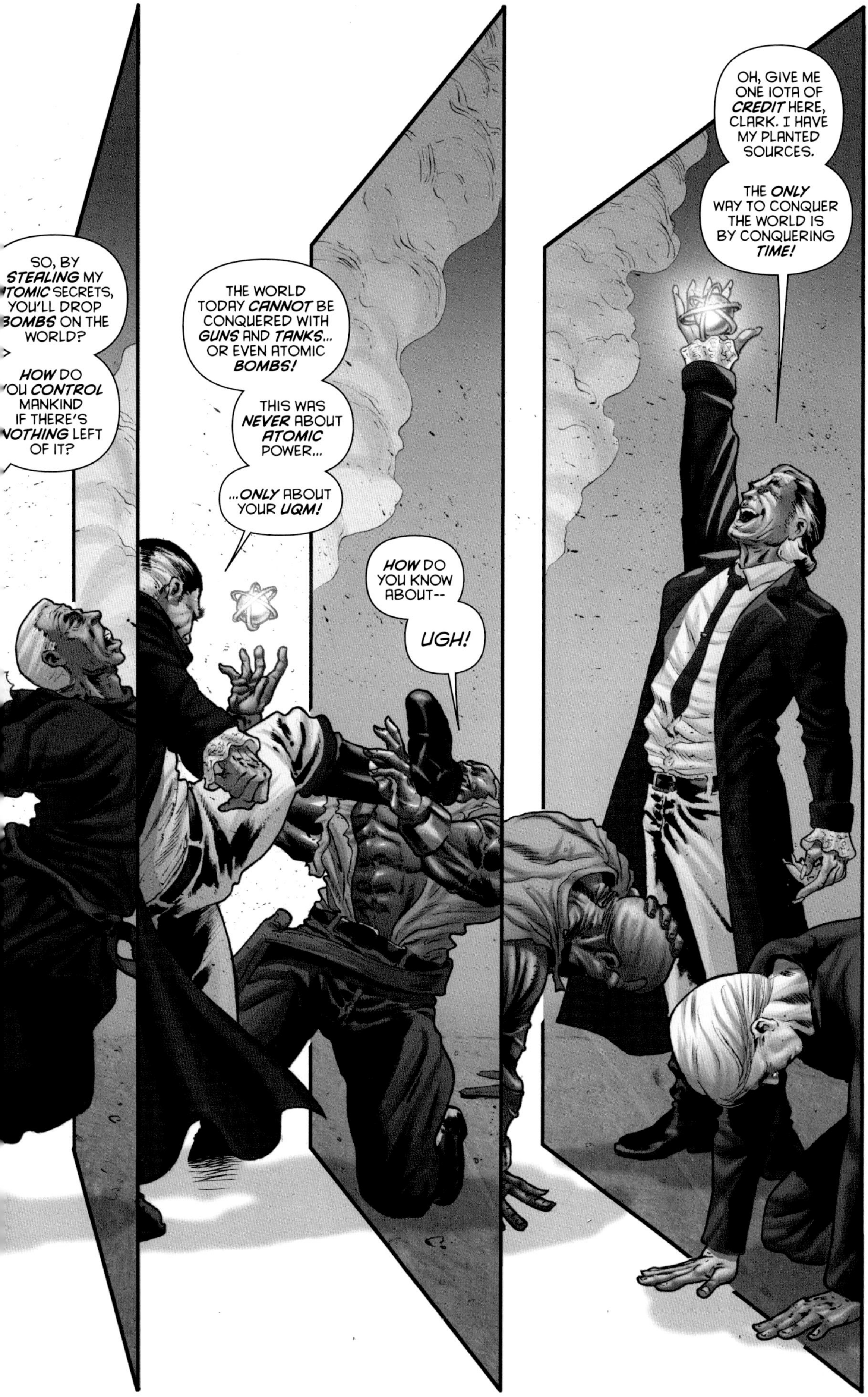
SO, BY STEALING MY ATOMIC SECRETS, YOU'LL DROP BOMBS ON THE WORLD?
HOW DO YOU CONTROL MANKIND IF THERE'S NOTHING LEFT OF IT?
THE WORLD TODAY CANNOT BE CONQUERED WITH GUNS AND TANKS... OR EVEN ATOMIC BOMBS!
THIS WAS NEVER ABOUT ATOMIC POWER...
...ONLY ABOUT YOUR UQM!
HOW DO YOU KNOW ABOUT--
UGH!
OH, GIVE ME ONE IOTA OF CREDIT HERE, CLARK. I HAVE MY PLANTED SOURCES.
THE ONLY WAY TO CONQUER THE WORLD IS BY CONQUERING TIME!

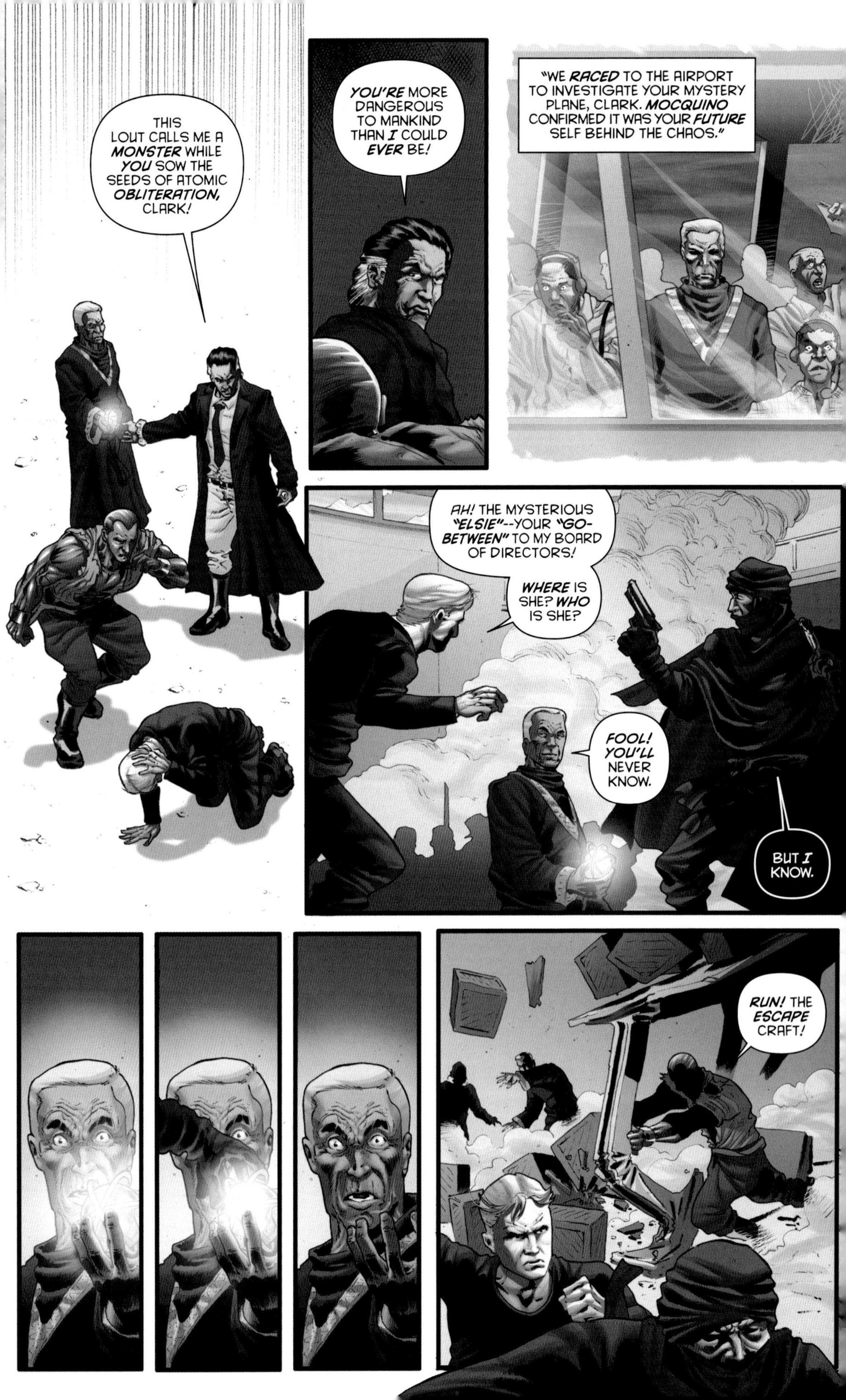
THIS LOUT CALLS ME A MONSTER WHILE YOU SOW THE SEEDS OF ATOMIC OBLITERATION, CLARK!
YOU'RE MORE DANGEROUS TO MANKIND THAN I COULD EVER BE!
"WE RACED TO THE AIRPORT TO INVESTIGATE YOUR MYSTERY PLANE, CLARK. MOCQUINO CONFIRMED IT WAS YOUR FUTURE SELF BEHIND THE CHAOS."
AH! THE MYSTERIOUS "ELSIE"--YOUR "GO-BETWEEN" TO MY BOARD OF DIRECTORS!
WHERE IS SHE? WHO IS SHE?
FOOL! YOU'LL NEVER KNOW.
BUT I KNOW.
RUN! THE ESCAPE CRAFT!

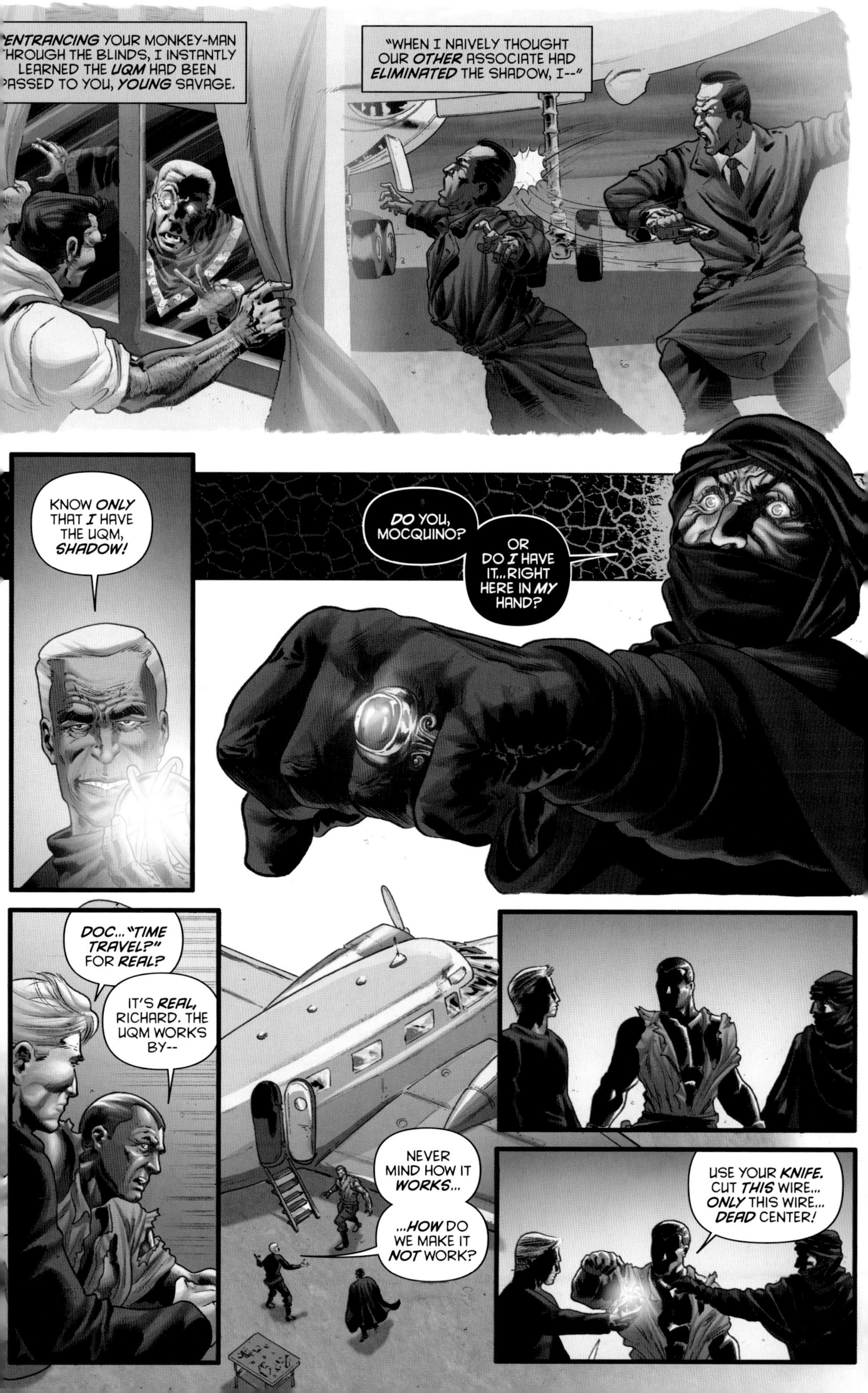
"ENTRANCING YOUR MONKEY-MAN THROUGH THE BLINDS, I INSTANTLY LEARNED THE UQM HAD BEEN PASSED TO YOU, YOUNG SAVAGE.
"WHEN I NAIVELY THOUGHT OUR OTHER ASSOCIATE HAD ELIMINATED THE SHADOW, I--"
KNOW ONLY THAT I HAVE THE UQM, SHADOW!
DO YOU, MOCQUINO?
OR DO I HAVE IT...RIGHT HERE IN MY HAND?
DOC... "TIME TRAVEL?" FOR REAL?
IT'S REAL, RICHARD. THE UQM WORKS BY--
NEVER MIND HOW IT WORKS...
...HOW DO WE MAKE IT NOT WORK?
USE YOUR KNIFE. CUT THIS WIRE... ONLY THIS WIRE... DEAD CENTER!

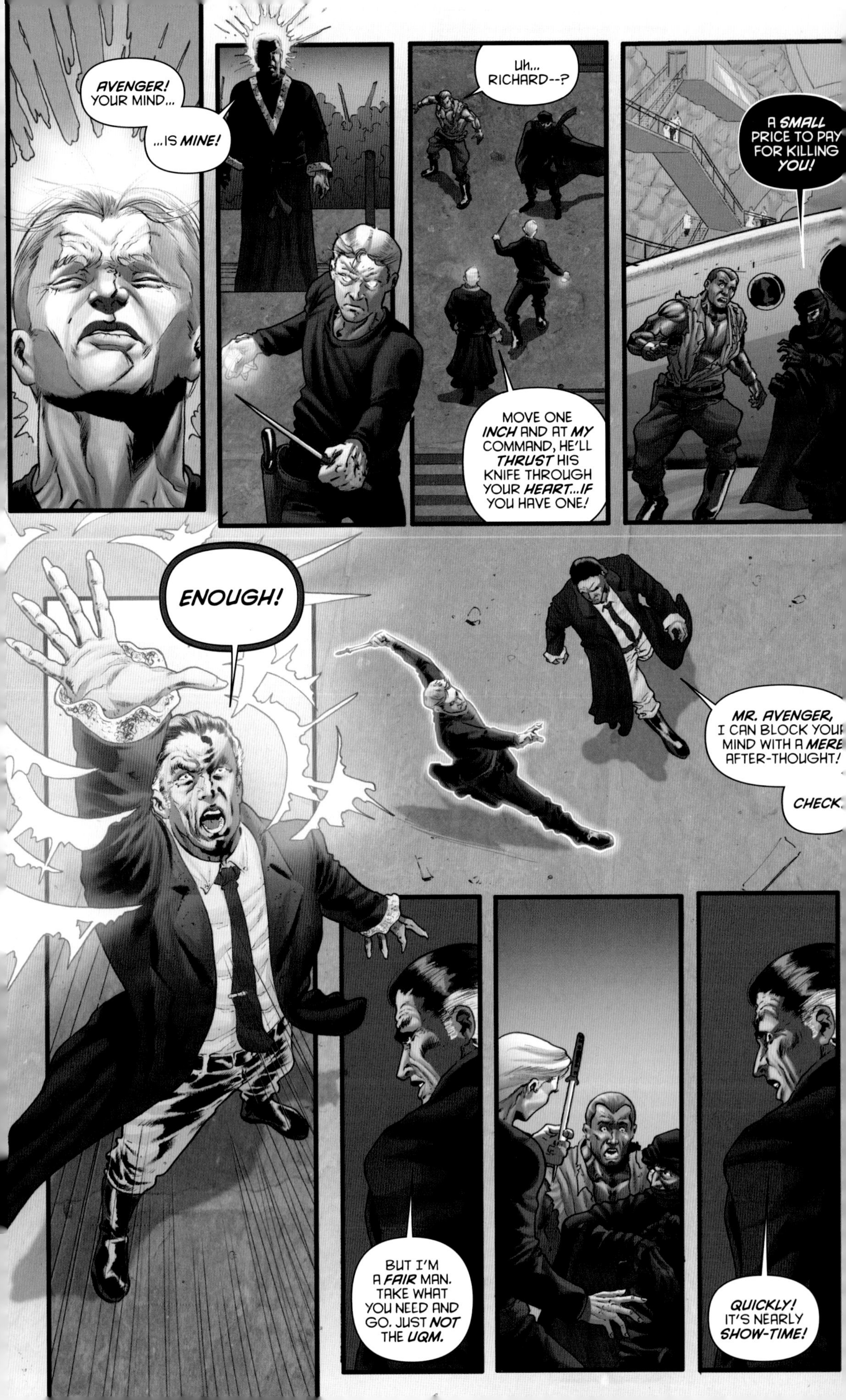
AVENGER! YOUR MIND...
...IS MINE!
UH... RICHARD--?
MOVE ONE INCH AND AT MY COMMAND, HE'LL THRUST HIS KNIFE THROUGH YOUR HEART...IF YOU HAVE ONE!
A SMALL PRICE TO PAY FOR KILLING YOU!
ENOUGH!
MR. AVENGER, I CAN BLOCK YOUR MIND WITH A MERE AFTER-THOUGHT!
CHECK.
BUT I'M A FAIR MAN. TAKE WHAT YOU NEED AND GO. JUST NOT THE UQM.
QUICKLY! IT'S NEARLY SHOW-TIME!

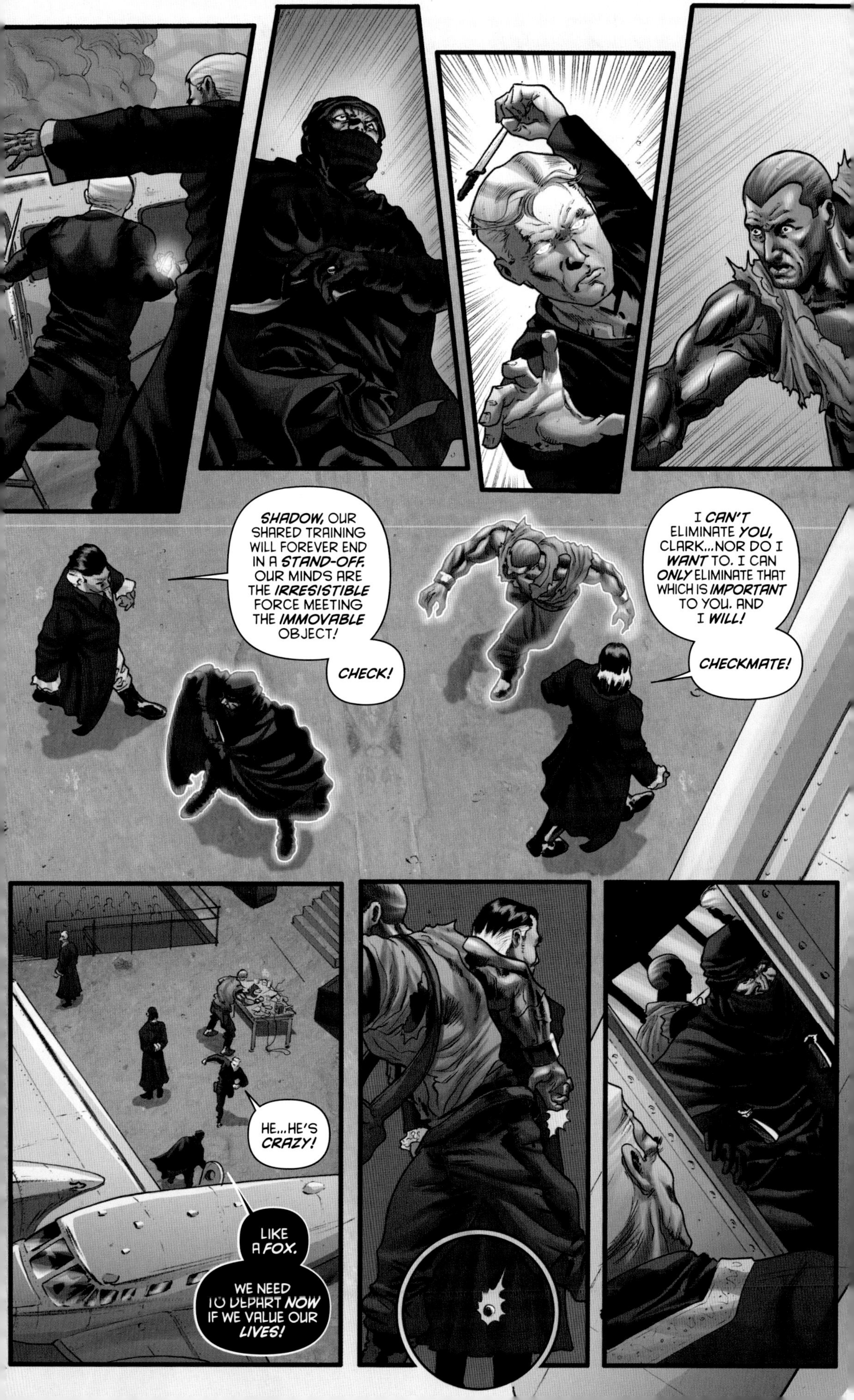

SHADOW, OUR SHARED TRAINING WILL FOREVER END IN A STAND-OFF. OUR MINDS ARE THE IRRESISTIBLE FORCE MEETING THE IMMOVABLE OBJECT!
CHECK!
I CAN'T ELIMINATE YOU, CLARK...NOR DO I WANT TO. I CAN ONLY ELIMINATE THAT WHICH IS IMPORTANT TO YOU. AND I WILL!
CHECKMATE!
HE...HE'S CRAZY!
LIKE A FOX.
WE NEED TO DEPART NOW IF WE VALUE OUR LIVES!

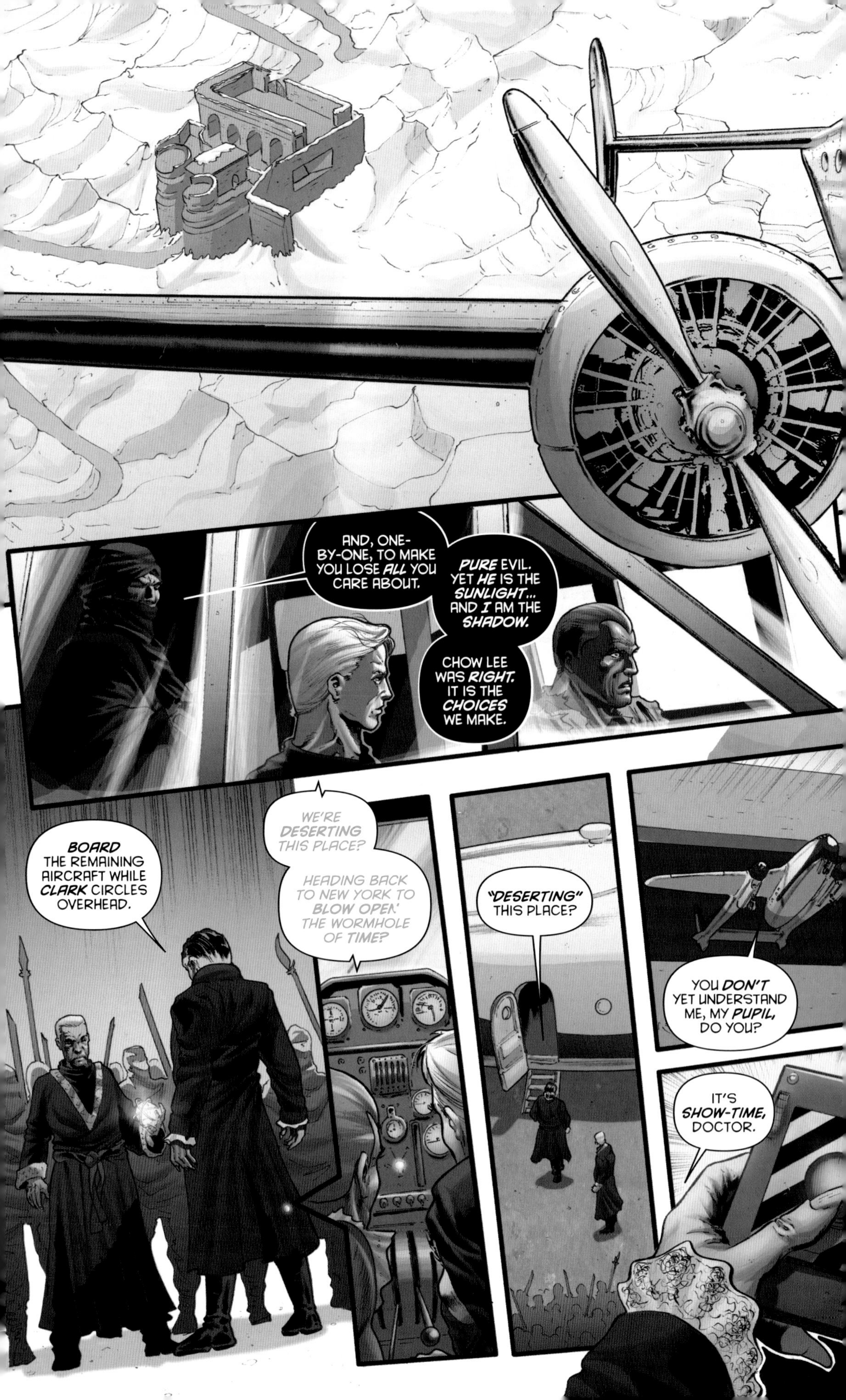
AND, ONE-BY-ONE, TO MAKE YOU LOSE ALL YOU CARE ABOUT.
PURE EVIL. YET HE IS THE SUNLIGHT... AND I AM THE SHADOW.
CHOW LEE WAS RIGHT. IT IS THE CHOICES WE MAKE.
BOARD THE REMAINING AIRCRAFT WHILE CLARK CIRCLES OVERHEAD.
WE'RE DESERTING THIS PLACE?
HEADING BACK TO NEW YORK TO 'BLOW OPEN' THE WORMHOLE OF TIME?
"DESERTING" THIS PLACE?
YOU DON'T YET UNDERSTAND ME, MY PUPIL, DO YOU?
IT'S SHOW-TIME, DOCTOR.

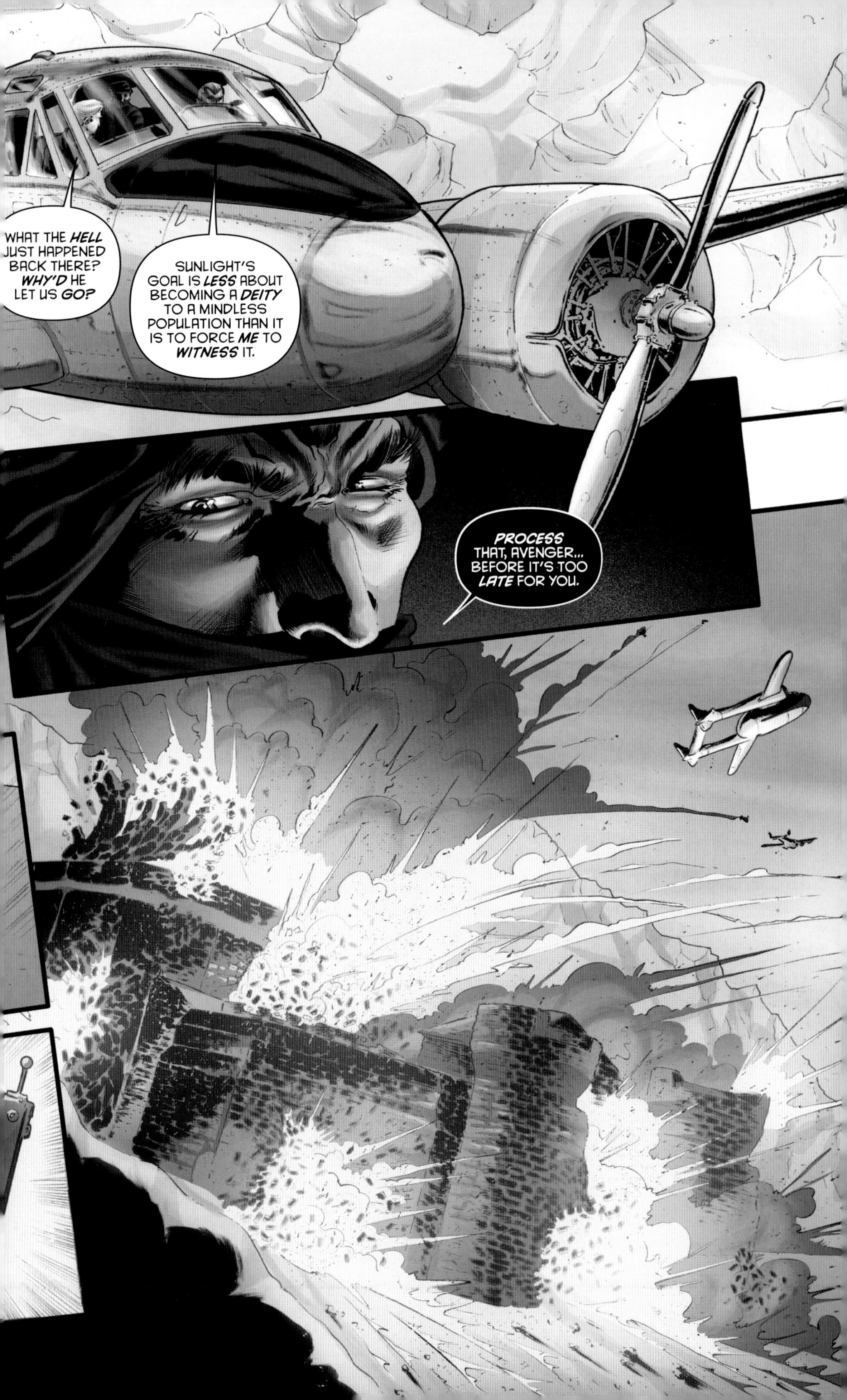

WHAT THE HELL JUST HAPPENED BACK THERE? WHY'D HE LET US GO?
SUNLIGHT'S GOAL IS LESS ABOUT BECOMING A DEITY TO A MINDLESS POPULATION THAN IT IS TO FORCE ME TO WITNESS IT.
PROCESS THAT, AVENGER... BEFORE IT'S TOO LATE FOR YOU.

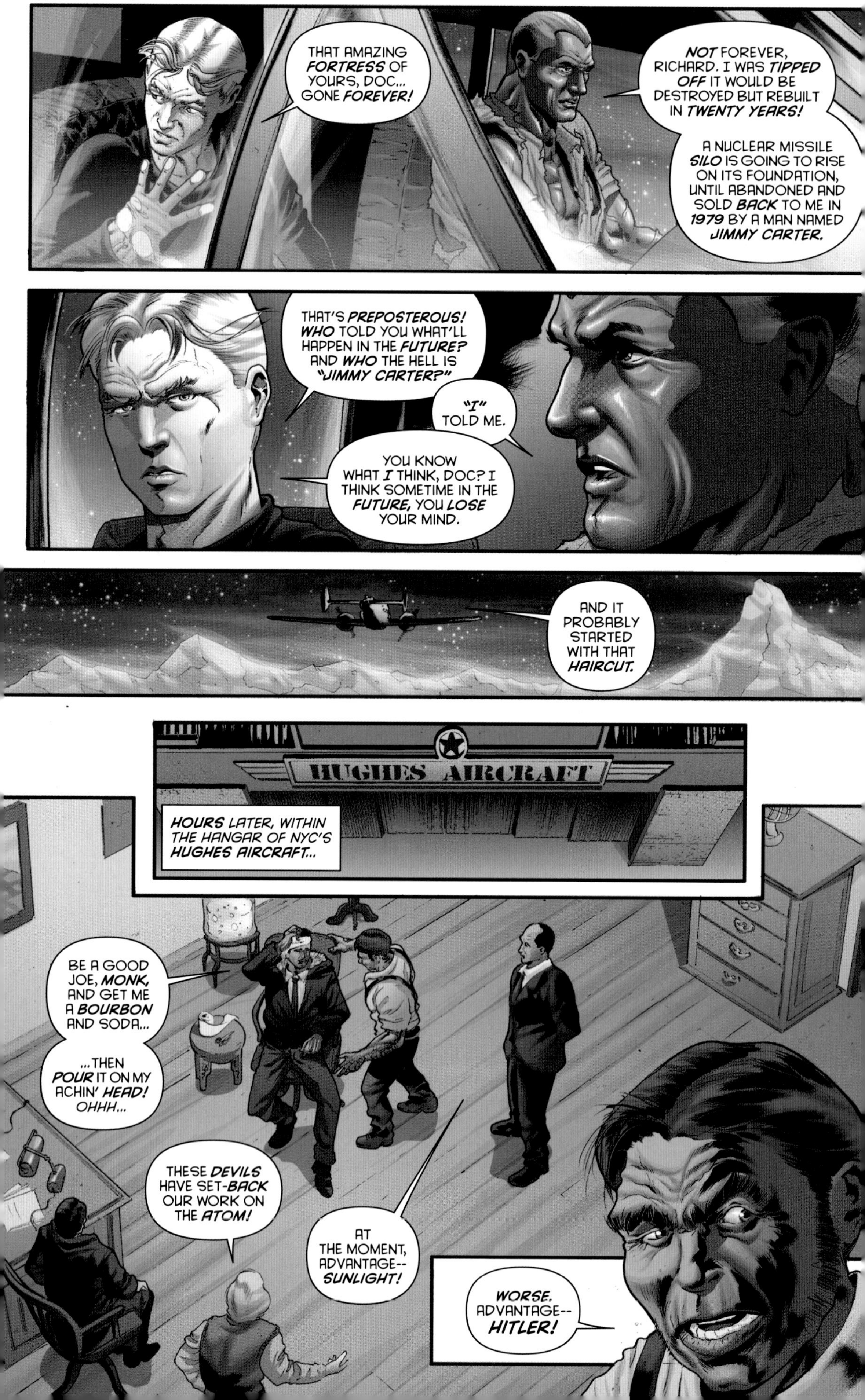
THAT AMAZING FORTRESS OF YOURS, DOC... GONE FOREVER!
NOT FOREVER, RICHARD. I WAS TIPPED OFF IT WOULD BE DESTROYED BUT REBUILT IN TWENTY YEARS!
A NUCLEAR MISSILE SILO IS GOING TO RISE ON ITS FOUNDATION, UNTIL ABANDONED AND SOLD BACK TO ME IN 1979 BY A MAN NAMED JIMMY CARTER.
THAT'S PREPOSTEROUS! WHO TOLD YOU WHAT'LL HAPPEN IN THE FUTURE? AND WHO THE HELL IS "JIMMY CARTER?"
"I" TOLD ME.
YOU KNOW WHAT I THINK, DOC? I THINK SOMETIME IN THE FUTURE, YOU LOSE YOUR MIND.
AND IT PROBABLY STARTED WITH THAT HAIRCUT.
HUGHES AIRCRAFT
HOURS LATER, WITHIN THE HANGAR OF NYC'S HUGHES AIRCRAFT...
BE A GOOD JOE, MONK, AND GET ME A BOURBON AND SODA...
...THEN POUR IT ON MY ACHIN' HEAD! OHHH...
THESE DEVILS HAVE SET-BACK OUR WORK ON THE ATOM!
AT THE MOMENT, ADVANTAGE-- SUNLIGHT!
WORSE. ADVANTAGE-- HITLER!

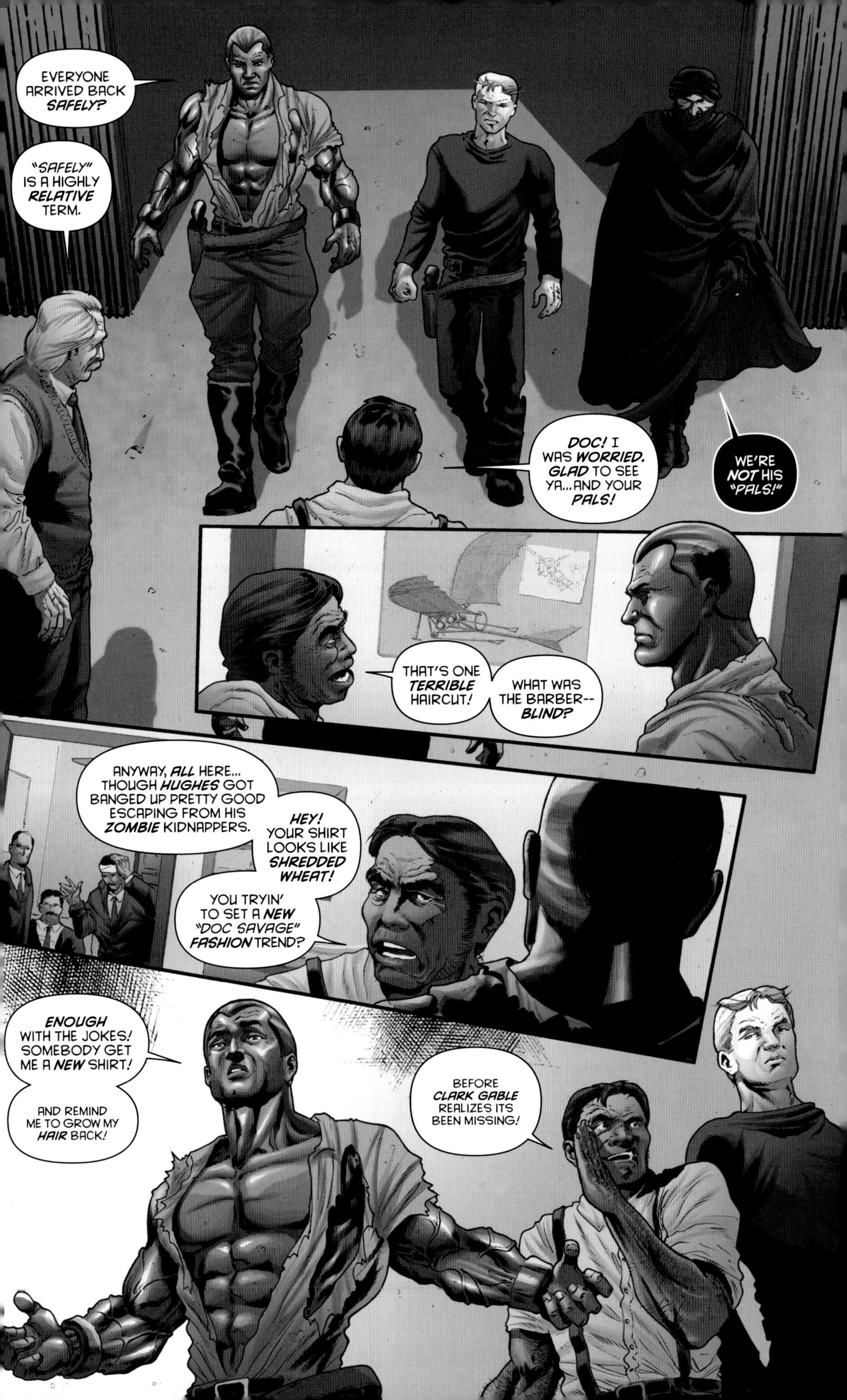
EVERYONE ARRIVED BACK SAFELY?
"SAFELY" IS A HIGHLY RELATIVE TERM.
DOC! I WAS WORRIED. GLAD TO SEE YA...AND YOUR PALS!
WE'RE NOT HIS "PALS!"
THAT'S ONE TERRIBLE HAIRCUT!
WHAT WAS THE BARBER--BLIND?
ANYWAY, ALL HERE... THOUGH HUGHES GOT BANGED UP PRETTY GOOD ESCAPING FROM HIS ZOMBIE KIDNAPPERS.
HEY! YOUR SHIRT LOOKS LIKE SHREDDED WHEAT!
YOU TRYIN' TO SET A NEW "DOC SAVAGE" FASHION TREND?
ENOUGH WITH THE JOKES! SOMEBODY GET ME A NEW SHIRT!
AND REMIND ME TO GROW MY HAIR BACK!
BEFORE CLARK GABLE REALIZES ITS BEEN MISSING!

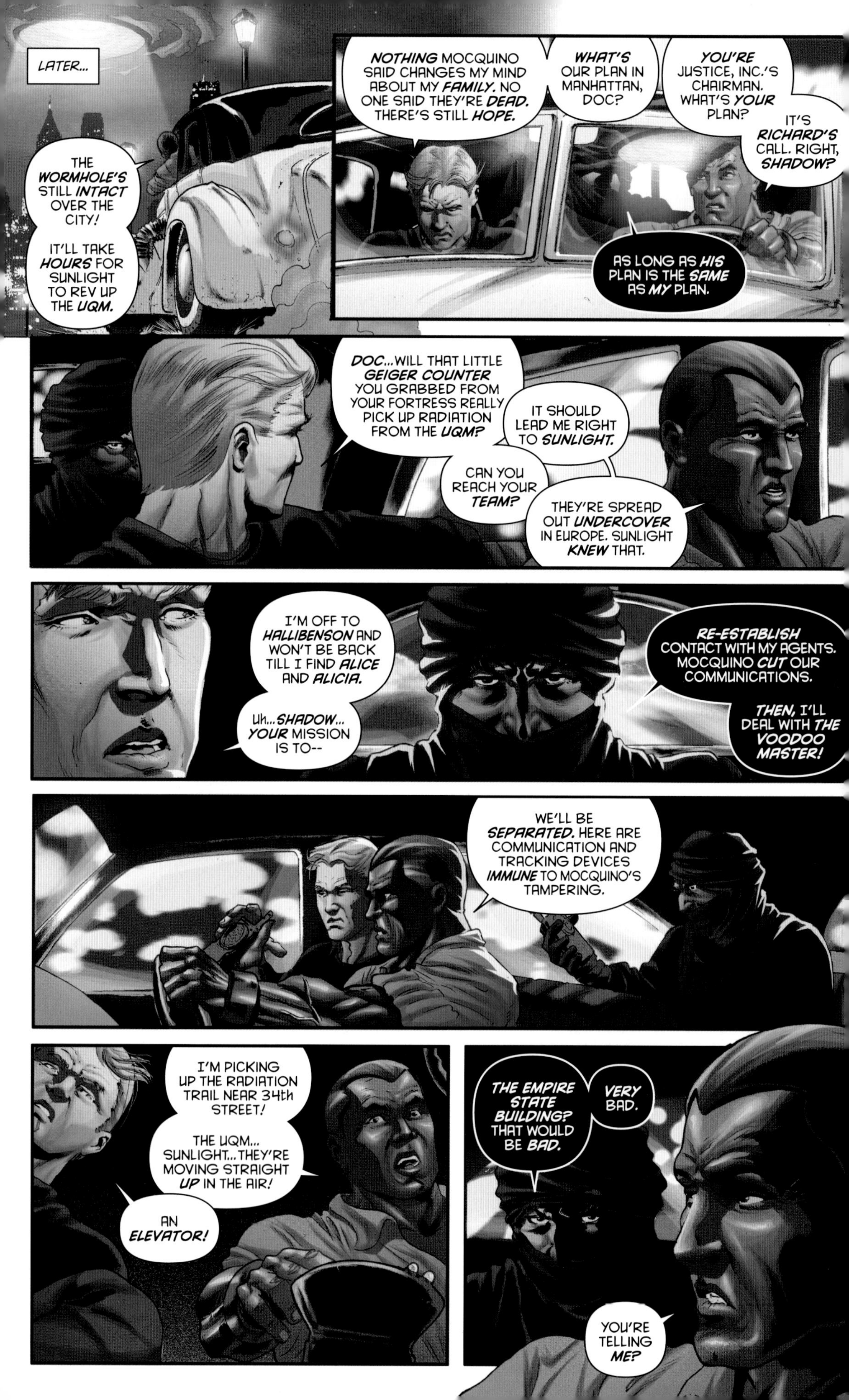
LATER...
THE WORMHOLE'S STILL INTACT OVER THE CITY!
IT'LL TAKE HOURS FOR SUNLIGHT TO REV UP THE UQM.
NOTHING MOCQUINO SAID CHANGES MY MIND ABOUT MY FAMILY. NO ONE SAID THEY'RE DEAD. THERE'S STILL HOPE.
WHAT'S OUR PLAN IN MANHATTAN, DOC?
YOU'RE JUSTICE, INC.'S CHAIRMAN. WHAT'S YOUR PLAN?
IT'S RICHARD'S CALL. RIGHT, SHADOW?
AS LONG AS HIS PLAN IS THE SAME AS MY PLAN.
DOC...WILL THAT LITTLE GEIGER COUNTER YOU GRABBED FROM YOUR FORTRESS REALLY PICK UP RADIATION FROM THE UQM?
IT SHOULD LEAD ME RIGHT TO SUNLIGHT.
CAN YOU REACH YOUR TEAM?
THEY'RE SPREAD OUT UNDERCOVER IN EUROPE. SUNLIGHT KNEW THAT.
I'M OFF TO HALLIBENSON AND WON'T BE BACK TILL I FIND ALICE AND ALICIA.
Uh...SHADOW... YOUR MISSION IS TO--
RE-ESTABLISH CONTACT WITH MY AGENTS. MOCQUINO CUT OUR COMMUNICATIONS.
THEN, I'LL DEAL WITH THE VOODOO MASTER!
WE'LL BE SEPARATED. HERE ARE COMMUNICATION AND TRACKING DEVICES IMMUNE TO MOCQUINO'S TAMPERING.
I'M PICKING UP THE RADIATION TRAIL NEAR 34th STREET!
THE UQM... SUNLIGHT... THEY'RE MOVING STRAIGHT UP IN THE AIR!
AN ELEVATOR!
THE EMPIRE STATE BUILDING? THAT WOULD BE BAD.
VERY BAD.
YOU'RE TELLING ME?

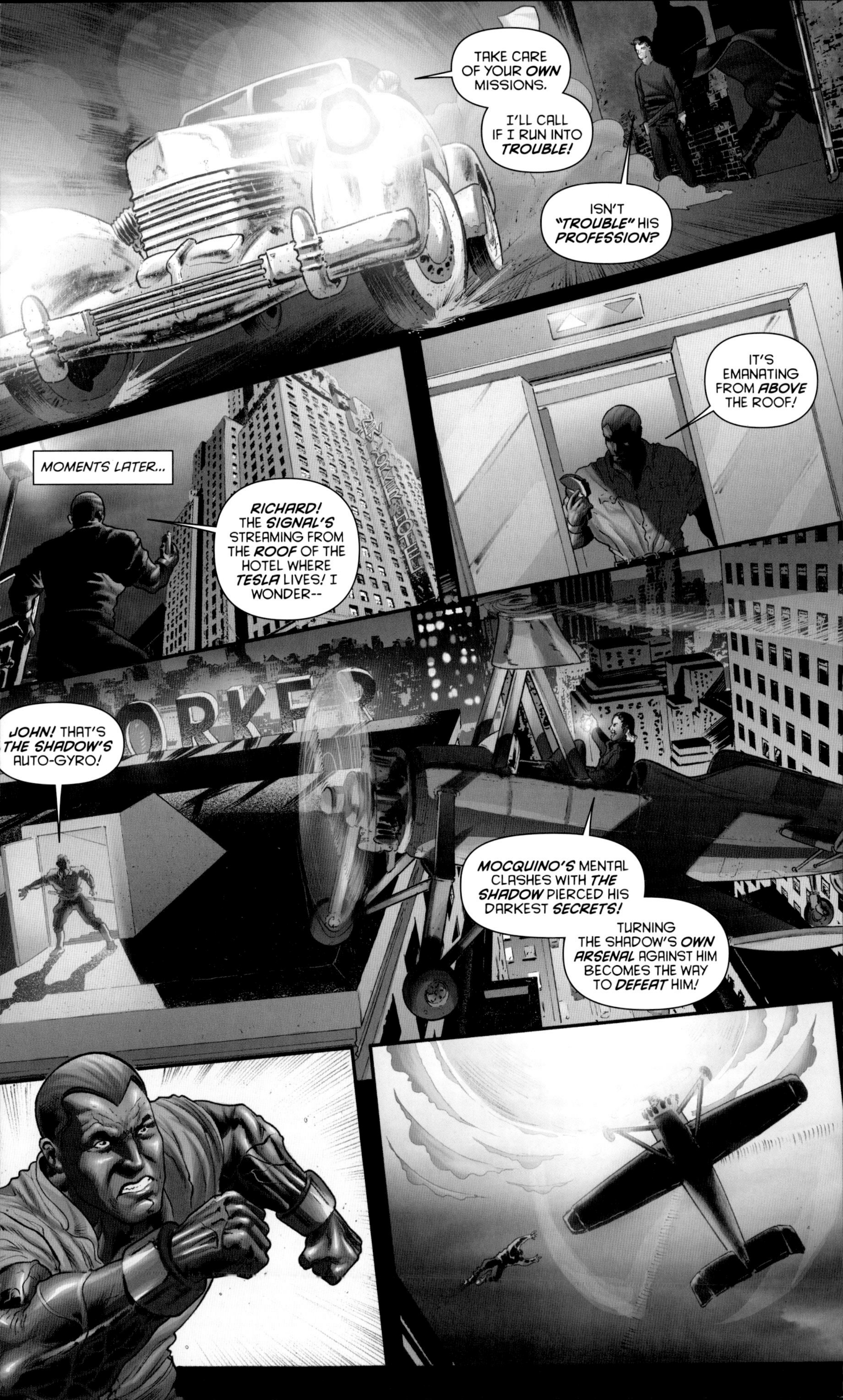
TAKE CARE OF YOUR *OWN* MISSIONS.
I'LL CALL IF I RUN INTO *TROUBLE!*
ISN'T *"TROUBLE"* HIS *PROFESSION?*
IT'S EMANATING FROM *ABOVE* THE ROOF!
MOMENTS LATER...
RICHARD! THE *SIGNAL'S* STREAMING FROM THE *ROOF* OF THE HOTEL WHERE *TESLA* LIVES! I WONDER--
JOHN! THAT'S *THE SHADOW'S* AUTO-GYRO!
MOCQUINO'S MENTAL CLASHES WITH *THE SHADOW* PIERCED HIS DARKEST *SECRETS!*
TURNING THE SHADOW'S *OWN ARSENAL* AGAINST HIM BECOMES THE WAY TO *DEFEAT* HIM!

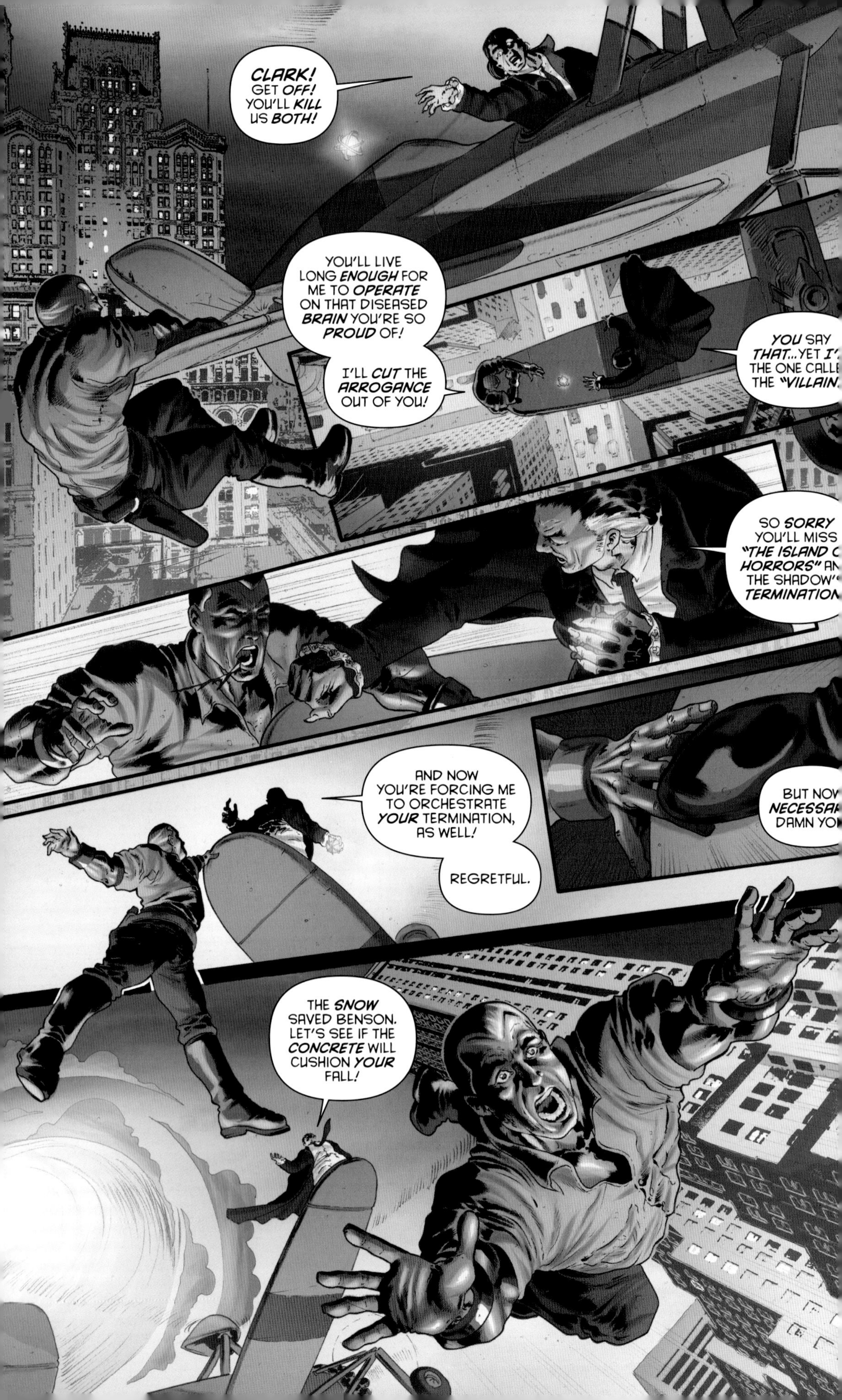

CLARK! GET OFF! YOU'LL KILL US BOTH!
YOU'LL LIVE LONG ENOUGH FOR ME TO OPERATE ON THAT DISEASED BRAIN YOU'RE SO PROUD OF!
I'LL CUT THE ARROGANCE OUT OF YOU!
YOU SAY THAT...YET I'
THE ONE CALL
THE "VILLAIN.
SO SORRY YOU'LL MISS
"THE ISLAND O
HORRORS" AN
THE SHADOW'S
TERMINATION
AND NOW YOU'RE FORCING ME TO ORCHESTRATE YOUR TERMINATION, AS WELL!
REGRETFUL.
BUT NOW
NECESSAR
DAMN YO
THE SNOW SAVED BENSON. LET'S SEE IF THE CONCRETE WILL CUSHION YOUR FALL!

FIVE

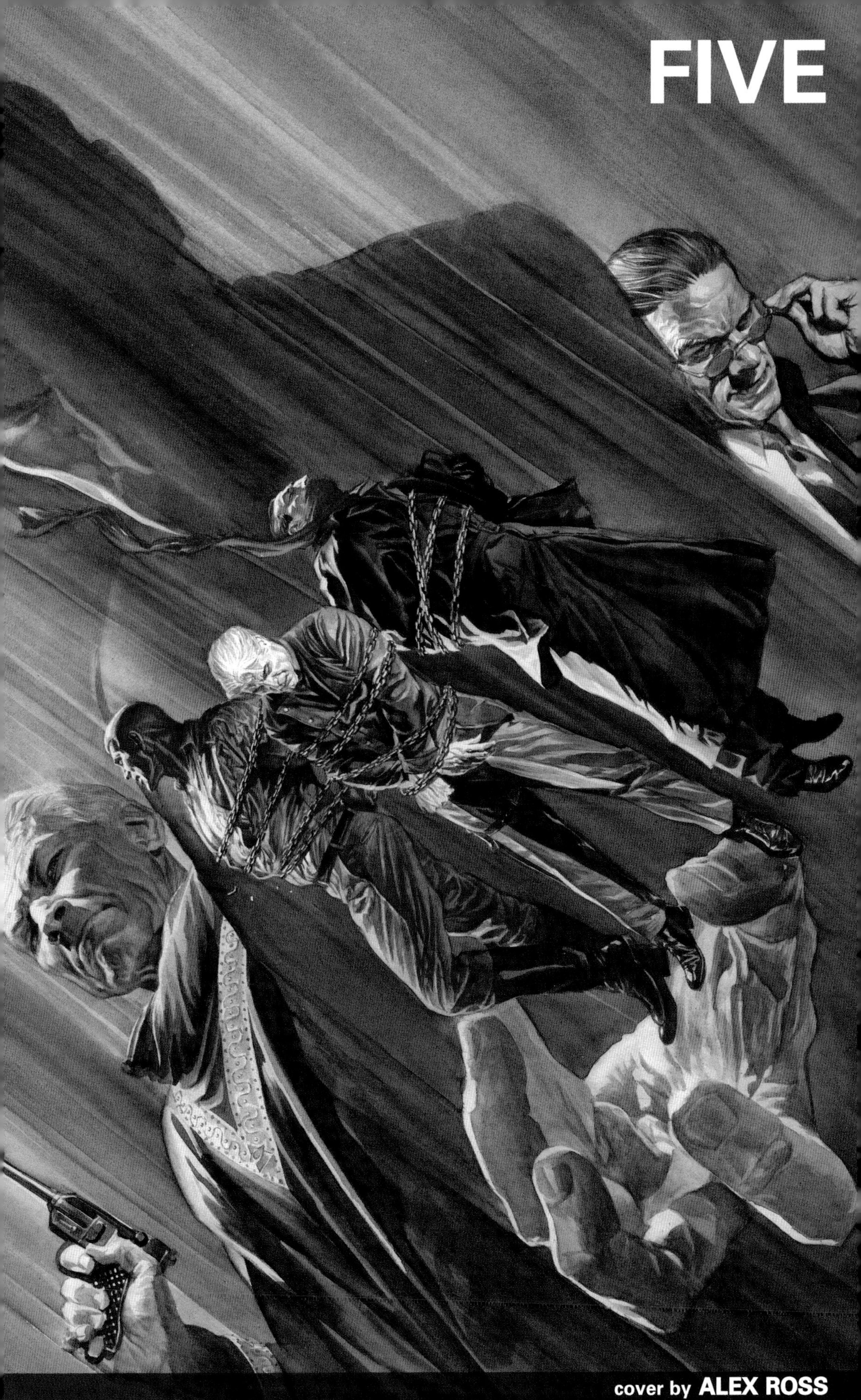

cover by **ALEX ROSS**

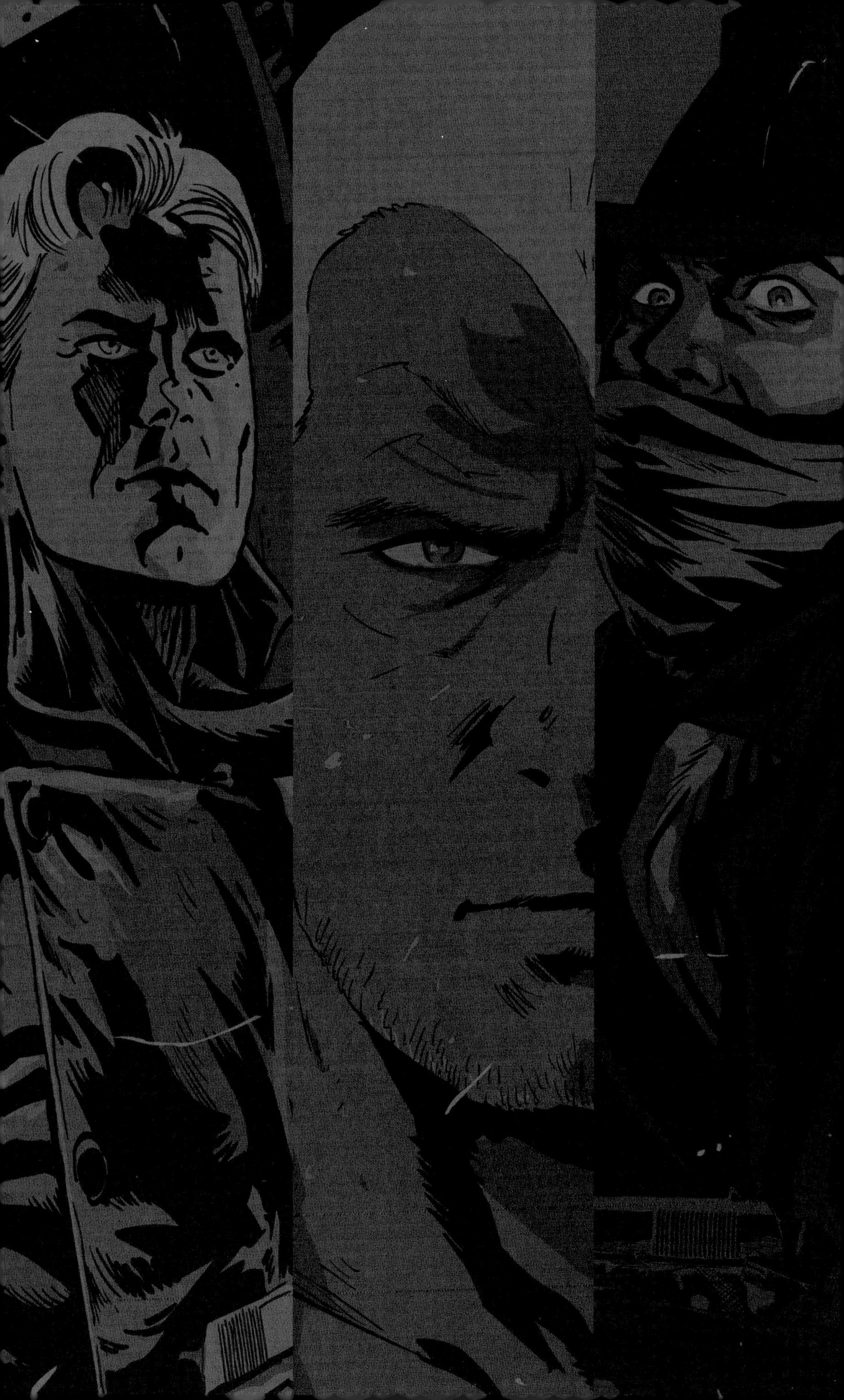

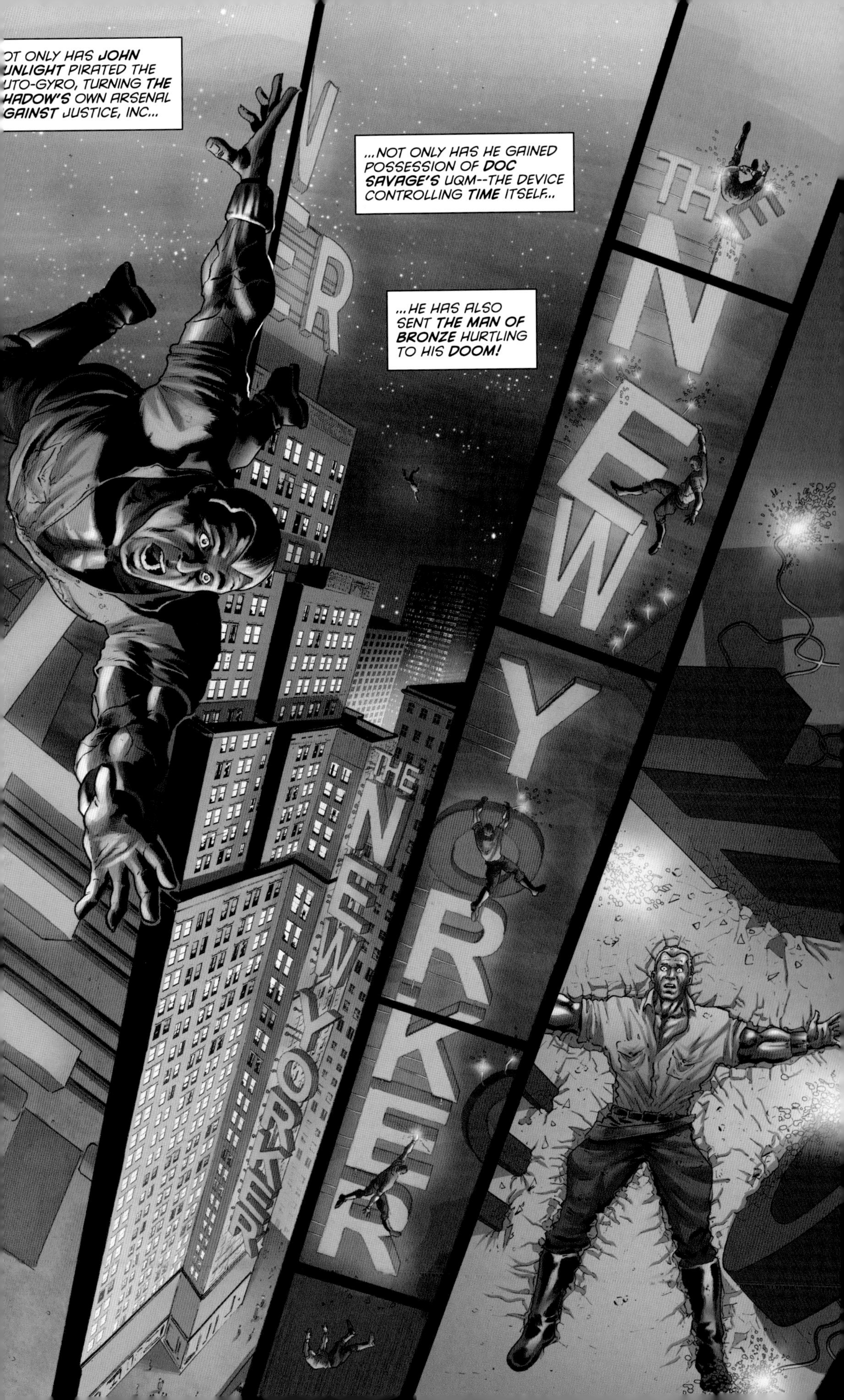
OT ONLY HAS JOHN UNLIGHT PIRATED THE UTO-GYRO, TURNING THE HADOW'S OWN ARSENAL GAINST JUSTICE, INC...
...NOT ONLY HAS HE GAINED POSSESSION OF DOC SAVAGE'S UQM--THE DEVICE CONTROLLING TIME ITSELF...
...HE HAS ALSO SENT THE MAN OF BRONZE HURTLING TO HIS DOOM!
THE NEW YORKER

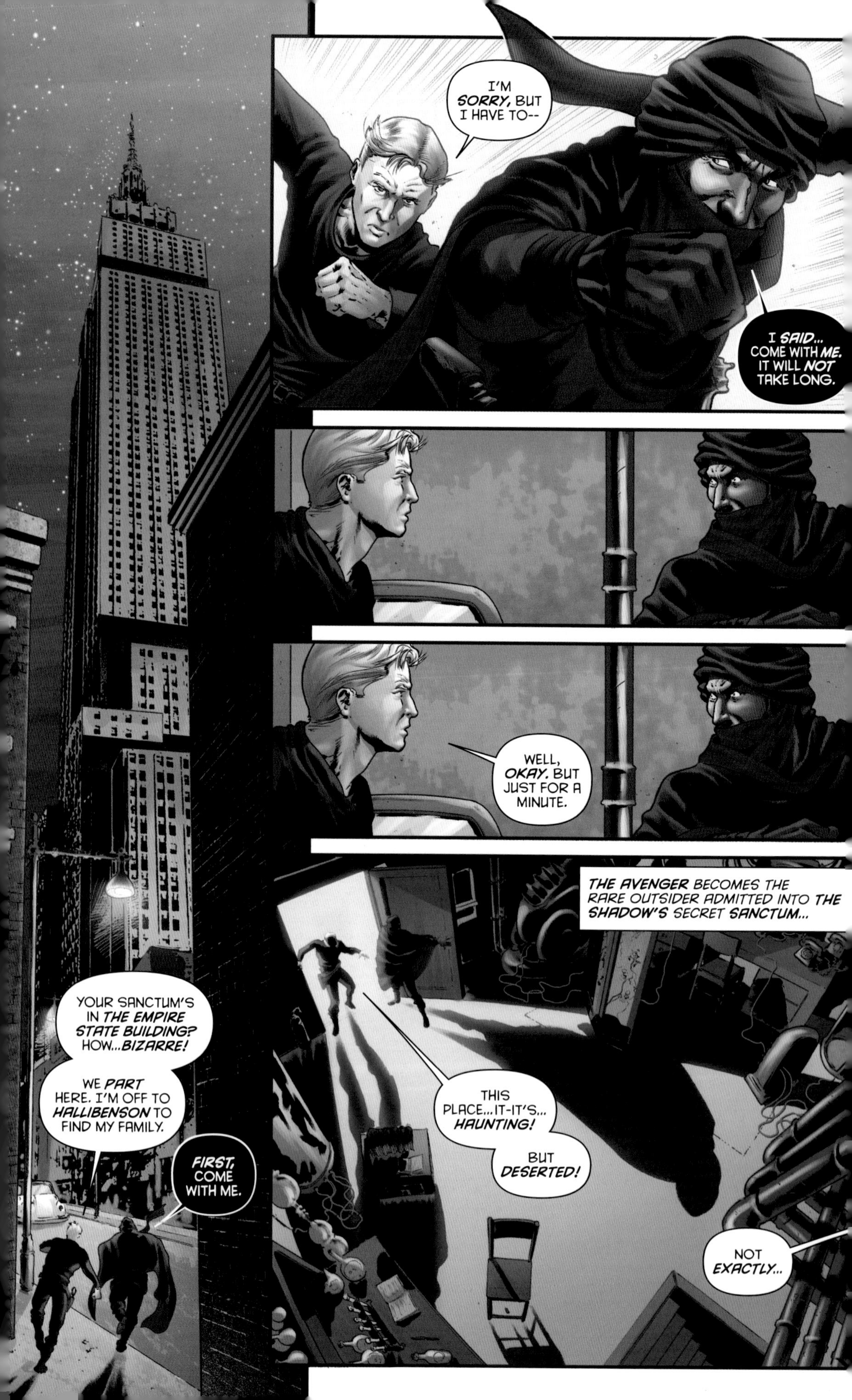

I'M SORRY, BUT I HAVE TO--
I SAID... COME WITH ME. IT WILL NOT TAKE LONG.
WELL, OKAY. BUT JUST FOR A MINUTE.
YOUR SANCTUM'S IN THE EMPIRE STATE BUILDING? HOW...BIZARRE!
WE PART HERE. I'M OFF TO HALLIBENSON TO FIND MY FAMILY.
FIRST, COME WITH ME.
THE AVENGER BECOMES THE RARE OUTSIDER ADMITTED INTO THE SHADOW'S SECRET SANCTUM...
THIS PLACE...IT-IT'S... HAUNTING!
BUT DESERTED!
NOT EXACTLY...

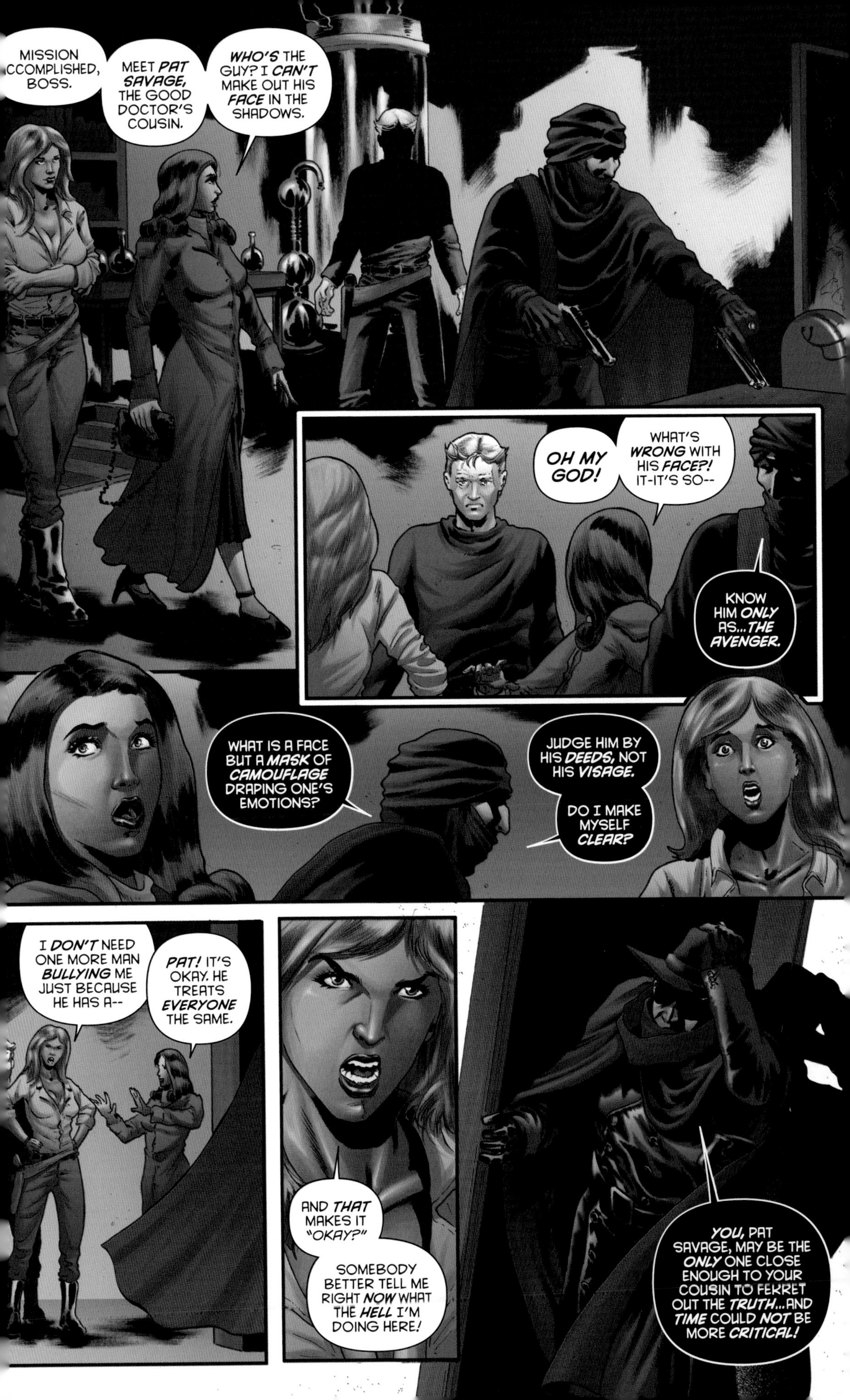

MISSION CCOMPLISHED, BOSS.
MEET *PAT SAVAGE,* THE GOOD DOCTOR'S COUSIN.
WHO'S THE GUY? I *CAN'T* MAKE OUT HIS *FACE* IN THE SHADOWS.
OH MY GOD!
WHAT'S *WRONG* WITH HIS *FACE?!* IT-IT'S SO--
KNOW HIM *ONLY* AS... *THE AVENGER.*
WHAT IS A FACE BUT A *MASK* OF *CAMOUFLAGE* DRAPING ONE'S EMOTIONS?
JUDGE HIM BY HIS *DEEDS,* NOT HIS *VISAGE.*
DO I MAKE MYSELF *CLEAR?*
I *DON'T* NEED ONE MORE MAN *BULLYING* ME JUST BECAUSE HE HAS A--
PAT! IT'S OKAY. HE TREATS *EVERYONE* THE SAME.
AND *THAT* MAKES IT *"OKAY?"*
SOMEBODY BETTER TELL ME RIGHT *NOW* WHAT THE *HELL* I'M DOING HERE!
YOU, PAT SAVAGE, MAY BE THE *ONLY* ONE CLOSE ENOUGH TO YOUR COUSIN TO FERRET OUT THE *TRUTH*...AND *TIME* COULD *NOT* BE MORE *CRITICAL!*

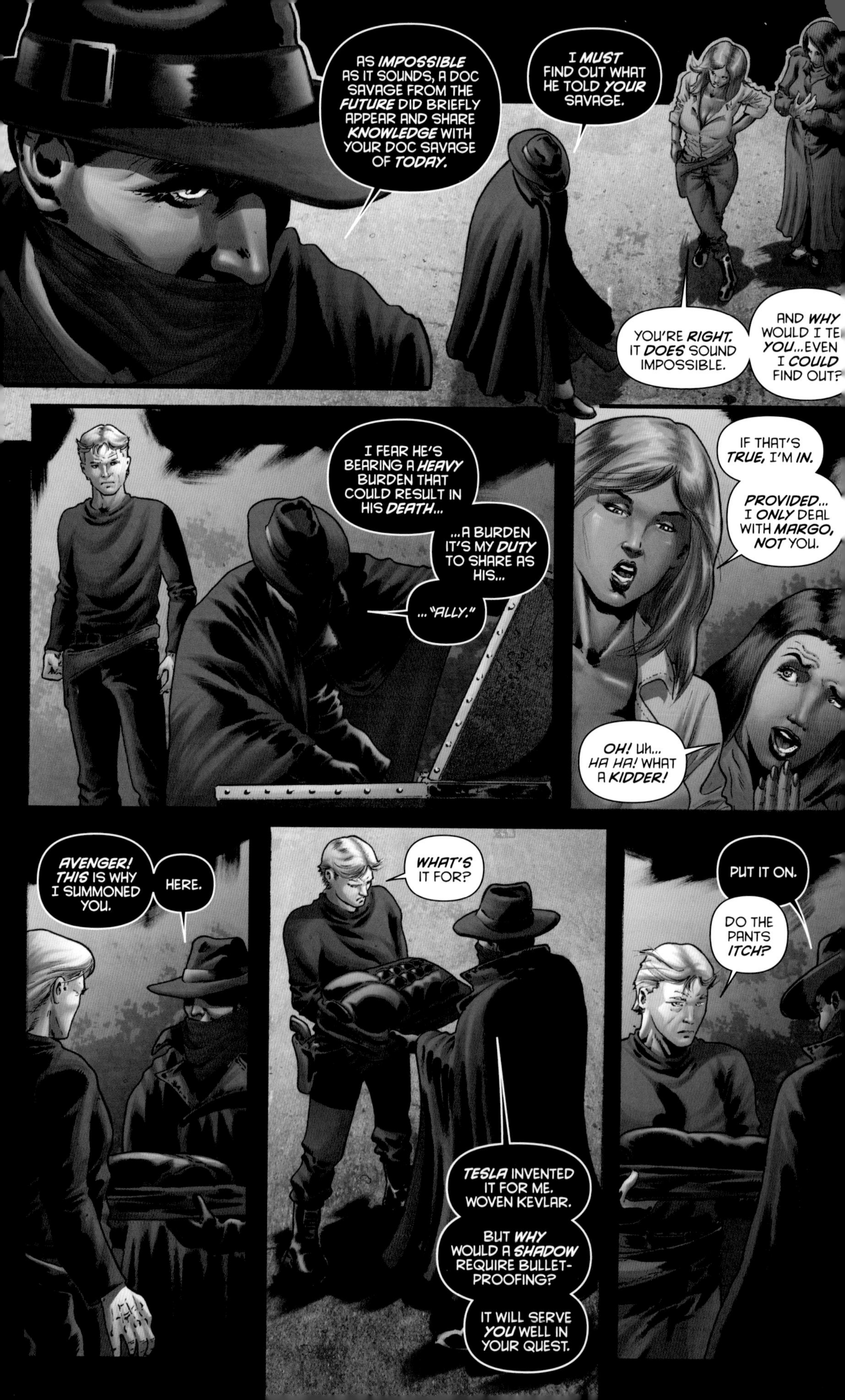
AS IMPOSSIBLE AS IT SOUNDS, A DOC SAVAGE FROM THE FUTURE DID BRIEFLY APPEAR AND SHARE KNOWLEDGE WITH YOUR DOC SAVAGE OF TODAY.
I MUST FIND OUT WHAT HE TOLD YOUR SAVAGE.
YOU'RE RIGHT. IT DOES SOUND IMPOSSIBLE.
AND WHY WOULD I TE YOU...EVEN I COULD FIND OUT?
I FEAR HE'S BEARING A HEAVY BURDEN THAT COULD RESULT IN HIS DEATH...
...A BURDEN IT'S MY DUTY TO SHARE AS HIS...
..."ALLY."
IF THAT'S TRUE, I'M IN.
PROVIDED... I ONLY DEAL WITH MARGO, NOT YOU.
OH! Uh... HA HA! WHAT A KIDDER!
AVENGER! THIS IS WHY I SUMMONED YOU.
HERE.
WHAT'S IT FOR?
TESLA INVENTED IT FOR ME. WOVEN KEVLAR.
BUT WHY WOULD A SHADOW REQUIRE BULLET-PROOFING?
IT WILL SERVE YOU WELL IN YOUR QUEST.
PUT IT ON.
DO THE PANTS ITCH?

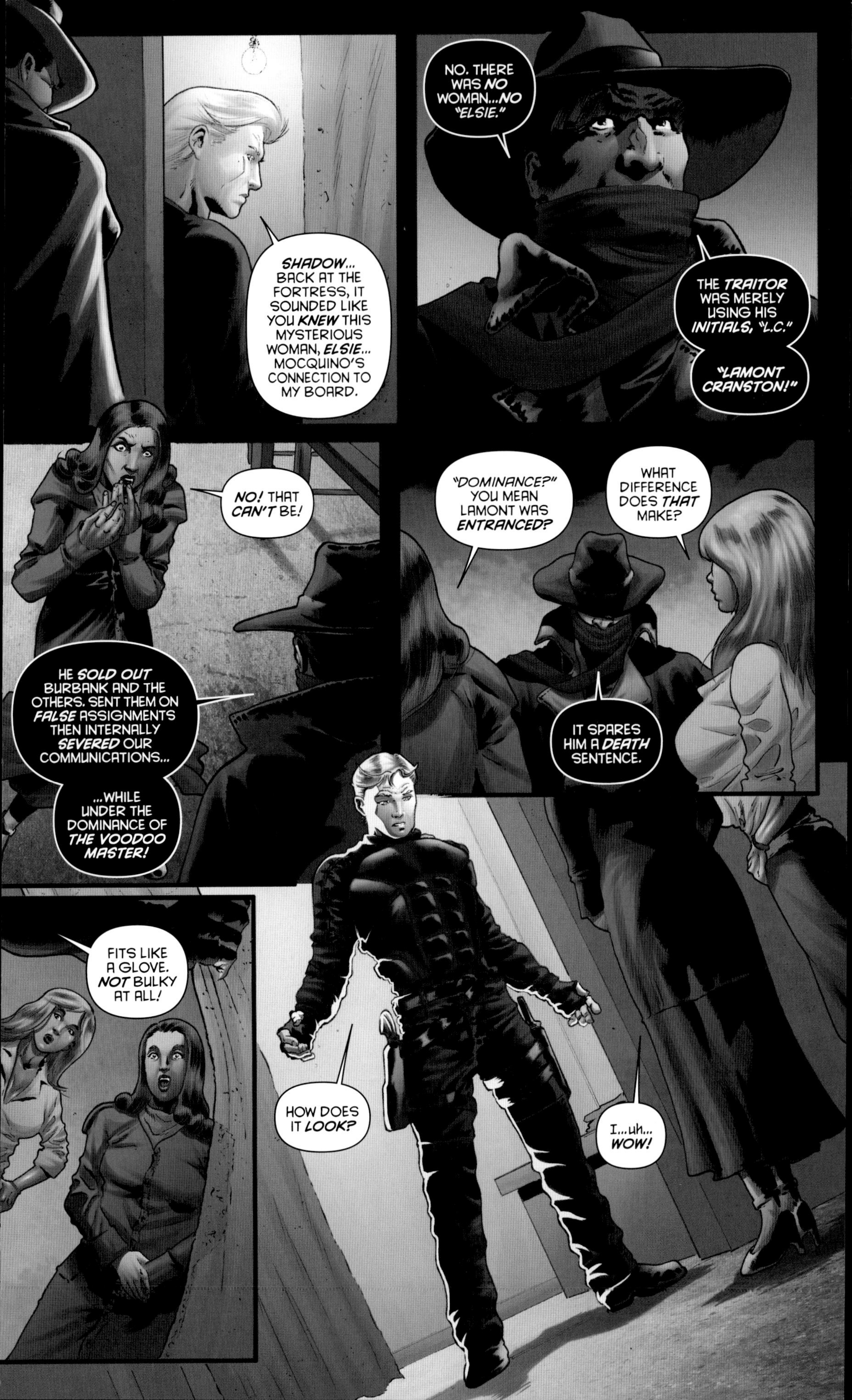
SHADOW... BACK AT THE FORTRESS, IT SOUNDED LIKE YOU KNEW THIS MYSTERIOUS WOMAN, ELSIE... MOCQUINO'S CONNECTION TO MY BOARD.
NO. THERE WAS NO WOMAN...NO "ELSIE."
THE TRAITOR WAS MERELY USING HIS INITIALS, "L.C."
"LAMONT CRANSTON!"
NO! THAT CAN'T BE!
HE SOLD OUT BURBANK AND THE OTHERS. SENT THEM ON FALSE ASSIGNMENTS THEN INTERNALLY SEVERED OUR COMMUNICATIONS...
...WHILE UNDER THE DOMINANCE OF THE VOODOO MASTER!
"DOMINANCE?" YOU MEAN LAMONT WAS ENTRANCED?
WHAT DIFFERENCE DOES THAT MAKE?
IT SPARES HIM A DEATH SENTENCE.
FITS LIKE A GLOVE. NOT BULKY AT ALL!
HOW DOES IT LOOK?
I...uh... WOW!

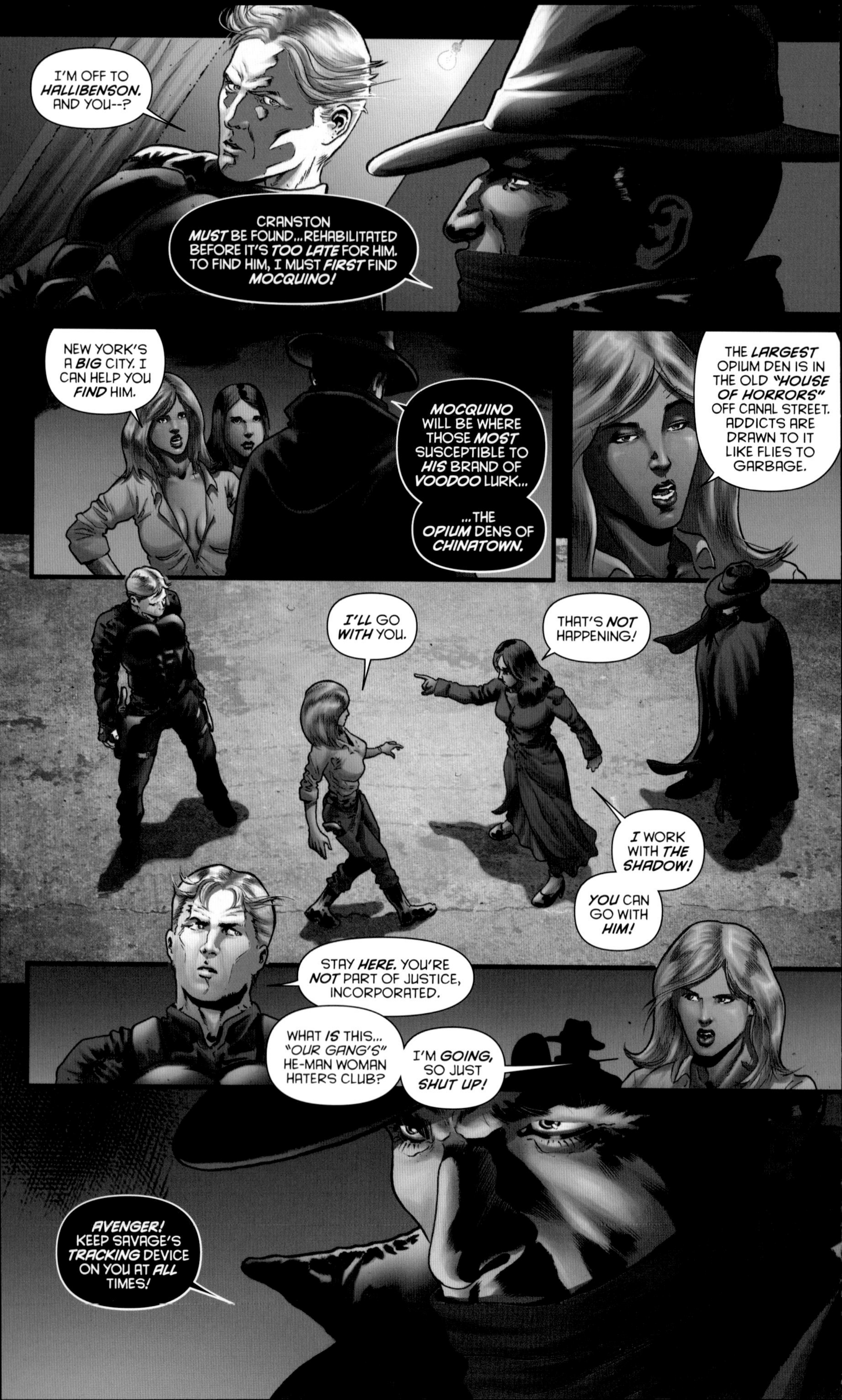
I'M OFF TO HALLIBENSON. AND YOU--?
CRANSTON MUST BE FOUND...REHABILITATED BEFORE IT'S TOO LATE FOR HIM. TO FIND HIM, I MUST FIRST FIND MOCQUINO!
NEW YORK'S A BIG CITY. I CAN HELP YOU FIND HIM.
MOCQUINO WILL BE WHERE THOSE MOST SUSCEPTIBLE TO HIS BRAND OF VOODOO LURK...
...THE OPIUM DENS OF CHINATOWN.
THE LARGEST OPIUM DEN IS IN THE OLD "HOUSE OF HORRORS" OFF CANAL STREET. ADDICTS ARE DRAWN TO IT LIKE FLIES TO GARBAGE.
I'LL GO WITH YOU.
THAT'S NOT HAPPENING!
I WORK WITH THE SHADOW!
YOU CAN GO WITH HIM!
STAY HERE. YOU'RE NOT PART OF JUSTICE, INCORPORATED.
WHAT IS THIS... "OUR GANG'S" HE-MAN WOMAN HATERS CLUB?
I'M GOING, SO JUST SHUT UP!
AVENGER! KEEP SAVAGE'S TRACKING DEVICE ON YOU AT ALL TIMES!

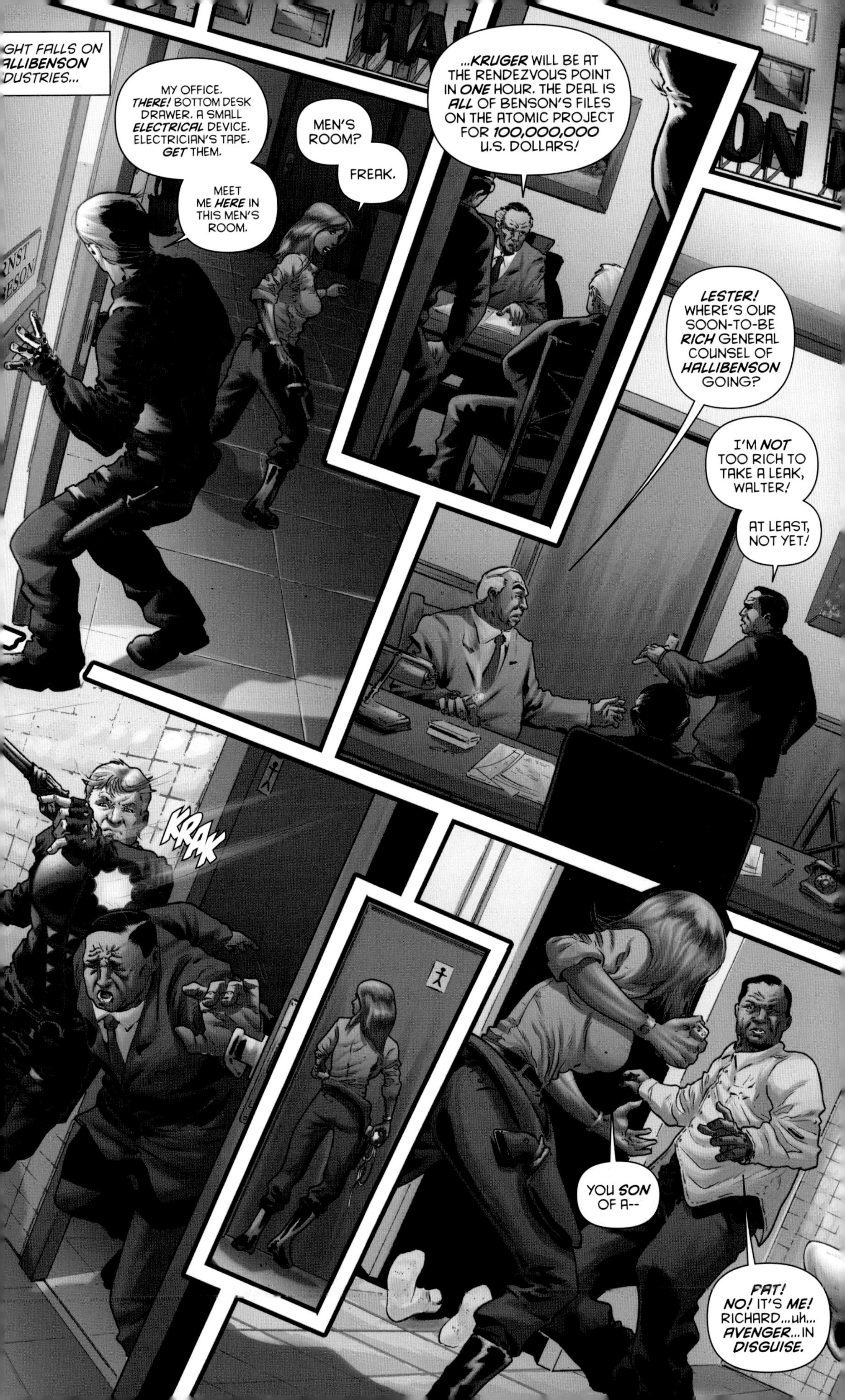

GHT FALLS ON HALLIBENSON DUSTRIES...
MY OFFICE. THERE! BOTTOM DESK DRAWER. A SMALL ELECTRICAL DEVICE. ELECTRICIAN'S TAPE. GET THEM.
MEET ME HERE IN THIS MEN'S ROOM.
MEN'S ROOM?
FREAK.
...KRUGER WILL BE AT THE RENDEZVOUS POINT IN ONE HOUR. THE DEAL IS ALL OF BENSON'S FILES ON THE ATOMIC PROJECT FOR 100,000,000 U.S. DOLLARS!
LESTER! WHERE'S OUR SOON-TO-BE RICH GENERAL COUNSEL OF HALLIBENSON GOING?
I'M NOT TOO RICH TO TAKE A LEAK, WALTER!
AT LEAST, NOT YET!
KRAK
YOU SON OF A--
FAT! NO! IT'S ME! RICHARD...uh... AVENGER...IN DISGUISE.

IN MERE MINUTES...

THAT'S THE MOST *REMARKABLE* DISGUISE I'VE EVER *SEEN! WHERE'D* YOU FIND THE MAKE-UP AND--?

I'LL EXPLAIN LATER.

NOW, LET'S SEE IF I CAN *ACTUALLY* PULL THIS OFF!

LESTER! ABOUT TIME! SEE WHAT HAPPENS AFTER AGE *FIFTY?*

ENOUGH NONSENSE! *KRUGER* IS HITLER'S *SPY* IN AMERICA. THERE *CANNOT* BE A MISSTEP WITH HIM!

DO WE HAVE *EVERYTHING* WE PROMISED?

WE DO *NOW.* WHEN BENSON *DIED,* WE SECURED THE COURT ORDER TO *OPEN* HIS SAFE DEPOSIT BOX. AND IT WAS *ALL* THERE. BUT I STILL FEEL *BAD* ABOUT--

ANY *HEIRS* WOULD'VE HAD THE *RIGHT* TO OPEN THAT BOX.

HIS *WIFE* GOT WHAT SHE *DESERVED!*

THE PRIG TOSSED HER *DRINK* IN MY FACE AT THE OFFICE XMAS PARTY! TO *HELL* WITH HER!

BUT DID WE *REALLY* HAVE TO TOSS THE *LITTLE GIRL,* TOO?

"WE" DIDN'T, WALTER! MOCQUINO'S MESMERIZED *CREW* AND *PASSENGERS* DID.

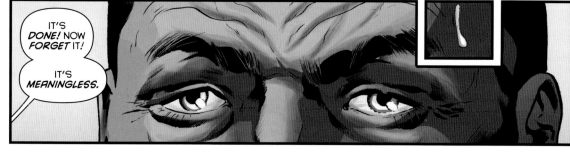

IT'S *DONE!* NOW *FORGET* IT!

IT'S *MEANINGLESS.*

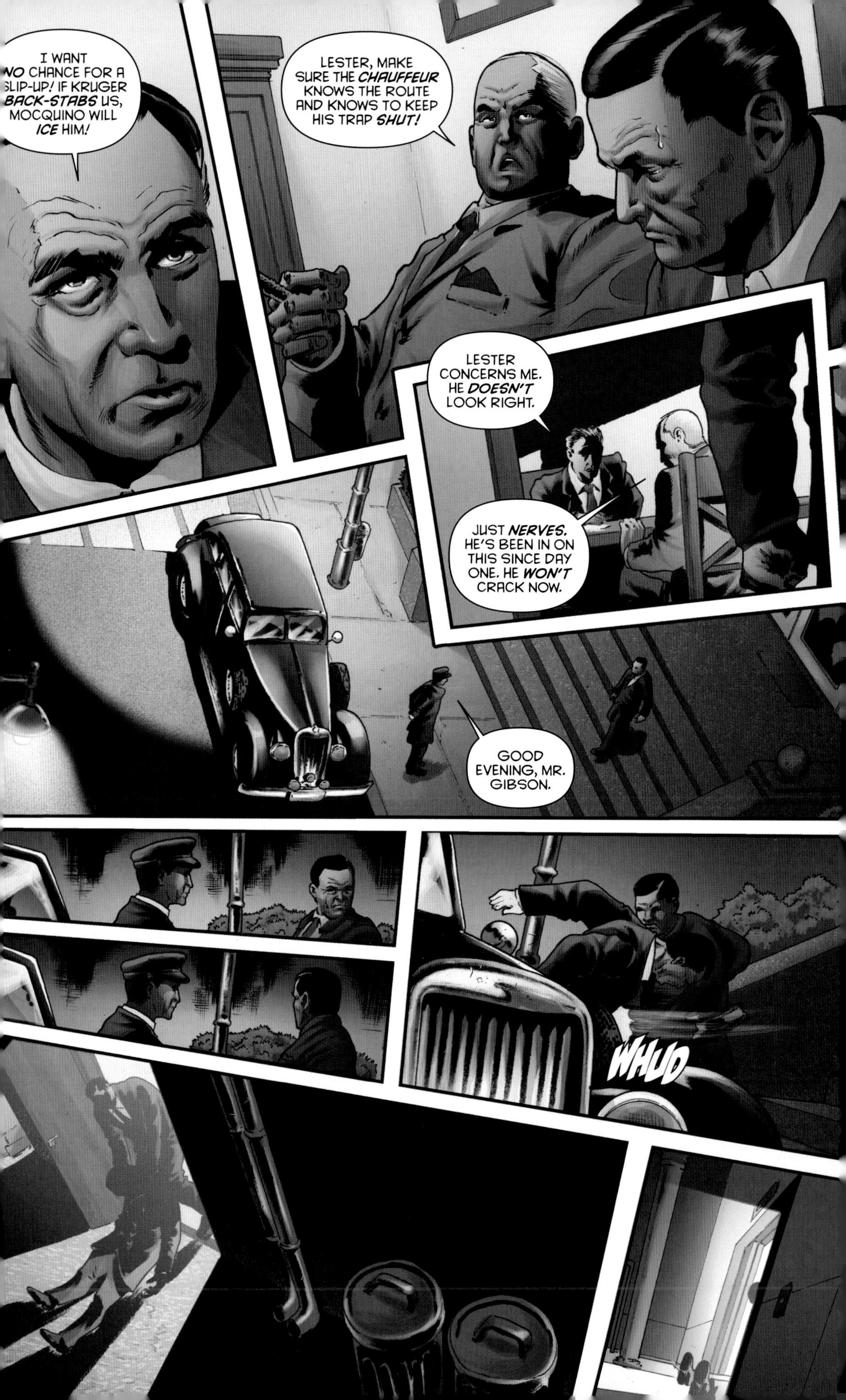
I WANT NO CHANCE FOR A SLIP-UP! IF KRUGER BACK-STABS US, MOCQUINO WILL ICE HIM!
LESTER, MAKE SURE THE CHAUFFEUR KNOWS THE ROUTE AND KNOWS TO KEEP HIS TRAP SHUT!
LESTER CONCERNS ME. HE DOESN'T LOOK RIGHT.
JUST NERVES. HE'S BEEN IN ON THIS SINCE DAY ONE. HE WON'T CRACK NOW.
GOOD EVENING, MR. GIBSON.
WHUD

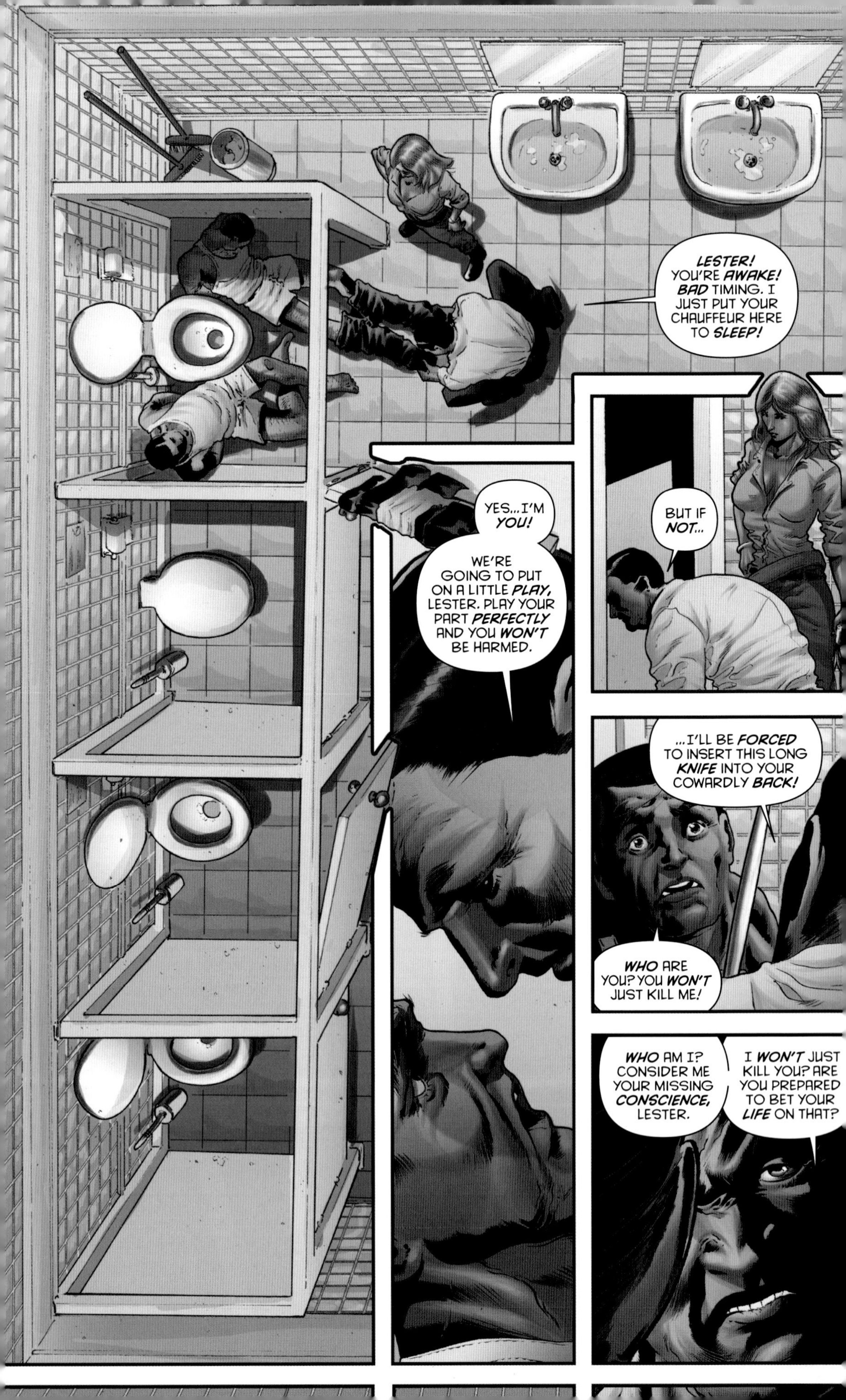
LESTER! YOU'RE AWAKE! BAD TIMING. I JUST PUT YOUR CHAUFFEUR HERE TO SLEEP!
YES...I'M YOU!
WE'RE GOING TO PUT ON A LITTLE PLAY, LESTER. PLAY YOUR PART PERFECTLY AND YOU WON'T BE HARMED.
BUT IF NOT...
...I'LL BE FORCED TO INSERT THIS LONG KNIFE INTO YOUR COWARDLY BACK!
WHO ARE YOU? YOU WON'T JUST KILL ME!
WHO AM I? CONSIDER ME YOUR MISSING CONSCIENCE, LESTER.
I WON'T JUST KILL YOU? ARE YOU PREPARED TO BET YOUR LIFE ON THAT?

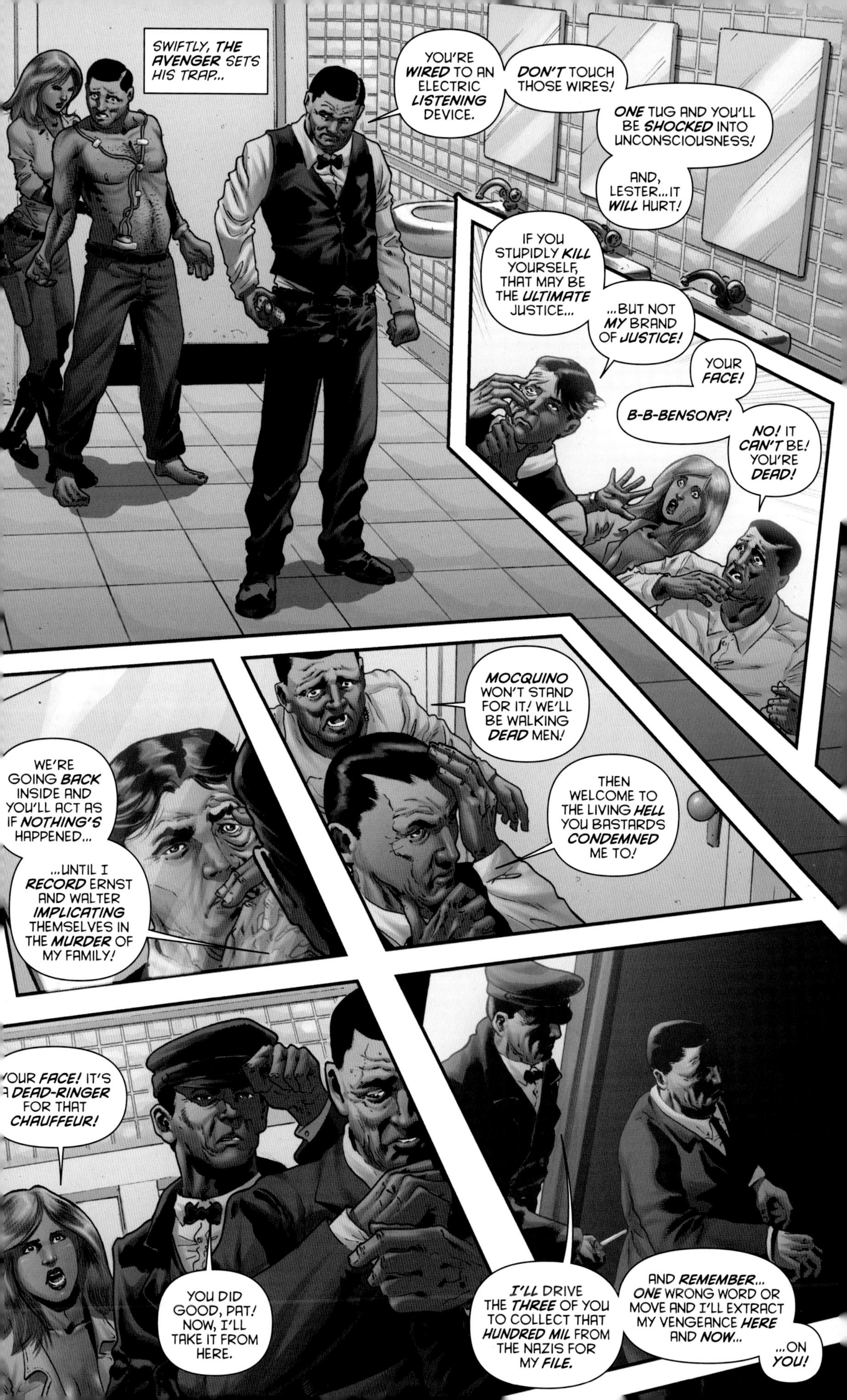
SWIFTLY, THE AVENGER SETS HIS TRAP...
YOU'RE WIRED TO AN ELECTRIC LISTENING DEVICE.
DON'T TOUCH THOSE WIRES!
ONE TUG AND YOU'LL BE SHOCKED INTO UNCONSCIOUSNESS!
AND, LESTER...IT WILL HURT!
IF YOU STUPIDLY KILL YOURSELF, THAT MAY BE THE ULTIMATE JUSTICE...
...BUT NOT MY BRAND OF JUSTICE!
YOUR FACE!
B-B-BENSON?!
NO! IT CAN'T BE! YOU'RE DEAD!
WE'RE GOING BACK INSIDE AND YOU'LL ACT AS IF NOTHING'S HAPPENED...
...UNTIL I RECORD ERNST AND WALTER IMPLICATING THEMSELVES IN THE MURDER OF MY FAMILY!
MOCQUINO WON'T STAND FOR IT! WE'LL BE WALKING DEAD MEN!
THEN WELCOME TO THE LIVING HELL YOU BASTARDS CONDEMNED ME TO!
YOUR FACE! IT'S A DEAD-RINGER FOR THAT CHAUFFEUR!
YOU DID GOOD, PAT! NOW, I'LL TAKE IT FROM HERE.
I'LL DRIVE THE THREE OF YOU TO COLLECT THAT HUNDRED MIL FROM THE NAZIS FOR MY FILE.
AND REMEMBER... ONE WRONG WORD OR MOVE AND I'LL EXTRACT MY VENGEANCE HERE AND NOW...
...ON YOU!

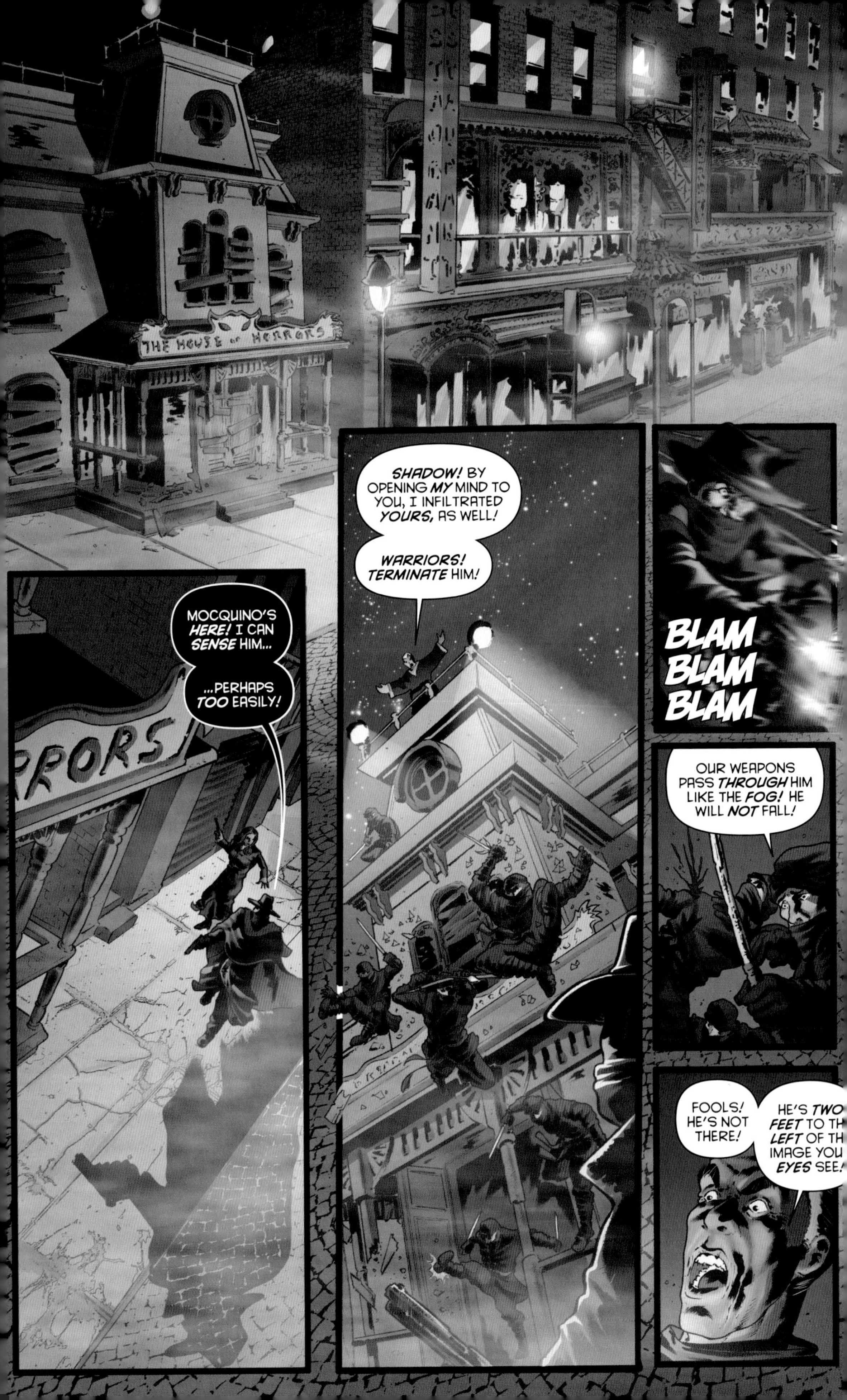
THE HOUSE OF HORRORS
MOCQUINO'S HERE! I CAN SENSE HIM...
...PERHAPS TOO EASILY!
RRORS
SHADOW! BY OPENING MY MIND TO YOU, I INFILTRATED YOURS, AS WELL!
WARRIORS! TERMINATE HIM!
BLAM BLAM BLAM
OUR WEAPONS PASS THROUGH HIM LIKE THE FOG! HE WILL NOT FALL!
FOOLS! HE'S NOT THERE!
HE'S TWO FEET TO TH LEFT OF TH IMAGE YOU EYES SEE!

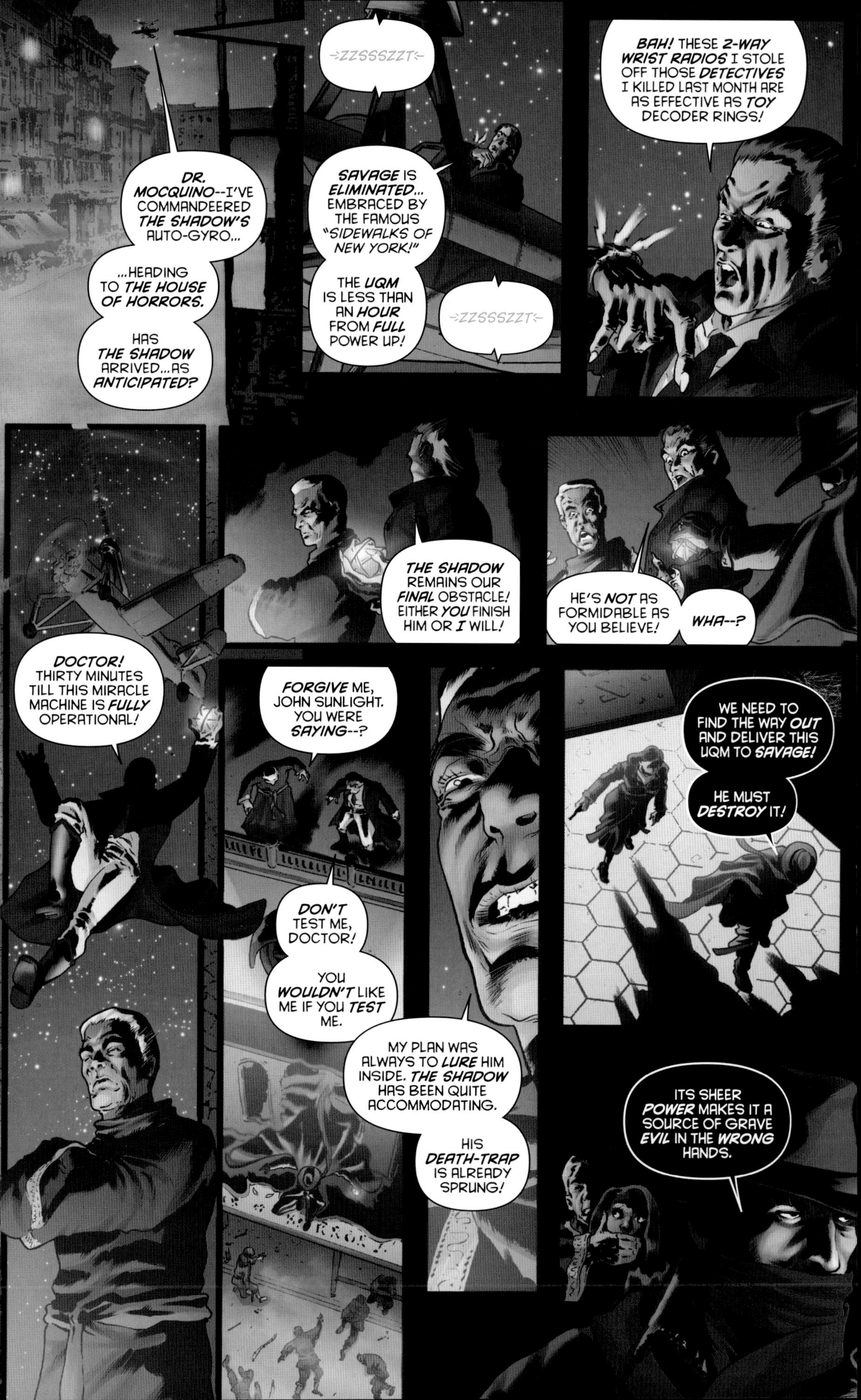
DR. MOCQUINO--I'VE COMMANDEERED THE SHADOW'S AUTO-GYRO...
...HEADING TO THE HOUSE OF HORRORS.
HAS THE SHADOW ARRIVED...AS ANTICIPATED?
ZZSSSSZZT
SAVAGE IS ELIMINATED... EMBRACED BY THE FAMOUS "SIDEWALKS OF NEW YORK!"
THE UQM IS LESS THAN AN HOUR FROM FULL POWER UP!
ZZSSSSZZT
BAH! THESE 2-WAY WRIST RADIOS I STOLE OFF THOSE DETECTIVES I KILLED LAST MONTH ARE AS EFFECTIVE AS TOY DECODER RINGS!
THE SHADOW REMAINS OUR FINAL OBSTACLE! EITHER YOU FINISH HIM OR I WILL!
HE'S NOT AS FORMIDABLE AS YOU BELIEVE!
WHA--?
DOCTOR! THIRTY MINUTES TILL THIS MIRACLE MACHINE IS FULLY OPERATIONAL!
FORGIVE ME, JOHN SUNLIGHT. YOU WERE SAYING--?
DON'T TEST ME, DOCTOR!
YOU WOULDN'T LIKE ME IF YOU TEST ME.
MY PLAN WAS ALWAYS TO LURE HIM INSIDE. THE SHADOW HAS BEEN QUITE ACCOMMODATING.
HIS DEATH-TRAP IS ALREADY SPRUNG!
WE NEED TO FIND THE WAY OUT AND DELIVER THIS UQM TO SAVAGE!
HE MUST DESTROY IT!
ITS SHEER POWER MAKES IT A SOURCE OF GRAVE EVIL IN THE WRONG HANDS.

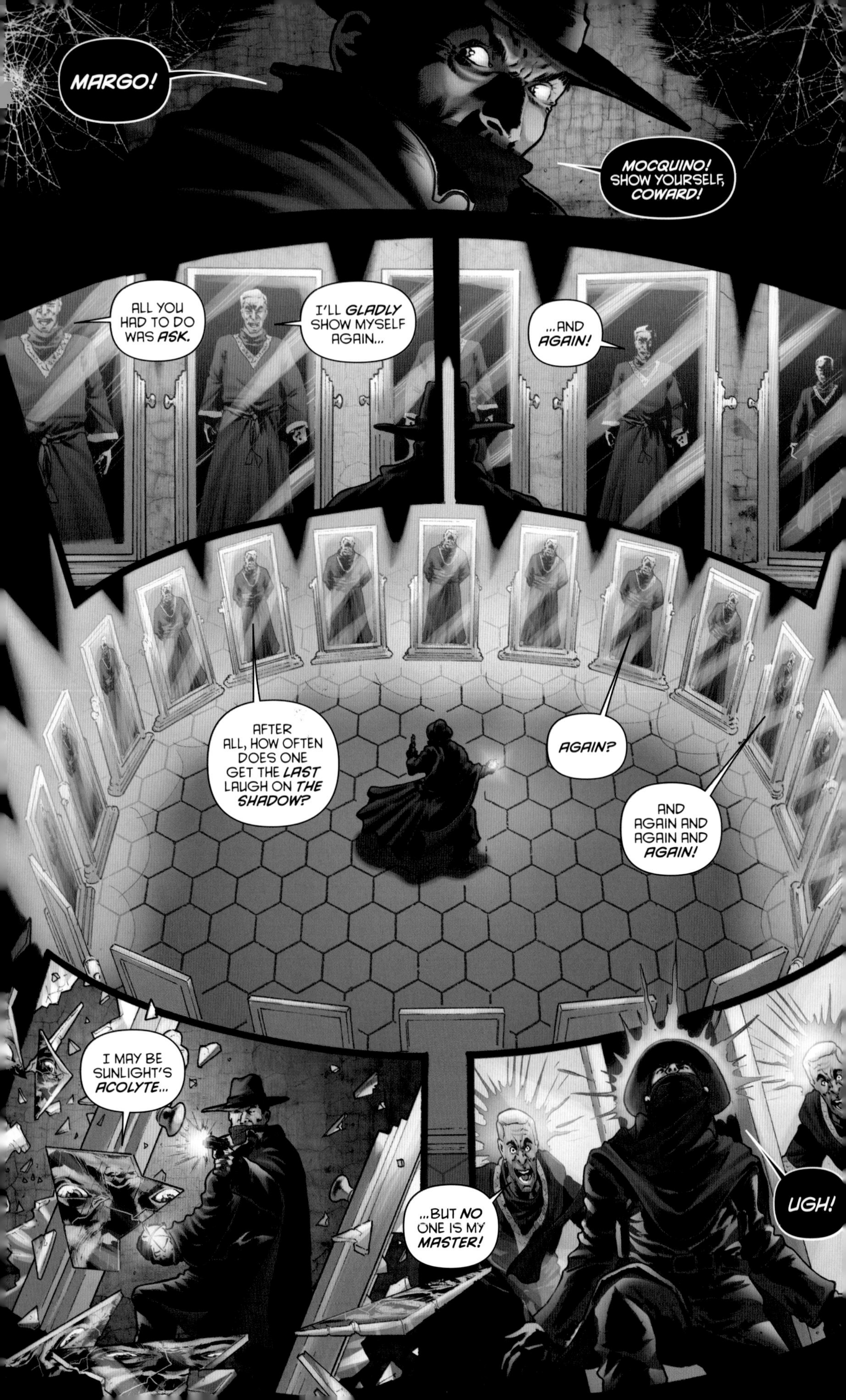
MARGO!
MOCQUINO! SHOW YOURSELF, COWARD!
ALL YOU HAD TO DO WAS ASK.
I'LL GLADLY SHOW MYSELF AGAIN...
...AND AGAIN!
AFTER ALL, HOW OFTEN DOES ONE GET THE LAST LAUGH ON THE SHADOW?
AGAIN?
AND AGAIN AND AGAIN AND AGAIN!
I MAY BE SUNLIGHT'S ACOLYTE...
...BUT NO ONE IS MY MASTER!
UGH!

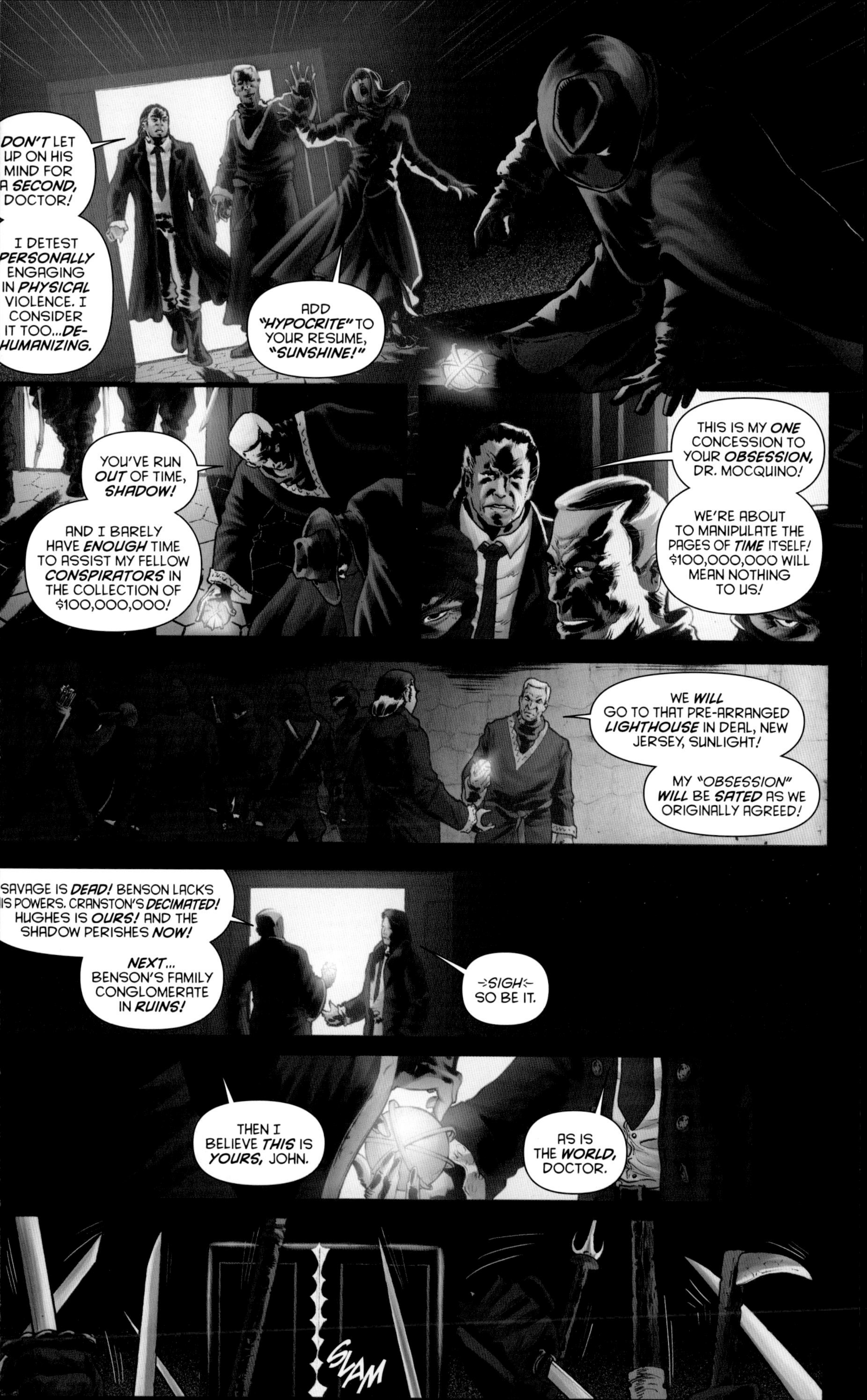
DON'T LET UP ON HIS MIND FOR A SECOND, DOCTOR!
I DETEST PERSONALLY ENGAGING IN PHYSICAL VIOLENCE. I CONSIDER IT TOO...DE-HUMANIZING.
ADD "HYPOCRITE" TO YOUR RESUME, "SUNSHINE!"
YOU'VE RUN OUT OF TIME, SHADOW!
AND I BARELY HAVE ENOUGH TIME TO ASSIST MY FELLOW CONSPIRATORS IN THE COLLECTION OF $100,000,000!
THIS IS MY ONE CONCESSION TO YOUR OBSESSION, DR. MOCQUINO!
WE'RE ABOUT TO MANIPULATE THE PAGES OF TIME ITSELF! $100,000,000 WILL MEAN NOTHING TO US!
WE WILL GO TO THAT PRE-ARRANGED LIGHTHOUSE IN DEAL, NEW JERSEY, SUNLIGHT!
MY "OBSESSION" WILL BE SATED AS WE ORIGINALLY AGREED!
SAVAGE IS DEAD! BENSON LACKS HIS POWERS. CRANSTON'S DECIMATED! HUGHES IS OURS! AND THE SHADOW PERISHES NOW!
NEXT... BENSON'S FAMILY CONGLOMERATE IN RUINS!
-SIGH- SO BE IT.
THEN I BELIEVE THIS IS YOURS, JOHN.
AS IS THE WORLD, DOCTOR.
SLAM

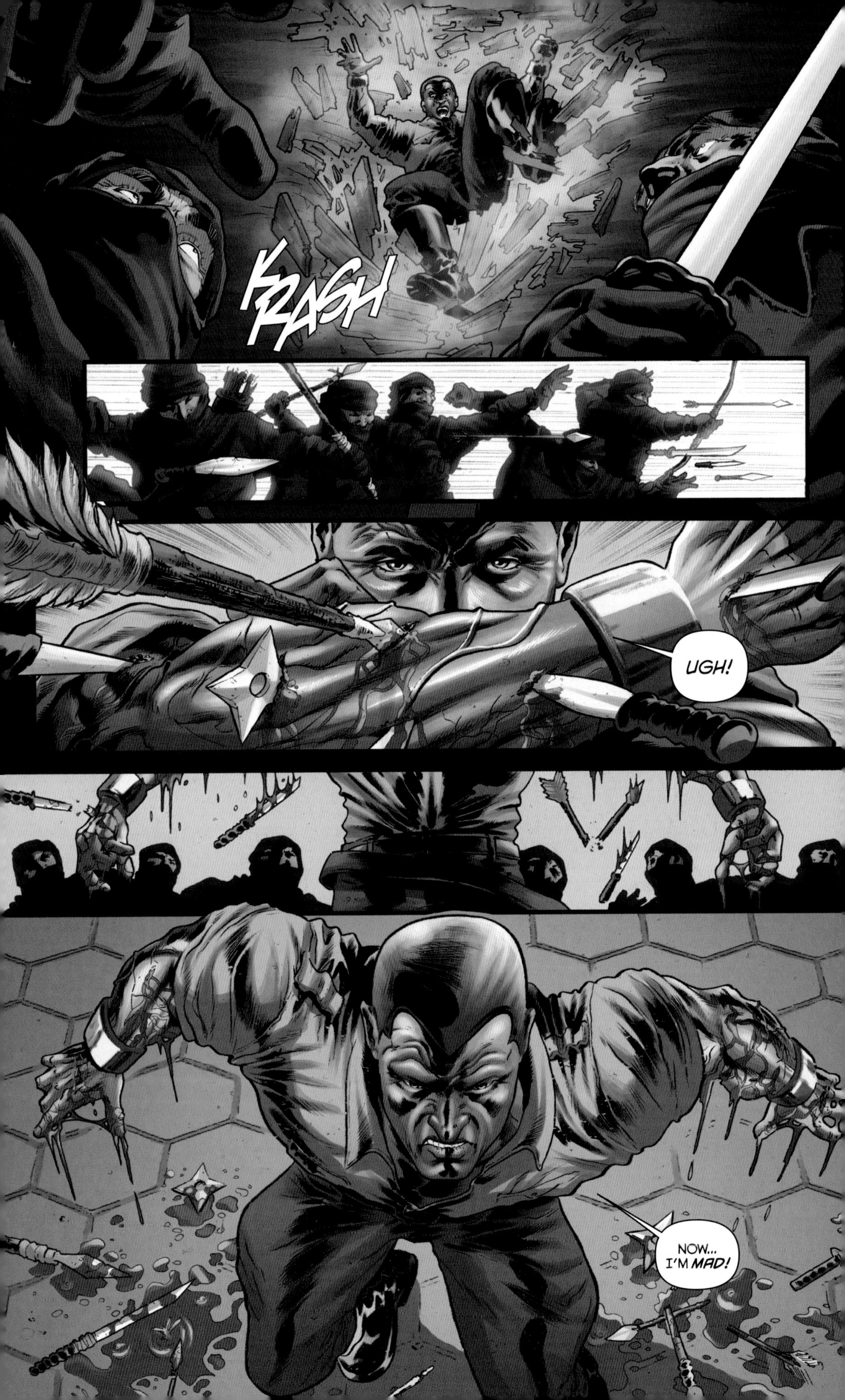
KRASH
UGH!
NOW... I'M MAD!

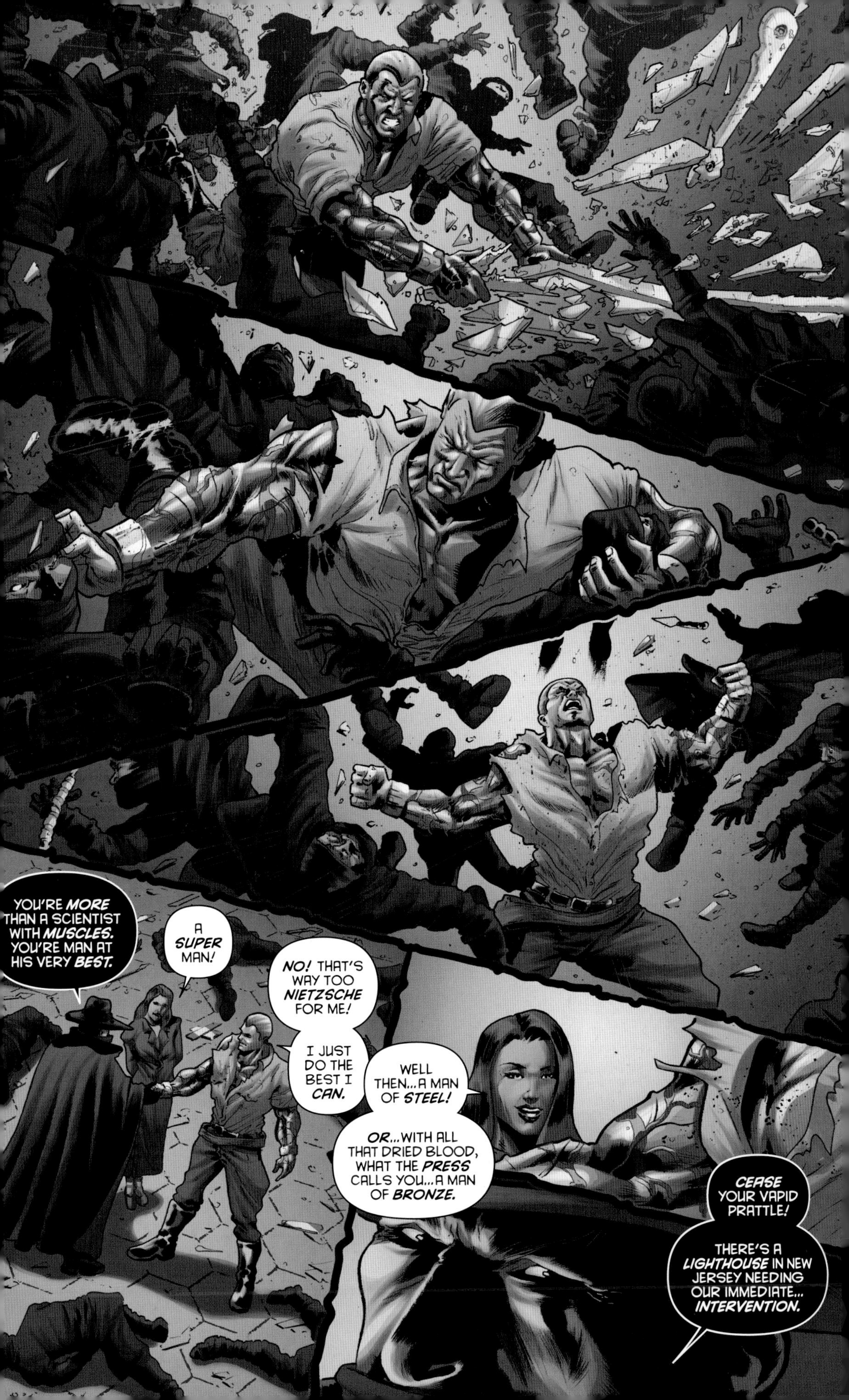
YOU'RE MORE THAN A SCIENTIST WITH MUSCLES. YOU'RE MAN AT HIS VERY BEST.
A SUPER MAN!
NO! THAT'S WAY TOO NIETZSCHE FOR ME!
I JUST DO THE BEST I CAN.
WELL THEN...A MAN OF STEEL!
OR...WITH ALL THAT DRIED BLOOD, WHAT THE PRESS CALLS YOU...A MAN OF BRONZE.
CEASE YOUR VAPID PRATTLE!
THERE'S A LIGHTHOUSE IN NEW JERSEY NEEDING OUR IMMEDIATE... INTERVENTION.

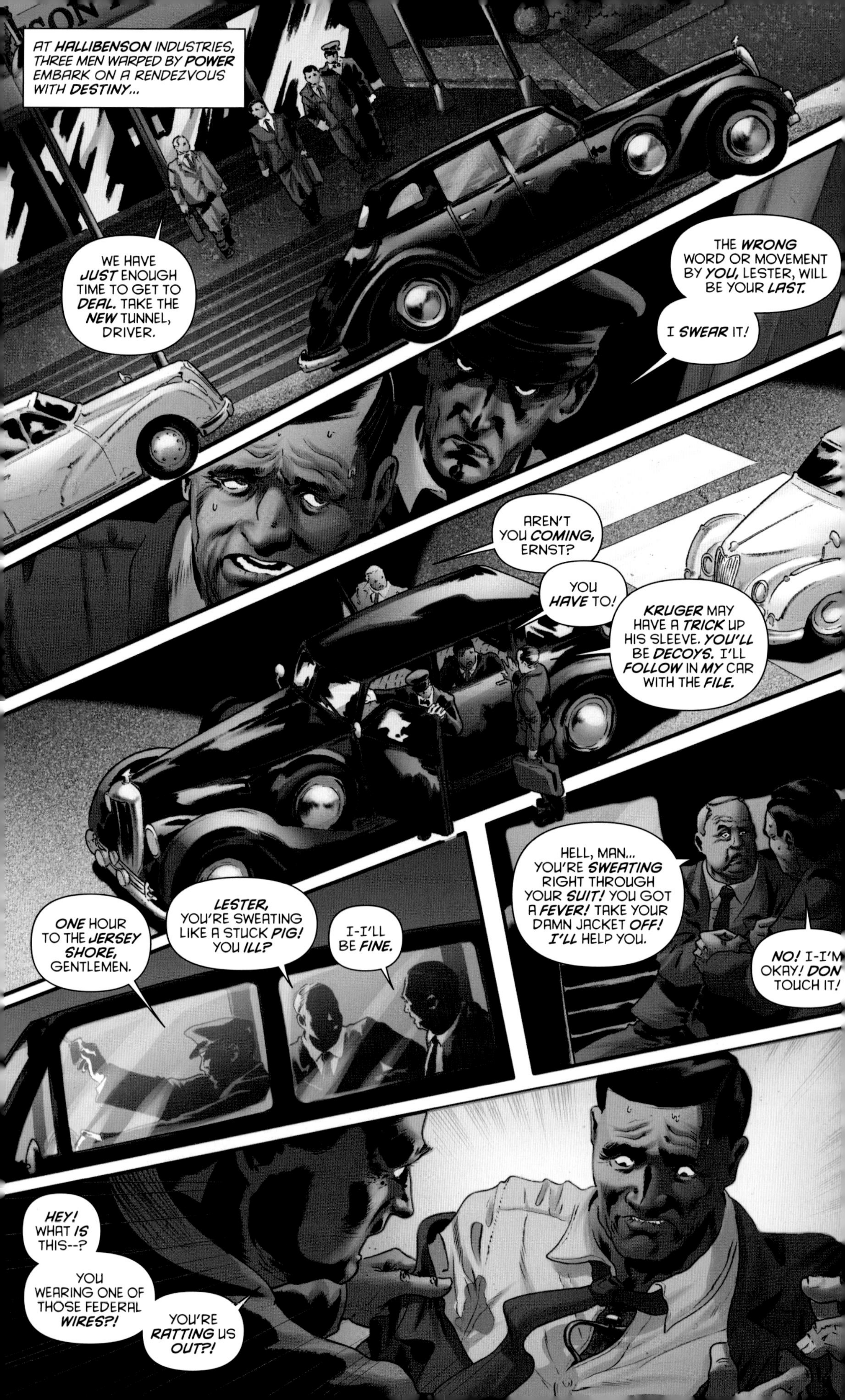

AT HALLIBENSON INDUSTRIES, THREE MEN WARPED BY POWER EMBARK ON A RENDEZVOUS WITH DESTINY...
WE HAVE JUST ENOUGH TIME TO GET TO DEAL. TAKE THE NEW TUNNEL, DRIVER.
THE WRONG WORD OR MOVEMENT BY YOU, LESTER, WILL BE YOUR LAST.
I SWEAR IT!
AREN'T YOU COMING, ERNST?
YOU HAVE TO!
KRUGER MAY HAVE A TRICK UP HIS SLEEVE. YOU'LL BE DECOYS. I'LL FOLLOW IN MY CAR WITH THE FILE.
ONE HOUR TO THE JERSEY SHORE, GENTLEMEN.
LESTER, YOU'RE SWEATING LIKE A STUCK PIG! YOU ILL?
I-I'LL BE FINE.
HELL, MAN... YOU'RE SWEATING RIGHT THROUGH YOUR SUIT! YOU GOT A FEVER! TAKE YOUR DAMN JACKET OFF! I'LL HELP YOU.
NO! I-I'M OKAY! DON'T TOUCH IT!
HEY! WHAT IS THIS--?
YOU WEARING ONE OF THOSE FEDERAL WIRES?!
YOU'RE RATTING US OUT?!

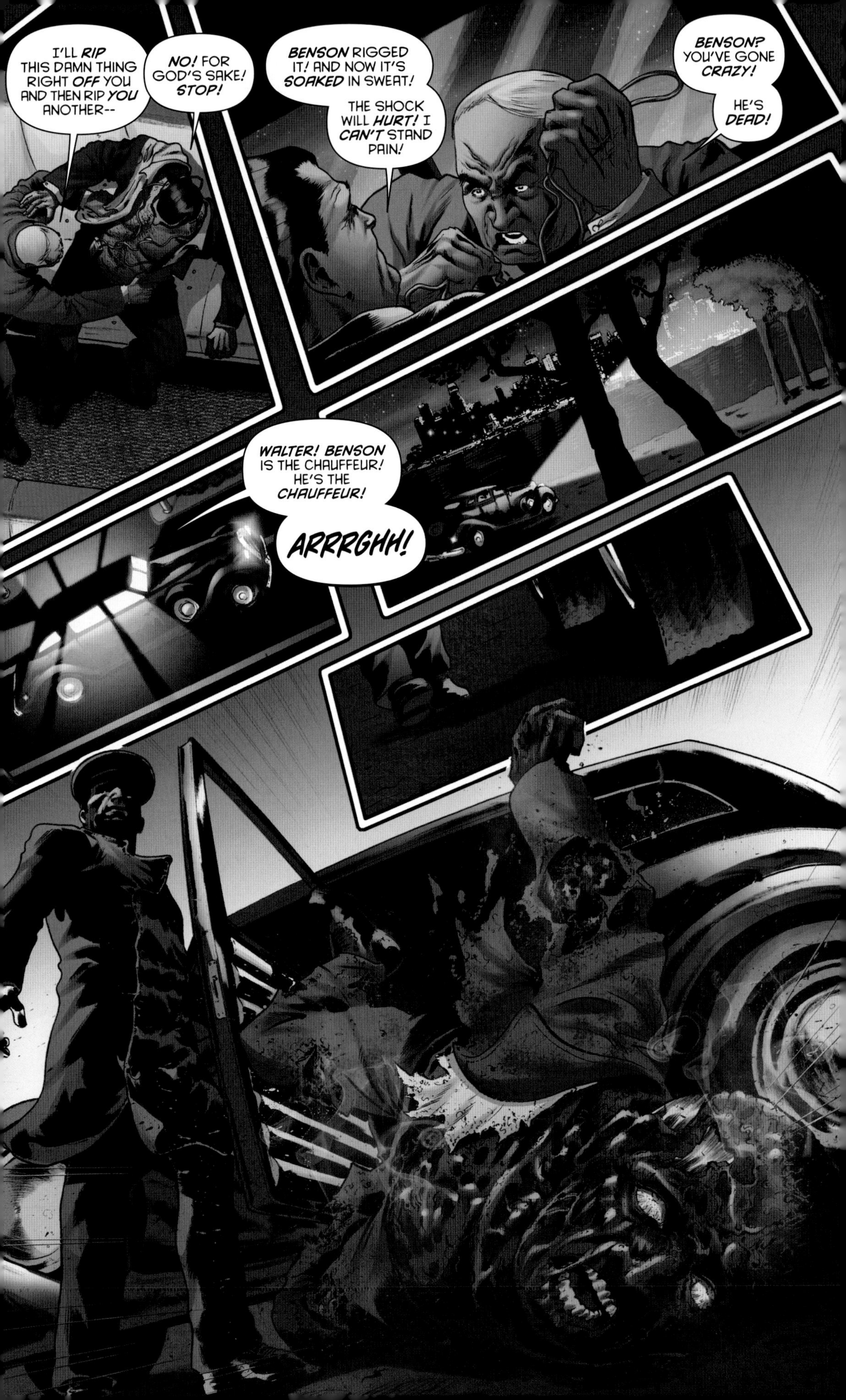
I'LL RIP THIS DAMN THING RIGHT OFF YOU AND THEN RIP YOU ANOTHER--
NO! FOR GOD'S SAKE! STOP!
BENSON RIGGED IT! AND NOW IT'S SOAKED IN SWEAT!
THE SHOCK WILL HURT! I CAN'T STAND PAIN!
BENSON? YOU'VE GONE CRAZY!
HE'S DEAD!
WALTER! BENSON IS THE CHAUFFEUR! HE'S THE CHAUFFEUR!
ARRRGHH!

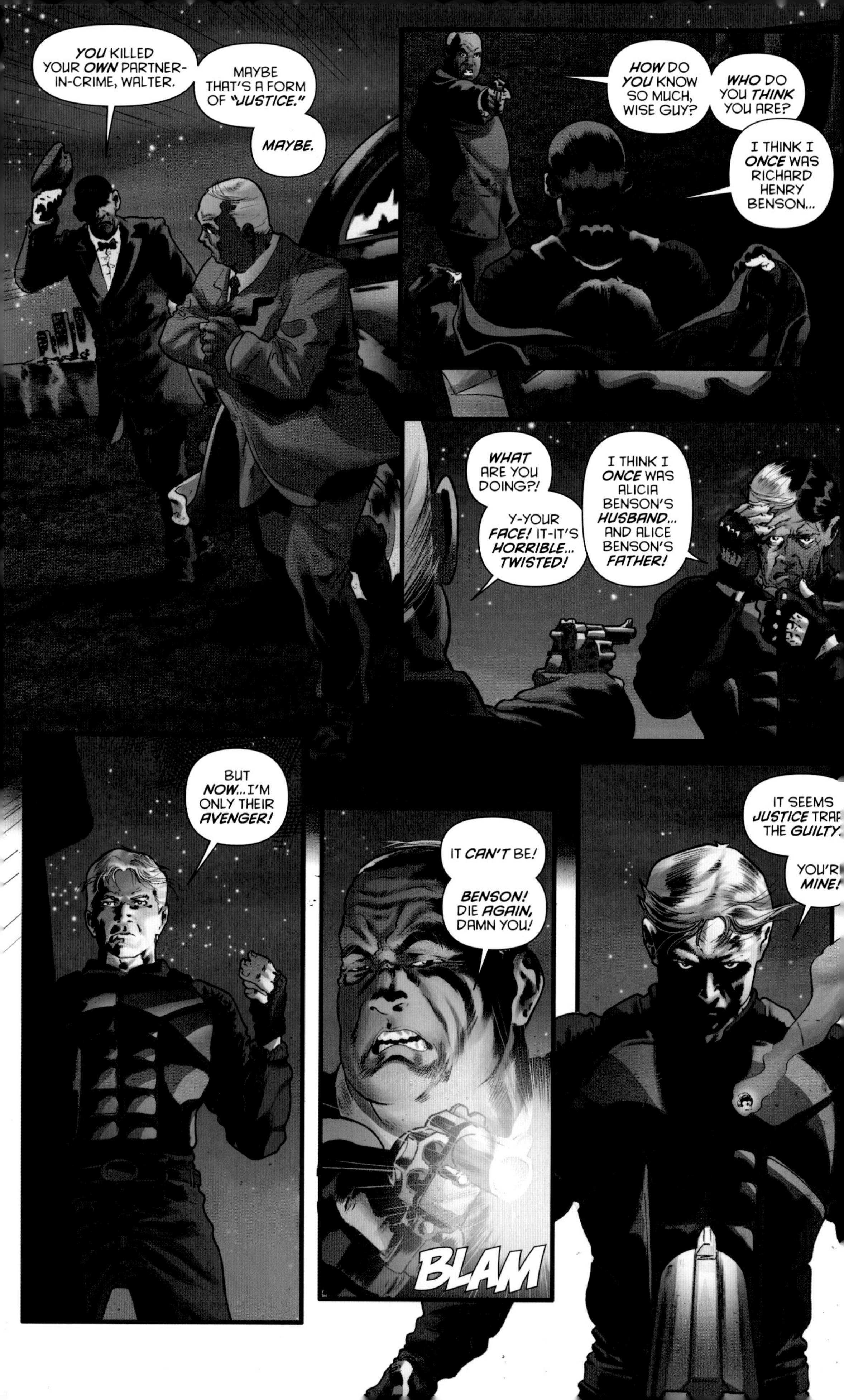
YOU KILLED YOUR OWN PARTNER-IN-CRIME, WALTER.
MAYBE THAT'S A FORM OF "JUSTICE."
MAYBE.
HOW DO YOU KNOW SO MUCH, WISE GUY?
WHO DO YOU THINK YOU ARE?
I THINK I ONCE WAS RICHARD HENRY BENSON...
WHAT ARE YOU DOING?!
Y-YOUR FACE! IT-IT'S HORRIBLE... TWISTED!
I THINK I ONCE WAS ALICIA BENSON'S HUSBAND... AND ALICE BENSON'S FATHER!
BUT NOW...I'M ONLY THEIR AVENGER!
IT CAN'T BE!
BENSON! DIE AGAIN, DAMN YOU!
BLAM
IT SEEMS JUSTICE TRAP THE GUILTY.
YOU'R MINE!

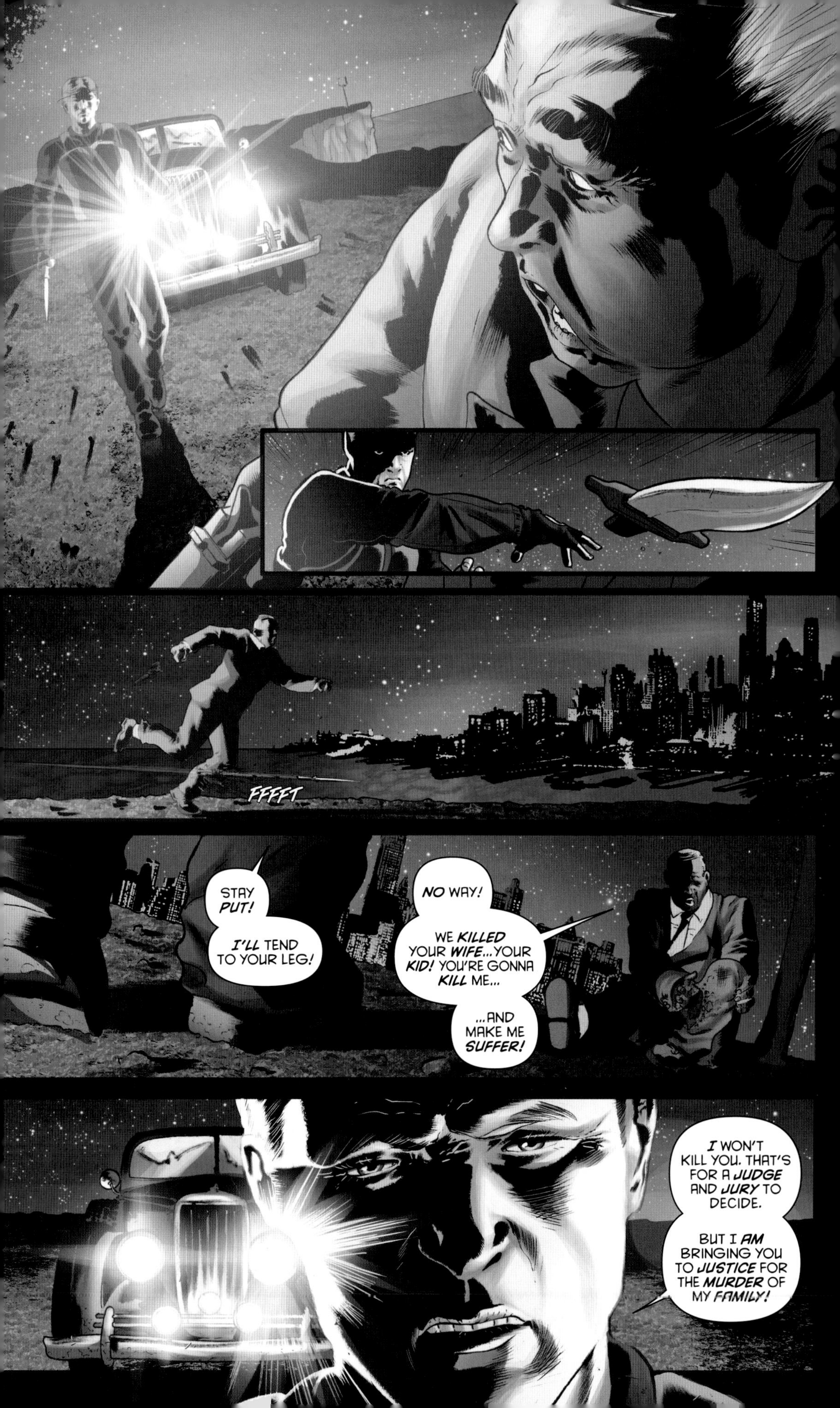
FFFFT
STAY PUT!
I'LL TEND TO YOUR LEG!
NO WAY!
WE KILLED YOUR WIFE...YOUR KID! YOU'RE GONNA KILL ME...
...AND MAKE ME SUFFER!
I WON'T KILL YOU. THAT'S FOR A JUDGE AND JURY TO DECIDE.
BUT I AM BRINGING YOU TO JUSTICE FOR THE MURDER OF MY FAMILY!

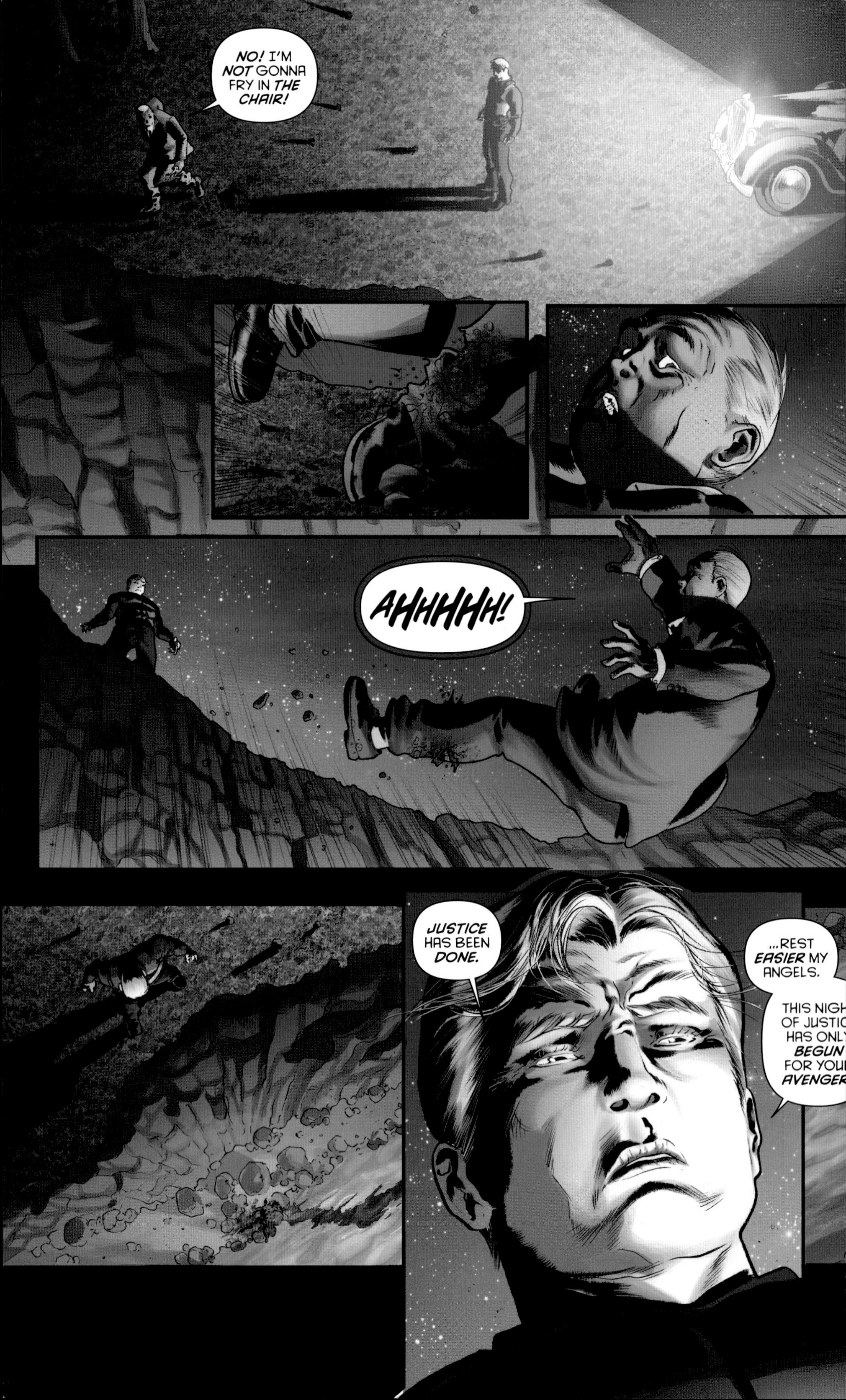

NO! I'M NOT GONNA FRY IN THE CHAIR!
AHHHHH!
JUSTICE HAS BEEN DONE.
...REST EASIER MY ANGELS.
THIS NIGH OF JUSTIC HAS ONLY BEGUN FOR YOUR AVENGER

SIX

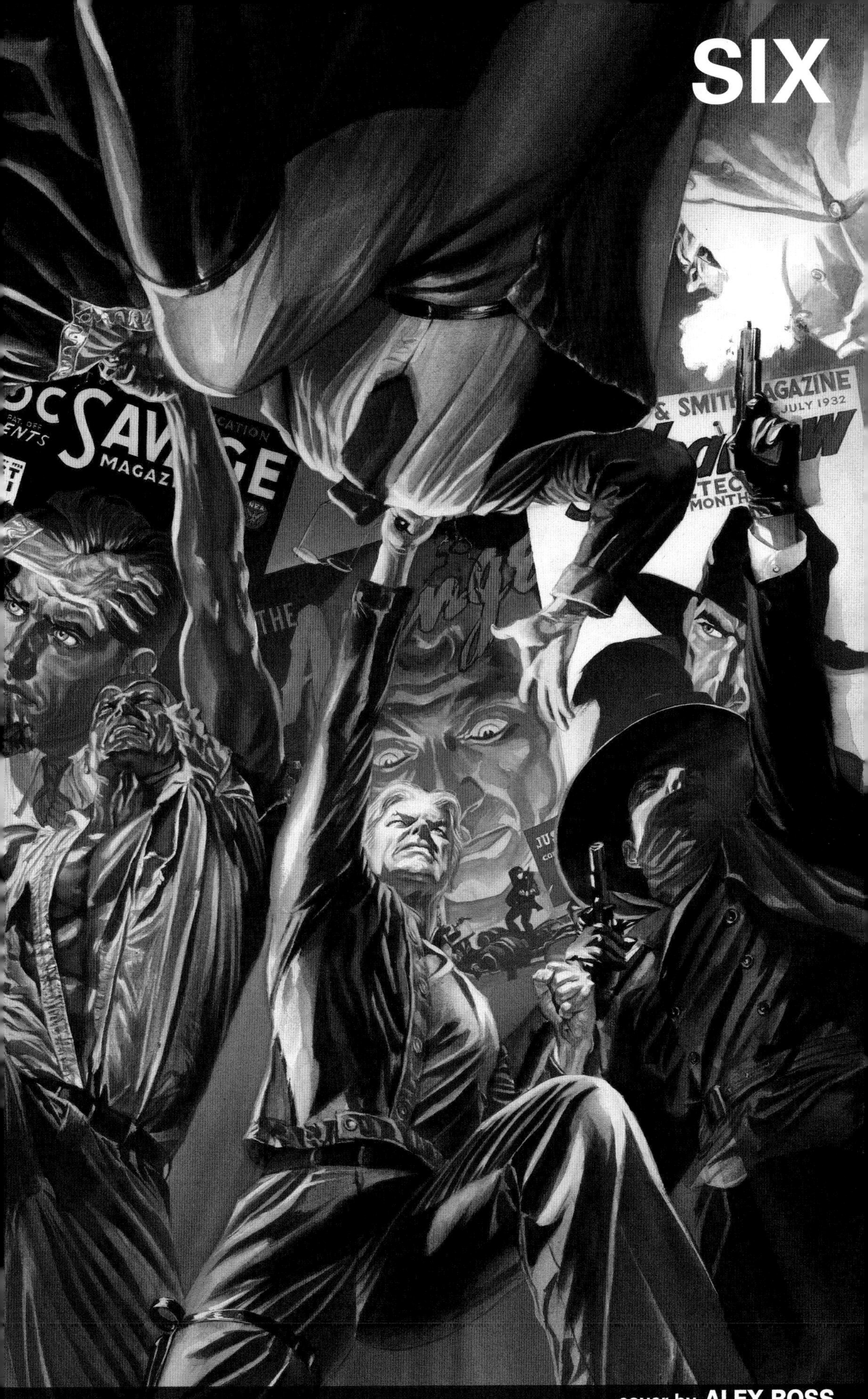
JULY 1932

cover by **ALEX ROSS**

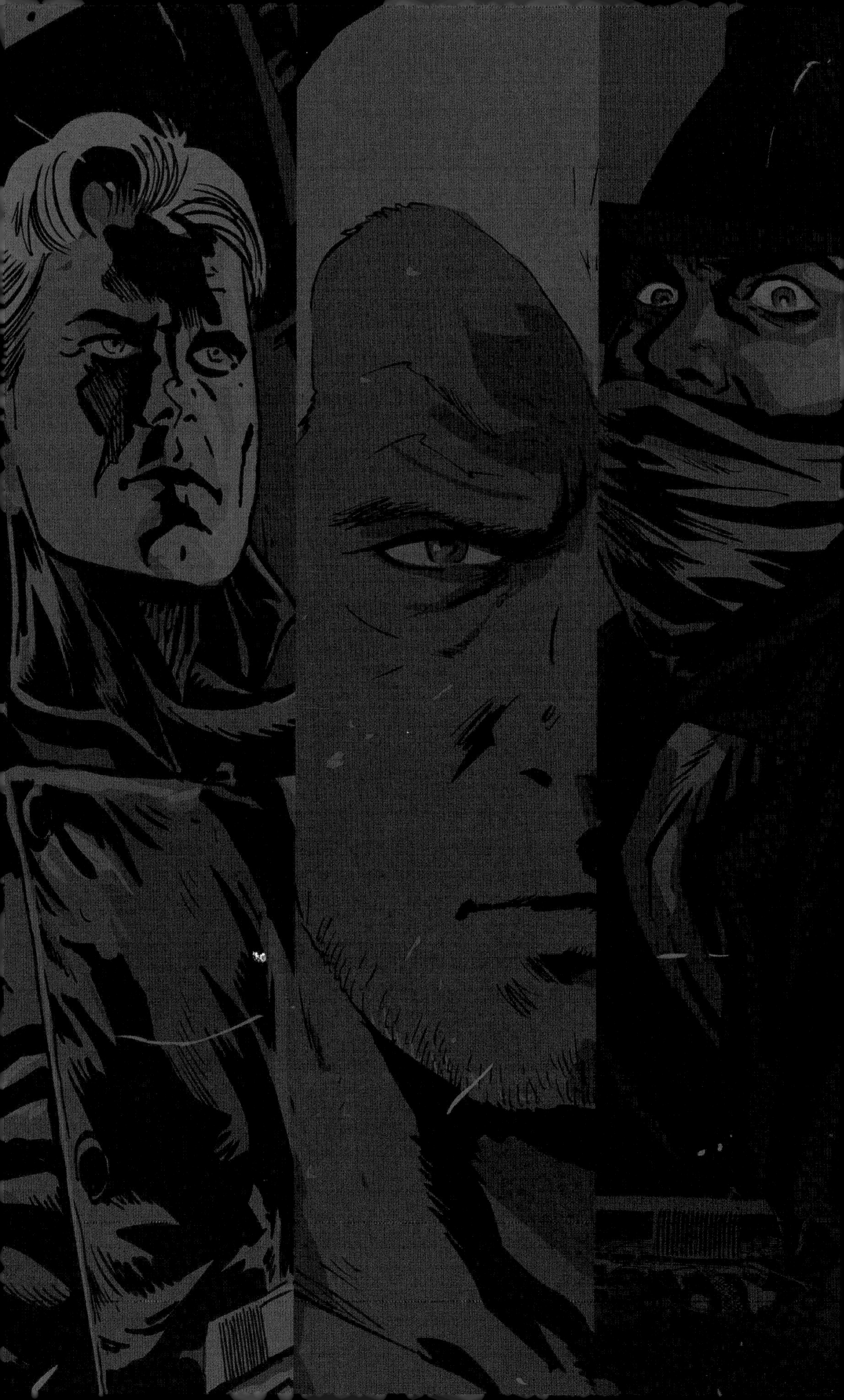

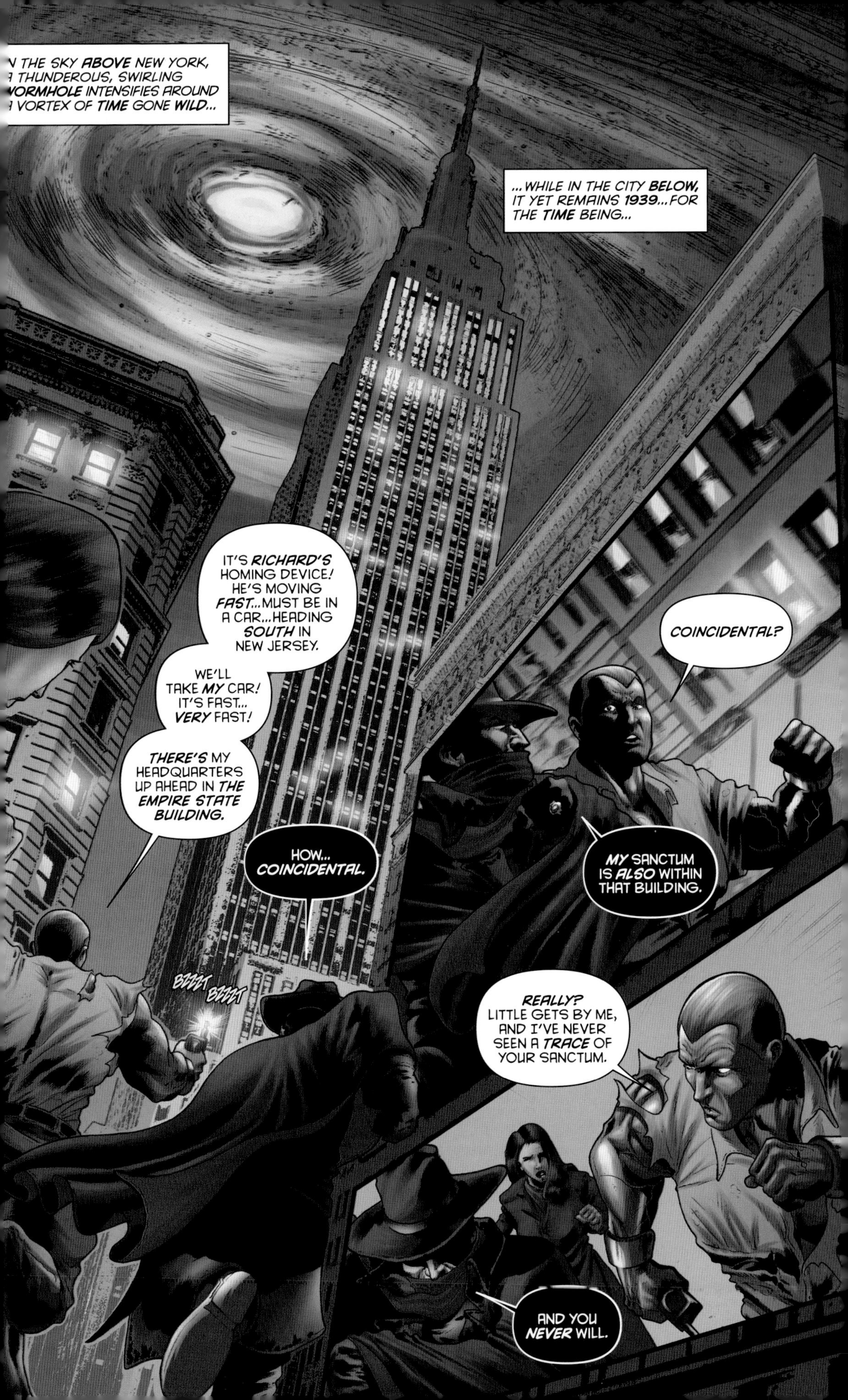
N THE SKY ABOVE NEW YORK, A THUNDEROUS, SWIRLING WORMHOLE INTENSIFIES AROUND A VORTEX OF TIME GONE WILD...
...WHILE IN THE CITY BELOW, IT YET REMAINS 1939...FOR THE TIME BEING...
IT'S RICHARD'S HOMING DEVICE! HE'S MOVING FAST...MUST BE IN A CAR...HEADING SOUTH IN NEW JERSEY.
WE'LL TAKE MY CAR! IT'S FAST... VERY FAST!
THERE'S MY HEADQUARTERS UP AHEAD IN THE EMPIRE STATE BUILDING.
HOW... COINCIDENTAL.
BZZZT BZZZT
COINCIDENTAL?
MY SANCTUM IS ALSO WITHIN THAT BUILDING.
REALLY? LITTLE GETS BY ME, AND I'VE NEVER SEEN A TRACE OF YOUR SANCTUM.
AND YOU NEVER WILL.

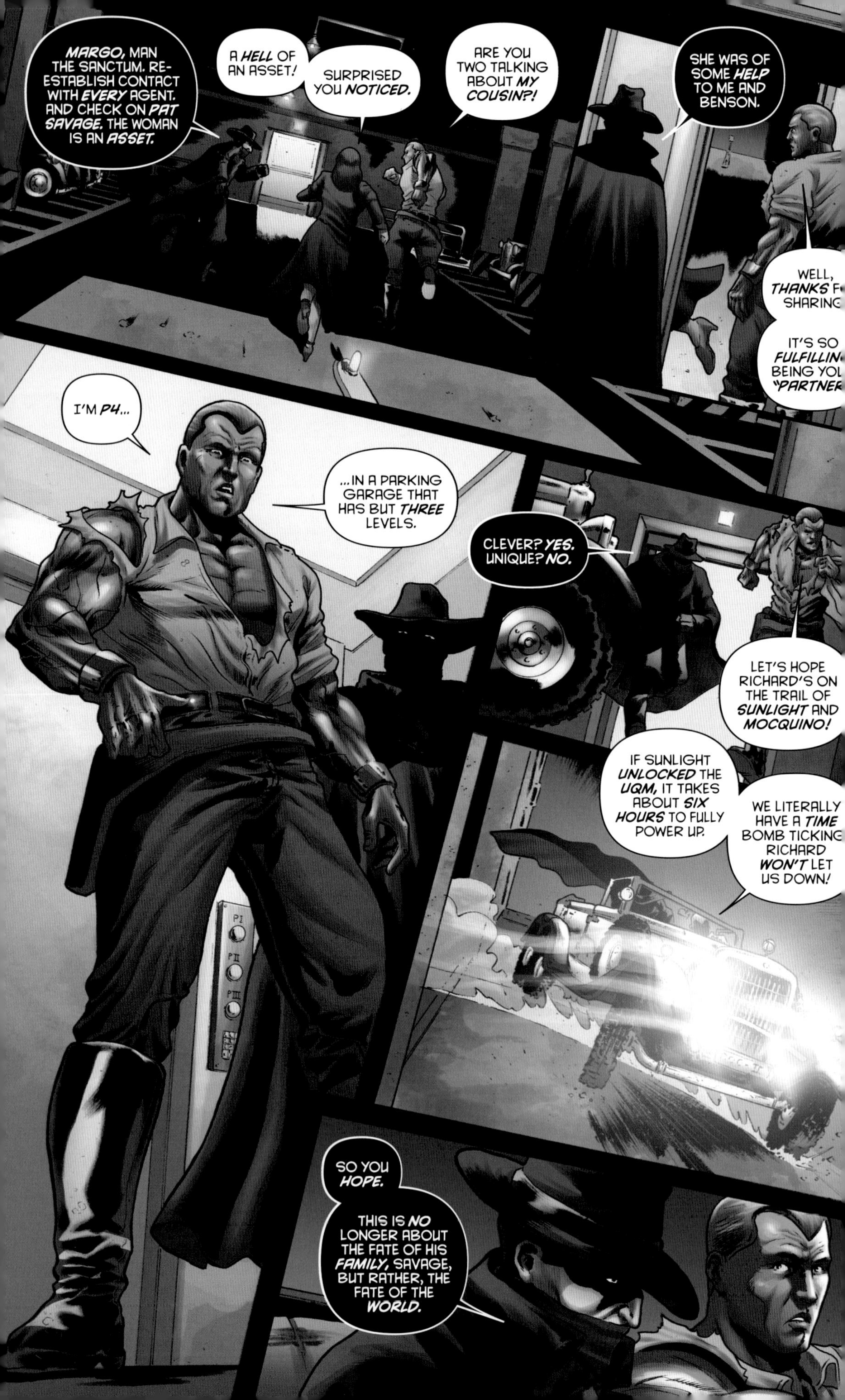
MARGO, MAN THE SANCTUM. RE-ESTABLISH CONTACT WITH EVERY AGENT. AND CHECK ON PAT SAVAGE. THE WOMAN IS AN ASSET.
A HELL OF AN ASSET!
SURPRISED YOU NOTICED.
ARE YOU TWO TALKING ABOUT MY COUSIN?!
SHE WAS OF SOME HELP TO ME AND BENSON.
WELL, THANKS F
SHARING
IT'S SO FULFILLIN
BEING YOU
"PARTNER
I'M P4...
...IN A PARKING GARAGE THAT HAS BUT THREE LEVELS.
CLEVER? YES. UNIQUE? NO.
LET'S HOPE RICHARD'S ON THE TRAIL OF SUNLIGHT AND MOCQUINO!
IF SUNLIGHT UNLOCKED THE UQM, IT TAKES ABOUT SIX HOURS TO FULLY POWER UP.
WE LITERALLY HAVE A TIME BOMB TICKING
RICHARD WON'T LET US DOWN!
SO YOU HOPE.
THIS IS NO LONGER ABOUT THE FATE OF HIS FAMILY, SAVAGE, BUT RATHER, THE FATE OF THE WORLD.
PI
PII
PIII

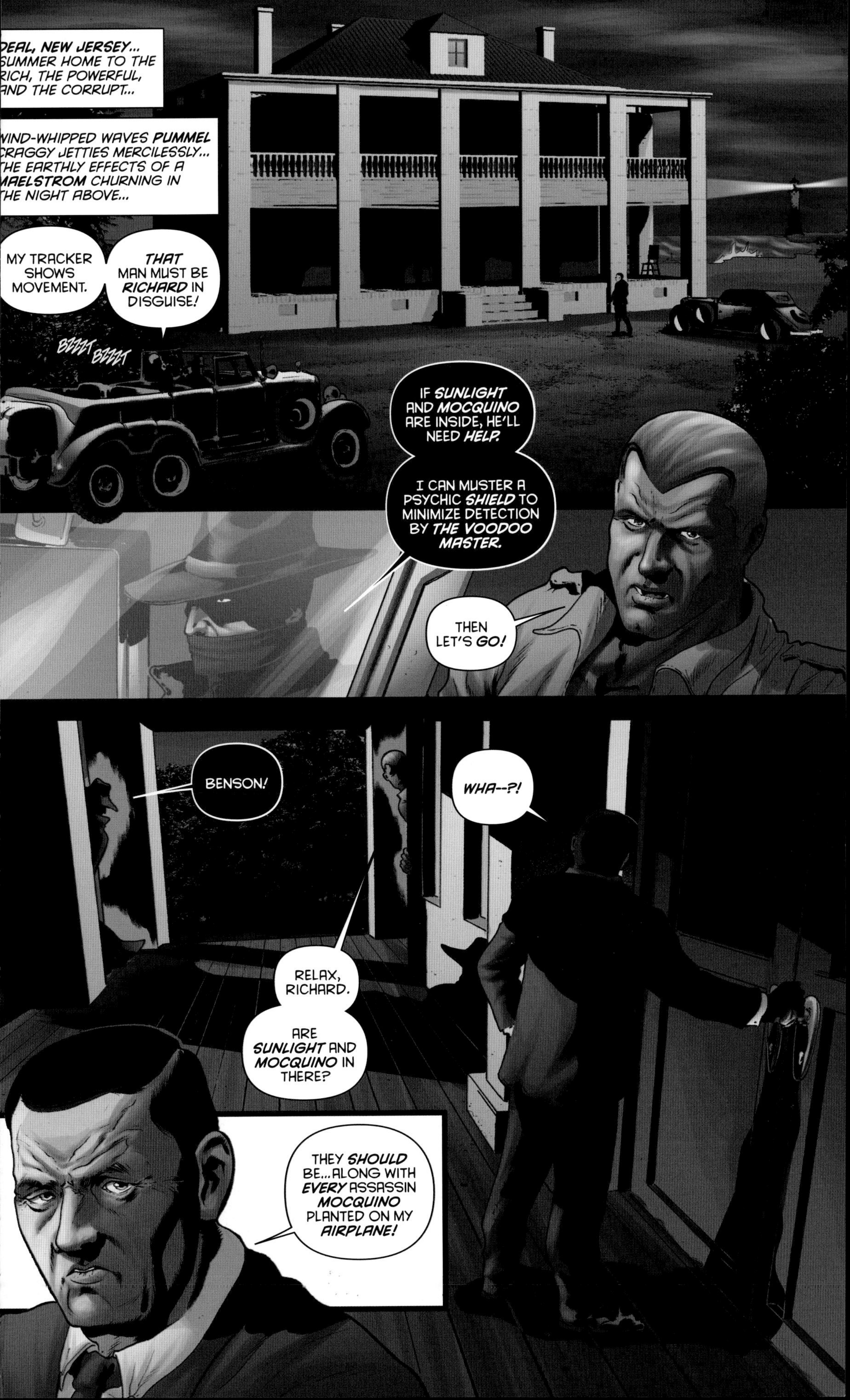
DEAL, NEW JERSEY... SUMMER HOME TO THE RICH, THE POWERFUL, AND THE CORRUPT...
WIND-WHIPPED WAVES PUMMEL CRAGGY JETTIES MERCILESSLY... THE EARTHLY EFFECTS OF A MAELSTROM CHURNING IN THE NIGHT ABOVE...
MY TRACKER SHOWS MOVEMENT.
THAT MAN MUST BE RICHARD IN DISGUISE!
BZZZT BZZZT
IF SUNLIGHT AND MOCQUINO ARE INSIDE, HE'LL NEED HELP.
I CAN MUSTER A PSYCHIC SHIELD TO MINIMIZE DETECTION BY THE VOODOO MASTER.
THEN LET'S GO!
BENSON!
WHA--?!
RELAX, RICHARD.
ARE SUNLIGHT AND MOCQUINO IN THERE?
THEY SHOULD BE...ALONG WITH EVERY ASSASSIN MOCQUINO PLANTED ON MY AIRPLANE!

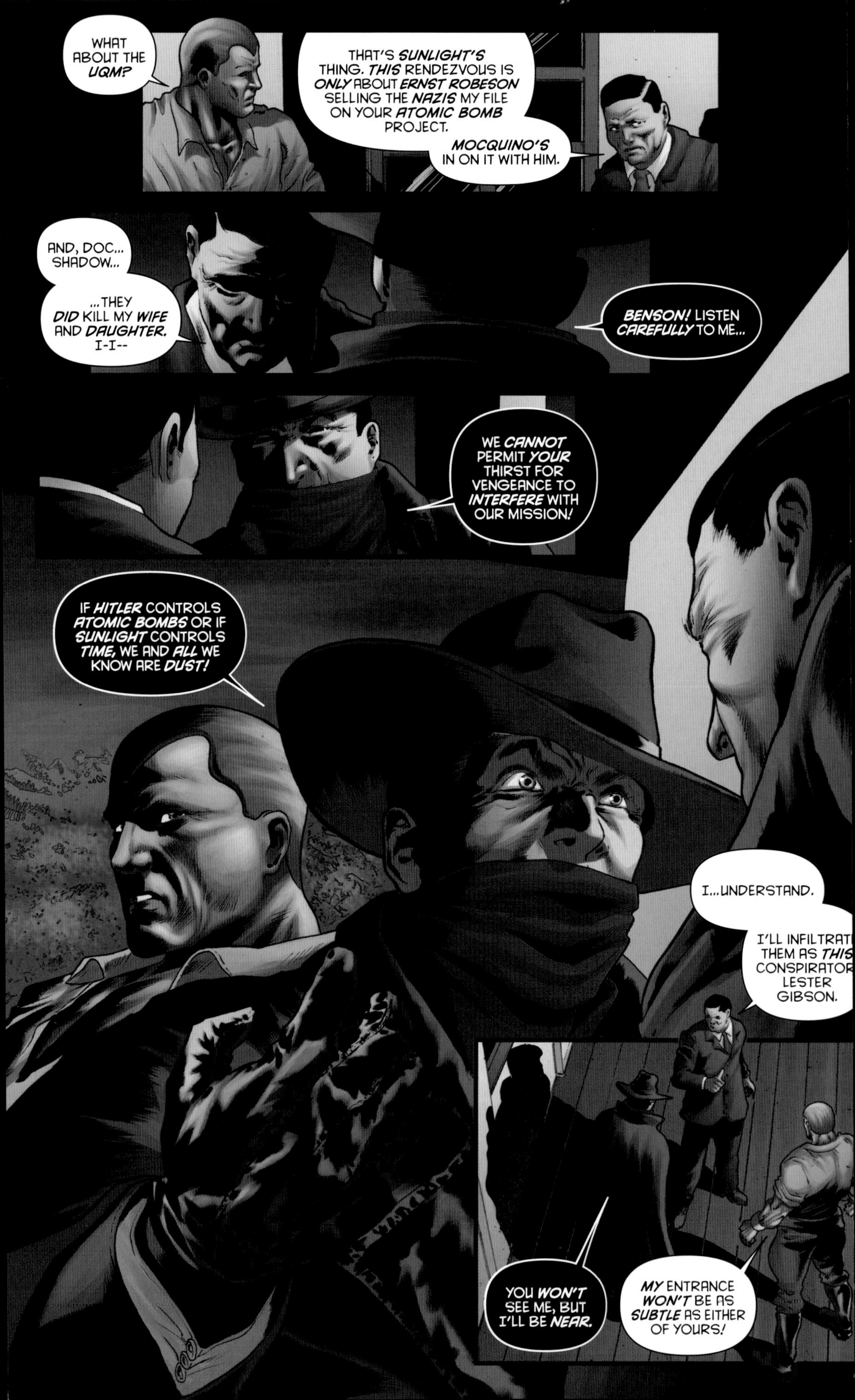
WHAT ABOUT THE UQM?
THAT'S SUNLIGHT'S THING. THIS RENDEZVOUS IS ONLY ABOUT ERNST ROBESON SELLING THE NAZIS MY FILE ON YOUR ATOMIC BOMB PROJECT.
MOCQUINO'S IN ON IT WITH HIM.
AND, DOC... SHADOW...
...THEY DID KILL MY WIFE AND DAUGHTER. I-I--
BENSON! LISTEN CAREFULLY TO ME...
WE CANNOT PERMIT YOUR THIRST FOR VENGEANCE TO INTERFERE WITH OUR MISSION!
IF HITLER CONTROLS ATOMIC BOMBS OR IF SUNLIGHT CONTROLS TIME, WE AND ALL WE KNOW ARE DUST!
I...UNDERSTAND.
I'LL INFILTRAT THEM AS THIS CONSPIRATOR LESTER GIBSON.
YOU WON'T SEE ME, BUT I'LL BE NEAR.
MY ENTRANCE WON'T BE AS SUBTLE AS EITHER OF YOURS!

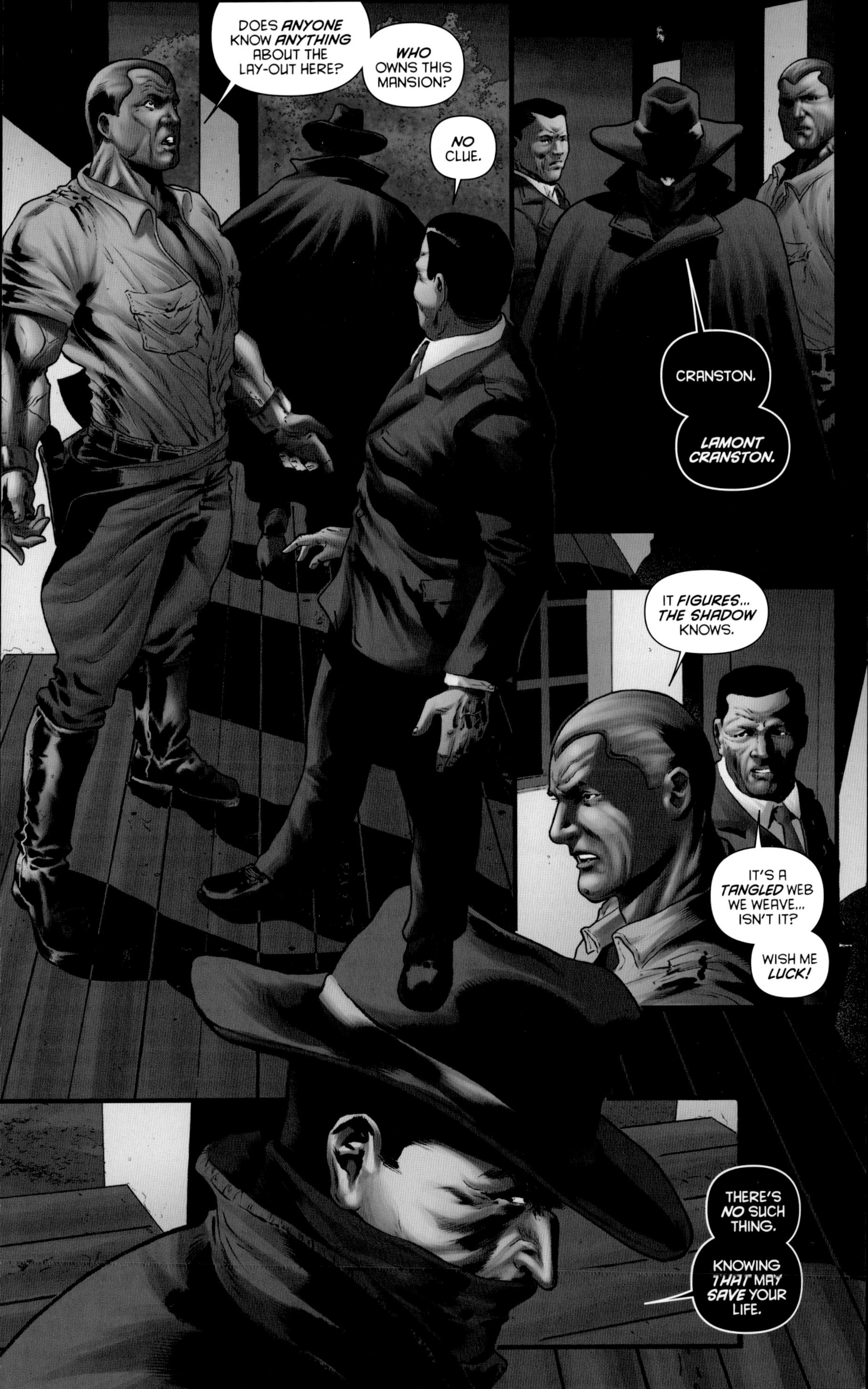
DOES ANYONE KNOW ANYTHING ABOUT THE LAY-OUT HERE?
WHO OWNS THIS MANSION?
NO CLUE.
CRANSTON.
LAMONT CRANSTON.
IT FIGURES... THE SHADOW KNOWS.
IT'S A TANGLED WEB WE WEAVE... ISN'T IT?
WISH ME LUCK!
THERE'S NO SUCH THING.
KNOWING THAT MAY SAVE YOUR LIFE.

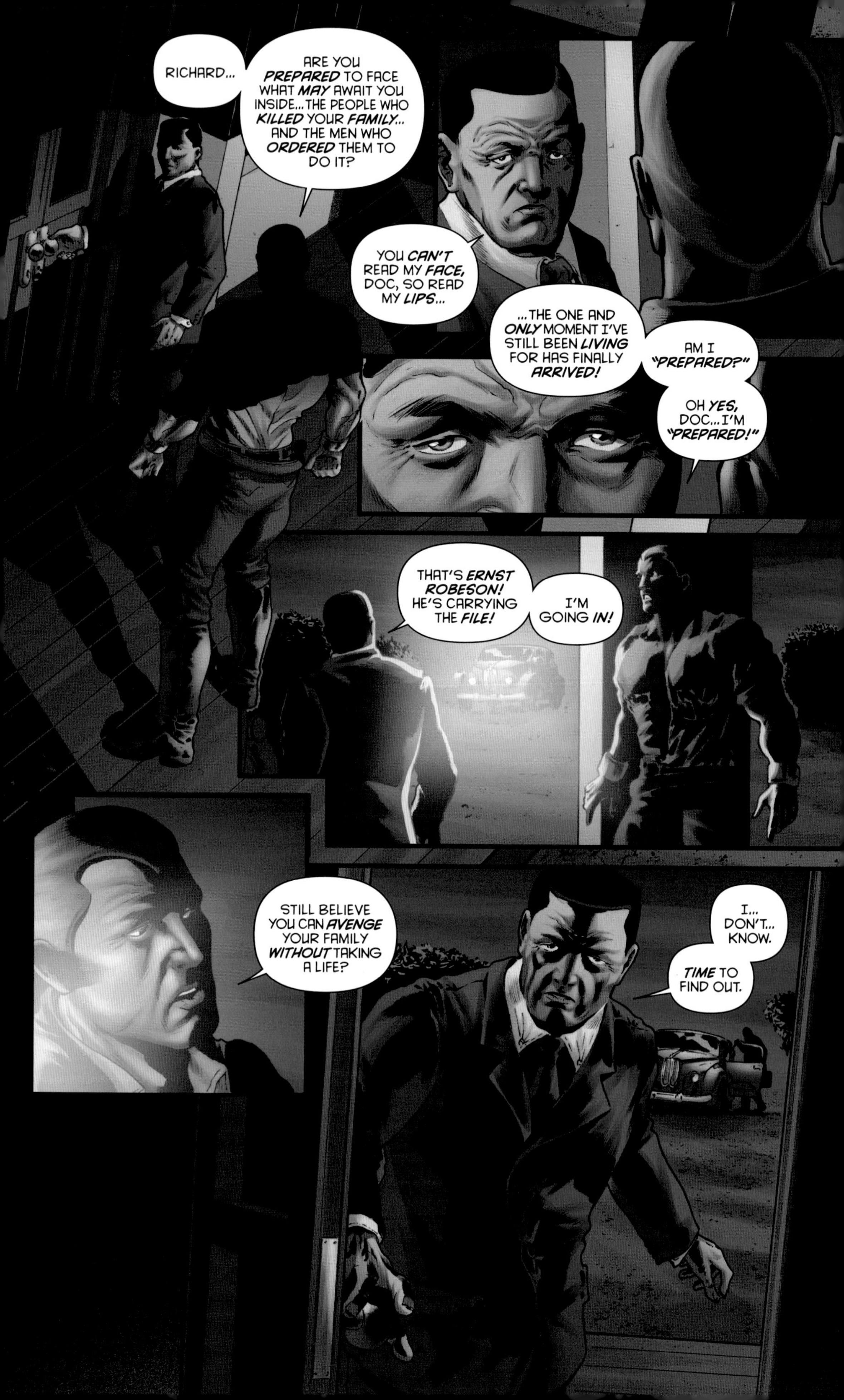
RICHARD...
ARE YOU *PREPARED* TO FACE WHAT *MAY* AWAIT YOU INSIDE...THE PEOPLE WHO *KILLED* YOUR *FAMILY*... AND THE MEN WHO *ORDERED* THEM TO DO IT?
YOU *CAN'T* READ MY *FACE,* DOC, SO READ MY *LIPS*...
...THE ONE AND *ONLY* MOMENT I'VE STILL BEEN *LIVING* FOR HAS FINALLY *ARRIVED!*
AM I *"PREPARED?"*
OH *YES,* DOC...I'M *"PREPARED!"*
THAT'S *ERNST ROBESON!* HE'S CARRYING THE *FILE!*
I'M GOING *IN!*
STILL BELIEVE YOU CAN *AVENGE* YOUR FAMILY *WITHOUT* TAKING A LIFE?
I... DON'T... KNOW.
TIME TO FIND OUT.

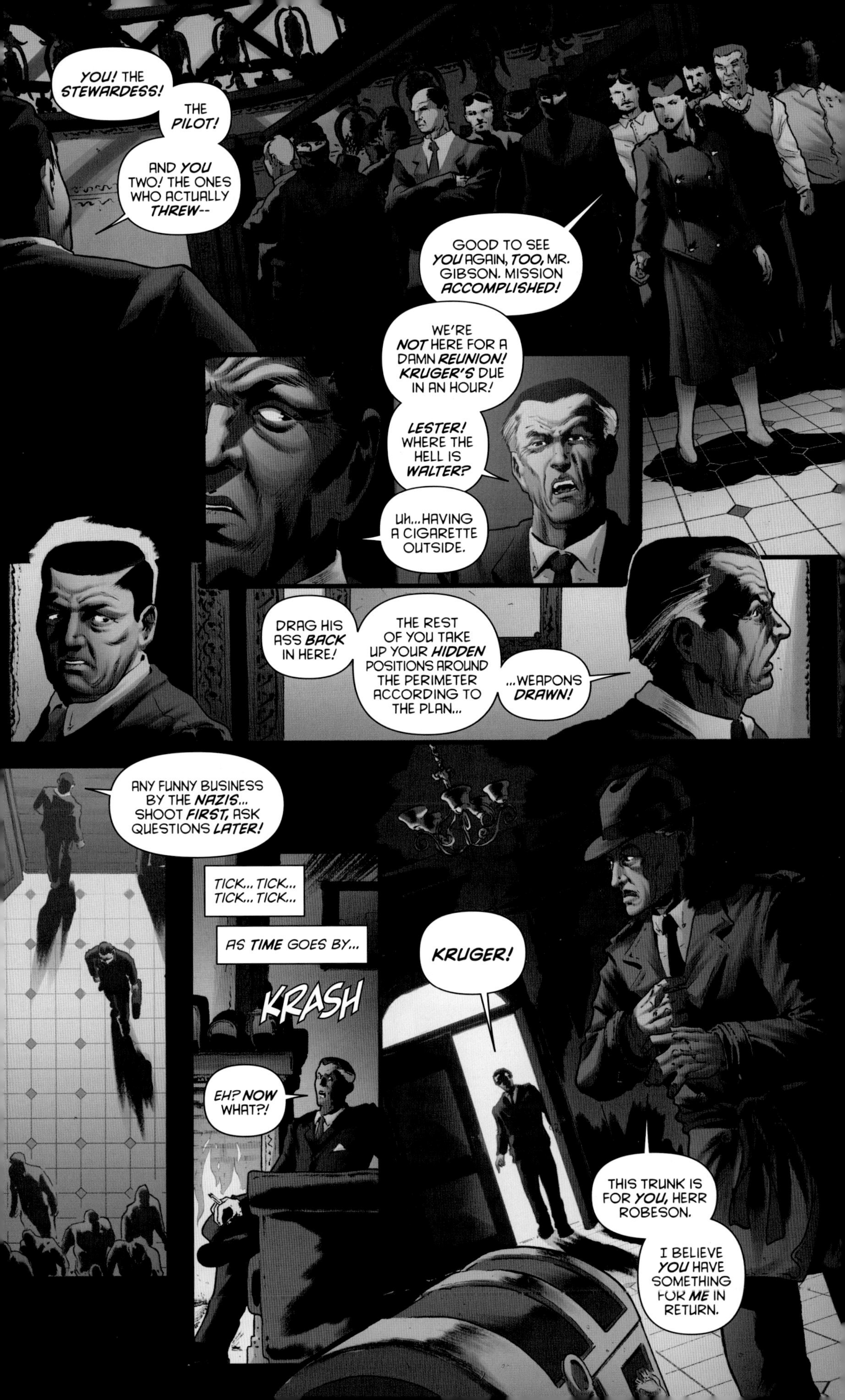
YOU! THE STEWARDESS!
THE PILOT!
AND YOU TWO! THE ONES WHO ACTUALLY THREW--
GOOD TO SEE YOU AGAIN, TOO, MR. GIBSON. MISSION ACCOMPLISHED!
WE'RE NOT HERE FOR A DAMN REUNION! KRUGER'S DUE IN AN HOUR!
LESTER! WHERE THE HELL IS WALTER?
UH...HAVING A CIGARETTE OUTSIDE.
DRAG HIS ASS BACK IN HERE!
THE REST OF YOU TAKE UP YOUR HIDDEN POSITIONS AROUND THE PERIMETER ACCORDING TO THE PLAN...
...WEAPONS DRAWN!
ANY FUNNY BUSINESS BY THE NAZIS... SHOOT FIRST, ASK QUESTIONS LATER!
TICK...TICK... TICK...TICK...
AS TIME GOES BY...
KRASH
EH? NOW WHAT?!
KRUGER!
THIS TRUNK IS FOR YOU, HERR ROBESON.
I BELIEVE YOU HAVE SOMETHING FOR ME IN RETURN.

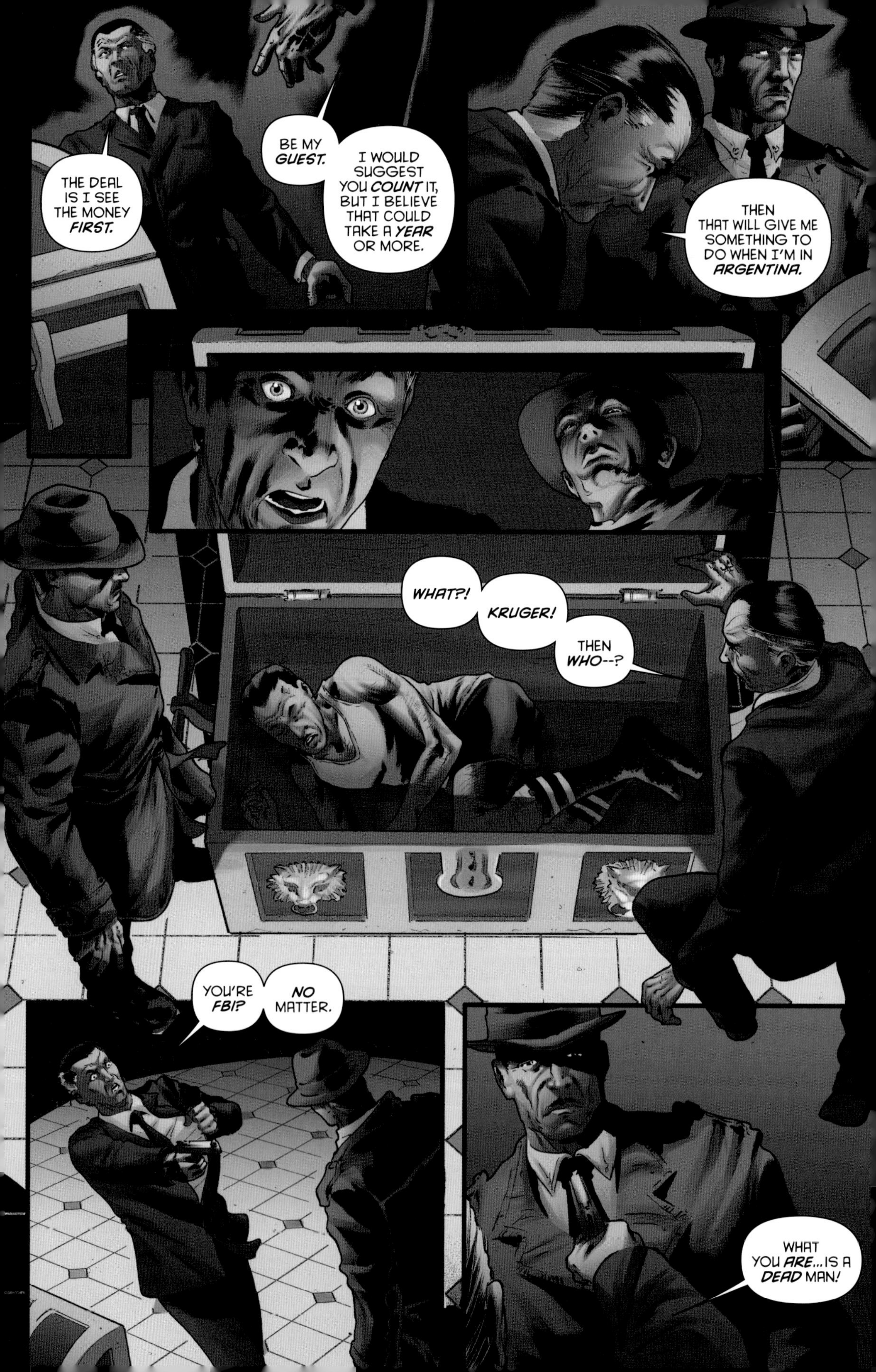
THE DEAL IS I SEE THE MONEY *FIRST.*
BE MY *GUEST.*
I WOULD SUGGEST YOU *COUNT* IT, BUT I BELIEVE THAT COULD TAKE A *YEAR* OR MORE.
THEN THAT WILL GIVE ME SOMETHING TO DO WHEN I'M IN *ARGENTINA.*
WHAT?!
KRUGER!
THEN *WHO--?*
YOU'RE *FBI?*
NO MATTER.
WHAT YOU *ARE*...IS A *DEAD* MAN!

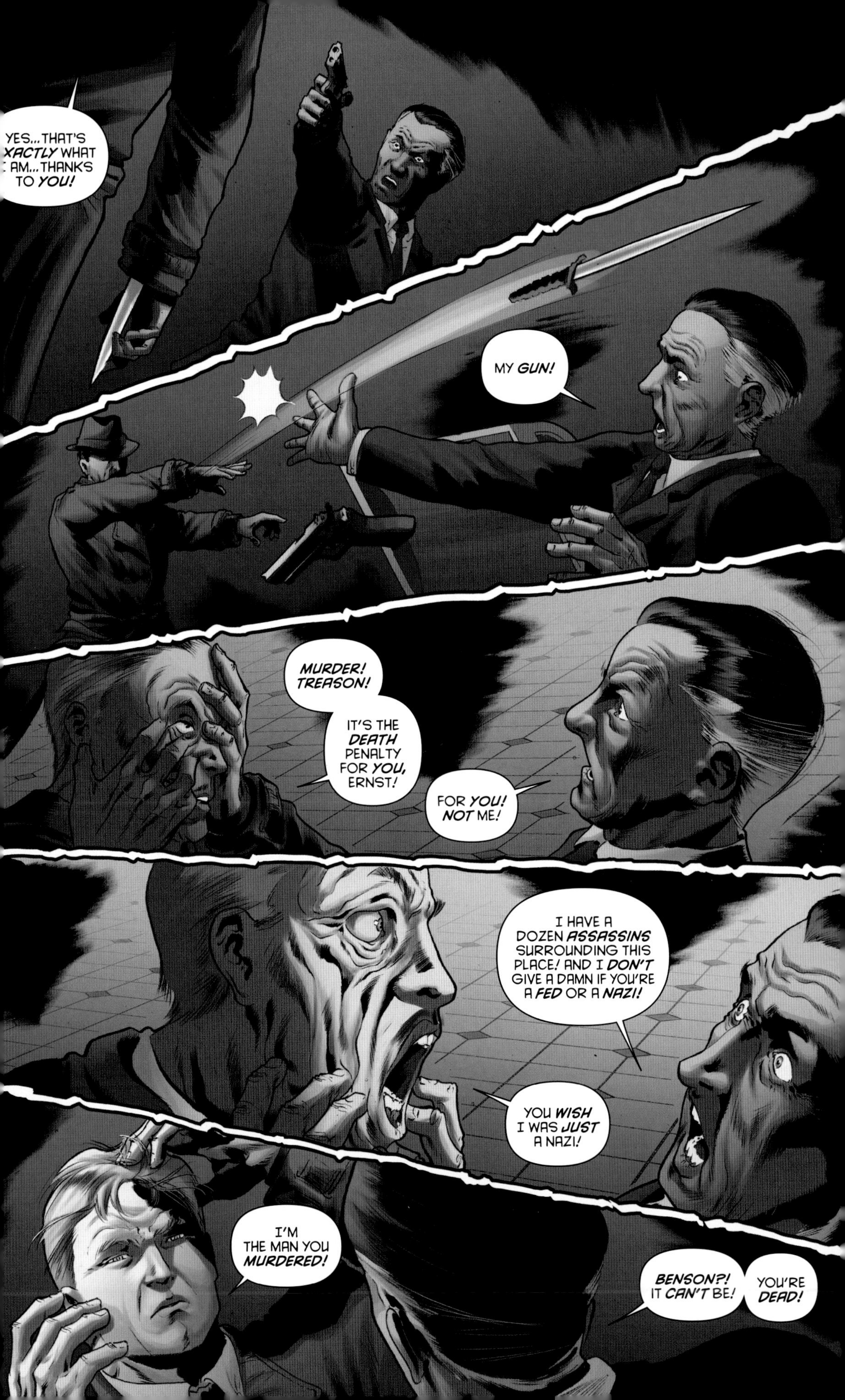
YES... THAT'S XACTLY WHAT I AM... THANKS TO YOU!
MY GUN!
MURDER! TREASON!
IT'S THE DEATH PENALTY FOR YOU, ERNST!
FOR YOU! NOT ME!
I HAVE A DOZEN ASSASSINS SURROUNDING THIS PLACE! AND I DON'T GIVE A DAMN IF YOU'RE A FED OR A NAZI!
YOU WISH I WAS JUST A NAZI!
I'M THE MAN YOU MURDERED!
BENSON?! IT CAN'T BE!
YOU'RE DEAD!

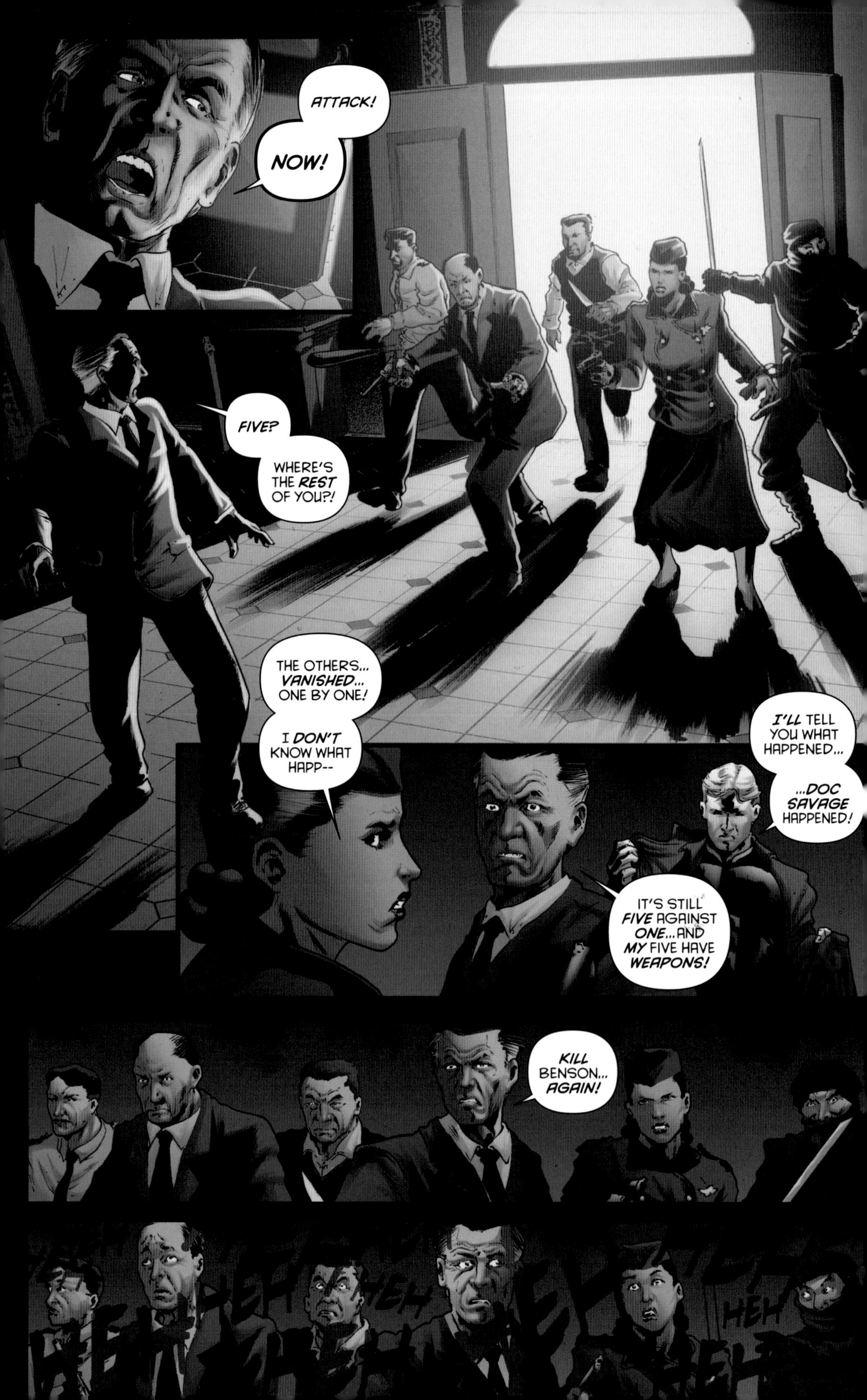
ATTACK!
NOW!
FIVE?
WHERE'S THE REST OF YOU?!
THE OTHERS... VANISHED... ONE BY ONE!
I DON'T KNOW WHAT HAPP--
I'LL TELL YOU WHAT HAPPENED...
...DOC SAVAGE HAPPENED!
IT'S STILL FIVE AGAINST ONE...AND MY FIVE HAVE WEAPONS!
KILL BENSON... AGAIN!
HEH HEH HEH

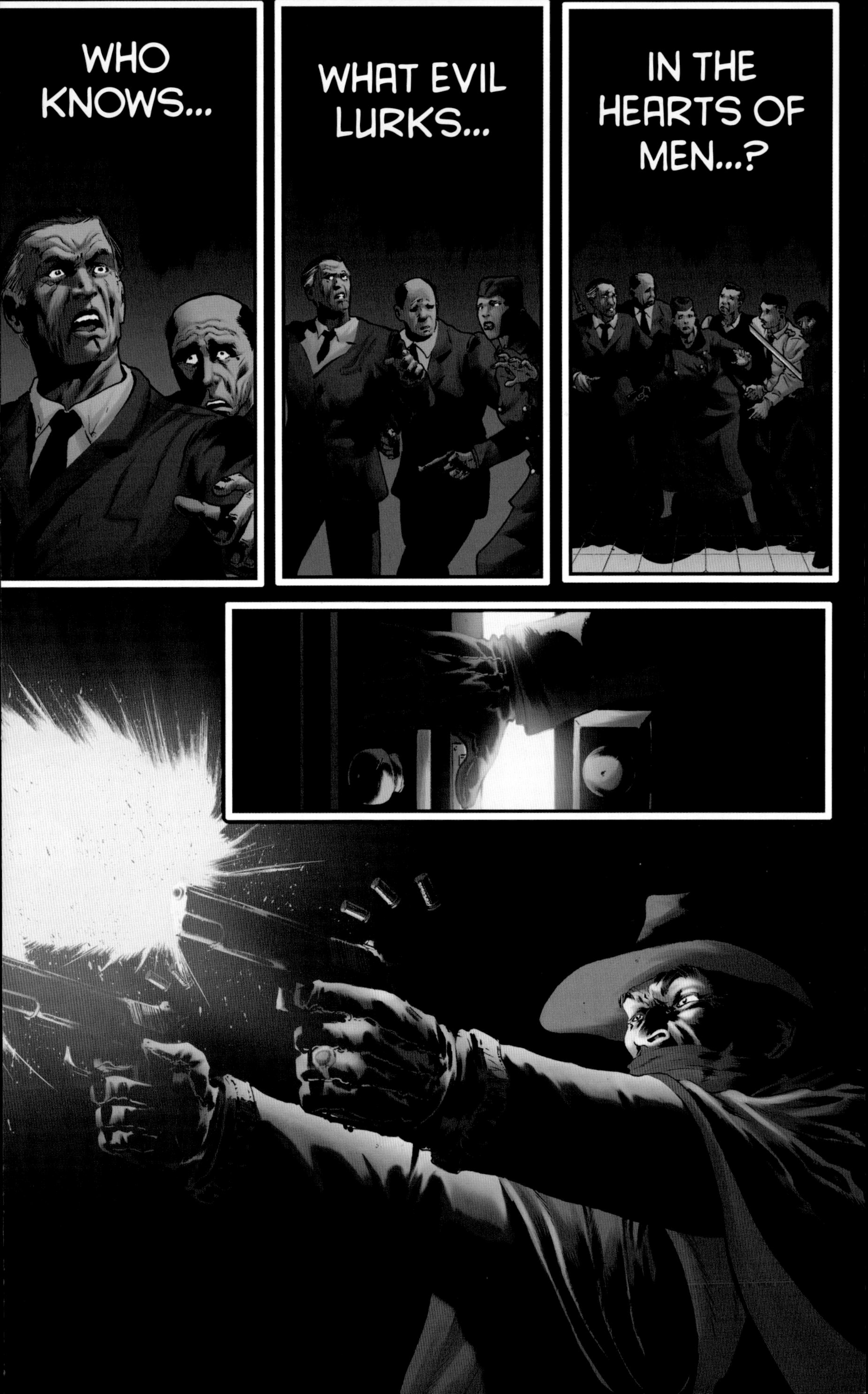
WHO KNOWS...
WHAT EVIL LURKS...
IN THE HEARTS OF MEN...?

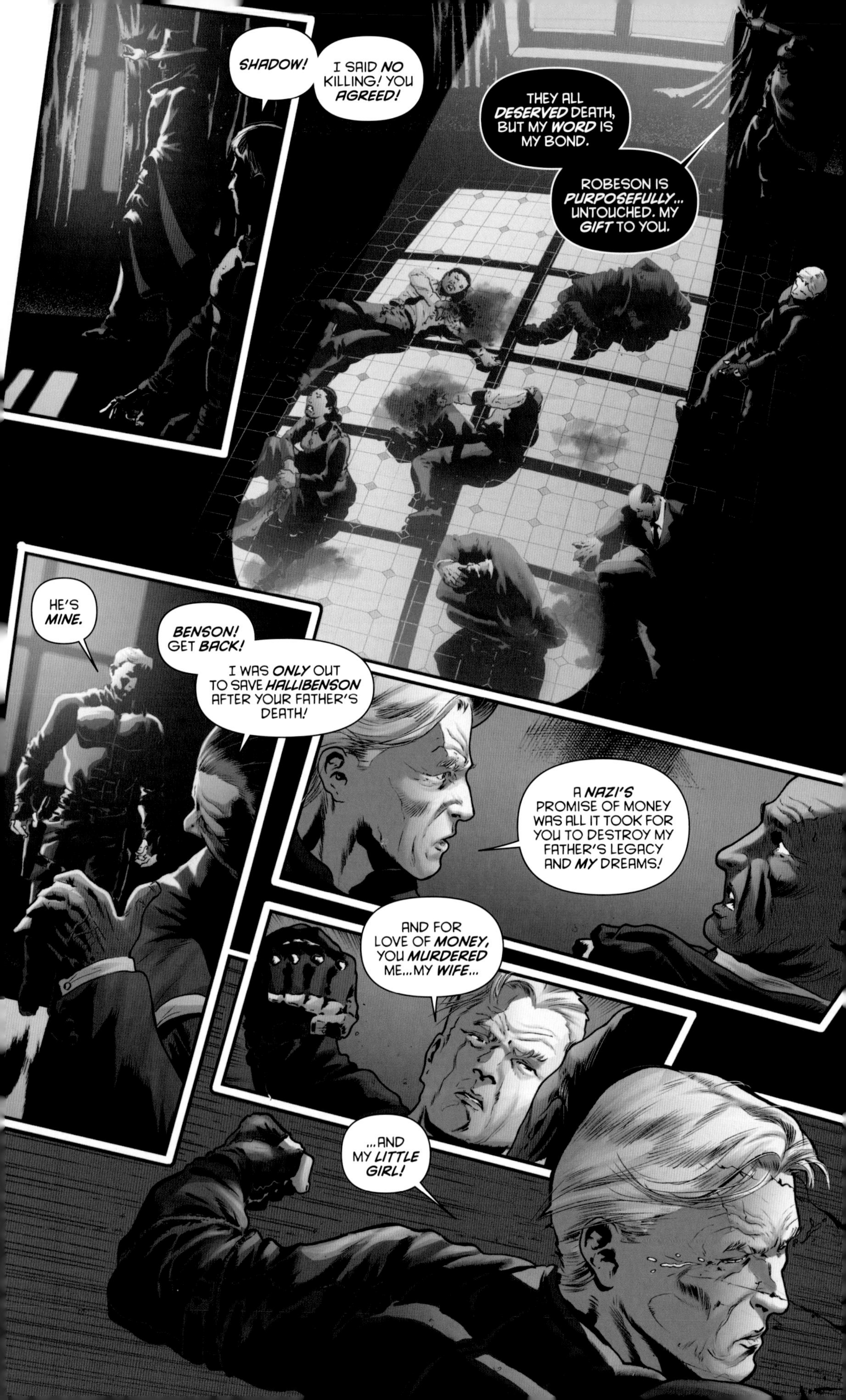
SHADOW!
I SAID NO KILLING! YOU AGREED!
THEY ALL DESERVED DEATH, BUT MY WORD IS MY BOND.
ROBESON IS PURPOSEFULLY... UNTOUCHED. MY GIFT TO YOU.
HE'S MINE.
BENSON! GET BACK!
I WAS ONLY OUT TO SAVE HALLIBENSON AFTER YOUR FATHER'S DEATH!
A NAZI'S PROMISE OF MONEY WAS ALL IT TOOK FOR YOU TO DESTROY MY FATHER'S LEGACY AND MY DREAMS!
AND FOR LOVE OF MONEY, YOU MURDERED ME...MY WIFE...
...AND MY LITTLE GIRL!

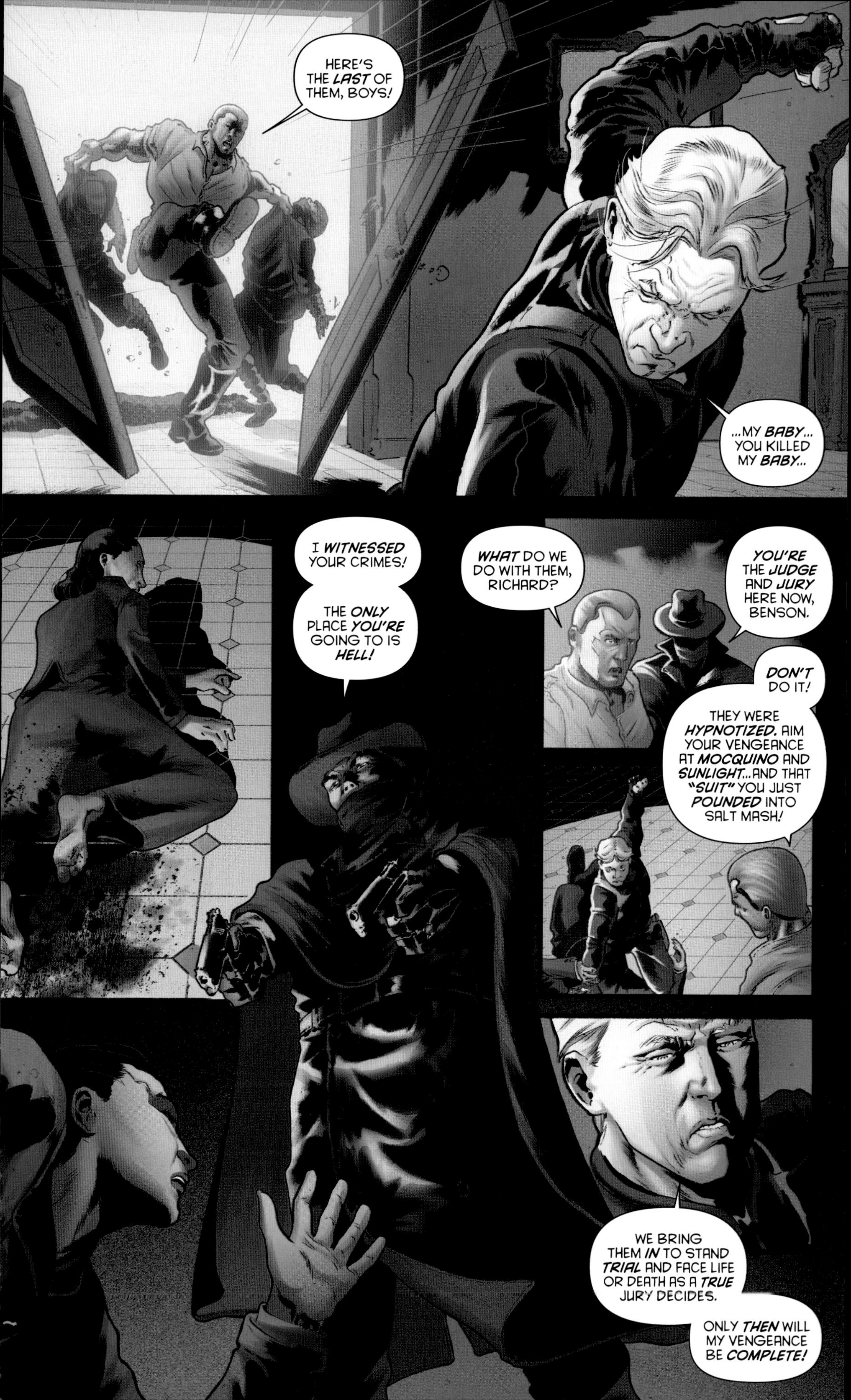
HERE'S THE LAST OF THEM, BOYS!
...MY BABY... YOU KILLED MY BABY...
I WITNESSED YOUR CRIMES!
THE ONLY PLACE YOU'RE GOING TO IS HELL!
WHAT DO WE DO WITH THEM, RICHARD?
YOU'RE THE JUDGE AND JURY HERE NOW, BENSON.
DON'T DO IT!
THEY WERE HYPNOTIZED. AIM YOUR VENGEANCE AT MOCQUINO AND SUNLIGHT...AND THAT "SUIT" YOU JUST POUNDED INTO SALT MASH!
WE BRING THEM IN TO STAND TRIAL AND FACE LIFE OR DEATH AS A TRUE JURY DECIDES.
ONLY THEN WILL MY VENGEANCE BE COMPLETE!

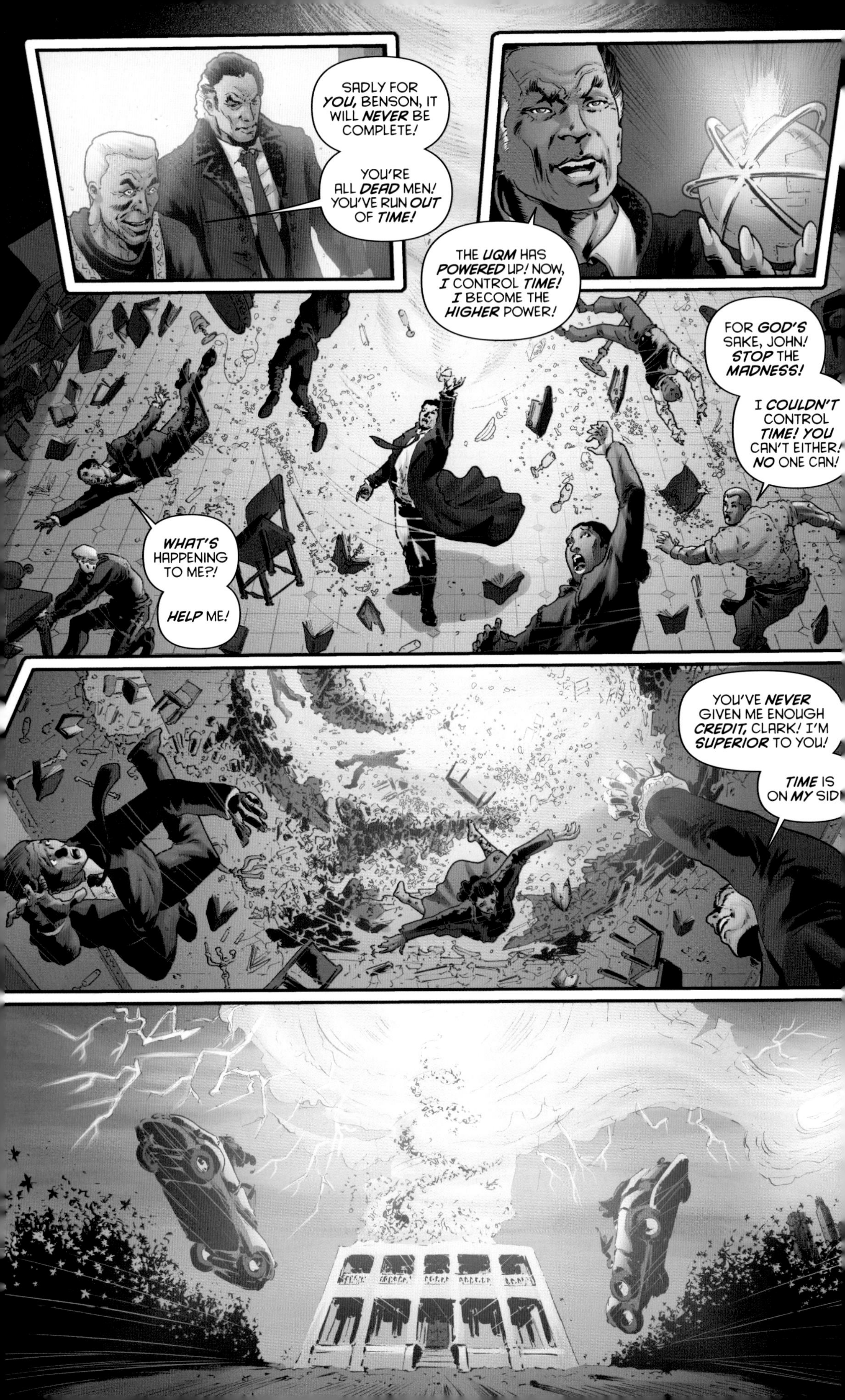
SADLY FOR YOU, BENSON, IT WILL NEVER BE COMPLETE!
YOU'RE ALL DEAD MEN! YOU'VE RUN OUT OF TIME!
THE UQM HAS POWERED UP! NOW, I CONTROL TIME! I BECOME THE HIGHER POWER!
FOR GOD'S SAKE, JOHN! STOP THE MADNESS!
I COULDN'T CONTROL TIME! YOU CAN'T EITHER! NO ONE CAN!
WHAT'S HAPPENING TO ME?!
HELP ME!
YOU'VE NEVER GIVEN ME ENOUGH CREDIT, CLARK! I'M SUPERIOR TO YOU!
TIME IS ON MY SID

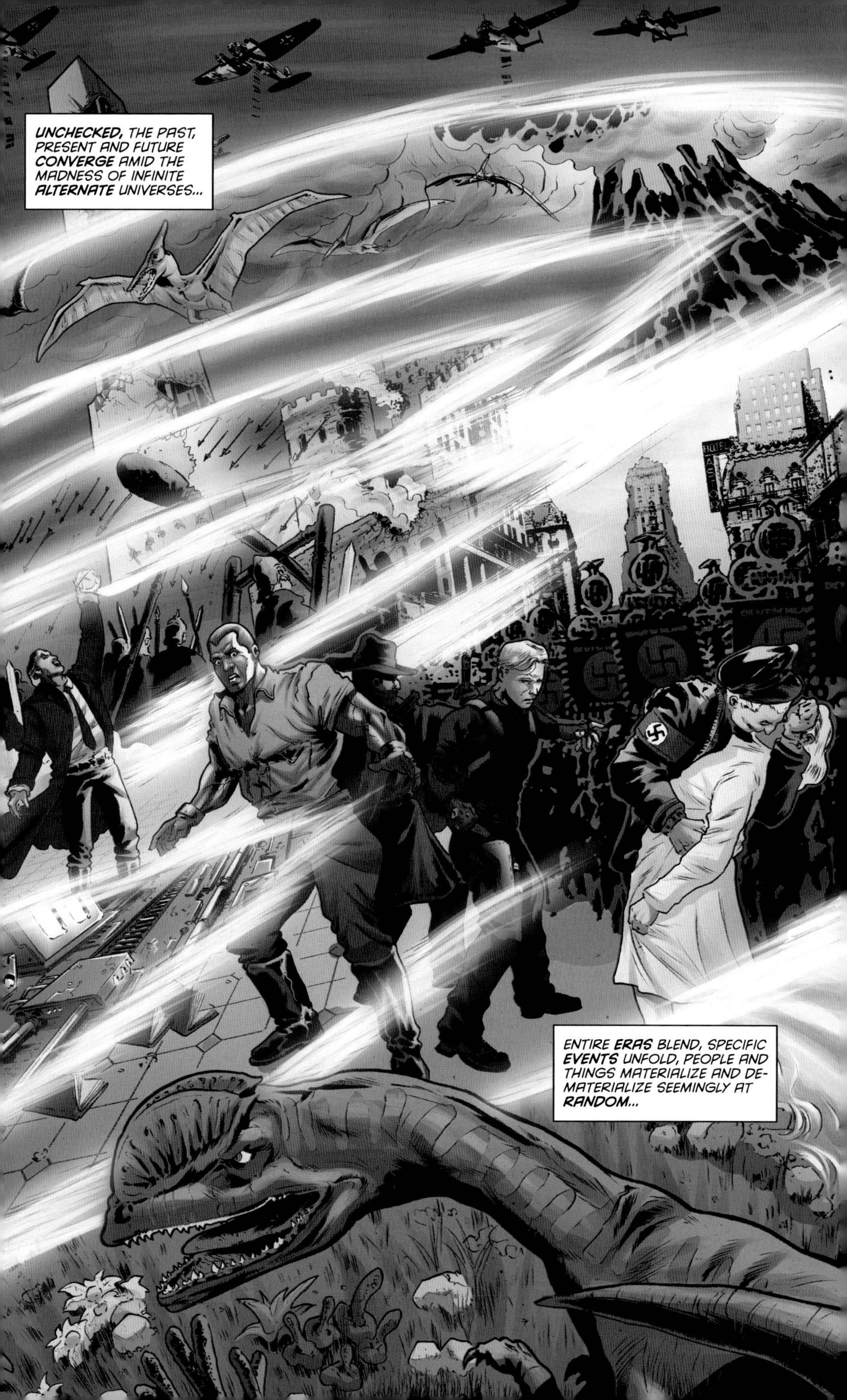
UNCHECKED, THE PAST, PRESENT AND FUTURE CONVERGE AMID THE MADNESS OF INFINITE ALTERNATE UNIVERSES...
ENTIRE ERAS BLEND, SPECIFIC EVENTS UNFOLD, PEOPLE AND THINGS MATERIALIZE AND DE-MATERIALIZE SEEMINGLY AT RANDOM...

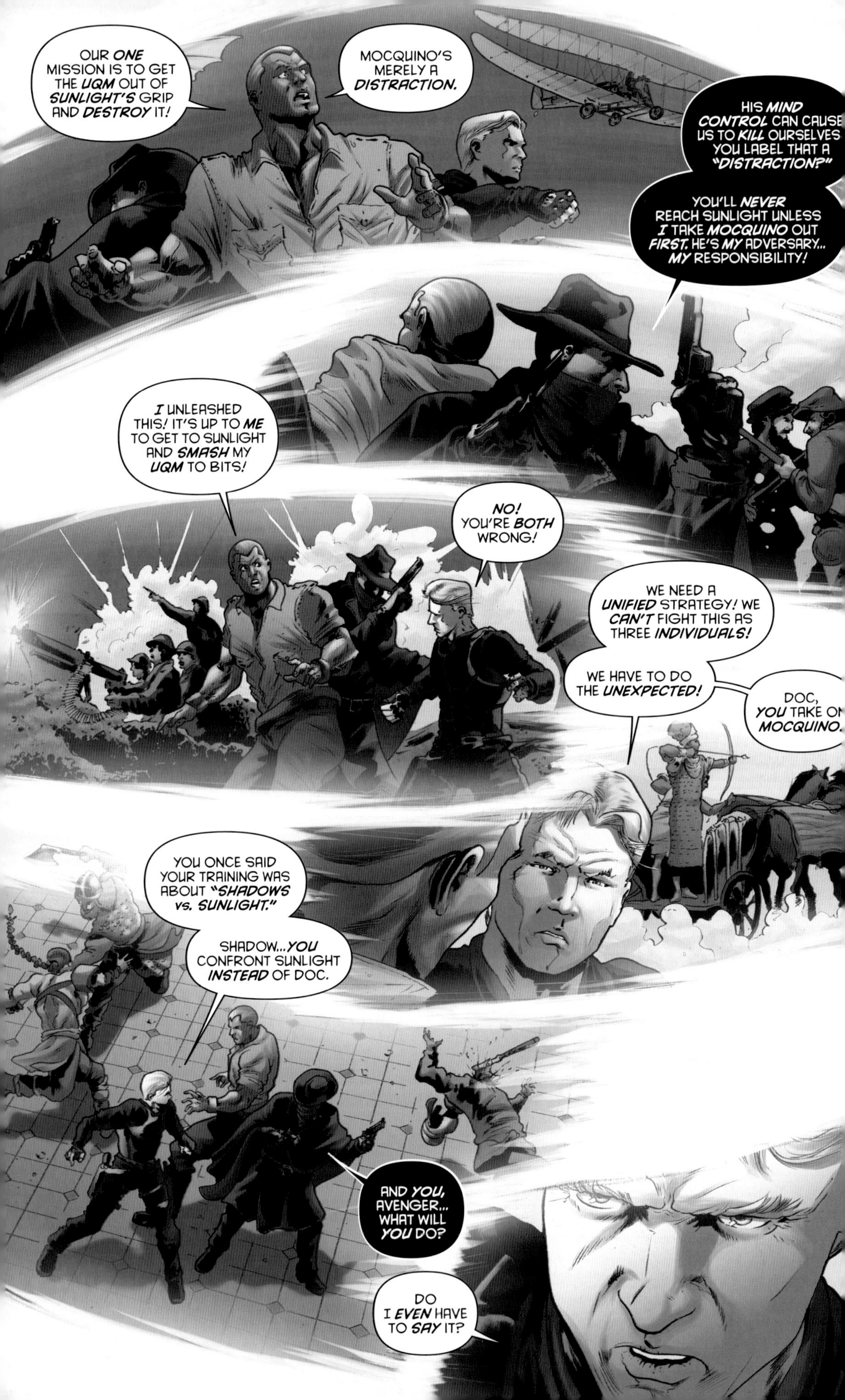
OUR ONE MISSION IS TO GET THE UQM OUT OF SUNLIGHT'S GRIP AND DESTROY IT!
MOCQUINO'S MERELY A DISTRACTION.
HIS MIND CONTROL CAN CAUSE US TO KILL OURSELVES YOU LABEL THAT A "DISTRACTION?"
YOU'LL NEVER REACH SUNLIGHT UNLESS I TAKE MOCQUINO OUT FIRST. HE'S MY ADVERSARY... MY RESPONSIBILITY!
I UNLEASHED THIS! IT'S UP TO ME TO GET TO SUNLIGHT AND SMASH MY UQM TO BITS!
NO! YOU'RE BOTH WRONG!
WE NEED A UNIFIED STRATEGY! WE CAN'T FIGHT THIS AS THREE INDIVIDUALS!
WE HAVE TO DO THE UNEXPECTED!
DOC, YOU TAKE ON MOCQUINO.
YOU ONCE SAID YOUR TRAINING WAS ABOUT "SHADOWS vs. SUNLIGHT."
SHADOW...YOU CONFRONT SUNLIGHT INSTEAD OF DOC.
AND YOU, AVENGER... WHAT WILL YOU DO?
DO I EVEN HAVE TO SAY IT?

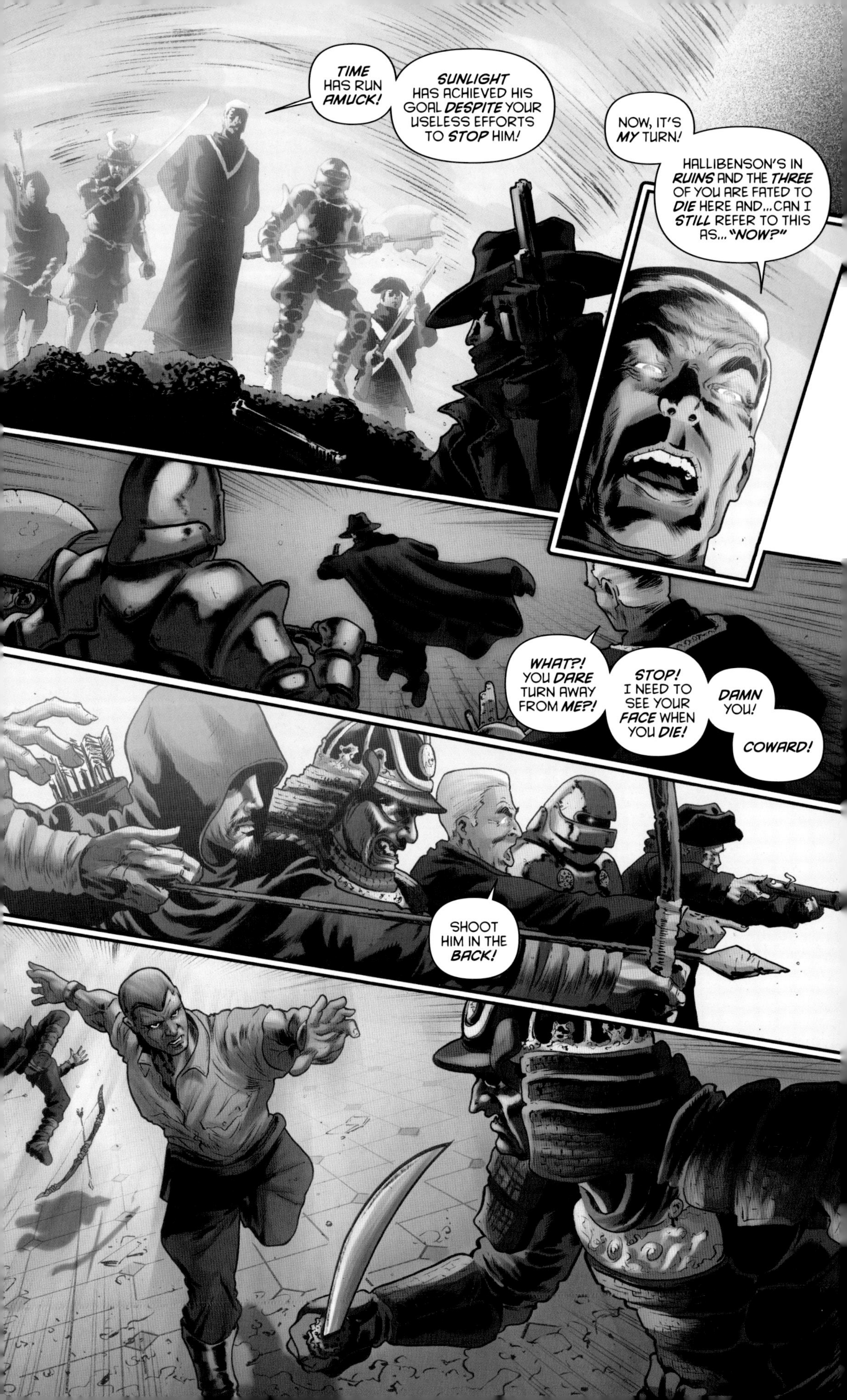
TIME HAS RUN AMUCK!
SUNLIGHT HAS ACHIEVED HIS GOAL DESPITE YOUR USELESS EFFORTS TO STOP HIM!
NOW, IT'S MY TURN!
HALLIBENSON'S IN RUINS AND THE THREE OF YOU ARE FATED TO DIE HERE AND...CAN I STILL REFER TO THIS AS... "NOW?"
WHAT?! YOU DARE TURN AWAY FROM ME?!
STOP! I NEED TO SEE YOUR FACE WHEN YOU DIE!
DAMN YOU!
COWARD!
SHOOT HIM IN THE BACK!

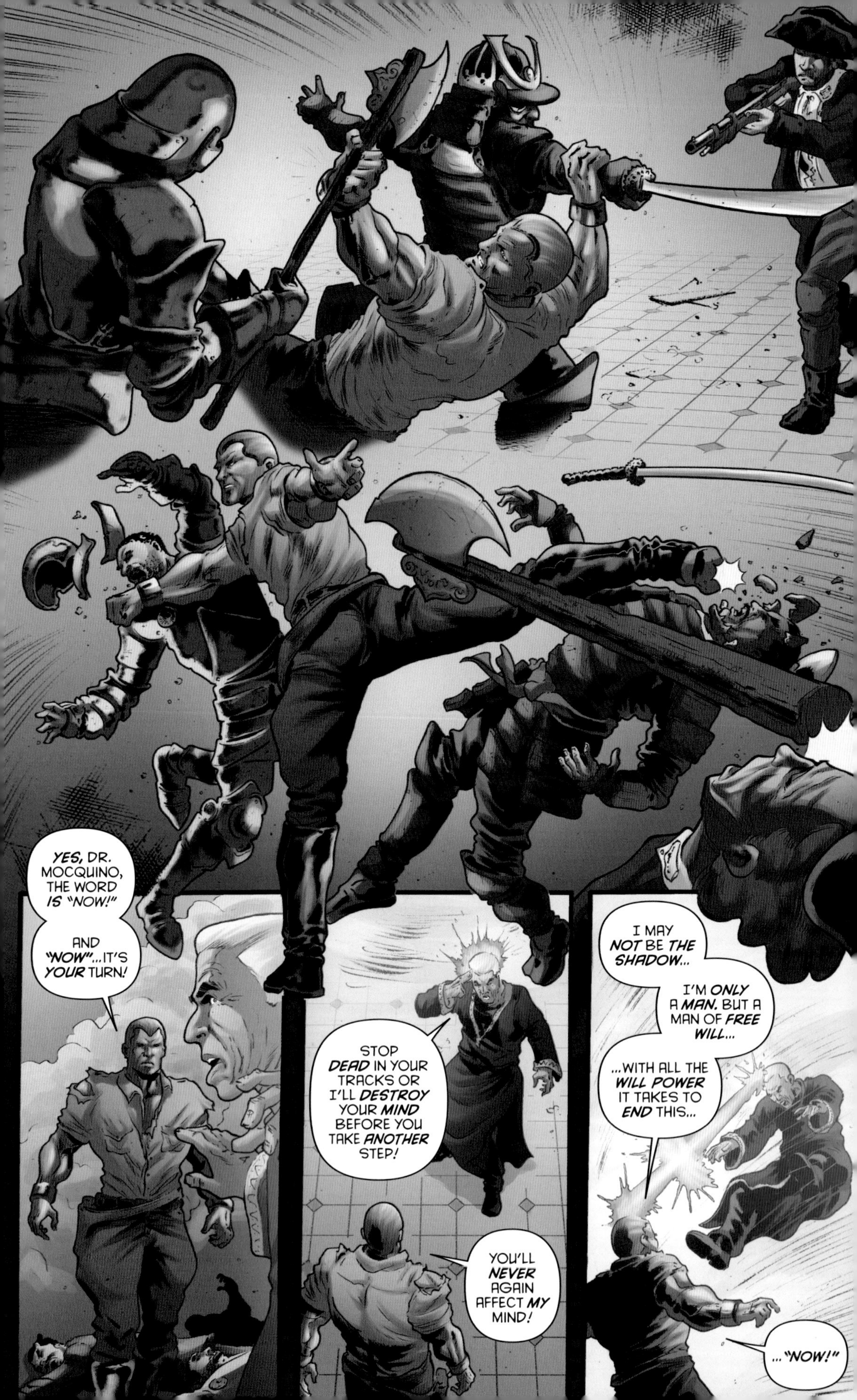

YES, DR. MOCQUINO, THE WORD IS "NOW!"
AND "NOW"... IT'S YOUR TURN!
STOP DEAD IN YOUR TRACKS OR I'LL DESTROY YOUR MIND BEFORE YOU TAKE ANOTHER STEP!
YOU'LL NEVER AGAIN AFFECT MY MIND!
I MAY NOT BE THE SHADOW...
I'M ONLY A MAN. BUT A MAN OF FREE WILL...
...WITH ALL THE WILL POWER IT TAKES TO END THIS...
..."NOW!"

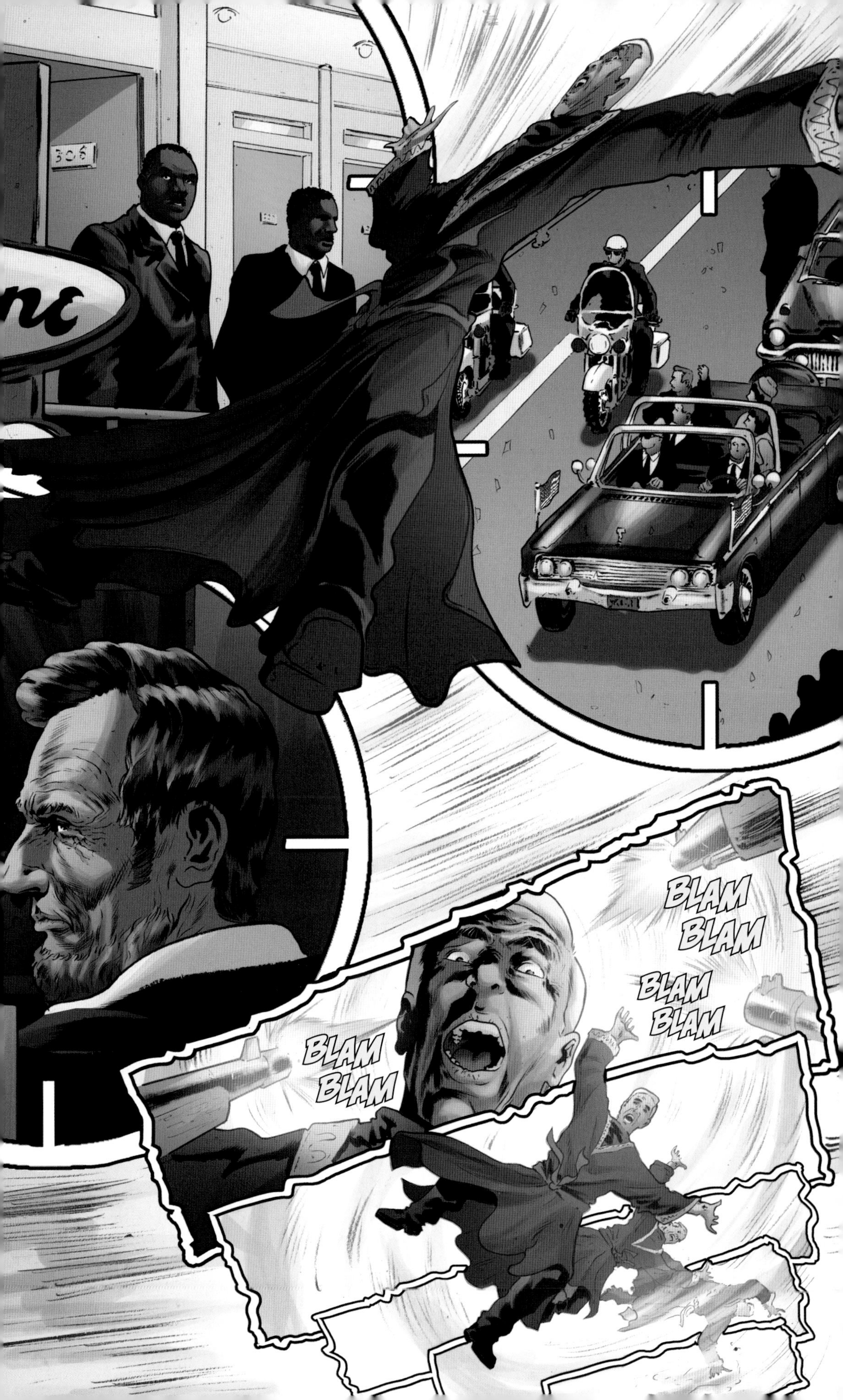

306
BLAM
BLAM
BLAM
BLAM
BLAM
BLAM

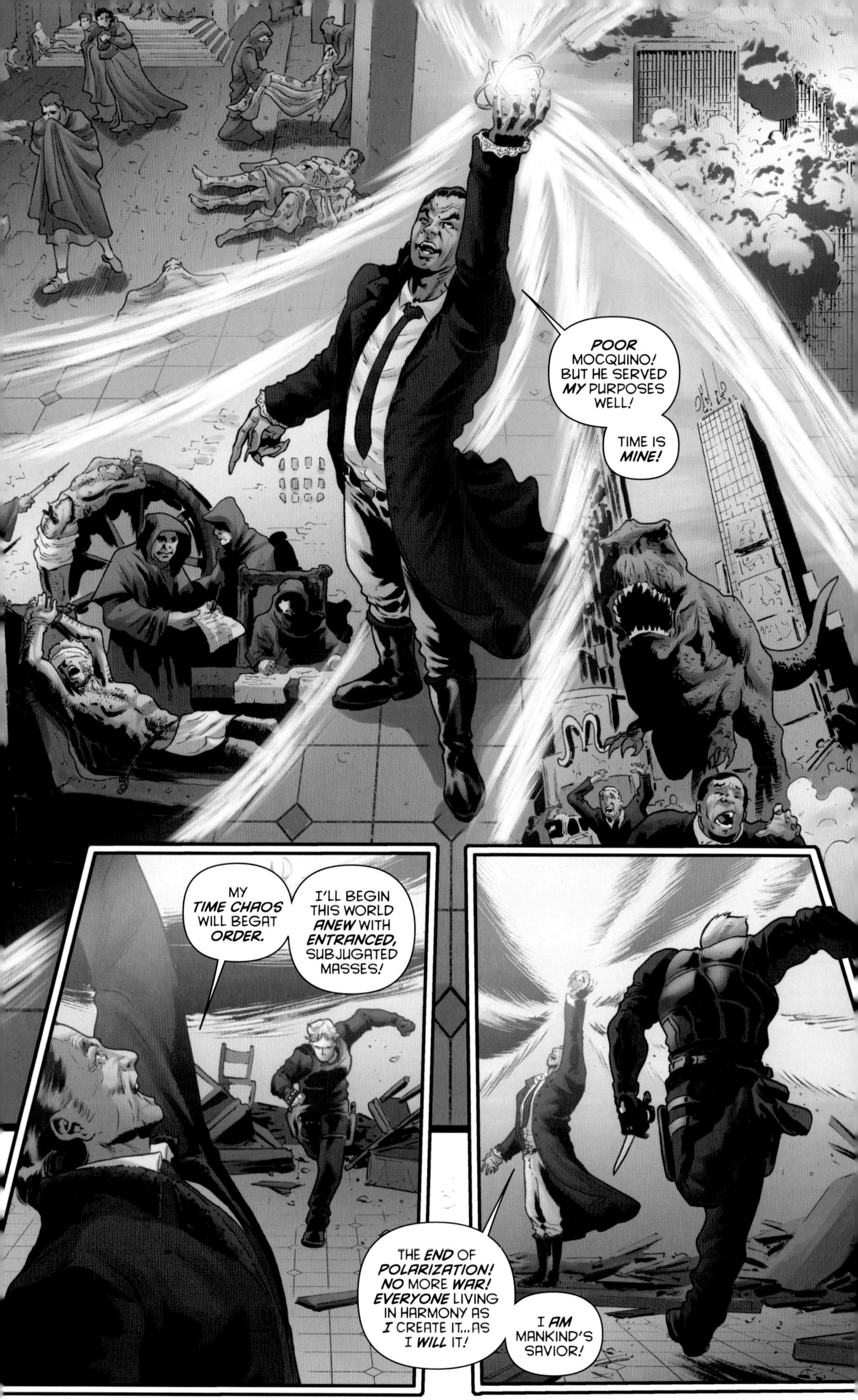
POOR MOCQUINO! BUT HE SERVED MY PURPOSES WELL!
TIME IS MINE!
MY TIME CHAOS WILL BEGAT ORDER.
I'LL BEGIN THIS WORLD ANEW WITH ENTRANCED, SUBJUGATED MASSES!
THE END OF POLARIZATION! NO MORE WAR! EVERYONE LIVING IN HARMONY AS I CREATE IT...AS I WILL IT!
I AM MANKIND'S SAVIOR!

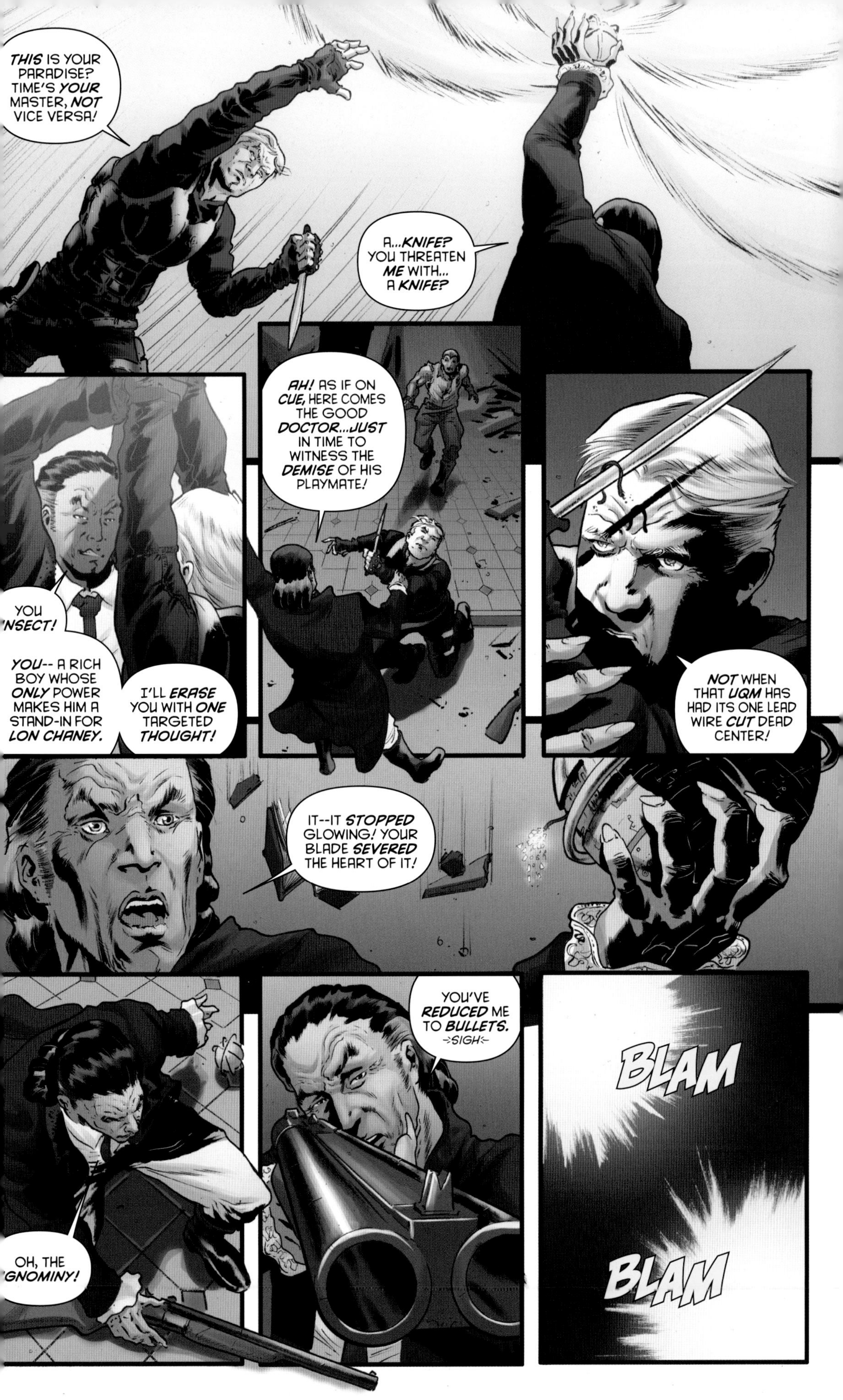

THIS IS YOUR PARADISE? TIME'S YOUR MASTER, NOT VICE VERSA!
A...KNIFE? YOU THREATEN ME WITH... A KNIFE?
YOU 'NSECT!
YOU-- A RICH BOY WHOSE ONLY POWER MAKES HIM A STAND-IN FOR LON CHANEY.
I'LL ERASE YOU WITH ONE TARGETED THOUGHT!
AH! AS IF ON CUE, HERE COMES THE GOOD DOCTOR...JUST IN TIME TO WITNESS THE DEMISE OF HIS PLAYMATE!
NOT WHEN THAT UQM HAS HAD ITS ONE LEAD WIRE CUT DEAD CENTER!
IT--IT STOPPED GLOWING! YOUR BLADE SEVERED THE HEART OF IT!
OH, THE 'GNOMINY!
YOU'VE REDUCED ME TO BULLETS.
SIGH
BLAM
BLAM

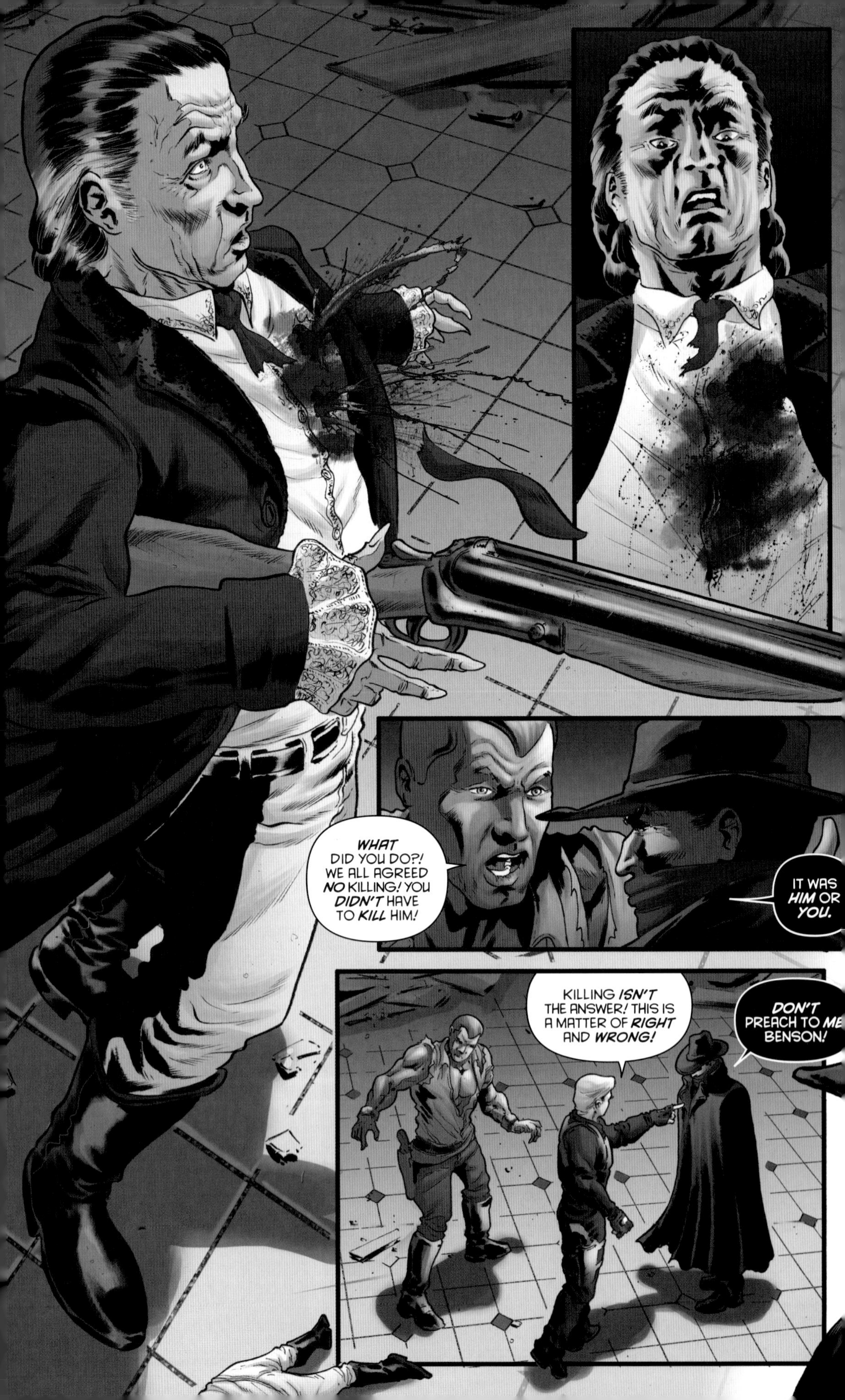

WHAT DID YOU DO?! WE ALL AGREED NO KILLING! YOU DIDN'T HAVE TO KILL HIM!
IT WAS HIM OR YOU.
KILLING ISN'T THE ANSWER! THIS IS A MATTER OF RIGHT AND WRONG!
DON'T PREACH TO ME BENSON!

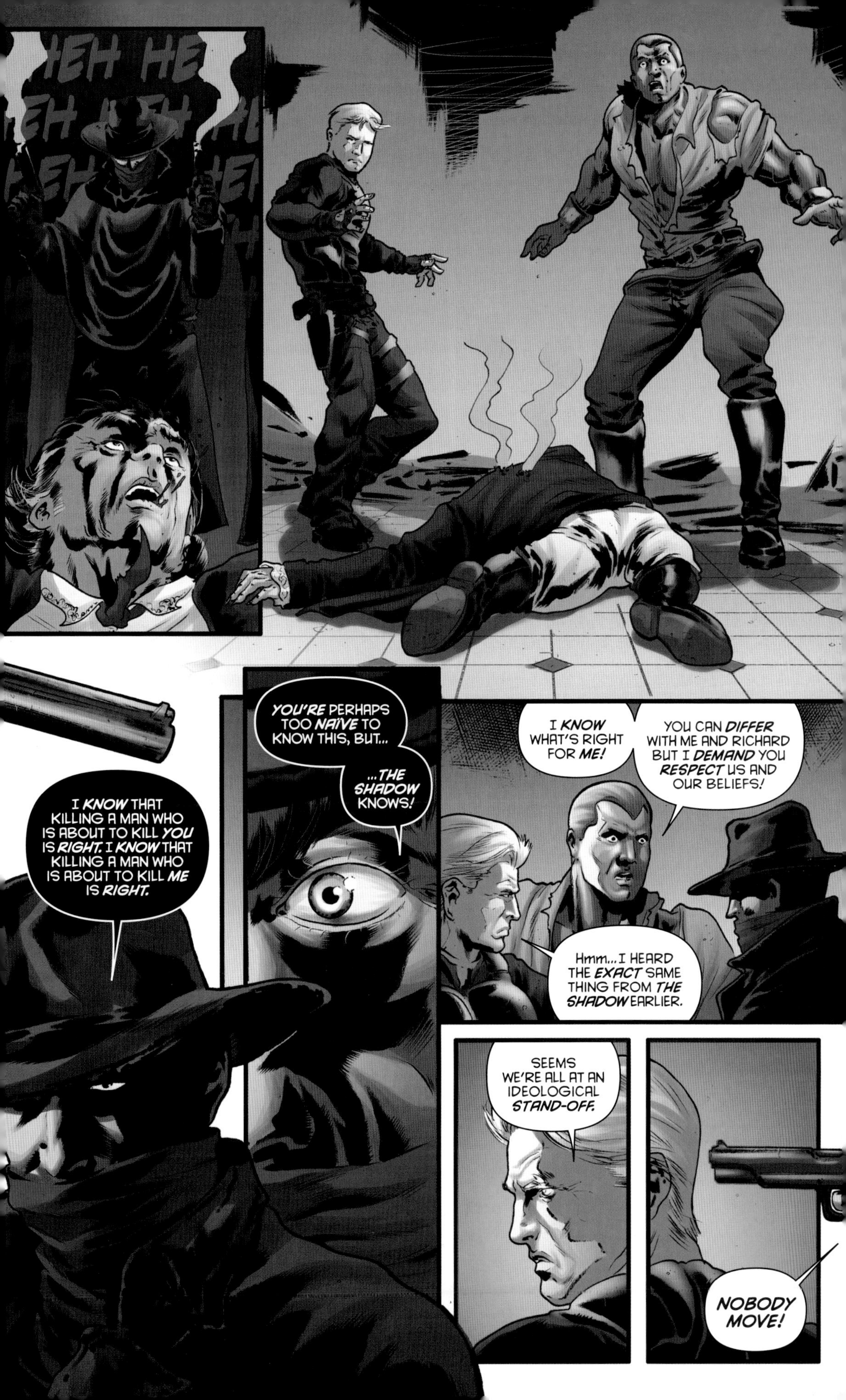
HEH HEH HEH HEH HEH HEH HEH
YOU'RE PERHAPS TOO NAÏVE TO KNOW THIS, BUT...
...THE SHADOW KNOWS!
I KNOW THAT KILLING A MAN WHO IS ABOUT TO KILL YOU IS RIGHT. I KNOW THAT KILLING A MAN WHO IS ABOUT TO KILL ME IS RIGHT.
I KNOW WHAT'S RIGHT FOR ME!
YOU CAN DIFFER WITH ME AND RICHARD BUT I DEMAND YOU RESPECT US AND OUR BELIEFS!
Hmm... I HEARD THE EXACT SAME THING FROM THE SHADOW EARLIER.
SEEMS WE'RE ALL AT AN IDEOLOGICAL STAND-OFF.
NOBODY MOVE!

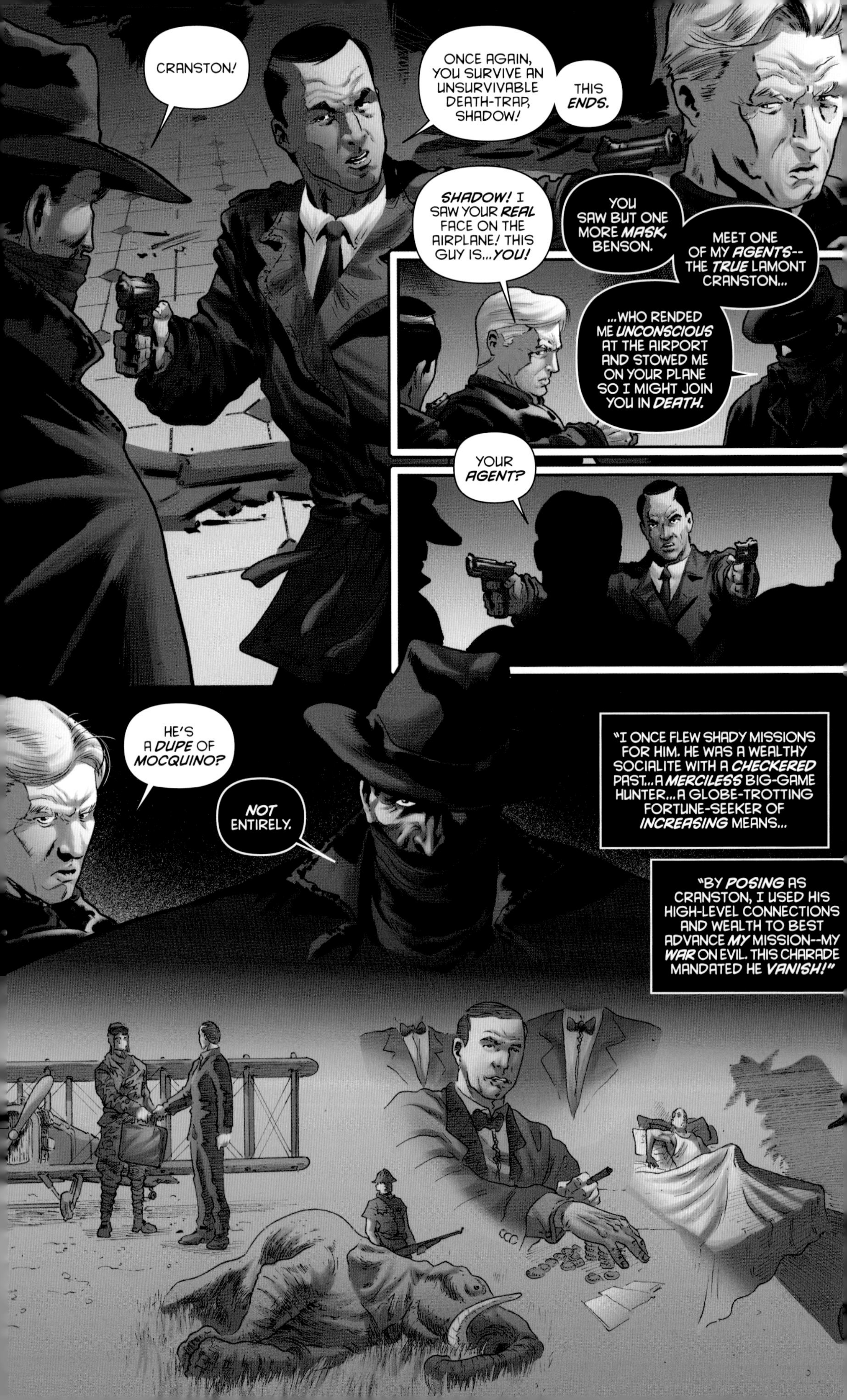
CRANSTON!
ONCE AGAIN, YOU SURVIVE AN UNSURVIVABLE DEATH-TRAP, SHADOW!
THIS ENDS.
SHADOW! I SAW YOUR REAL FACE ON THE AIRPLANE! THIS GUY IS...YOU!
YOU SAW BUT ONE MORE MASK, BENSON.
MEET ONE OF MY AGENTS-- THE TRUE LAMONT CRANSTON...
...WHO RENDED ME UNCONSCIOUS AT THE AIRPORT AND STOWED ME ON YOUR PLANE SO I MIGHT JOIN YOU IN DEATH.
YOUR AGENT?
HE'S A DUPE OF MOCQUINO?
NOT ENTIRELY.
"I ONCE FLEW SHADY MISSIONS FOR HIM. HE WAS A WEALTHY SOCIALITE WITH A CHECKERED PAST...A MERCILESS BIG-GAME HUNTER...A GLOBE-TROTTING FORTUNE-SEEKER OF INCREASING MEANS...
"BY POSING AS CRANSTON, I USED HIS HIGH-LEVEL CONNECTIONS AND WEALTH TO BEST ADVANCE MY MISSION--MY WAR ON EVIL. THIS CHARADE MANDATED HE VANISH!"

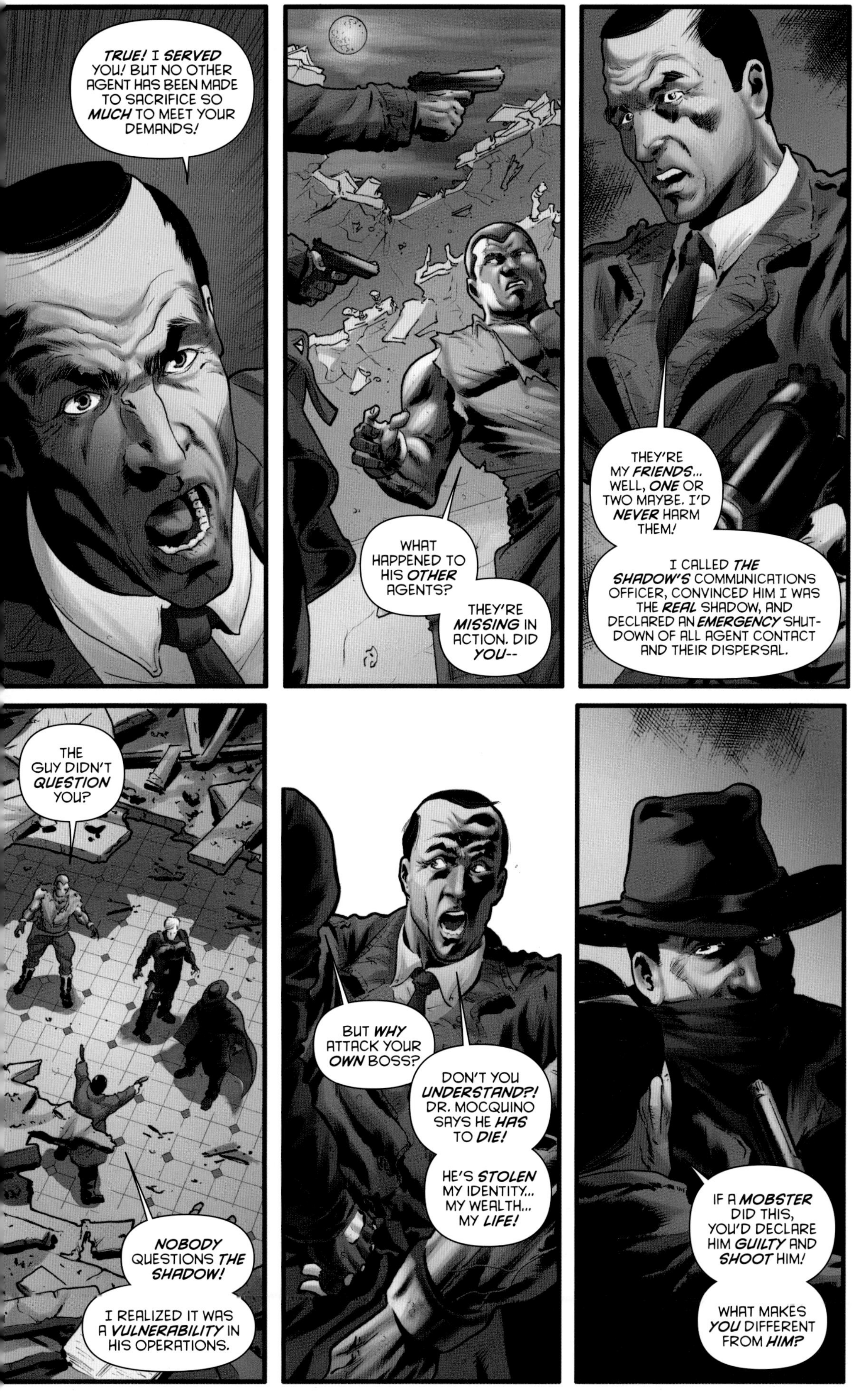
TRUE! I SERVED YOU! BUT NO OTHER AGENT HAS BEEN MADE TO SACRIFICE SO MUCH TO MEET YOUR DEMANDS!
WHAT HAPPENED TO HIS OTHER AGENTS?
THEY'RE MISSING IN ACTION. DID YOU--
THEY'RE MY FRIENDS... WELL, ONE OR TWO MAYBE. I'D NEVER HARM THEM!
I CALLED THE SHADOW'S COMMUNICATIONS OFFICER, CONVINCED HIM I WAS THE REAL SHADOW, AND DECLARED AN EMERGENCY SHUT-DOWN OF ALL AGENT CONTACT AND THEIR DISPERSAL.
THE GUY DIDN'T QUESTION YOU?
NOBODY QUESTIONS THE SHADOW!
I REALIZED IT WAS A VULNERABILITY IN HIS OPERATIONS.
BUT WHY ATTACK YOUR OWN BOSS?
DON'T YOU UNDERSTAND?! DR. MOCQUINO SAYS HE HAS TO DIE!
HE'S STOLEN MY IDENTITY... MY WEALTH... MY LIFE!
IF A MOBSTER DID THIS, YOU'D DECLARE HIM GUILTY AND SHOOT HIM!
WHAT MAKES YOU DIFFERENT FROM HIM?

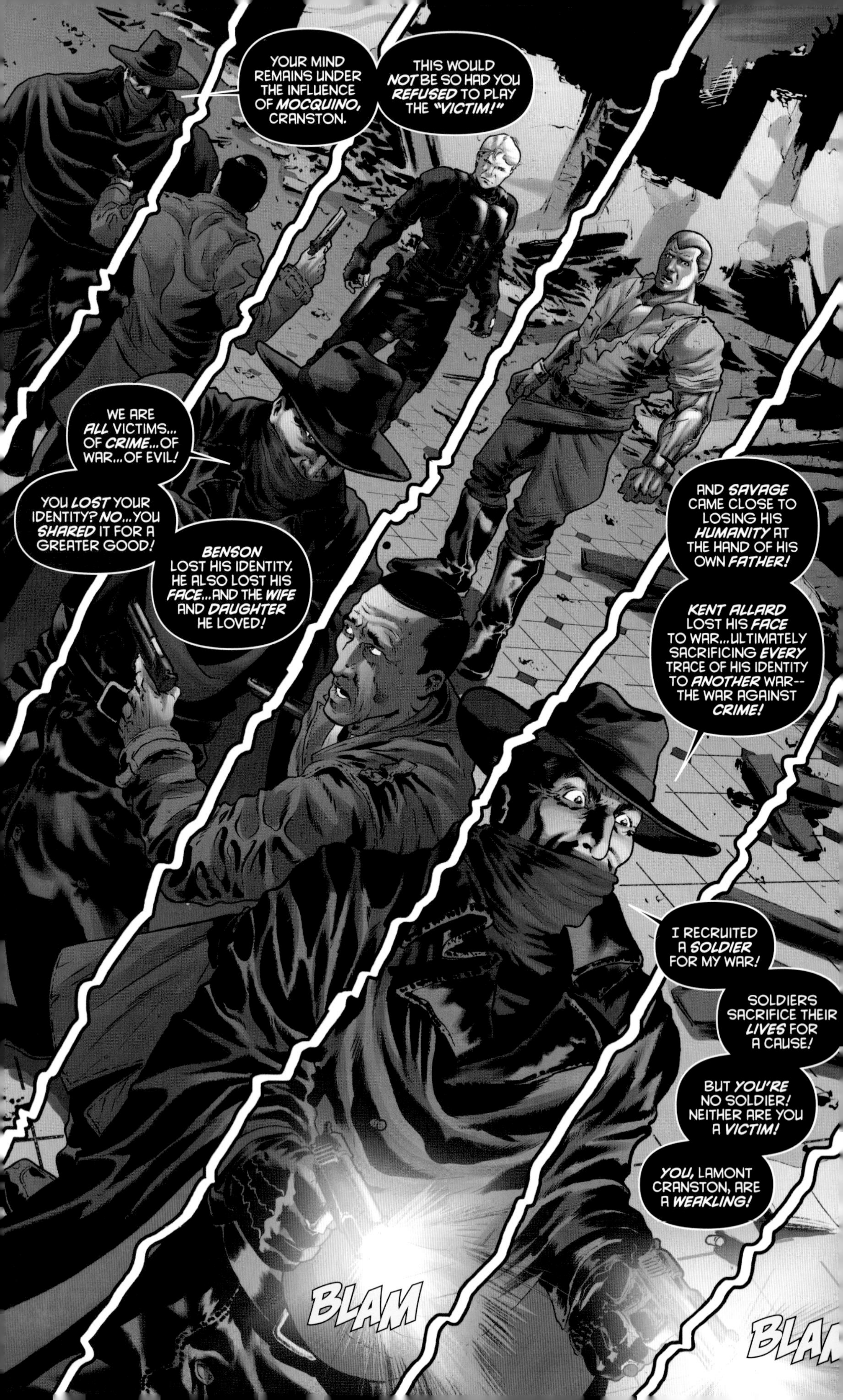
YOUR MIND REMAINS UNDER THE INFLUENCE OF MOCQUINO, CRANSTON.
THIS WOULD NOT BE SO HAD YOU REFUSED TO PLAY THE "VICTIM!"
WE ARE ALL VICTIMS... OF CRIME...OF WAR...OF EVIL!
YOU LOST YOUR IDENTITY? NO...YOU SHARED IT FOR A GREATER GOOD!
BENSON LOST HIS IDENTITY. HE ALSO LOST HIS FACE...AND THE WIFE AND DAUGHTER HE LOVED!
AND SAVAGE CAME CLOSE TO LOSING HIS HUMANITY AT THE HAND OF HIS OWN FATHER!
KENT ALLARD LOST HIS FACE TO WAR...ULTIMATELY SACRIFICING EVERY TRACE OF HIS IDENTITY TO ANOTHER WAR-- THE WAR AGAINST CRIME!
I RECRUITED A SOLDIER FOR MY WAR!
SOLDIERS SACRIFICE THEIR LIVES FOR A CAUSE!
BUT YOU'RE NO SOLDIER! NEITHER ARE YOU A VICTIM!
YOU, LAMONT CRANSTON, ARE A WEAKLING!
BLAM
BLAM

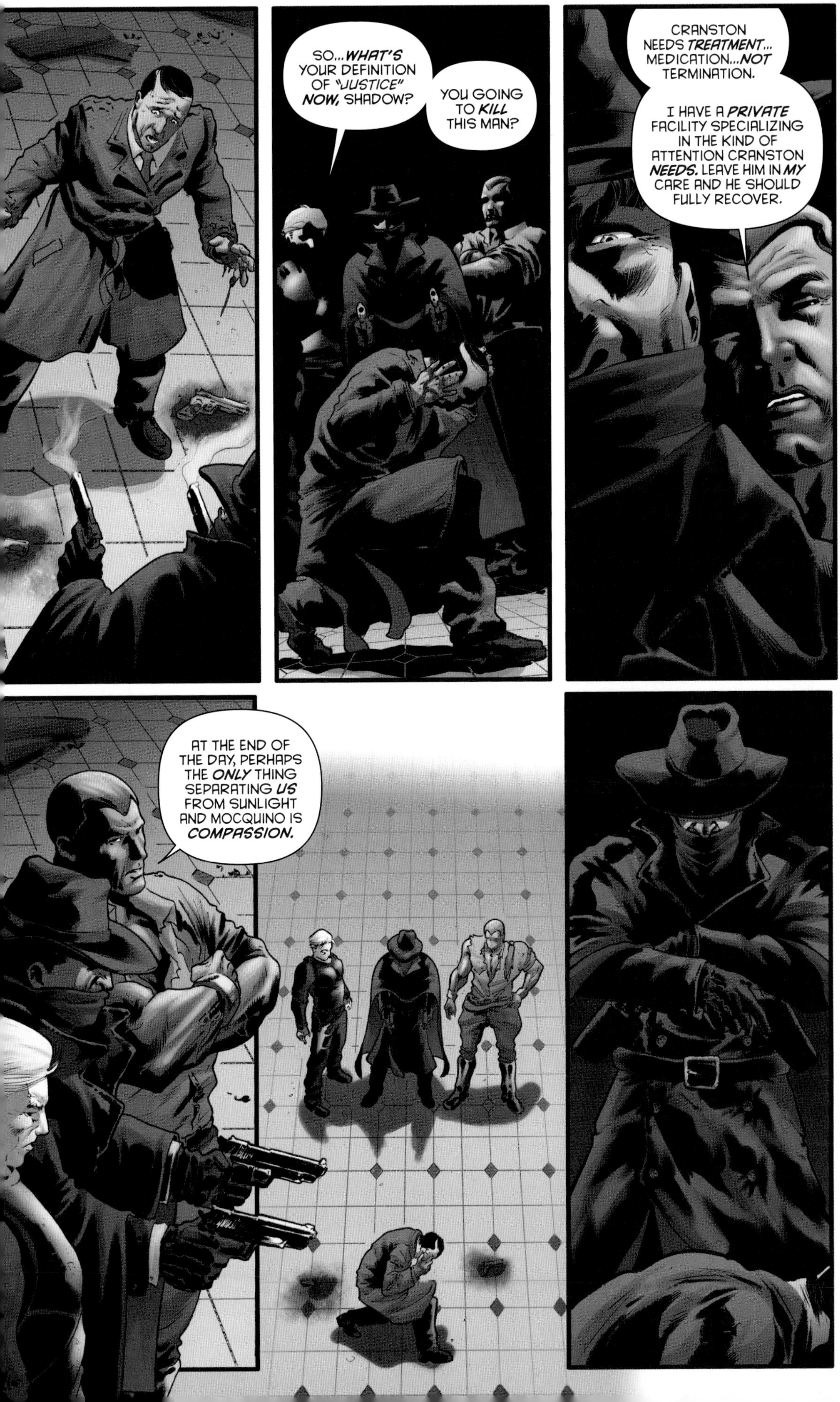

SO...WHAT'S YOUR DEFINITION OF "JUSTICE" NOW, SHADOW?
YOU GOING TO KILL THIS MAN?
CRANSTON NEEDS TREATMENT... MEDICATION...NOT TERMINATION.
I HAVE A PRIVATE FACILITY SPECIALIZING IN THE KIND OF ATTENTION CRANSTON NEEDS. LEAVE HIM IN MY CARE AND HE SHOULD FULLY RECOVER.
AT THE END OF THE DAY, PERHAPS THE ONLY THING SEPARATING US FROM SUNLIGHT AND MOCQUINO IS COMPASSION.

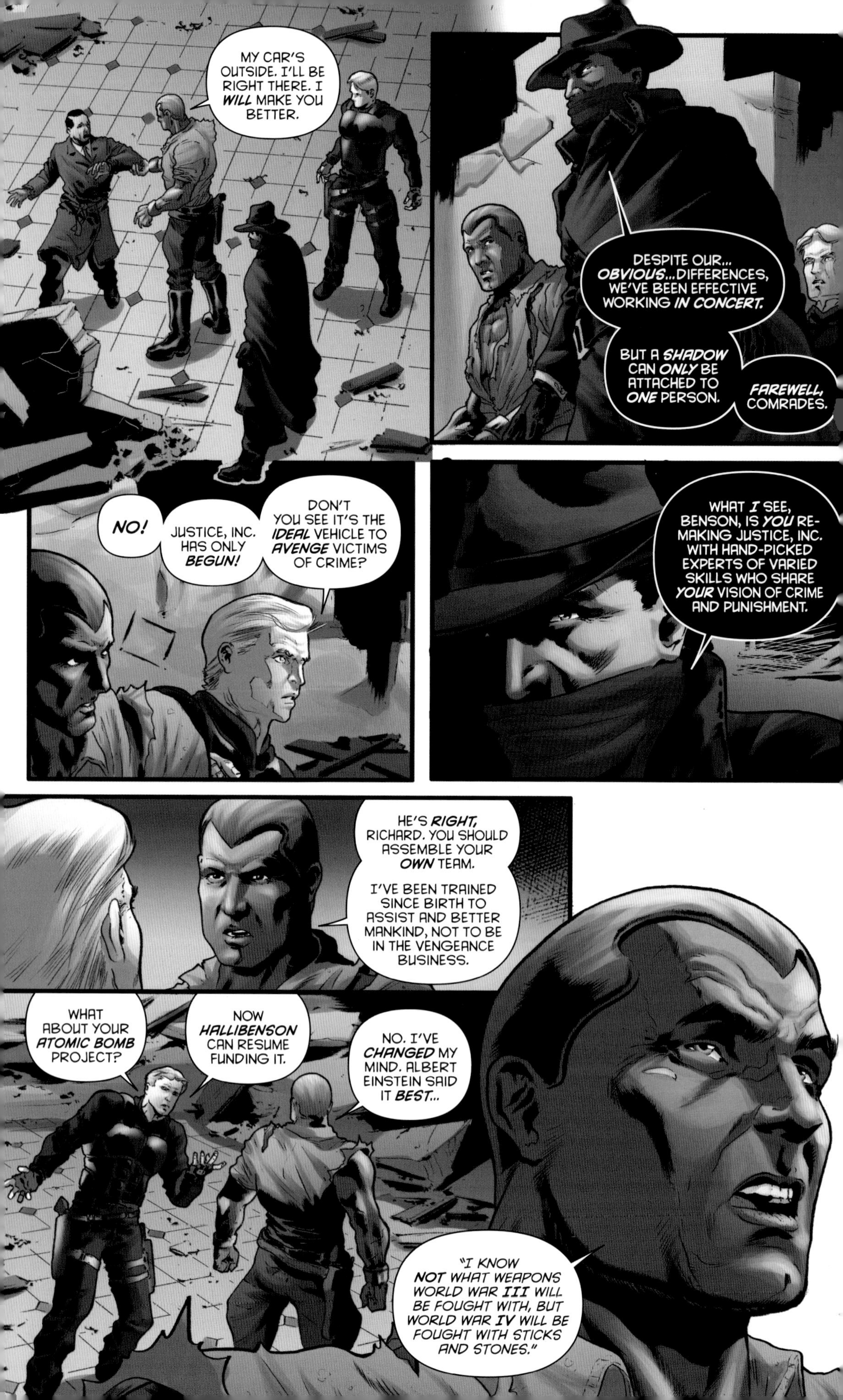
MY CAR'S OUTSIDE. I'LL BE RIGHT THERE. I *WILL* MAKE YOU BETTER.
DESPITE OUR... *OBVIOUS*...DIFFERENCES, WE'VE BEEN EFFECTIVE WORKING *IN CONCERT.*
BUT A *SHADOW* CAN *ONLY* BE ATTACHED TO *ONE* PERSON.
FAREWELL, COMRADES.
NO!
JUSTICE, INC. HAS ONLY *BEGUN!*
DON'T YOU SEE IT'S THE *IDEAL* VEHICLE TO *AVENGE* VICTIMS OF CRIME?
WHAT *I* SEE, BENSON, IS *YOU* RE-MAKING JUSTICE, INC. WITH HAND-PICKED EXPERTS OF VARIED SKILLS WHO SHARE *YOUR* VISION OF CRIME AND PUNISHMENT.
HE'S *RIGHT,* RICHARD. YOU SHOULD ASSEMBLE YOUR *OWN* TEAM.
I'VE BEEN TRAINED SINCE BIRTH TO ASSIST AND BETTER MANKIND, NOT TO BE IN THE VENGEANCE BUSINESS.
WHAT ABOUT YOUR *ATOMIC BOMB* PROJECT?
NOW *HALLIBENSON* CAN RESUME FUNDING IT.
NO. I'VE *CHANGED* MY MIND. ALBERT EINSTEIN SAID IT *BEST*...
"I KNOW *NOT* WHAT WEAPONS WORLD WAR *III* WILL BE FOUGHT WITH, BUT WORLD WAR *IV* WILL BE FOUGHT WITH STICKS AND STONES."

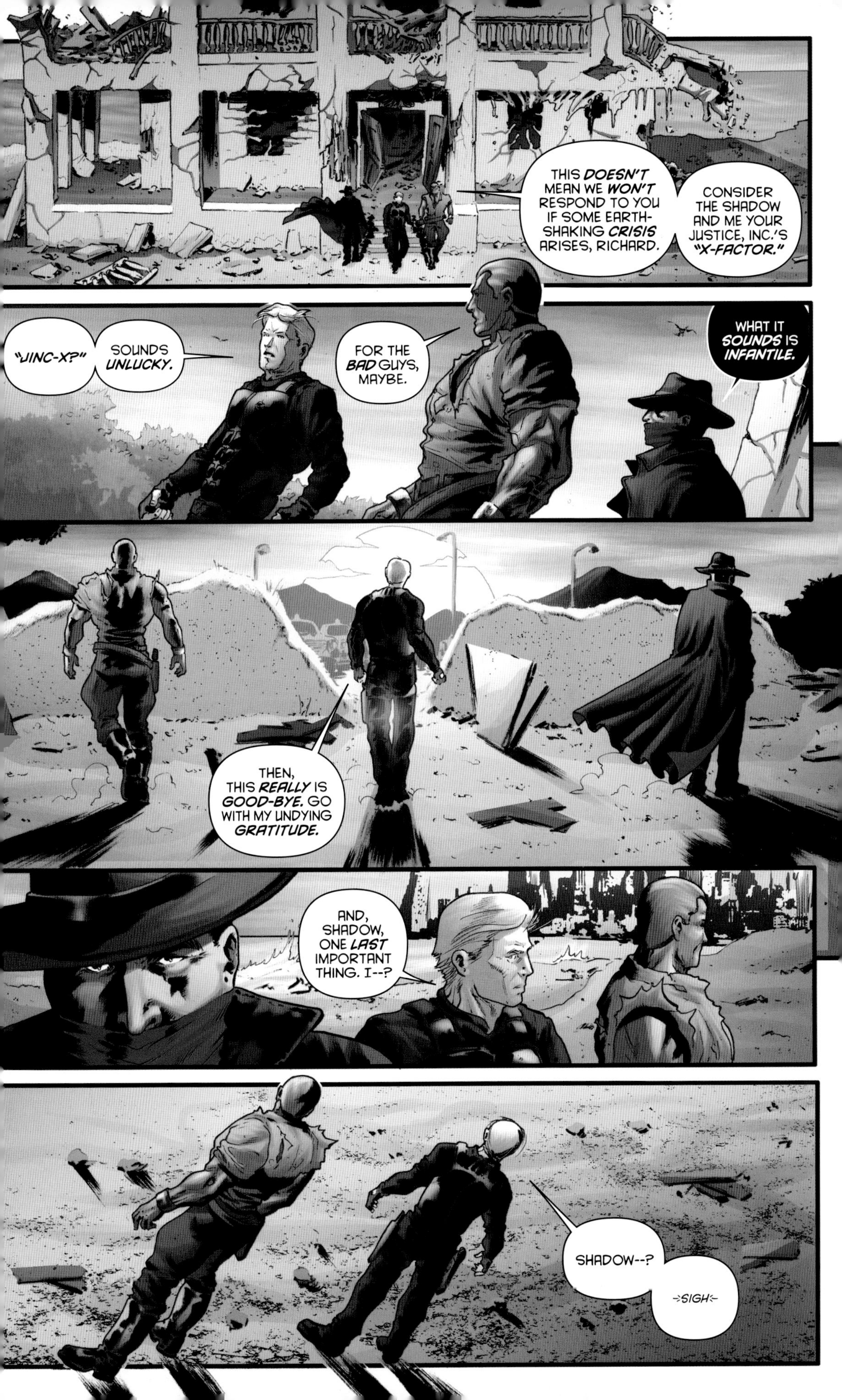
THIS DOESN'T MEAN WE WON'T RESPOND TO YOU IF SOME EARTH-SHAKING CRISIS ARISES, RICHARD.
CONSIDER THE SHADOW AND ME YOUR JUSTICE, INC.'S "X-FACTOR."
"JINC-X?"
SOUNDS UNLUCKY.
FOR THE BAD GUYS, MAYBE.
WHAT IT SOUNDS IS INFANTILE.
THEN, THIS REALLY IS GOOD-BYE. GO WITH MY UNDYING GRATITUDE.
AND, SHADOW, ONE LAST IMPORTANT THING. I--?
SHADOW--?
-SIGH-

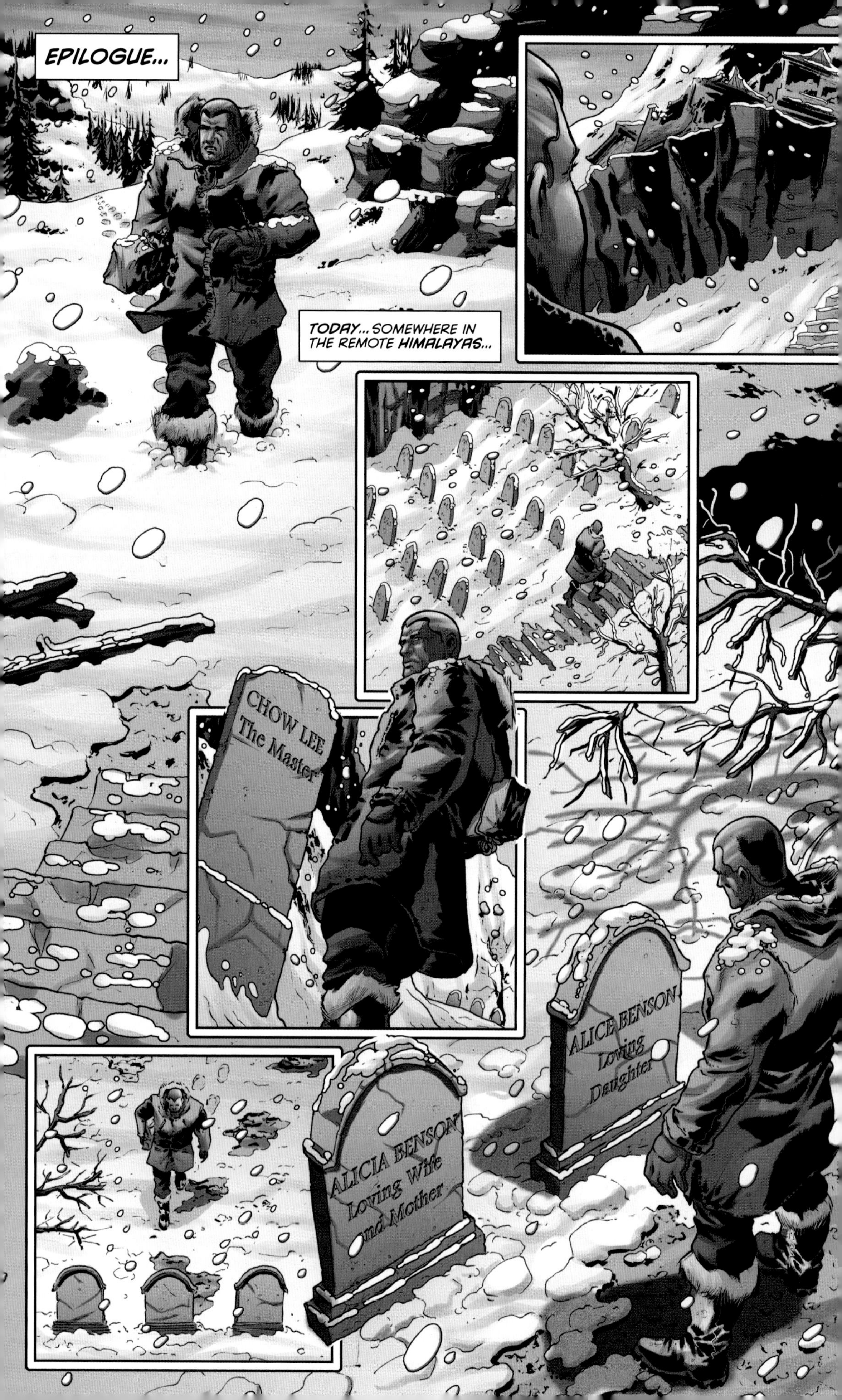
EPILOGUE...
TODAY... SOMEWHERE IN THE REMOTE HIMALAYAS...
CHOW LEE
The Master
ALICE BENSON
Loving Daughter
ALICIA BENSON
Loving Wife
and Mother

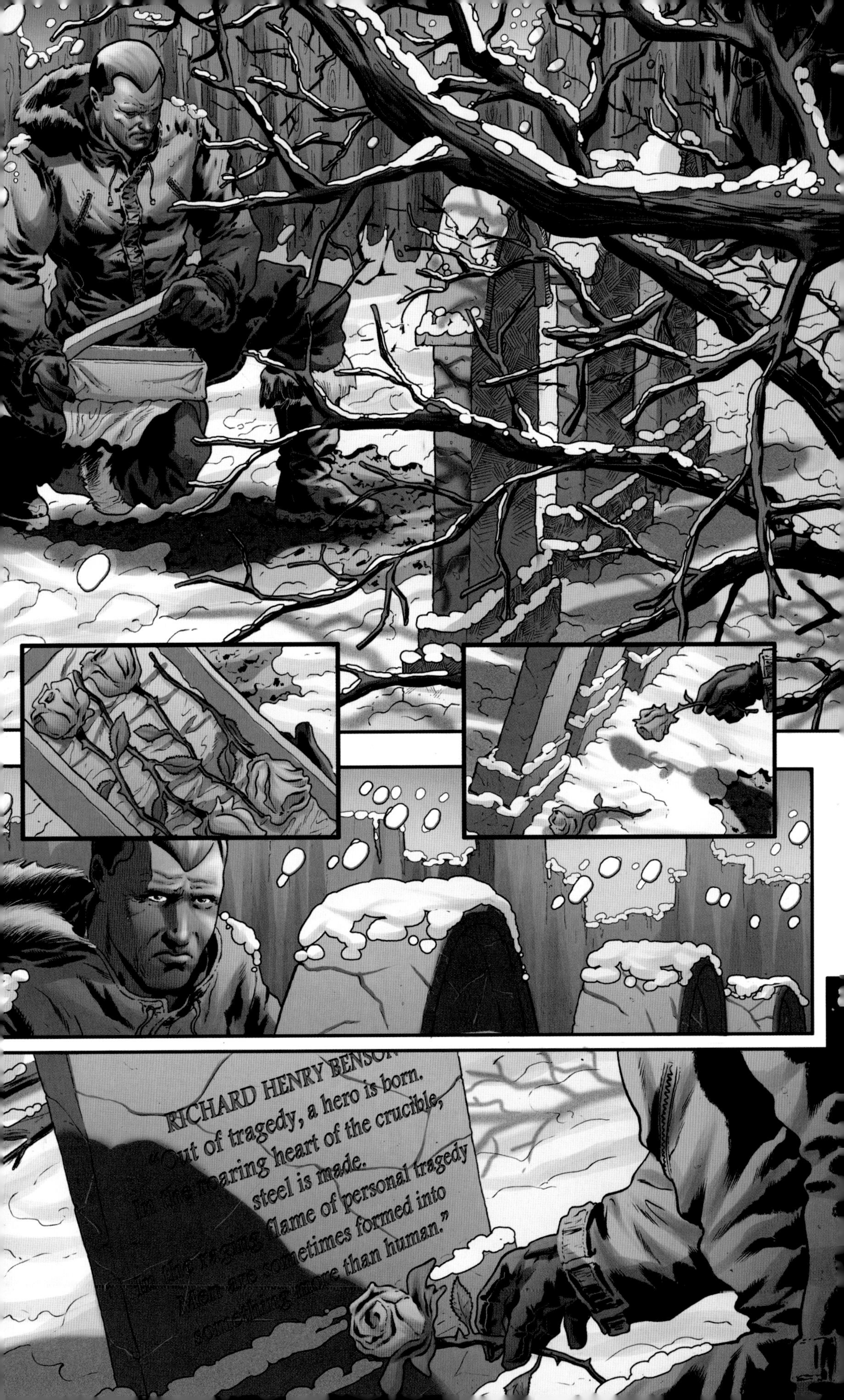

RICHARD HENRY BENSO
"Out of tragedy, a hero is born.
In the roaring heart of the crucible,
steel is made.
flame of personal tragedy
Men are sometimes formed into
something more than human."

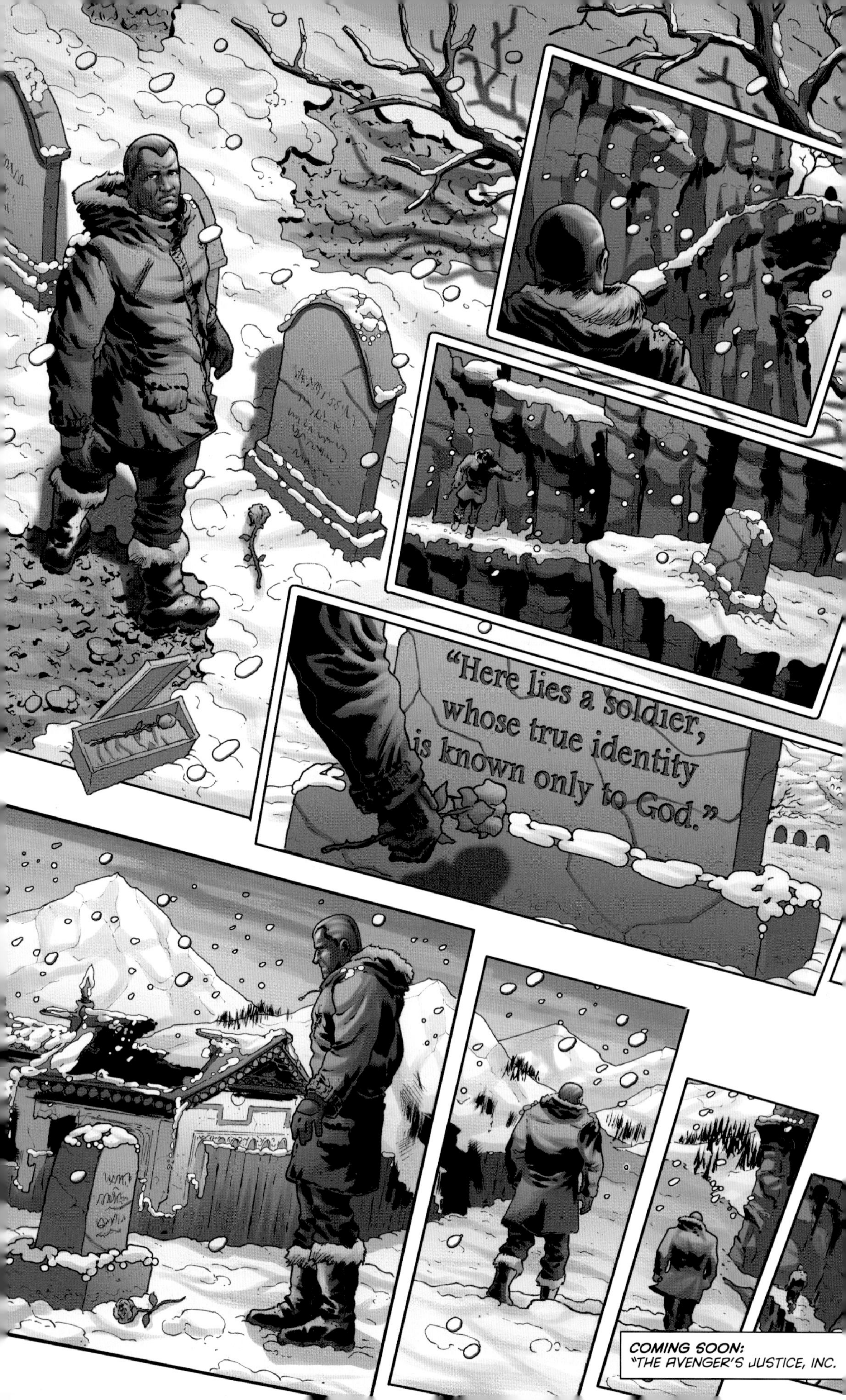
"Here lies a soldier,
whose true identity
is known only to God."
COMING SOON:
"THE AVENGER'S JUSTICE, INC.

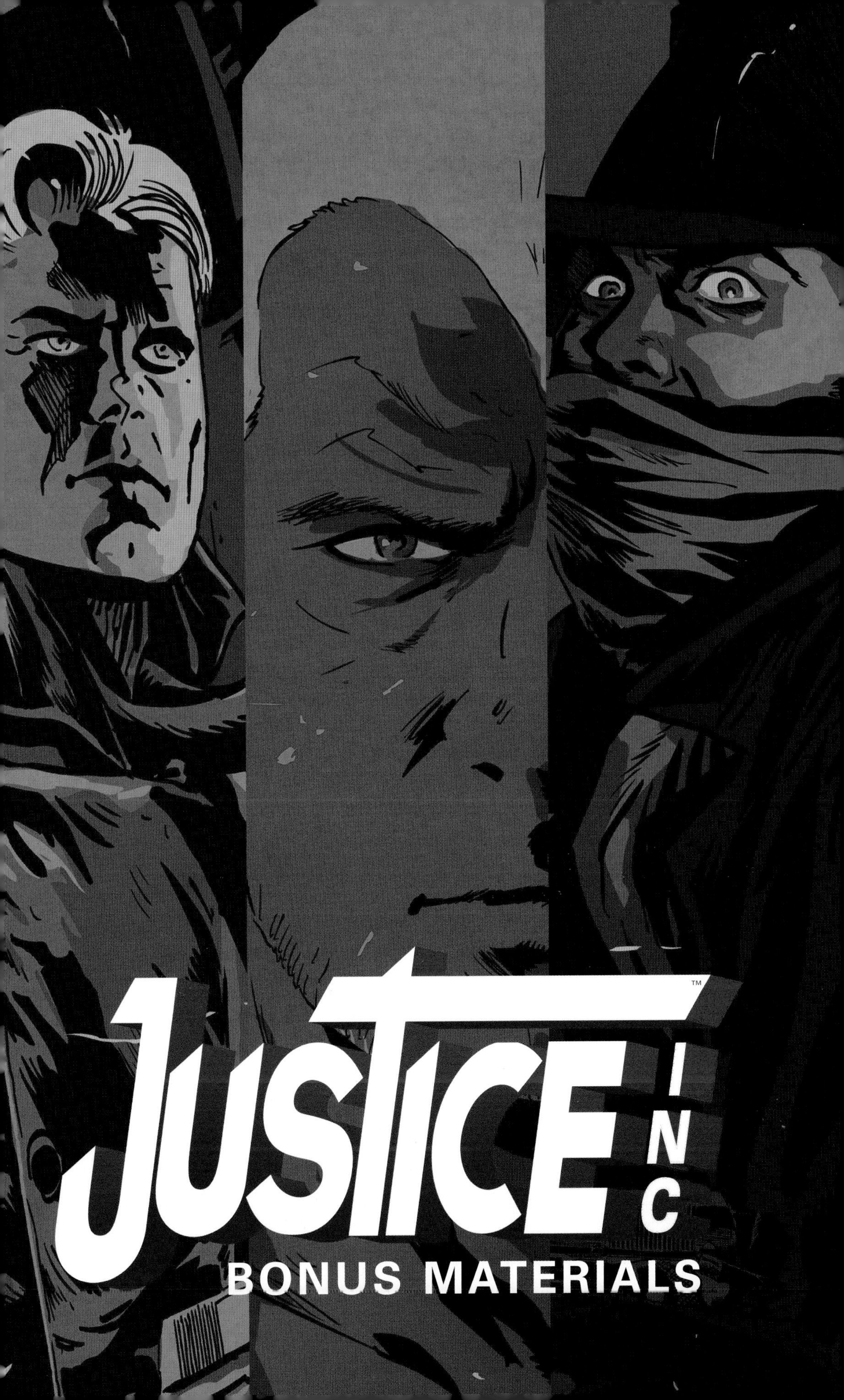
JUSTICE™ INC
BONUS MATERIALS

JUSTICE INC ™

FOOTNOTES TO HISTORY BY MICHAEL USLAN

ISSUE 1-1   **ISSUE 1-2**   **ISSUE 1-3**   **ISSUE 1-4**

ISSUE ONE - PAGE 1: Google the great facts and concerns and fictions connected to The Large Hadron Collider. It's truly science fiction come true. Not only has it found The Higgs Boson (God) Particle, but God knows what it may find with the generational enhancements coming to it between 2015 and 2040. For fun, read the story about the man who appeared there claiming to have been pulled in from the future. WHO could it be?

ISSUE ONE - PAGE 2: If you want to read the works of one of the great futurists a la Jules Verne, read the books (or at least the Classics Illustrated) of H.G. Wells: The Time Machine; The Invisible Man; The Island of Dr. Moreau; The First Men In The Moon; and his highly prophetic 1901 opus, Anticipations of the Reaction of Mechanical and Scientific Progress Upon Human Life and Thought.

ISSUE ONE - PAGE 3: The Universal Quantum Machine, aka the Universal Turing Machine, is real. Google it and if you can even begin to understand what it is capable of in layman's terms, you are deserving of a recurring co-star role on "The Big Bang Theory."

ISSUE ONE - PAGE 4: New York Municipal Airport would one day become LaGuardia Airport. Google Howard Hughes to learn how the rich and eccentric aviator, inventor, Hollywood mogul, and baron of big business, ended his life secluded in what he believed was a germ-free hotel room in Las Vegas, with his hair and nails grown chillingly long. Perhaps that's what happens when you become a "friend" to The Shadow.

SUE 1-7   ISSUE 1-9   ISSUE 1-12   ISSUE 1-17   ISSUE 1-20

ISSUE ONE - PAGE 7: Many claim that even beyond Shiwan Khan, Dr. Rodil Mocquindo, known in whispers as The Voodoo Master, was the most dangerous opponent ever faced by The Shadow. They fought each other to terrorizing conclusions on three occasions, as told in the bloody pulps: The Shadow #97, March 1936; The Shadow #102, May 1936; and The Shadow #151, June 1938.

ISSUE ONE - PAGE 9: Okay, so I admit "The Twilight Zone" was one of my favorite TV series of all time and I do pay homage to it in a few ways in this tale. Can you spot the tributes?

ISSUE ONE - PAGE 12: Yes, that P-39 Airacobra was a real state-of-the-art aircraft in 1939. Indiana Jones would have loved one.

ISSUE ONE - PAGE 17: For the story of how Howard Hughes helped Kent Allard get out of the Yucatan, see the graphic novel, "The Shadow/Green Hornet: Dark Nights.

ISSUE ONE - PAGE 20: Where did Timely Comics publisher, Martin Goodman, get the name for his landmark 1939 comic book, "Marvel Mystery Comics?" Did you know back then there was a popular motor oil called "Marvel Mystery Oil?" Truth is, again, stranger than fiction.

ISSUE TWO - PAGE 1: For the full effect of life in New York City 1939, Google The New York World's Fair 1939-40 and its symbols, The Trylon and Perisphere. This was on the site that later became The NY World's Fair of 1964-65 and on the spot where The Trylon and Perishere stood now stands The Unisphere. Today, the location is a very pretty park next to The Mets' Citifield and JFK Airport. The nearby airport today known as LaGuardia was called New York Municipal Airport back then. Superman made his first live action appearance ever at The World's Fair as DC Comics published two large commemorative comic books, "World's Fair 1939" (starring Superman and The Sandman) and a year later, "World's Fair 1940" (the cover of which was the first drawing of Superman and Batman together in the same scene, thus creating and defining what is today called "The DC Universe." "World's Fair Comics" would continue after the exhibition closed, initially under the altered title of "World's Best Comics," changed by the second issue to the legendary "World's Finest Comics." By the way, color home movies of

SSUE 2-1

Superman's appearance at The World's Fair may be found on Youtube.

ISSUE TWO - PAGE 1: If you were passing a corner newsstand in New York City during 1939, you might have plunked down a dime apiece and picked up a copy of Superman #1, Detective Comics #27 (first appearance of The Bat-Man), Adventure Comics #40 (a first appearance of The Sandman), and Marvel #1 (first paid public appearance of Sub-Mariner and first appearance of The Human Torch). What do you think that 40 cents worth of comic books would be worth today? I'm guessing in great condition, $3,750,000.

ISSUE TWO - PAGE 1: Eccentric millionaire Howard Hughes had an amazing and bizarre life from aviation pioneer to movie mogul to paranoid hermit. One movie about him I liked in particular was "Melvin and Howard," which made a star out of Mary Steenburgen. Read all about him, if you can.

ISSUE TWO - PAGE 1: J. Edgar Hoover was arguably the second most powerful man in America for decades next to the U.S. Presidents. From his days taking down the greatest criminals of the Depression era to his days as President Nixon's attack dog, Hoover ran The FBI with an iron fist and a bit of taffeta. For elaboration on the latter statement, I suggest you Google him.

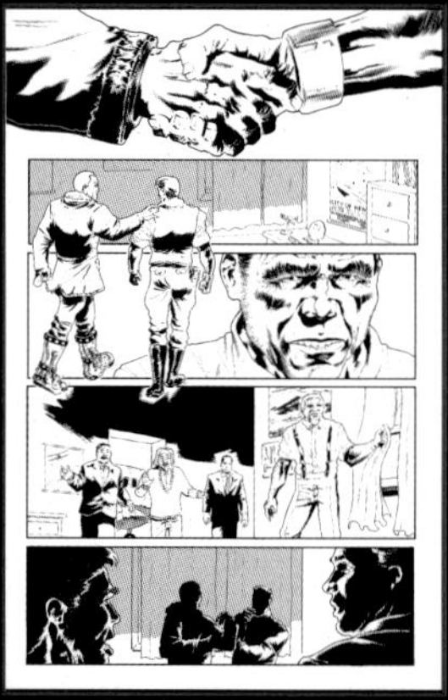
ISSUE 2-3

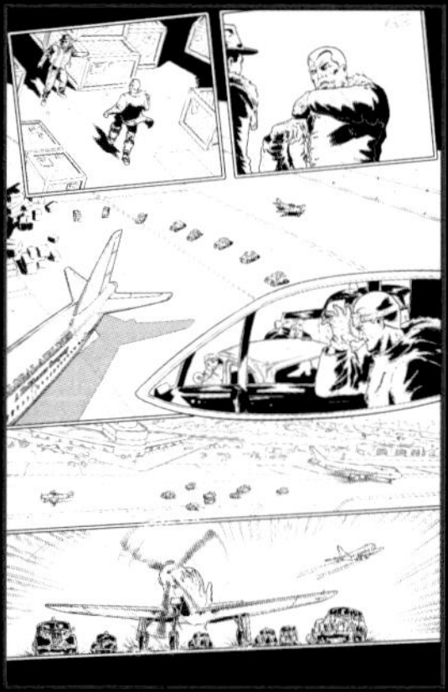
ISSUE 2-5

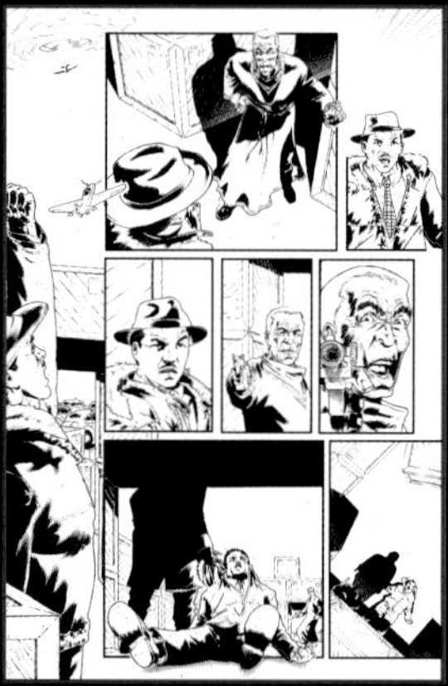
ISSUE 2-6

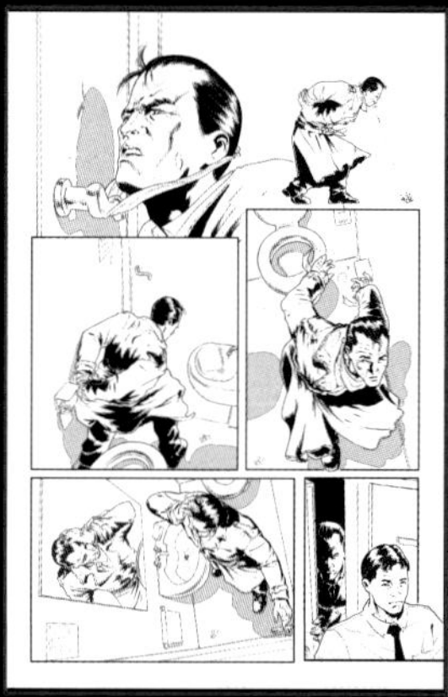
ISSUE 2-9

ISSUE TWO - PAGE 3: Meet: H.G. Wells, the futurist, visionary, and prophetic author of such great novels as THE TIME MACHINE, the invisible man, and THE ISLAND OF DOCTOR MOREAU; Albert Einstein, perhaps the smartest man who ever lived, who left us with his revolutionary Theory of Relativity which everyone knows is E=MC2 but nobody knows how to explain it; Enrico Fermi, a driving force behind the birth of atomic power and the historic Manhattan Project. Check them all out via Google.

ISSUE TWO - PAGE 5: The P-39 was a very cool airplane circa 1939. Giovanni's art accurately reflects what it looked like.

ISSUE TWO - PAGE 6: Dr. Roquil Mocquino, aka The Voodoo Master, was possibly the villain who came the closest to destroying The Shadow, and challenged him three times in the pulps: The Shadow #97 (March 1936), 102 (May 1936), and 151 (June 1938). These three classic novels have been reprinted by Anthony Tollin's Sanctum Books in his double novel editions of THE SHADOW Volume 3, Volume 10, and Volume 19, respectively.

ISSUE TWO - PAGE 9: For my ultimate word on "Datura" and its effects, read my 2003 graphic novel, BATMAN: DETECTIVE #27 (Plug!).

ISSUE TWO - PAGE 22: Have you considered whether or not Richard Henry Benson could be either considered or perceived to be a zombie in today's culture? I invite your thoughts.

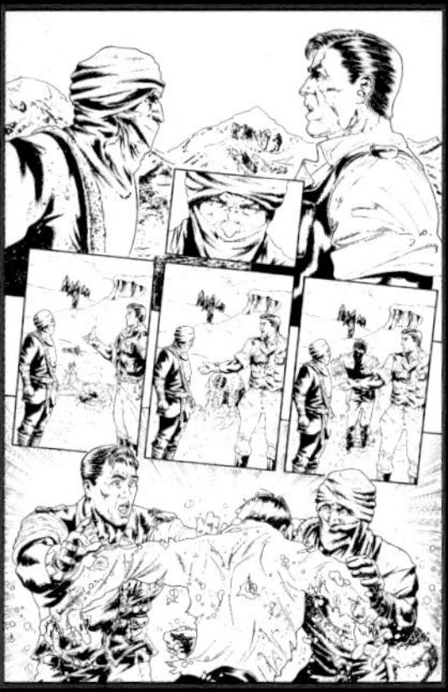

ISSUE 2-22

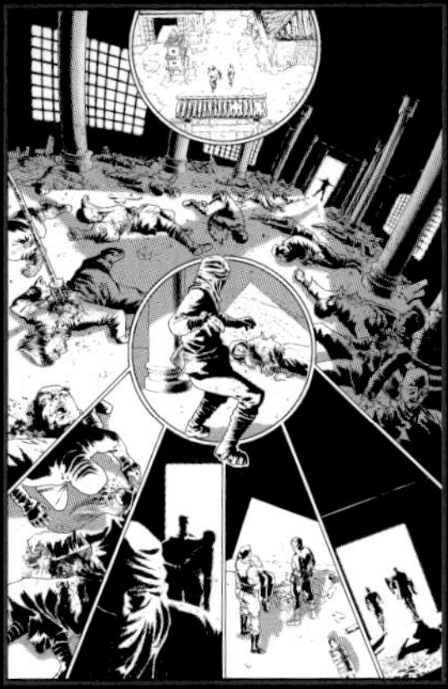

ISSUE 3-2

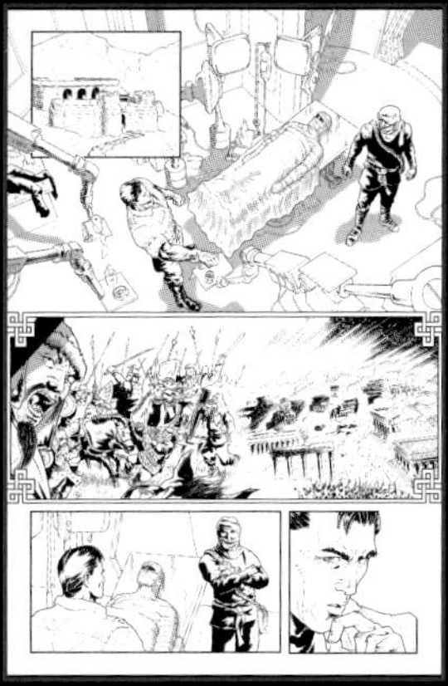

ISSUE 3-3

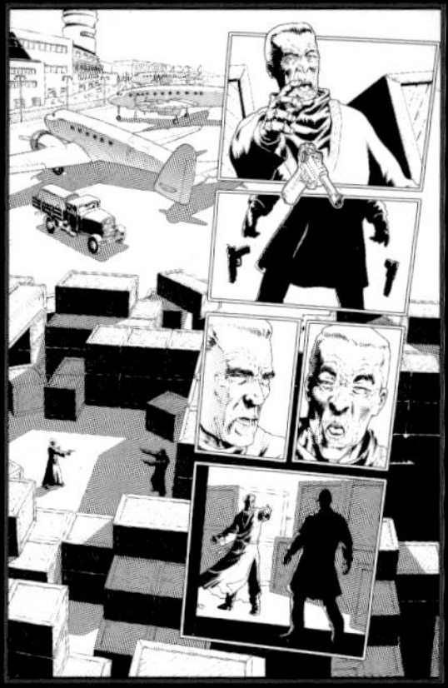

ISSUE 3-6

ISSUE 3 - PAGE 2: You mean you never heard of the plot to kidnap President Franklin D. Roosevelt in NY in 1939 by Shiwan Khan? Skip your history book and instead research this extraordinary incident in the graphic novel, THE SHADOW/GREEN HORNET: DARK NIGHTS. (Plug!)

ISSUE 3 - PAGE 3: Although literary license has been taken regarding eras, the Huns, the Visigoths and the Vandals were, indeed, barbarian tribes worthy of reading about! Google them for some fun reading from the battle-torn pages of history.

ISSUE 3 - PAGE 6: Although called New York Municipal Airport in 1939, today we call it LaGuardia Airport.

ISSUE 3 - PAGE 7: The Astor Bar in the Hotel Astor on Times Square was the place to see and be seen in New York in 1939.

ISSUE 3 - PAGE 8: The Explorers Club is real!

ISSUE 3 - PAGE 9: Howard Hughes, wealthy industrialist, famed aviator, movie producer and studio mogul, adventurer and innovator, became the world's wealthiest recluse in his later years.

ISSUE 3 - PAGE 10: Read more in "The Gotham Times" about this famous murder case first reported in May 1939.

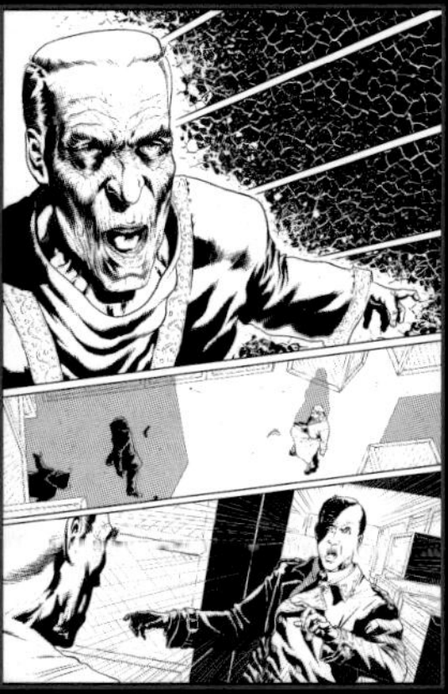

ISSUE 3-7

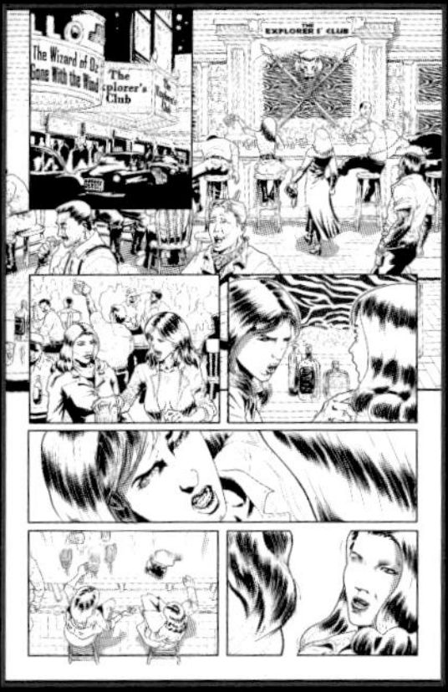
The Wizard of Oz
Gone With the Wind
THE EXPLORER'S CLUB

ISSUE 3-8

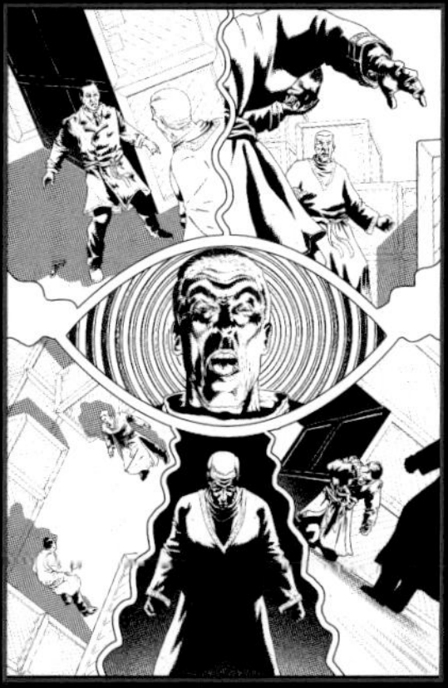

ISSUE 3-9

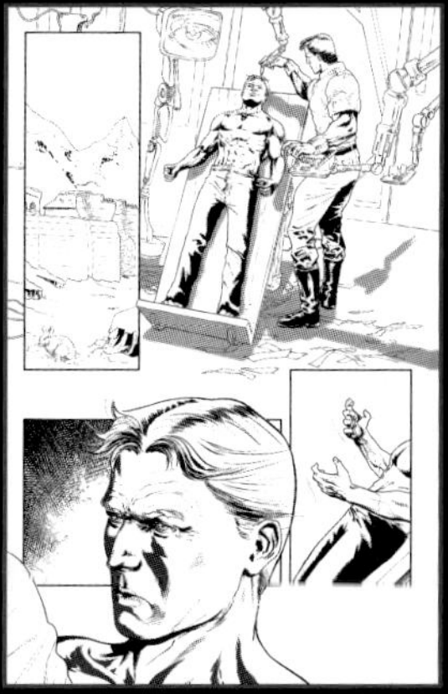

ISSUE 3-10

ISSUE 3 - PAGE 12: This year is the 100th anniversary of what was then called "The Great War" and has since been re-named "World War I." Colonel Kent Allard was, apparently, one of its victims, possibly physically, probably mentally.

ISSUE 3-12   ISSUE 4-1   ISSUE 4-18   ISSUE 4-19

ISSUE 4 - PAGE 1: John Sunlight, Doc Savage's master villain, appeared in two pulp adventures, "The Fortress of Solitude" in October 1938, and in "The Devil Genghis" in December 1938, both as reprinted in Anthony Tollin's Sanctum Book Series as DOC SAVAGE, Volume .

ISSUE 4 - PAGE 18: Jimmy Carter in 1939 was a fifteen year old high school student and peanut farmer in the tiny town of Plains, Georgia. In a truly All-American story, he was elected President of the United States in 1976 and, apparently in 1979, shut down an old U.S, nuclear missile silo under a nuclear non-proliferation treaty with the Soviet Union, and sold it to the site's original owner, Clark Savage, Jr.

ISSUE 4 - PAGE 19: The Danzig Corridor was in 1939 the object of desire for Adolph Hitler. His ultimatum, ultimately rejected, became his excuse to invade Poland in September 1939, a giant step forward in the march to World War II.

ISSUE 4 - PAGE 22: Scientist of the ages, Nikola Tesla, was, in fact, living in The New Yorker Hotel in New York City. The Auto-Gyro was his design and sold by him to The Shadow. It's base was the roof of the Hotel, a mere three blocks from The Empire State Building, home to The Shadow's Secret Sanctum and to the "offices" of Doc Savage's Hidalgo Trading Company… and perhaps, shortly, to a new Justice, Inc.

ISSUE 4 - PAGE 22: Coney Island's 1930's sensation, "The House of Horrors" directly inspired this "Island of Horrors."

ISSUE 4-22   ISSUE 5-1   ISSUE 5-3   ISSUE 5-4

ISSUE 5 · PAGE 1: John Sunlight originally appeared in the October 1938 issue of Doc Savage Magazine in a tale entitled, "Fortress of Solitude." His sequel appearance was in the December 1938 issue in a story called, "The Devil Genghis." Both have been reprinted in one trade paperback book published by Anthony Tollin entitled, "Doc Savage Double #1."

ISSUE 5 · PAGE 1: The Auto-Gyro of The Shadow and its inventor, Nikola Tesla, may be seen atop The New Yorker Hotel in the Dynamite graphic novel, "The Shadow/Green Hornet: Dark Nights."

ISSUE 5 · PAGE 3: Pat Savage, Doc's cousin, made her initial appearance in the January 1934 pulp story entitled, "The Brand of the Werewolf," as reprinted in Anthony Tollin's Sanctum Book Series as DOC SAVAGE, Volume 13.

ISSUE 5 · PAGES 3-4: Is anyone else a fan of Karen Allen in "Raiders of the Lost Ark?"

ISSUE 5 · PAGE 4: If you are unaware of the amazing career of scientist/inventor Nikola Tesla, get thee to the internet or your library and read all about his genius.

ISSUE 5-8   ISSUE 5-12   ISSUE 5-16   ISSUE 5-17

ISSUE 5 · PAGE 8: Question #1: Fresh from his role in "The Shadow/Green Hornet: Dark Nights," Kruger was clearly Hitler's favorite spy who would lose his life in late 1941 in the pages of what comic book?

ISSUE 5 · PAGE 12: Question #2: Which detectives did John Sunlight believe he killed in order to seize their high tech communication devices... two-way wrist radios.

ISSUE 5 · PAGE 15: Deal, New Jersey was also the scene of the climax of the original meeting between The DC Universe's Shadow and The Avenger in 1975's 11th issue of "The Shadow," written by yours truly. Coincidentally, it's the place where I grew up.

ISSUE 5 · PAGE 16: Doc's dramatic entrance influenced by Max Fleischer in his first "Superman" cartoon.

ISSUE 5 · PAGE 17: Did you know that the 1933 ads for Doc Savage Magazine headlined him as "Superman"... five years before the other guy landed on earth.

ISSUE 5 · PAGE 18: That fairly "new tunnel" they refer to is The Lincoln Tunnel, connecting New Jersey and New York City.

ISSUE 5 · PAGE 21: The cliffs of Weehawken, N.J. are also where the famous duel occurred

ISSUE 5 - PAGE 22: The title for our concluding issue 6 is a salute to the title of my original Shadow/Justice, Inc. 1975 story, "Night of The Avenger." And so the circle is complete.

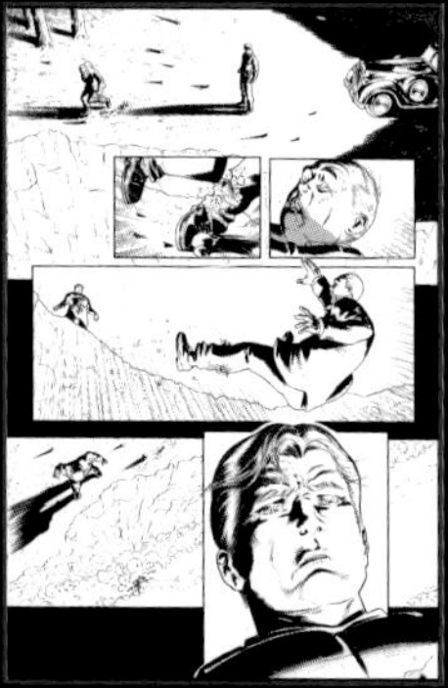
ISSUE 5-22

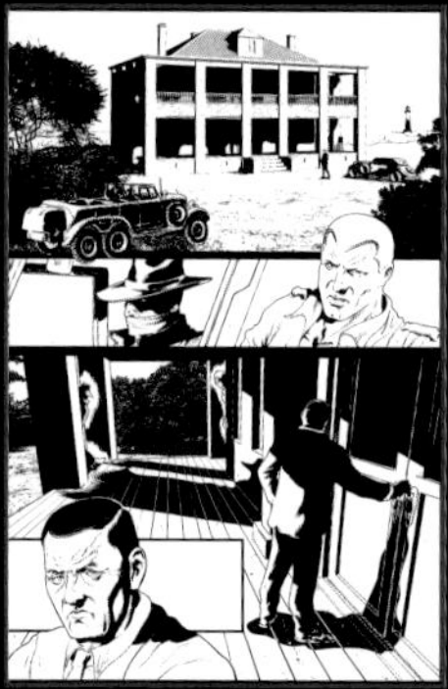
ISSUE 6-3

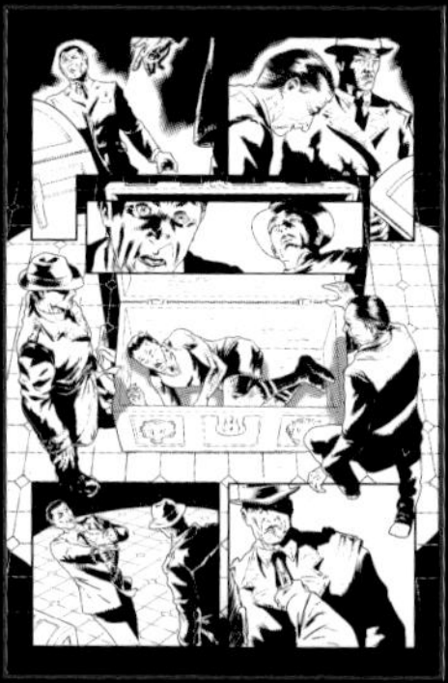
ISSUE 6-8

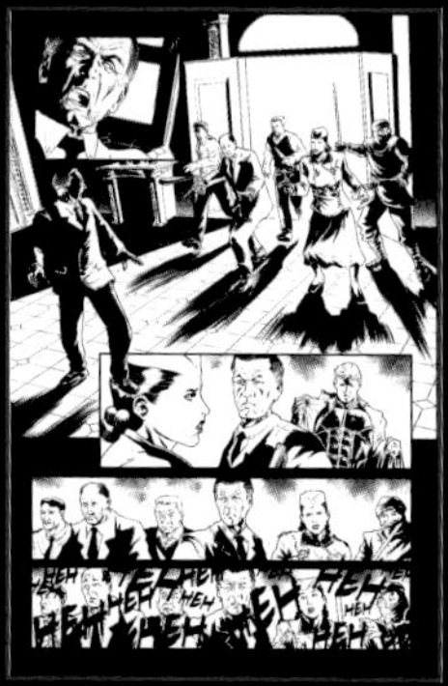
ISSUE 6-10

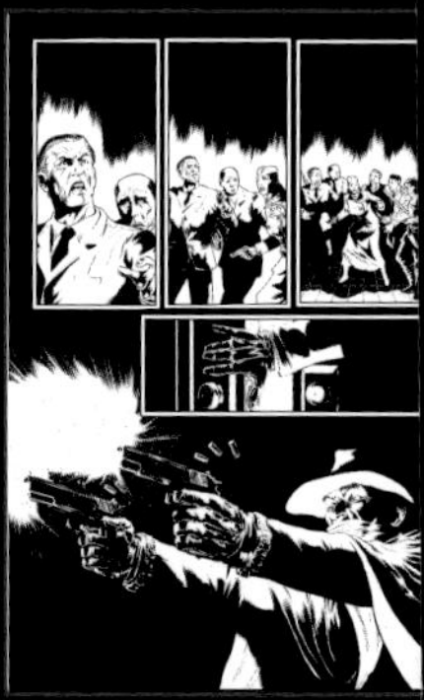
ISSUE 6-11

ISSUE 6- PAGE 3: Named after Deal, England, Deal, New Jersey is a real place... an upscale beachfront community north of Asbury Park. Originally known for its lavish wooden mansions, most of which have now been torn down and replaced by large contemporary homes. In an alternate universe, Deal was the scene of a violent encounter between The Shadow's agents and the men and women of Richard Henry Benson's Justice, Inc., as reported in the pages of DC Comics' "The Shadow" #11 from 1975 in a story not coincidentally entitled, "The Night of The Avenger!"

ISSUE 6 - PAGE 8: Herr Kruger has made a famous appearance in the pages of Dynamite's "The Shadow/Green Hornet: Dark Nights." He also made a very famous appearance in another comic book. 'Nuff said.

ISSUE 6 - PAGE 10 AND ELSEWHERE: I've been lucky enough to write the comic book adventures of both The Avenger and The Question (the latter in tandem with the legendary artist, Alex Toth). It always baffled me why in most of their adventures, though one looked like an albino zombie and the other seemed to have no face at all, nobody seemed to react in horror to either one's visage. I believe people would get scared in reaction to what they saw, and so that's what I write.

ISSUE 6 - PAGE 11: Okay, yes, this is an homage to the full page ad drawn by Bernie Wrightson (plus others) to advertise the coming 1970's DC Comics series, "The Shadow." A tip of the fedora to Berni, Mike Kaluta, Denny O'Neill, E.R. Cruz, Frank Robbins, Joe Kubert, and Allan Asherman.

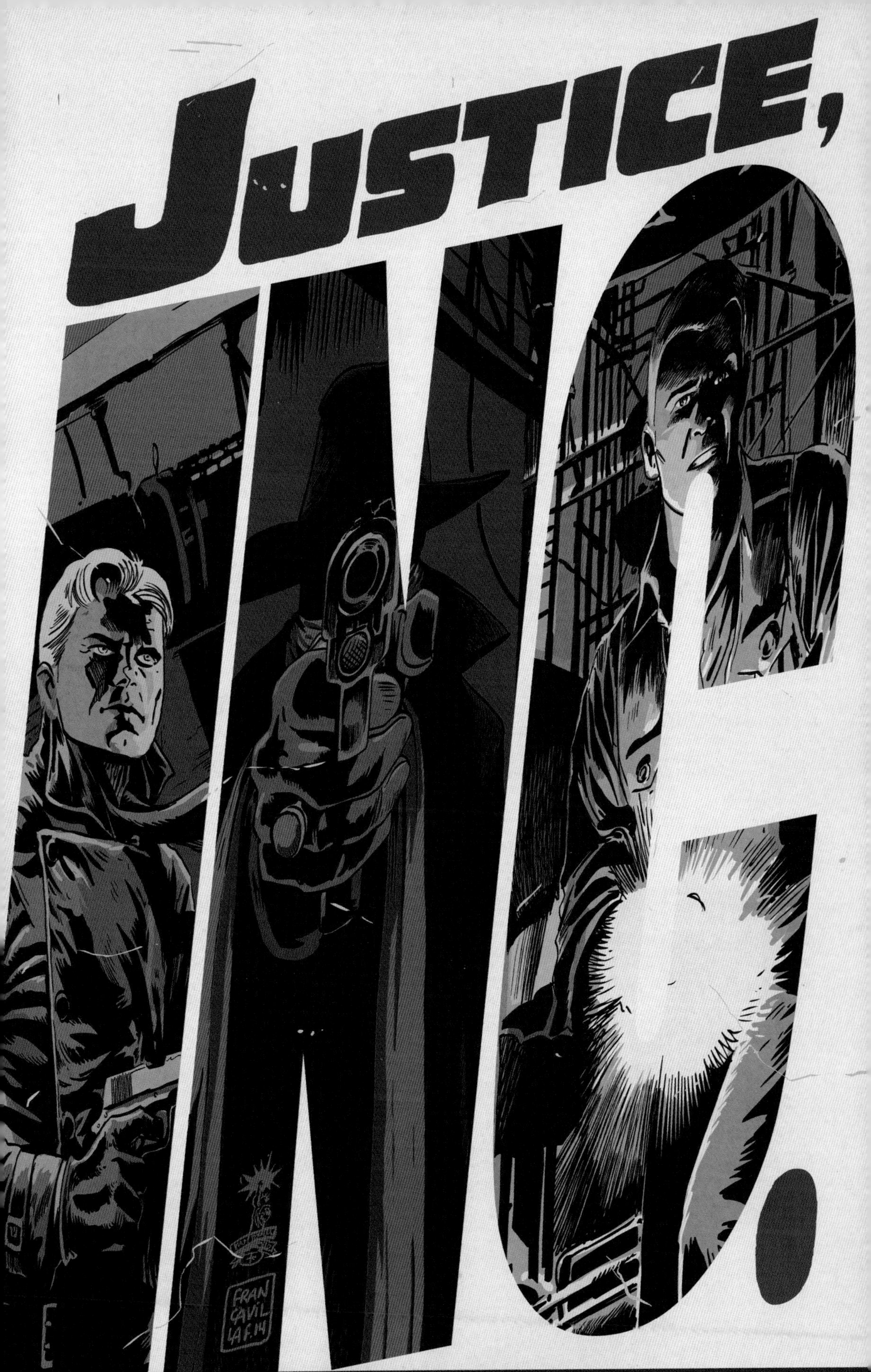
JUSTICE, INC.

issue #1 alternate cover
art by **FRANCESCO FRANCAVILLA**

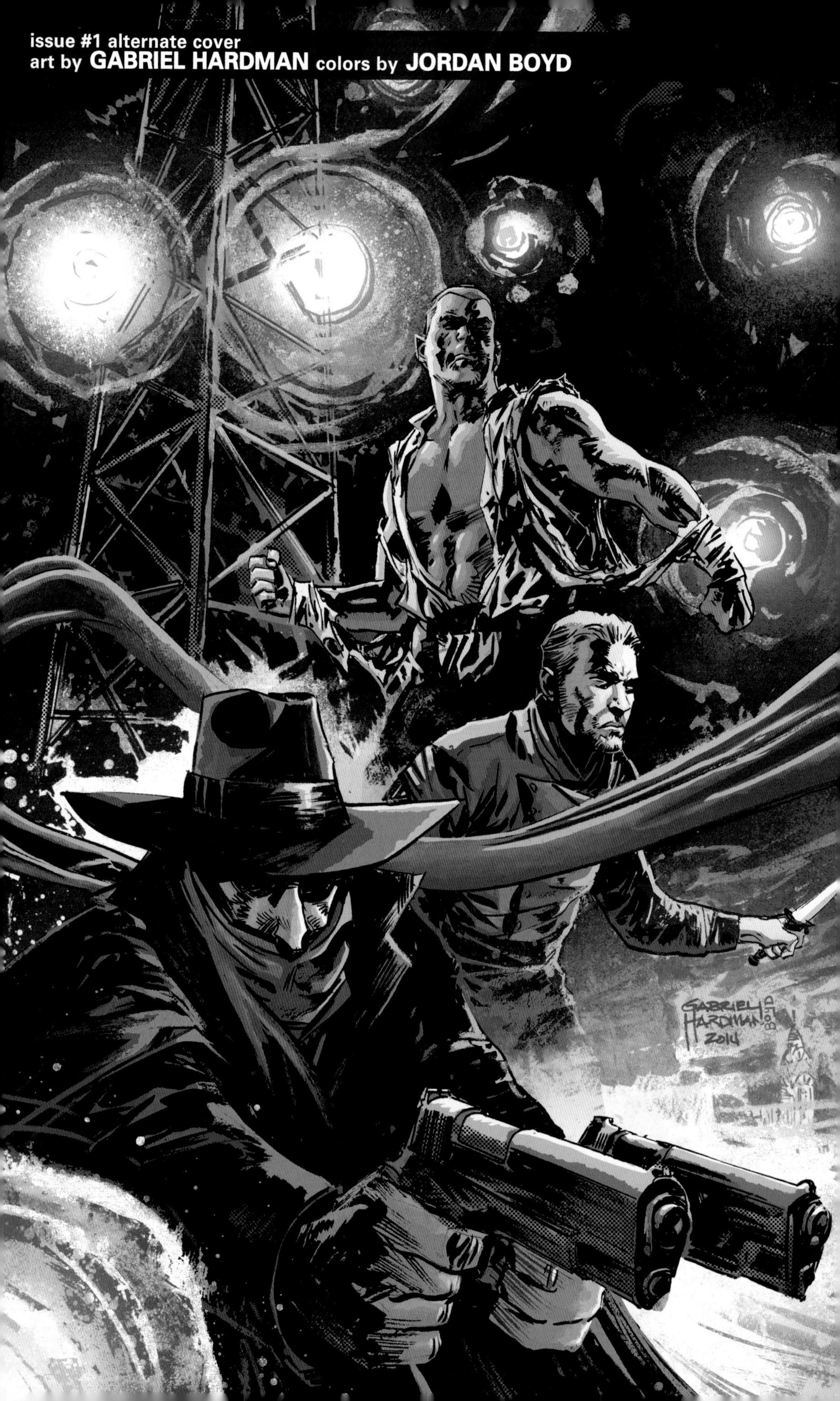
GABRIEL HARDMAN 2014

issue #1 alternate cover
art by **GABRIEL HARDMAN** colors by **JORDAN BOYD**

issue #1 alternate cover
art by **ARDIAN SYAF** inks by **GUILLERMO ORTEGA** colors by **KYLE RITTER**

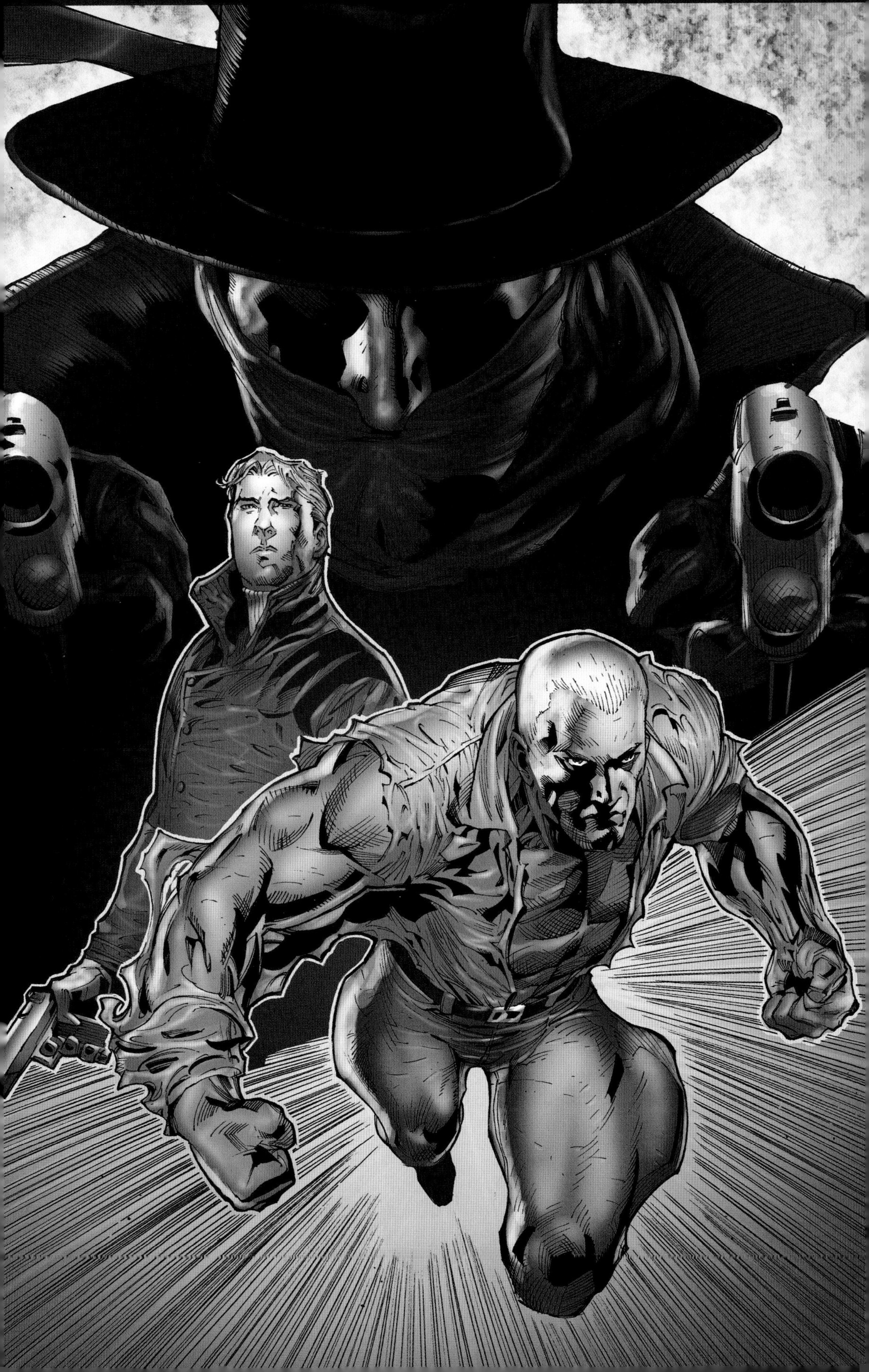

issue #1 alternate cover
art by **STEPHEN SEGOVIA** colors by **ELMER SANTOS**

issue #2 alternate cover
art by **FRANCESCO FRANCAVILLA**

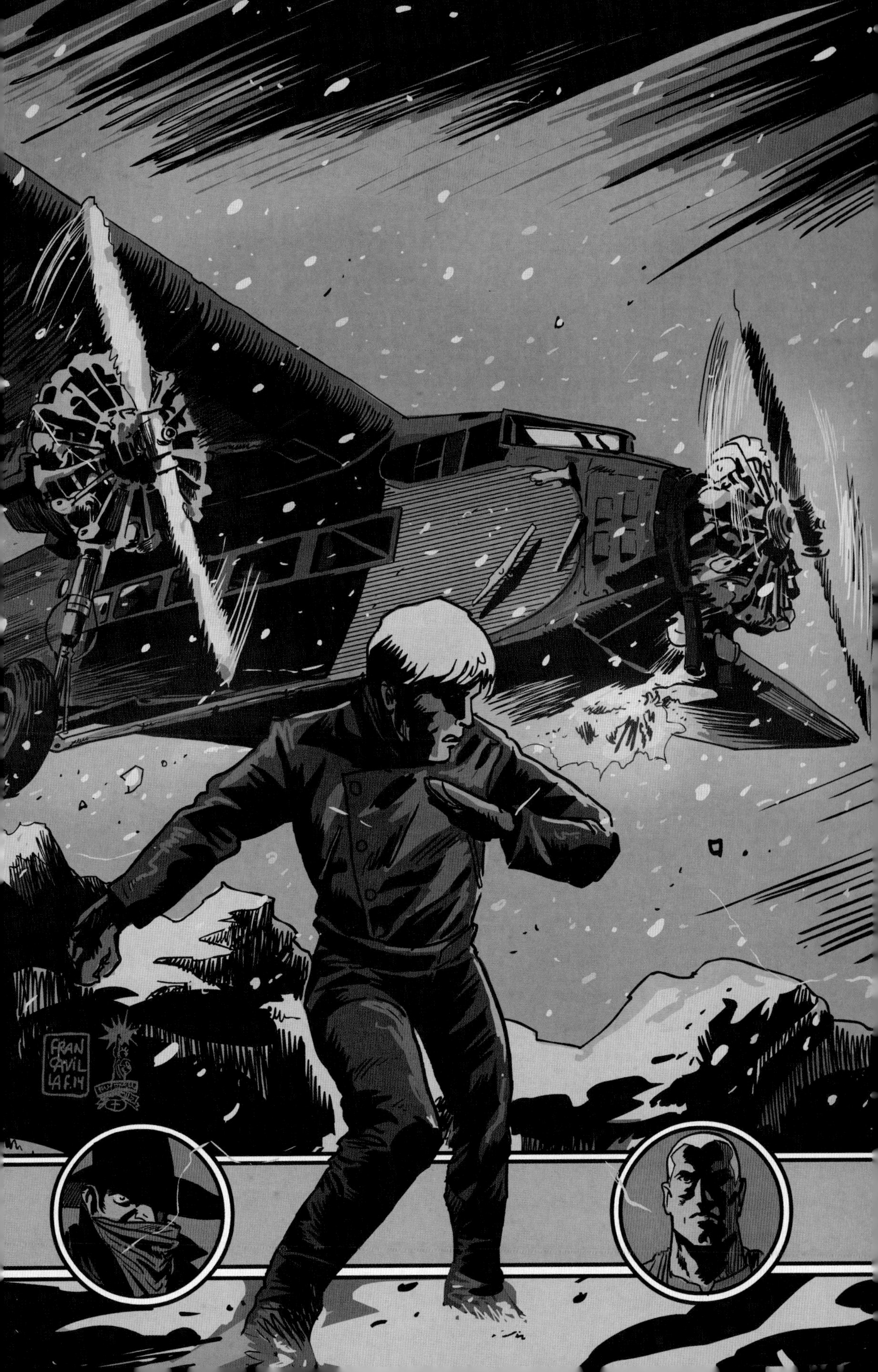
FRAN CAVIL LA F.14

issue #2 alternate cover
art by **GABRIEL HARDMAN** colors by **JORDAN BOYD**

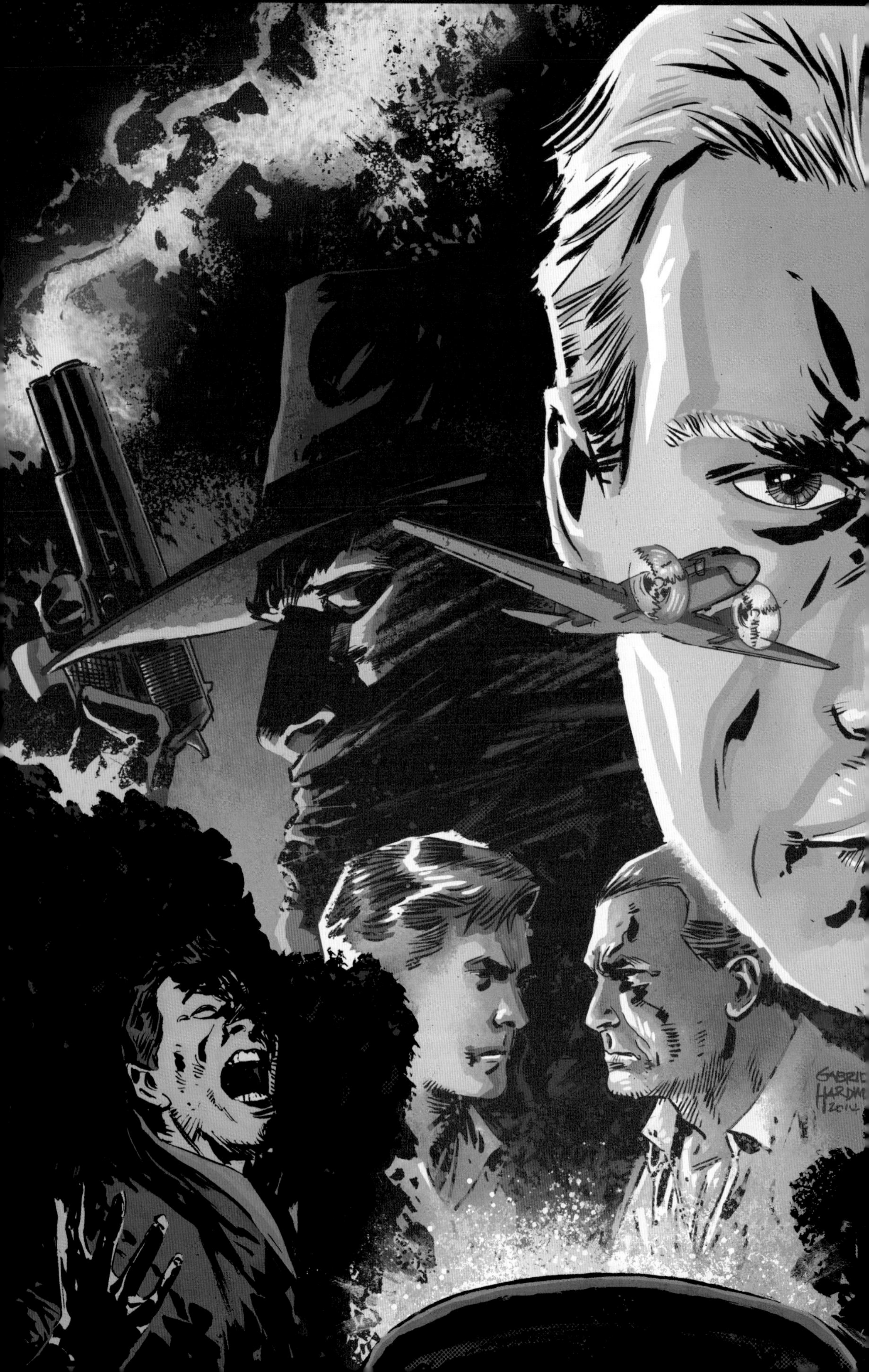
GABRIEL HARDMAN 2014

issue #2 alternate cover
art by **ARDIAN SYAF** inks by **GUILLERMO ORTEGA** colors by **KYLE RITTER**

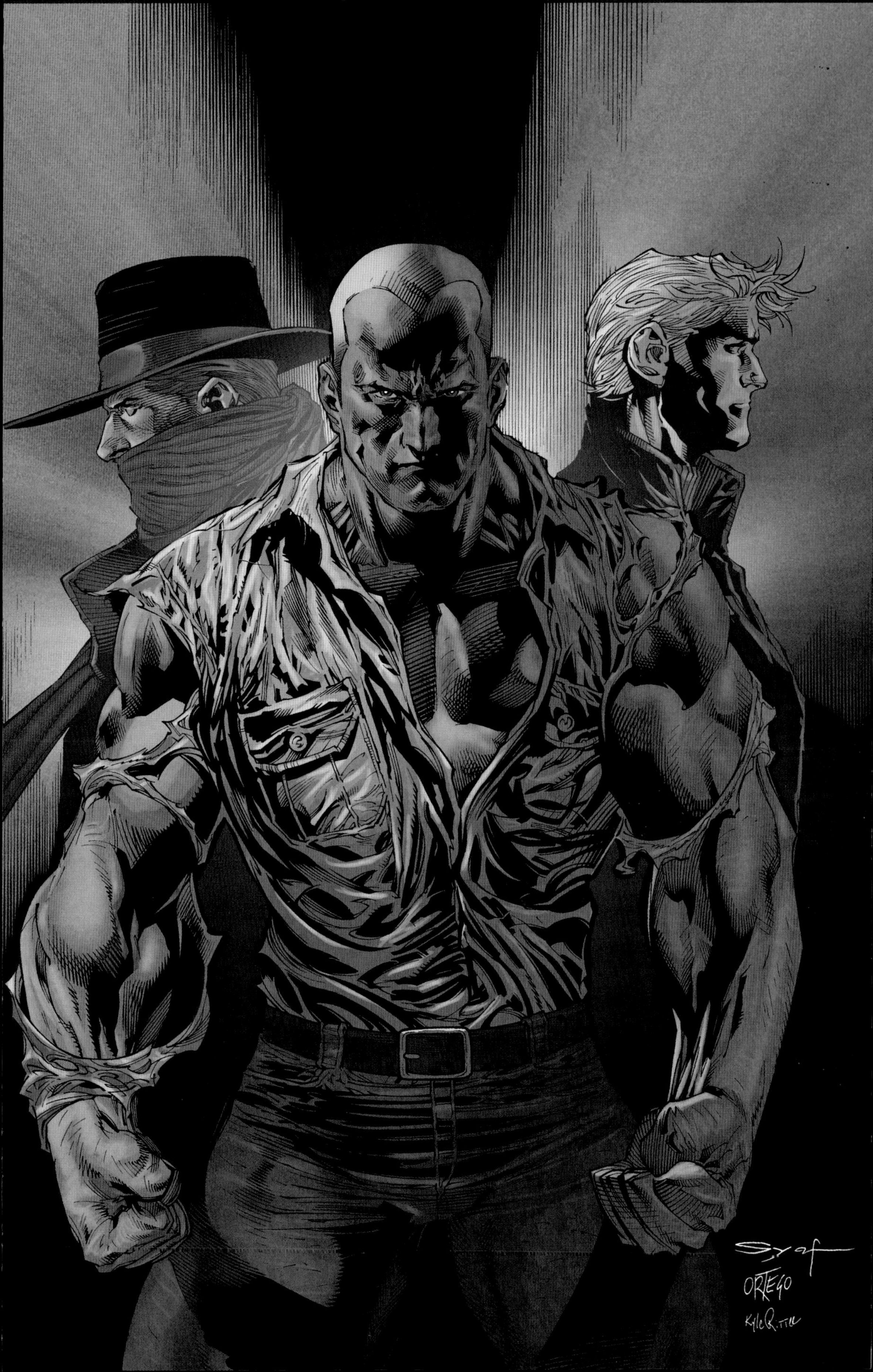

issue #3 alternate cover
art by **FRANCESCO FRANCAVILLA**

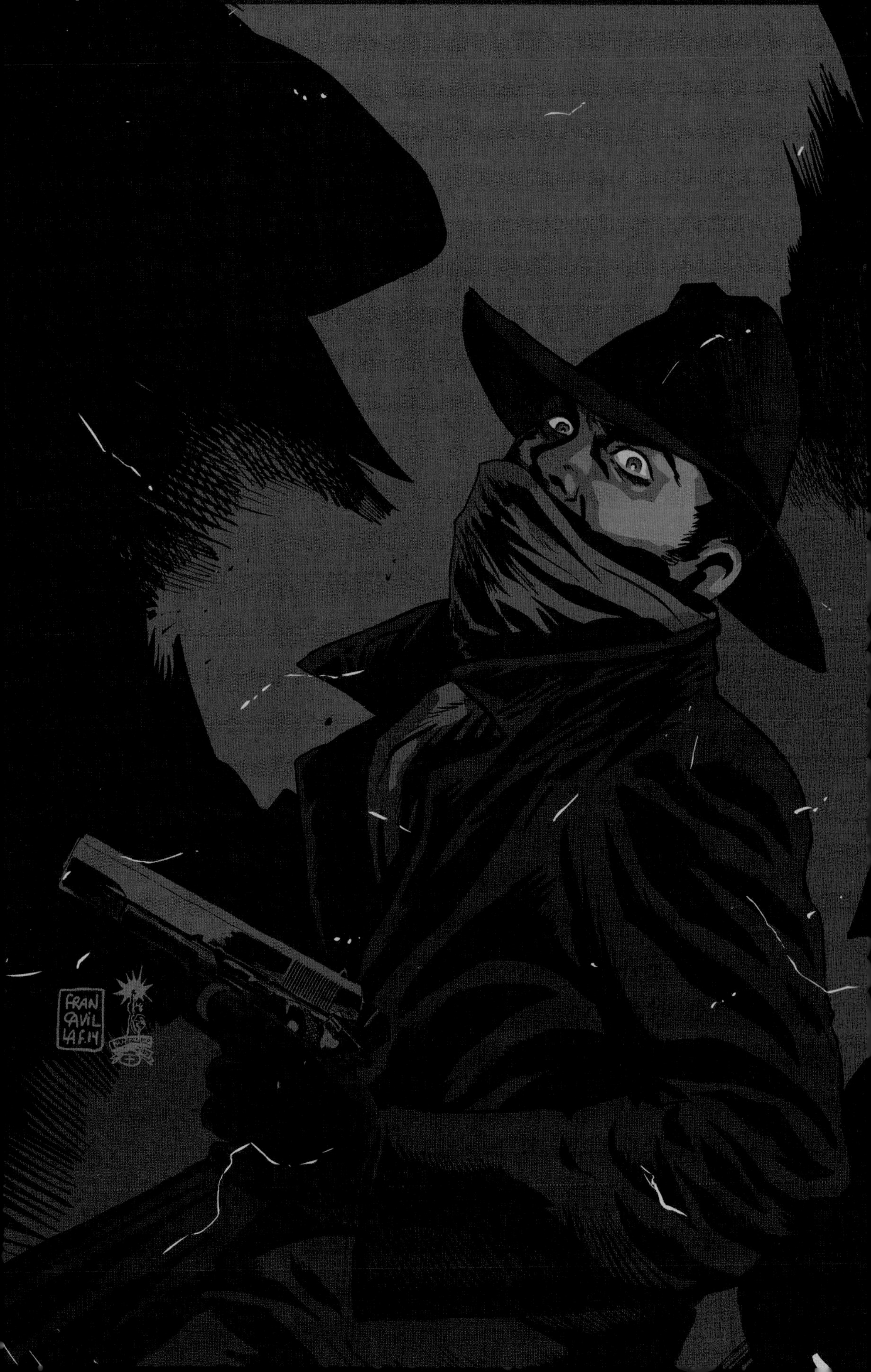
FRAN
CAVIL
LA F. 14

issue #3 alternate cover
art by **GABRIEL HARDMAN** colors by **JORDAN BOYD**

issue #3 alternate cover
art by **ARDIAN SYAF** inks by **GUILLERMO ORTEGA** colors by **KYLE RITTER**

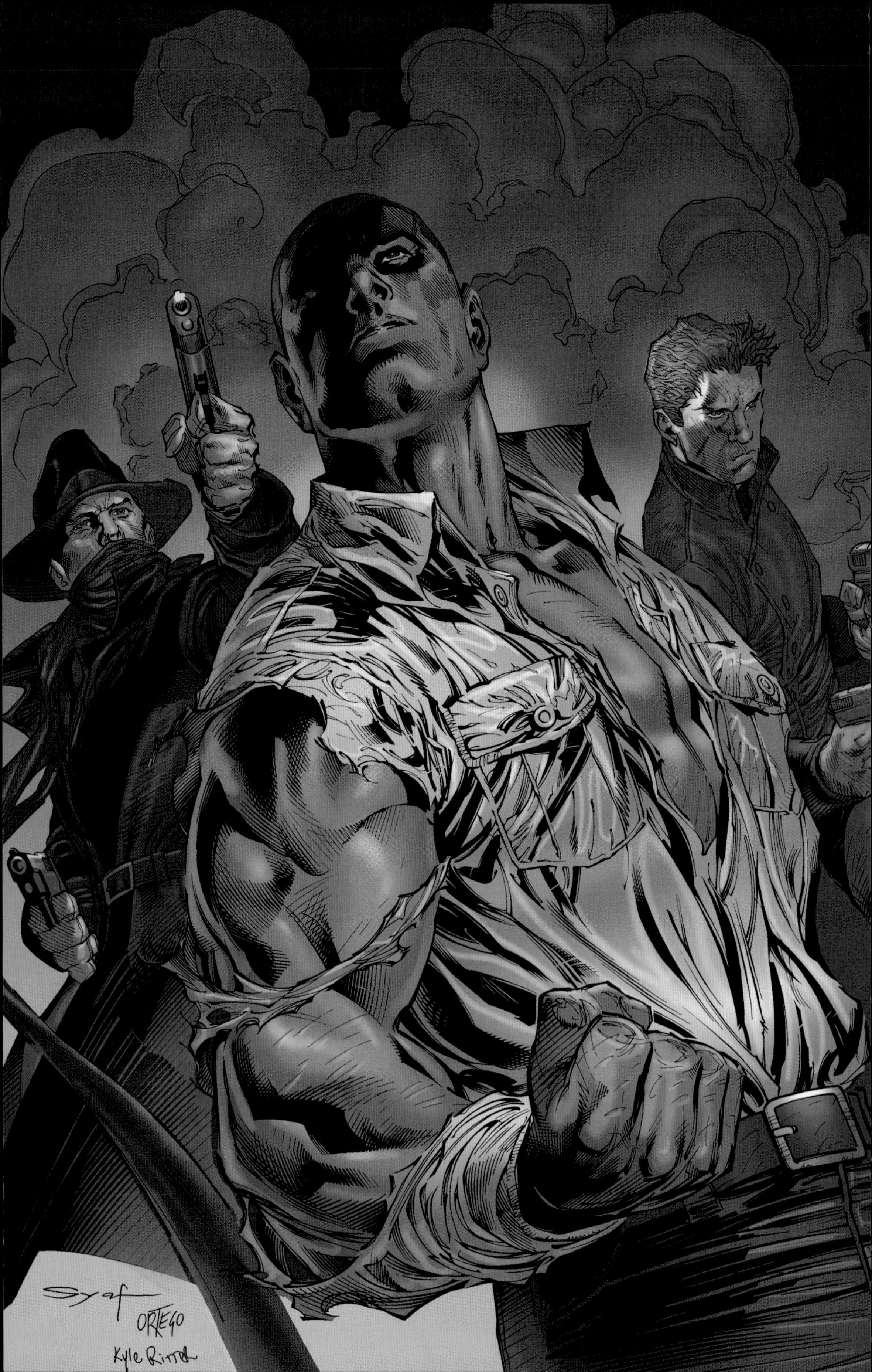
Syaf
ORTEGO
Kyle Ritter

issue #4 alternate cover
art by **FRANCESCO FRANCAVILLA**

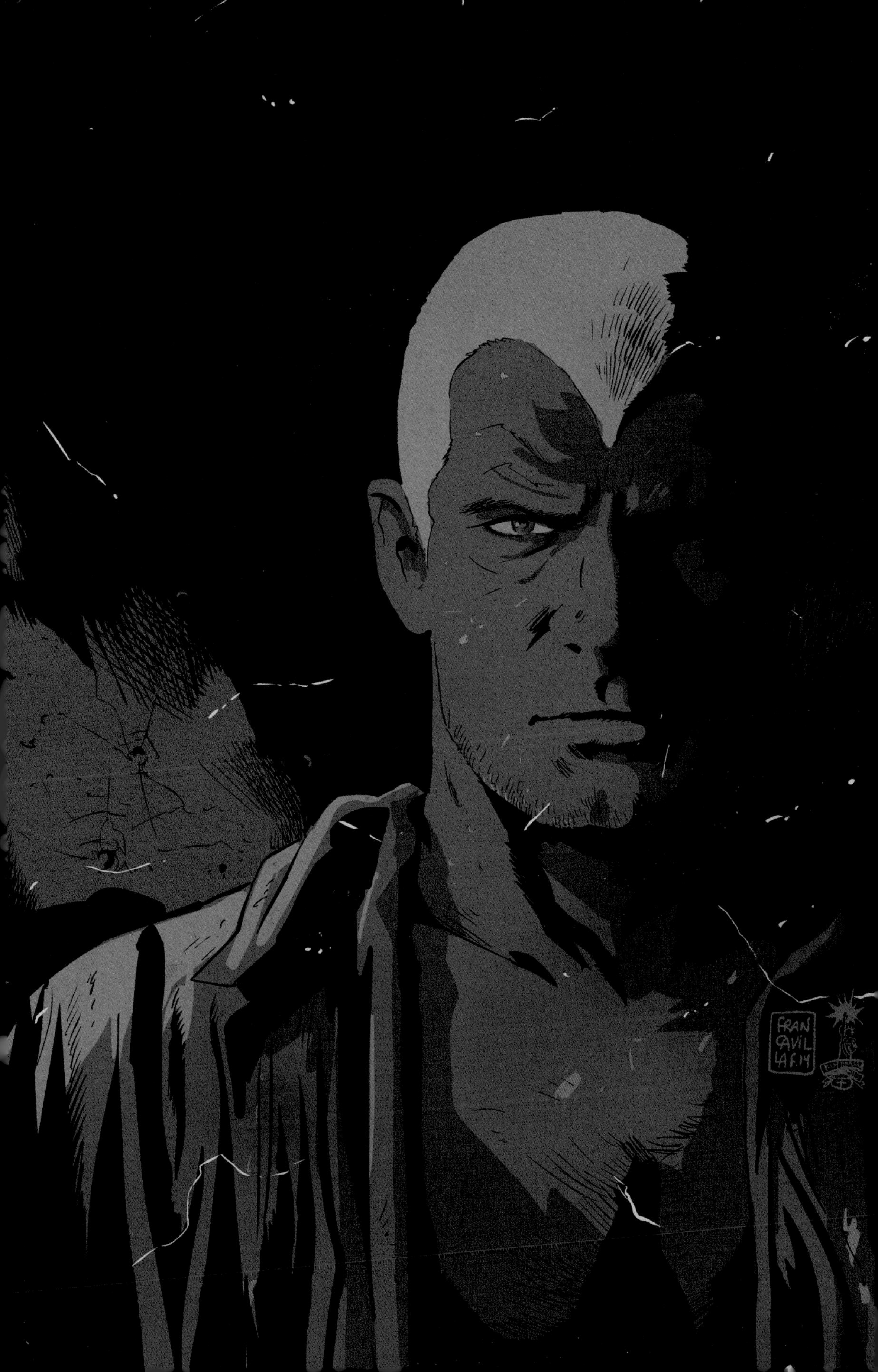
FRAN CAVIL LA F.14

issue #4 alternate cover
art by **GABRIEL HARDMAN** colors by **JORDAN BOYD**

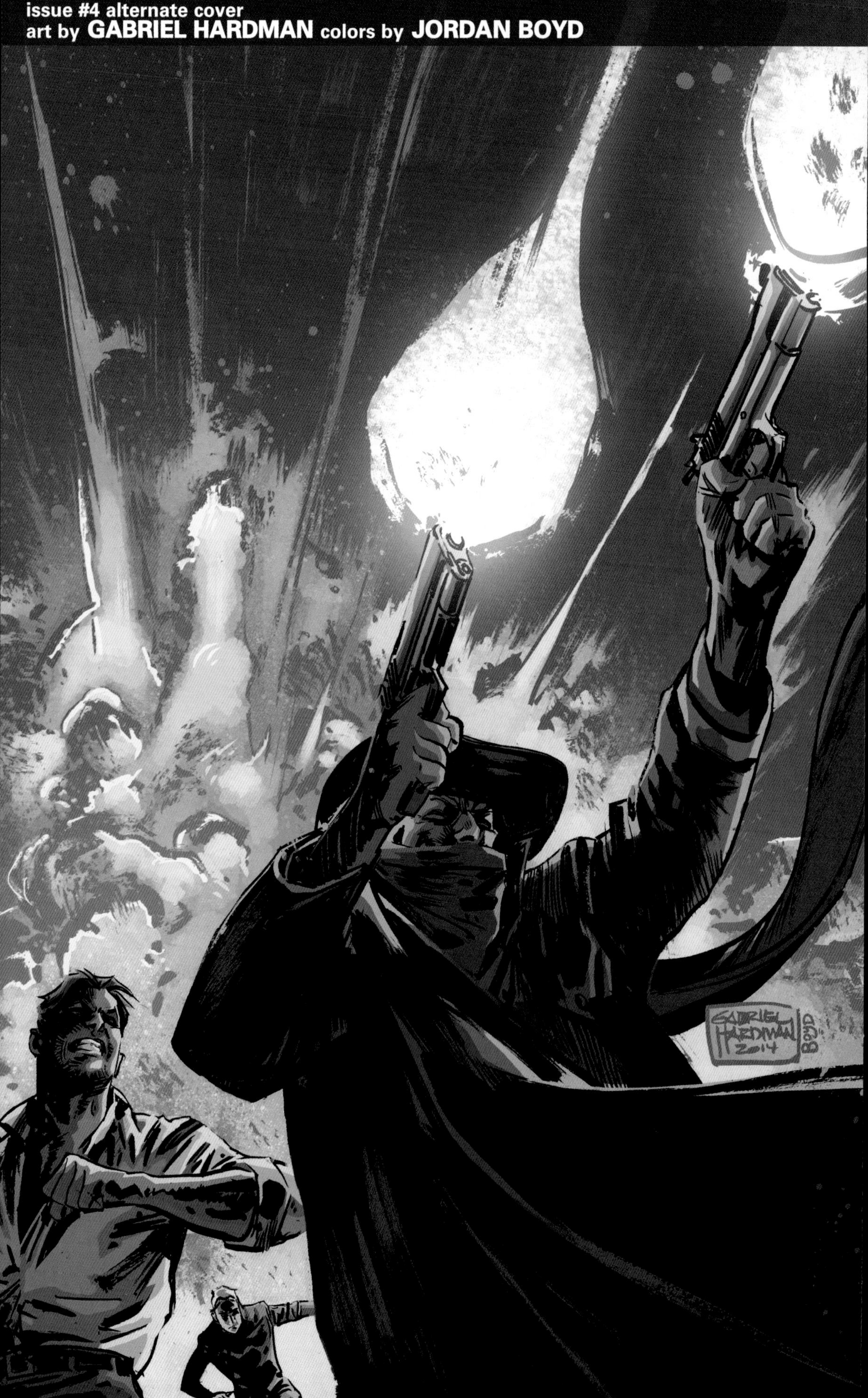
GABRIEL HARDMAN 2014
BOYD

issue #4 alternate cover
art by **ARDIAN SYAF** inks by **GUILLERMO ORTEGA** colors by **KYLE RITTER**

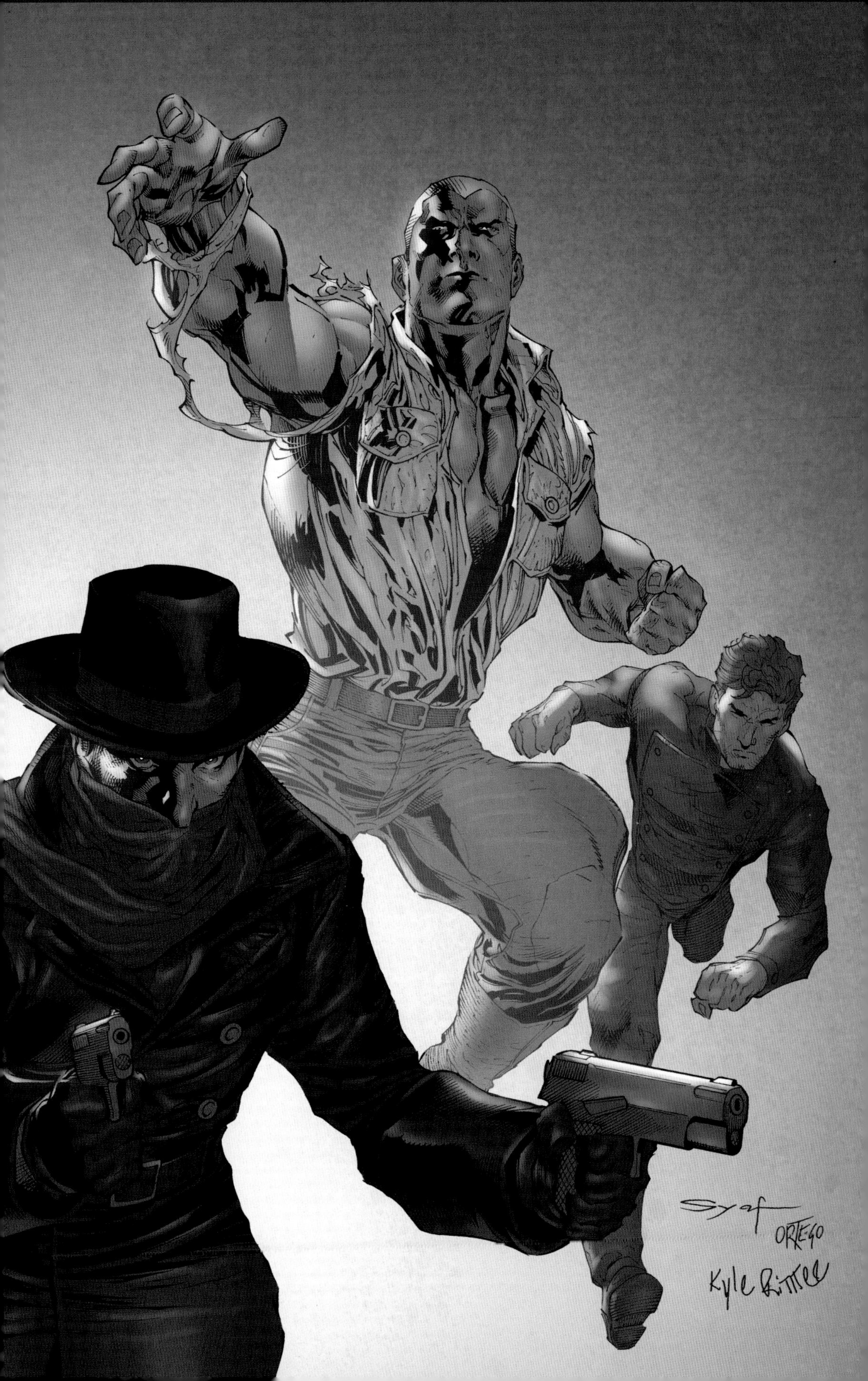
Syaf
ORTEGA
Kyle Ritter

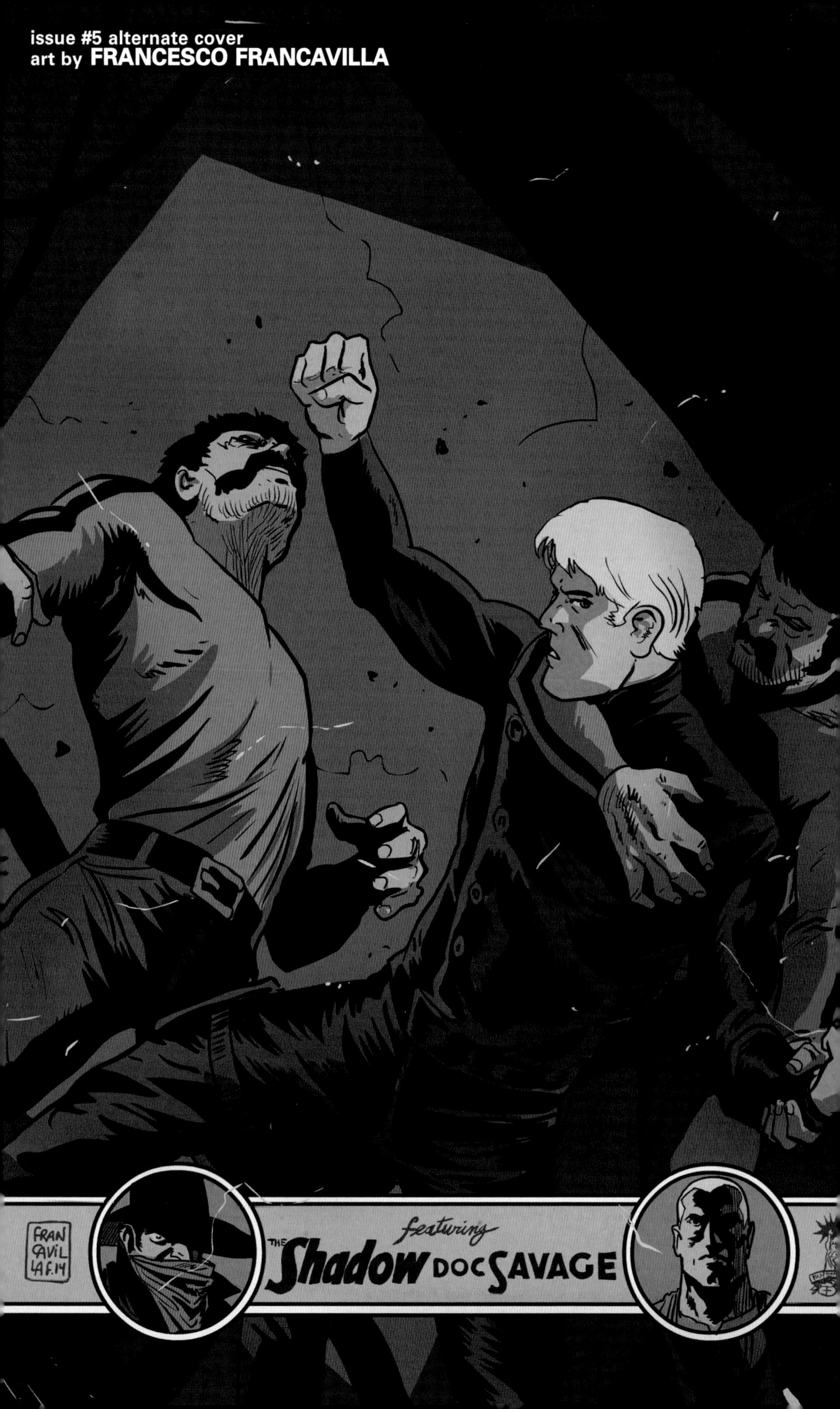
FRAN CAVIL LA F.14
featuring
THE Shadow DOC SAVAGE
issue #5 alternate cover
art by **FRANCESCO FRANCAVILLA**

issue #5 alternate cover
art by **GABRIEL HARDMAN** colors by **JORDAN BOYD**

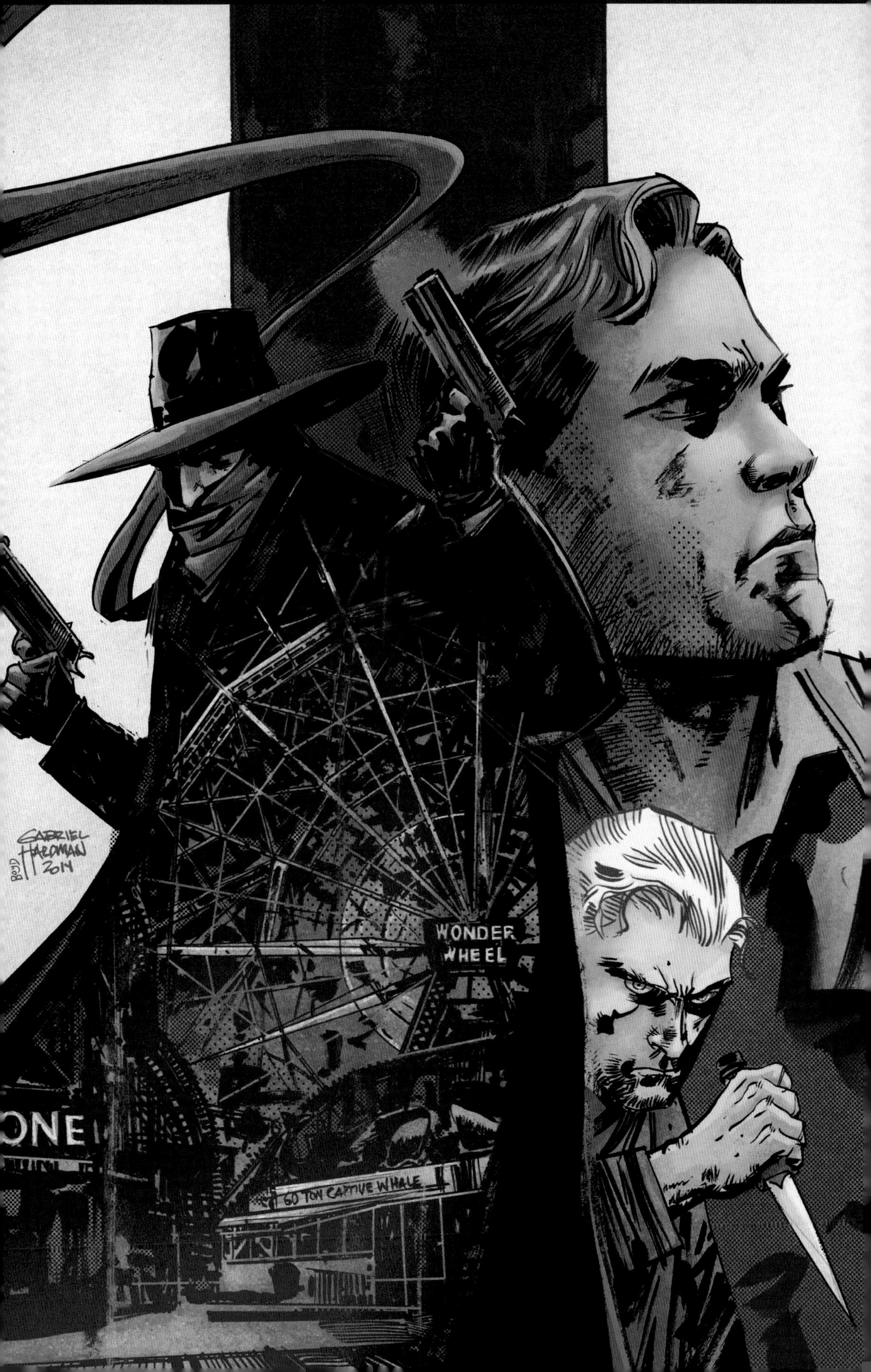
GABRIEL HARDMAN 2014
BOYD
WONDER WHEEL
ONE
60 TON CAPTIVE WHALE

issue #5 alternate cover
art by **ARDIAN SYAF** inks by **GUILLERMO ORTEGA** colors by **KYLE RITTER**

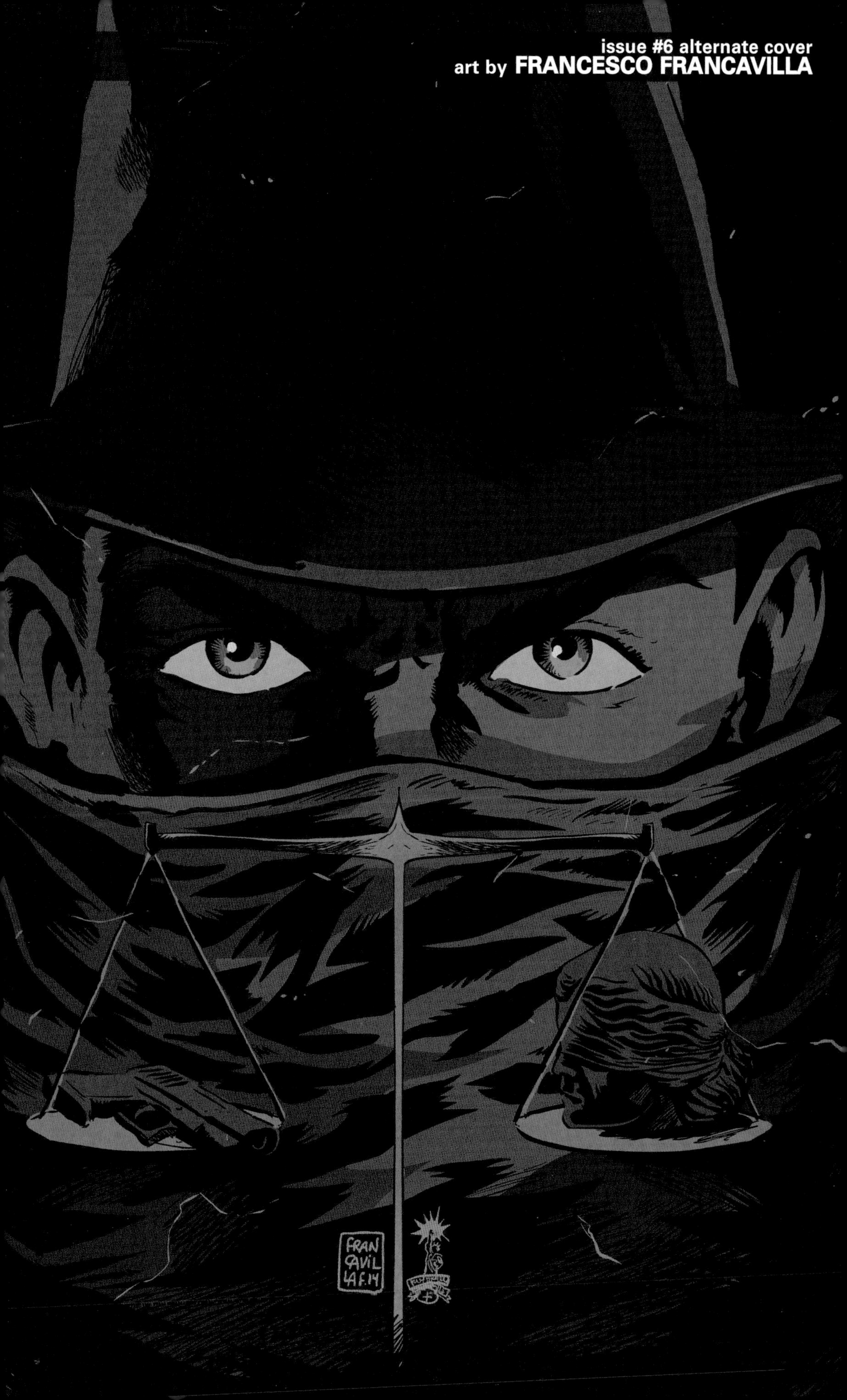
FRAN
CAVIL
LA F.14

issue #6 alternate cover
art by **FRANCESCO FRANCAVILLA**

issue #6 alternate cover
art by **GABRIEL HARDMAN** colors by **JORDAN BOYD**

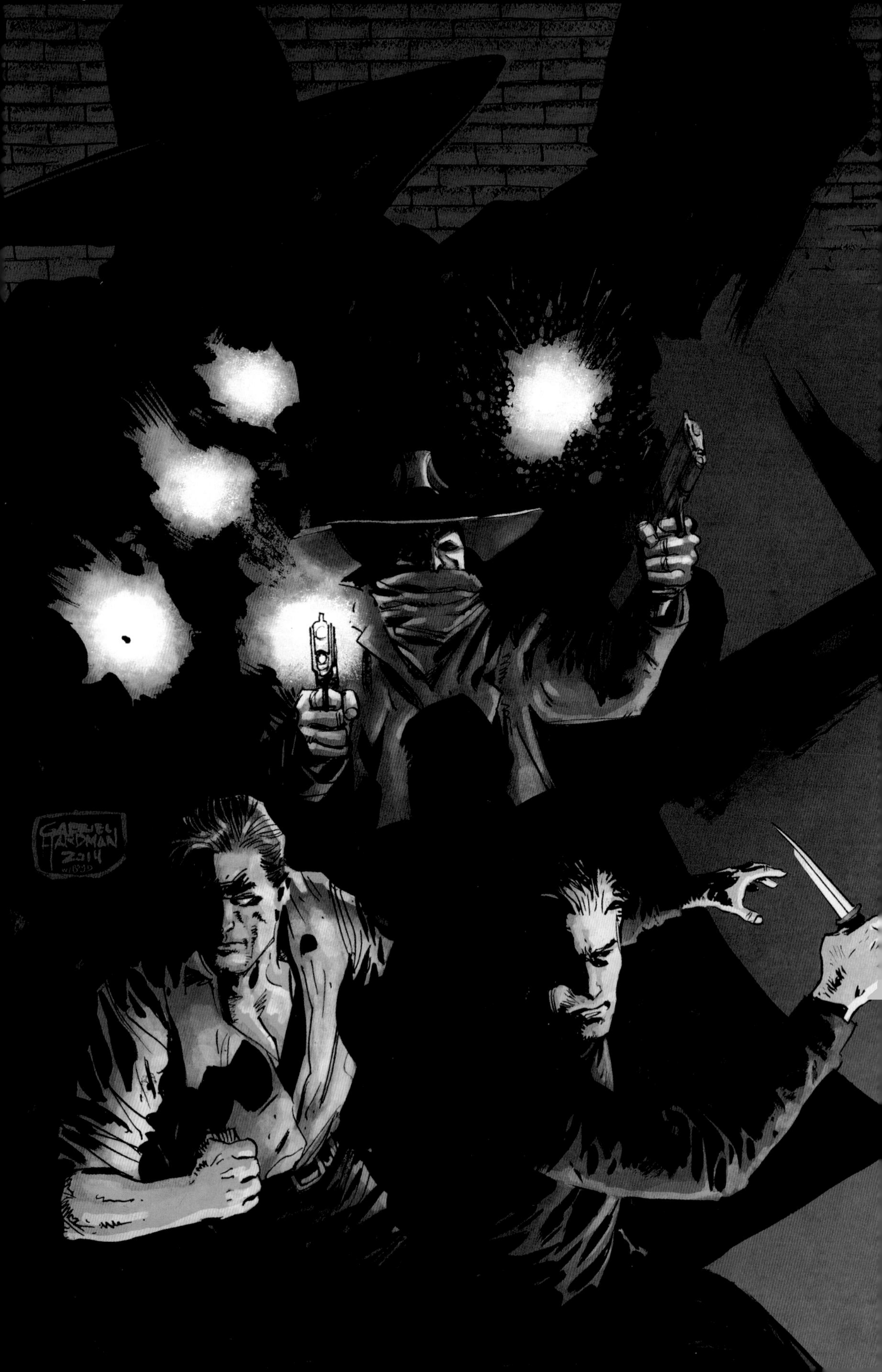
GABRIEL HARDMAN 2014

issue #6 alternate cover
art by **ARDIAN SYAF** inks by **GUILLERMO ORTEGA** colors by **KYLE RITTER**

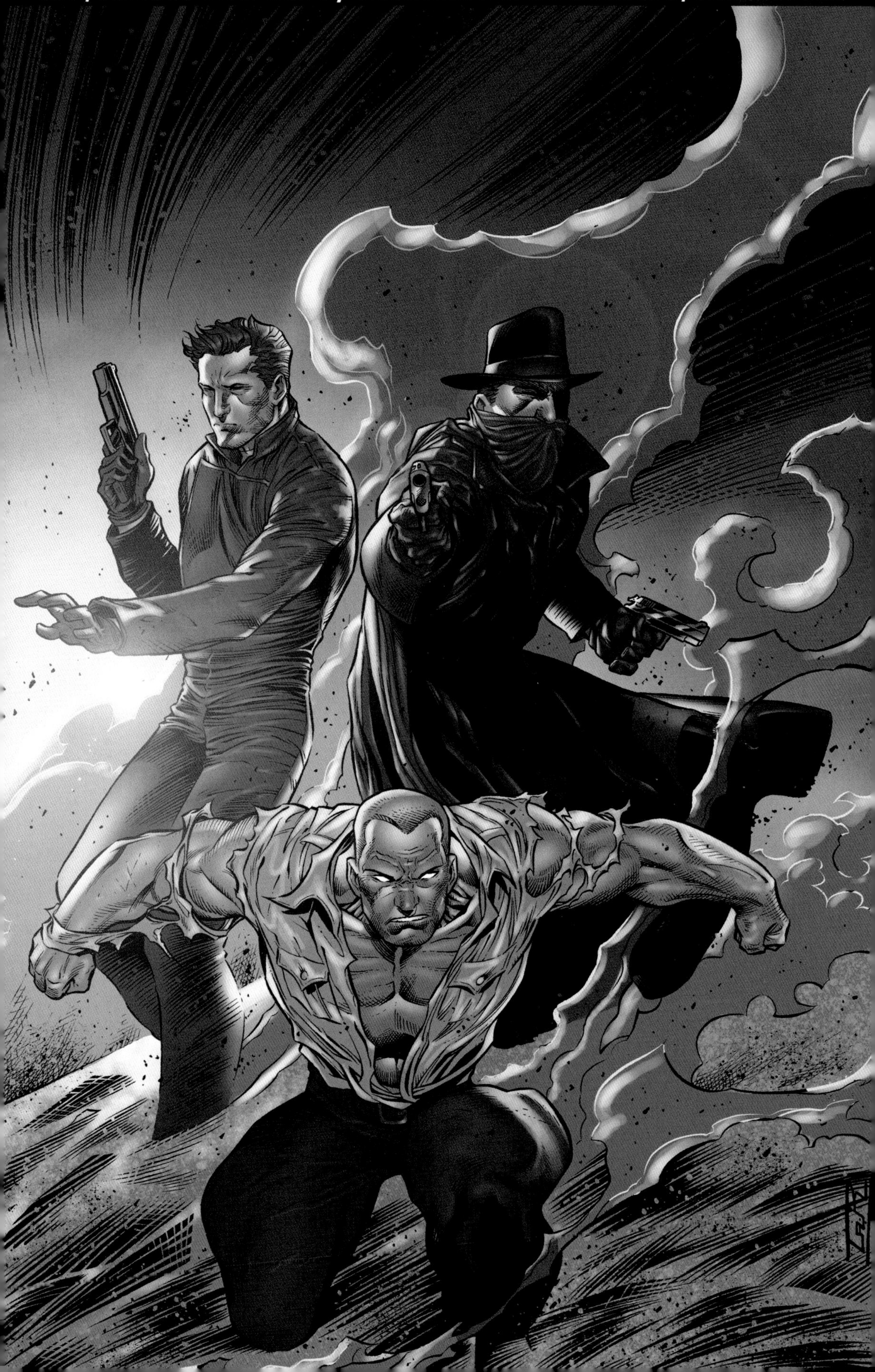

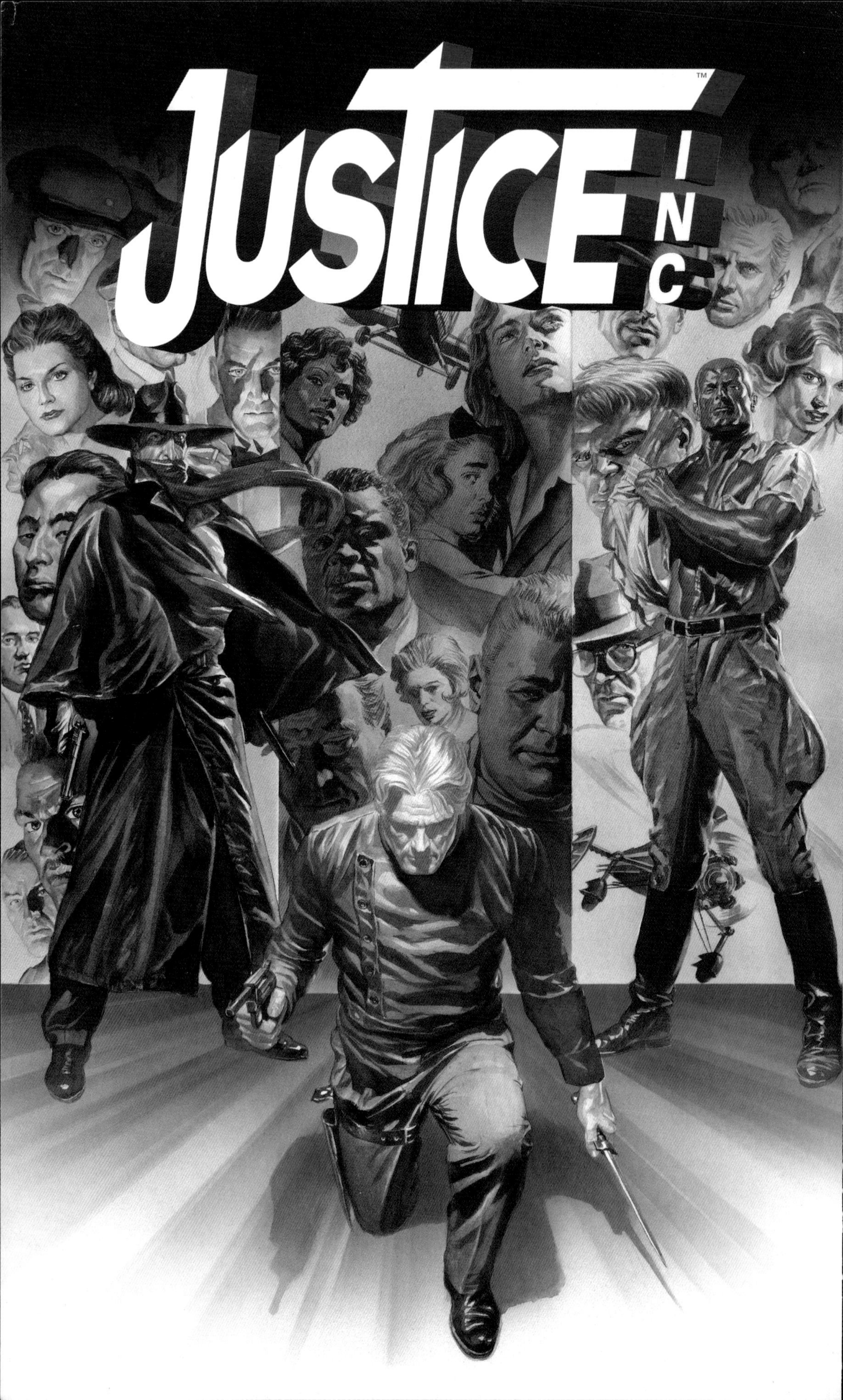
JUSTICE INC